A History of Sociology in Britain

**THE UNIVERSITY
OF BIRMINGHAM**

A History of Sociology in Britain

Science, Literature, and Society

A. H. Halsey

OXFORD
UNIVERSITY PRESS

OXFORD

UNIVERSITY PRESS

Great Clarendon Street, Oxford OX2 6DP

Oxford University Press is a department of the University of Oxford.
It furthers the University's objective of excellence in research, scholarship,
and education by publishing worldwide in

Oxford New York

Auckland Bangkok Buenos Aires Cape Town Chennai
Dar es Salaam Delhi Hong Kong Istanbul Karachi Kolkata
Kuala Lumpur Madrid Melbourne Mexico City Mumbai Nairobi
São Paulo Shanghai Taipei Tokyo Toronto

Oxford is a registered trade mark of Oxford University Press
in the UK and in certain other countries

Published in the United States
by Oxford University Press Inc., New York

© A. H. Halsey 2004

The moral rights of the author have been asserted
Database right Oxford University Press (maker)

First published 2004

British Library Cataloguing in Publication Data
Data available

Library of Congress Cataloging in Publication Data
Data available
ISBN 0-19-926660-3 (hbk.) 23058358
ISBN 0-19-926661-1 (pbk.)

1 3 5 7 9 10 8 6 4 2

Typeset by Newgen Imaging Systems (P) Ltd., Chennai, India
Printed in Great Britain
on acid-free paper by
Biddles Ltd., King's Lynn, Norfolk

PREFACE

'It is the fate of those who toil at the lower employments of life to be rather driven by the fear of evil than attracted by the prospect of good; to be exposed to censure, without hope of praise; to be disgraced by miscarriage, or punished for neglect, where success would have been without applause, and diligence without reward.' That was Samuel Johnson in 1755 writing the preface to his dictionary, whose object, his mother tongue, he went on, had been 'hitherto neglected, suffered to spread, under the direction of chance, into wild exuberance, resigned to the tyranny of time and fashion, and exposed to the corruptions of ignorance, and caprices of innovation'. Much the same may be said of sociology by both friends and enemies.

When colleagues forty years ago began to suggest that I write a history of sociology in Britain, I was reluctant. It was a job for retirement and it was the 1960s when there was much sociological research to do. Now, after fourteen years of 'retirement', there can be no excuse for further delay.

Having begun as an undergraduate at LSE in 1947, I specialized in the sociology of higher education (Halsey, 1995) and in the techniques of survey and the use of Official Statistics (Halsey and Webb, 2000), I have advised the Secretary of State for Education and served on the Council of the Social Science Research Council (SSRC). Moreover, I have held teaching and research posts in Liverpool, Birmingham, the Centre for Advanced Study of the Behavioural Sciences at Palo Alto, Harvard, Chicago, and Berkeley, as well as in Oxford. This may sound all very creditable and may perhaps induce credulity in the reader. But it is salutary to remember W. G. Runciman's introductory text (Runciman, 1998), which ends (p. 211) with the point that 'only through the practice of sociology and psychology can we hope to understand not only how far but also why Dio Chrysostom, a famously eloquent stoic philosopher of the first century AD, was right to ask: why oh why are human beings so hard to teach, but so easy to deceive?'

Personal Confession and the Truth of this History

It is up to the reader to decide on the truthfulness of this history, but here let me sketch the biography of the author. I have already written an autobiography (*No Discouragement*, Macmillan, 1996). I also recount in Chapter 4 my experiences as an undergraduate at LSE in the late 1940s. As to the origin of the subject, I am aware that words change their meanings through space and time and that this is true not least for 'sociology'. It is well known that Philip

Abrams, the late professor of the subject at the University of Durham, has argued for a kind of British exceptionalism—that sociology started so late in the British universities because there were alternative means of access to government and decision making in the relatively peaceful development of nineteenth-century Britain. R. N. Soffer (1978, 1982) later opposed Abrams's analysis, arguing that British sociology under Hobhouse and later Ginsberg had based itself on biological assumptions to contend that evolution entailed progress towards social consensus through the steady emergence of the rational will of individuals leading eventually to the unity of mankind. This so-called orthogenic version of the Darwinian theory of evolution dominated British sociology, deflected attention from social conflict, and therefore effectively eliminated sociologists as potential advisers on social reform. The contrast with American, German, or French experience between 1880 and 1920 was heavily drawn. In a later series of articles and a book (2002), Lawrence Goldman has challenged this view, seeing Britain (England) as not essentially different from the United States, Germany, France, or Italy in failing to develop academic sociology from the late-nineteenth to the mid-twentieth century. Where Goldman and Soffer differ is that Goldman forthrightly declares this a cause for congratulation rather than despair in the sense that, being motivated fundamentally by social reform, early sociologists were satisfied by their own interventions and successful in transforming industrial society by building up a network of empirically based reformist institutions inside and outside parliament, such that R. H. Tawney was eventually able to think of the state as a 'serviceable drudge'.

This was the atmosphere of my childhood—belief in the potency of politics. As a student I listened to David Glass's inaugural lecture of 1950, in which he envisaged that the main destination of sociology graduates would be in Whitehall and perhaps Westminster. My contemporaries and I were activists, full of enthusiasm for the reform of British society in the direction of the welfare state. What we had at LSE was an education that was *not* a training for sociology but a course in the understanding of society. Thus economics and statistics were prominent. Much of the old B.Sc. (Econ.) degree was oriented to the political management of an emerging welfare state, of macroeconomic planning informed by Keynes, of ethical socialism from R. H. Tawney's historical knowledge of industrialism, of reasoned 'piecemeal social engineering' from Popper.

I personally had enjoyed and endured an English upbringing steeped, such were the times, in individualism with, no doubt, its intellectual roots in Hobbes and Locke modified perhaps by T. H. Green, but even stronger roots in daily experience, though again modified for the working class by familism and the social or communal rituals of conformity such as the Sunday suit or the Monday washday. Thus we read Adam Smith's *Wealth of Nations* (1776) in parallel with Emile Durkheim's *Division of Labour* (1893), and, in my own case at any rate, realized what was the relation between the cult of the individual and the 'conscience collective'—the one the vehicle of reason, the other the source of moral obligation.

Of course, as post-war students we looked back on an inter-war childhood as a period of failed government policy with respect to the production (unemployment) and distribution (unequal wealth) of the nation. But with Beveridge and Bevan we saw the future state, as did Tawney, as a reliable instrument for the delivery of health, education, and welfare. I remember reading Ignatio Silone's novels at the time and noticing that his Italian counterparts of the inter-war grammar school scholarship boy were taught by Roman Catholic schoolmasters to hate the state and to worship a Garden of Eden called Russia. My working class, by contrast, thought of communism as associated with cucumber sandwiches on rectory lawns and Russia as a strange exotic tyranny.

Thus, Popper's attack on historicism was deeply impressive to me. The Hobhouse tradition of seeking laws of social development, though never explicitly mentioned by Popper, was thereby rendered suspect and we were prejudiced against it and converted to Popper's version of 'positivism' as well as, admittedly reluctantly, to piecemeal social engineering. Our activism also led us to quantitative surveys. Popper was not apparently a philosopher but a physicist interested in the methods of the social sciences. It was his conversion of philosophy into methodological problems that attracted us—all very abstract but most persuasive.

At the same time, along with an addiction to the normal athletic activities of a male (very late) adolescent, I had become steeped in English and European literature as part of the taken-for-granted equipment of political understanding of the day. In short, I was also a Victorian child, led by the promise of science to a new political and social order and inspired by idealistic novels and other arts to the creation, at last, of a new utopia. I have never subsequently lost these early orientations.

One argument for writing this book is to preserve institutional memory. I have been sadly reminded of the speed at which remembrance may fade in times of rapid change. In this case two particular forces have been at work—the expansion of the universities and the failure of bureaucracies to bring their records into rhythm with reality.[1] Thus, in connection with my survey of professors of sociology (living, retired, and dead), Professor Larraine wrote to me from Birmingham to tell me that he did not know that I had served there from 1954 to 1962. He was appointed in 1977. And questionnaires were returned to me from Leicester intended for Joe and Olive Banks marked 'Not known at this address'. They had retired in 1982. I tried again, using the private address at Husbands Bosworth in Leicestershire which I had last visited in the 1980s. This time the postman did remember, got the new address in Buxton from the neighbours, and sent on the questionnaire.

In 1970 in *Sociology* one of my predecessors, R. K. Kelsall of Sheffield University, reviewed the 'brave attempt' by another, G. D. Mitchell of Exeter University, to write the history of *A Hundred Years of Sociology*. He applied three

---

[1] Adequately to describe the contemporary 'system of tertiary education' would require the combined ironic genius of a modern Dickens, Veblen, and Kafka.

tests. Does the author succumb to the temptation of making brief mention of many sociologists or review at length the comparatively few? Is the choice of people and specialisms a wise one? Does the author stand back and analyse the recent past as convincingly as the more remote past? Mitchell failed all three of Kelsall's tests. He presents a catalogue of names, he leaves out Marx and barely mentions conflict theory or mathematical modelling, and he is more convincing about 1868 than about 1968.

Author and critic are now both dead. Now it is my turn to be judged. I have tried to overcome all Kelsall's hurdles. Only the reader can tell whether and to what extent I have done so. I fear especially for the third test. How to know the young or recent history are difficult challenges. As to the first, I have listed all the professors in my survey in Appendix 1.

I am most grateful to the Nuffield Trust and still more to the Leverhulme Foundation for grants in aid of this project, which enabled me to secure the secretarial services of Sarah McGuigan, the computing services of Jane Roberts, and the research services of Claire Donovan. And my debt is the greater to Nuffield College for providing the intellectual milieu and the library services headed by the ever helpful Elizabeth Martin, that have made the labour more enjoyable and less arduous than it would otherwise have been.

What follows is not a conventional nor even a genuine history in the sense of systematic interpretation of primary sources. But it does contain a survey of the professors of sociology in British universities, a collation of public statistics, and an analysis of citations and contents of the main sociological journals published in the United Kingdom. Claire Donovan has helped with a content analysis of published articles in British journals over the century, especially since 1950. The idea was to track the rise and fall of sociologies of this, that, and the other, such as the economy, the polity, education, race, or religion, and of ideological disputes over Marxism, feminism, ethnomethodology, eugenics, symbolic interactionism, functionalism, etc.

My acknowledgements are due to all the colleagues who answered my questionnaire, and those among them who were kind enough to be interviewed or to comment on a pilot version of the questionnaire. I am particularly grateful for the help of these colleagues who were kind enough to respond to my invitation to add their comments to the questionnaire and to all professors of sociology in the United Kingdom, especially Frank Webster (then at Birmingham) and Richard Jenkins (Sheffield) who sent me accounts of the history of their departments quoted in Chapter 5.

My thanks are also offered to Brian Harrison and his colleagues at the *New Dictionary of National Biography* for permission to draw on the entries which I have written about Morris Ginsberg, T. H. Marshall, W. J. H. Sprott, R. M. Titmuss, Charles Madge, and Barbara Wootton.

Special thanks are due to the seven essayists who have contributed the epilogue. I chose them as seven significant voices in contemporary sociology.

Finally, grateful thanks are offered to those friends and colleagues who read drafts of chapters, especially John Westergaard, who saved me from descending in several places to cohort-bound and egotistical prejudices, Julia Parker, who helped me immensely with her knowledge of social policy, Martin Trow, David Cox, and my daughter Ruth. Of course, none of them is responsible for any of my remaining miscredences, mistakes, or misrepresentations.

A. H. Halsey

Nuffield College
Oxford
December 2003

CONTENTS

LIST OF FIGURES

LIST OF TABLES

Part I

Context

Introduction

IN THE PREFACE we have offered a personal sketch of the atmosphere of the inter-war period (1919–39). Readers may have heard (10 November 2002) Jiang Zemin, the retiring Chairman of the Chinese Communist Party, urging his comrades to keep up with the times and to welcome capitalists into the Party! Could one believe one's ears? The point is that even about ten years ago, not only would the ghosts of Stalin and Chairman Mao have been aghast but no social scientist could conceivably have predicted such a pronouncement. No event so spectacular is to be found in the following pages. Yet, it is doubtful whether any of the handful of British sociologists in 1900 could have predicted that by 2000 as many as 2,000 sociologists would be teaching 24,000 students in the universities of the United Kingdom. This is the puzzle, both the facts and the predictive impossibility, which makes up the case for a history, institutional and intellectual, of this extraordinary expansion and its accompanying fragmentations. We shall elaborate the story in Chapter 5, and numerically in Appendix 2. As to the credibility of our own sensations, we must remind ourselves of the wise remark of John Eldridge that 'a sociology that does not cultivate an historical awareness cripples itself, since it cannot begin to encounter some of the central problems of explanation and interpretation' (Eldridge, 1980: 193).

What then, in a historical context, *is* sociology?[1] In any formal sense its beginnings were inchoate. The study of social relations? Yes, but as we proceed it will become clear that many approaches and definitions are, and have been, in contention. Sociology has no agreed boundaries or birthday. It is probably coincident with civilization. Its boundaries are shifting and disputed. Perhaps it is better to be pragmatic with Ralf Dahrendorf (1995) and say that sociology is what the London School of Economics and Political Science (LSE) does or did, just as Herbert Morrison affirmed that socialism is what Labour governments do, both remarks referring to the first half of the twentieth century.

Certainly, sociology as an academic subject in the United Kingdom began at LSE in 1907. That is a verifiable historical fact. Martin White, the Scottish philanthropist, gave £10,000 to found a chair of sociology, the very first; and it was instituted at LSE off the Aldwych. People, places, and events may be establishable. But if we ask the more difficult and more interesting question, what are the roots of sociology and what its connections to social research are, then we immediately enter the realm of conjecture, of dispute, and of uncertainty.

---

[1] Sociology has acquired a lexicon of strange words. Non-sociological readers will find an authoritative guide in *Sociology* edited by Gordon Marshall, 1994.

L. T. Hobhouse (1864–1929), the first and extremely hesitant holder of the chair, offered an answer in his inaugural lecture on 17 December 1907. Sociology had three sources in Western thought: political philosophy, the philosophy of history, and biological science. The Darwinian revolution and its Spencerian interpretation had dominated Hobhouse's youth and he had committed himself to an anti-Spencerian, collectivist view in the 1880s—the theory of orthogenic evolution—which was preoccupied with the idea of progress. He recognized a fourth institutional source for the general 'science of society' in the philosophers of the Scottish Enlightenment led by Adam Smith (Swingewood, 1970) in the eighteenth century and followed by John Stuart Mill in the nineteenth. If we add the names of Ferguson and Millar in Scotland, Herbert Spencer in Victorian England, and of Hobhouse's contemporaries Patrick Geddes and R. M. McIver also from Scotland, as well as such social researchers as Booth and Rowntree and the social accountancy of the statistical societies of Manchester, Bristol, and London, we can begin to see that a great tradition of sociological theory and research has existed in Britain stretching back at least to the beginnings of the Royal Society and the 'invisible college' of the seventeenth century.

Indeed, we have not only crossed disciplinary borders, but also national frontiers. For sociological thought has never been confined to twentieth-century Britain and never contained within Christian Europe; it has also extended to Islamic, Hindu, and Chinese civilizations. Sociology was given its name in the 1830s by the Frenchman Auguste Comte. The founding father before, so to speak, the naming ceremony was held by Comte and Durkheim as well as Aron to have been their eighteenth-century forbear Montesquieu. Others might cite the Islamic sage Ibn Kaldun. The *Old Testament* and the *Analects of Confucius* may be read as sociological studies. And origins are also to be found among the philosophers of Ancient Greece. Probably the very nature of human evolution makes the identification of a beginning impossible, depending as it does on social sensibility as well as human intelligence. Thus, sociological thought has grown with the evolution of *homo sapiens*.

The international character of sociology is evident in several ways. In this British study, there are particular illustrations: the national origins of the professors (Chapter 8), and of those cited by them as having contributed most to the subject in the twentieth century (Chapter 9), as well as the foreign countries studied by the incumbents of UK chairs. Professors born before 1930 included a third who were immigrants. Some were refugees from totalitarianism, others came for other reasons—Poggi from Italy, Andrewski from Poland, Martins from Portugal, Dahrendorf from Germany, Birnbaum from the United States. Reciprocally, some British-born sociologists have concentrated at least some of their research interests on countries overseas. Bottomore, Batstone, and Gallie on France, Albrow on Germany, Dore on Japan, Lane on Russia, Glass on India. It is noticeable too that command of the foreign tongues was more frequent among the older generations.

Still more remarkable was the international spread of cited luminaries of the subject. We shall see, in Chapter 9, that the Europeans, Weber, Durkheim, and

Simmel, led the field; but also Americans like Parsons, Merton, Mills, or Goffman and Germans like Habermas, or Frenchmen like Bourdieu or Boudon, have been cited more frequently even than Giddens who easily leads the contemporary native sociologists and is himself a 'global' figure, read world-wide. All the evidence confirms that sociology is, like any of the natural sciences, an international subject to which Britain has come perhaps belatedly and contentiously. We should not be surprised, for sociology is, and always was, an argumentative subject, living on the borders of politics and economics, always questioning received culture and custom.

In short, our history is artificially confined in time and space—to Britain in the twentieth century—with the understanding that the subject is international and has origins in earlier times. Sociology does not belong to twentieth-century Britain but reaches out to other civilizations and back to earlier centuries. Why then, the reader may properly ask, does the author restrict himself so drastically? The answer is twofold and, put bluntly, is ignorance and idleness. A Briton over eighty years old must be conscious of a limited remaining life. Frederick the Great is said to have horse-whipped soldiers of the Prussian Army with the cry of 'Into battle you dogs, do you want to live for ever?'[2] Moreover, my publisher is disinclined to such patience and such voluminousness. In any case my intention is a book, not a library.

So let us begin in studied arbitrariness with 1901. Not a particularly noteworthy year, though one in which Queen Victoria died and the Labour Party was born. The century that subsequently passed was one of unprecedented social change (Halsey and Webb, 2000). The country grew immensely more rich, its people lived longer, became more middle class, more ethnically varied, better educated, better housed, and more physically and socially mobile in absolute terms. Meanwhile, England lost a vast, if recently acquired, empire and also largely abandoned a religion stretching back over nearly two millennia. Yet, for all these momentous social changes, it can also be argued that social ideas and sociological explanations scarcely altered between 1900 and 2000.

From the tangled history of social thought in Europe five themes are elaborated in the chapters that follow. They are (i) the consequences of Darwin; (ii) the division between explanation and interpretation; (iii) the methods of study of society; (iv) the use of sociology in social policy; and (v) the LSE focus of institutionalization. Notice that only the last of these themes is peculiar to Britain, the early location of the subject at LSE.

Darwin

The American Bible belt apart, Darwin has conquered the Western world. The disciplines of microbiology and evolutionary psychology have expanded in universities and research laboratories in the twentieth century at a rate

---

[2] An equally apocryphal reply was muttered, 'No Sire, but at least until sundown'.

comparable with that of sociology. They offer exciting prospects to the young researcher in ways not matched by sociology. Yet, few know or ever knew that Darwin borrowed a crucial concept from Malthus: the famous and possibly singular example of a theory flowing from the social to the natural sciences. The general theory of population size was formulated in sociology by Malthus at the turn of the eighteenth and nineteenth centuries and migrated into biology by chance. Darwin wrote: 'In October 1838, that is, fifteen months after I had begun my systematic enquiry, I happened to read for amusement Malthus on Population, and being well prepared to appreciate the struggle for existence which everywhere goes on, from long continued observation of the habits of animals and plants, it at once struck me that under these circumstances favourable variations would tend to be preserved and unfavourable ones to be destroyed. The result would be the formation of new species. Here then, I had at last got a theory by which to work' (Darwin, 1887).

Darwin took over Malthus's notion that potential geometric progression of numbers was a consequence of the fecundity of species. In Chapter 3 of his *The Origin of Species*, he wrote: 'In looking at Nature, it is most necessary . . . never to forget that every single organic being may be said to be striving to the utmost to increase in numbers'. He was unsure as to the checks which restrained geometric progression in the real world but in putting forward four main categories of check he included only Malthus's 'positive' or ecological limiting forces and not his 'preventative' or sociological ones that refer to social interactions such as systems of marriage, communication, convention, or prestige which are shared by the members of a group. So the stage was set for explaining not only biological evolution through natural selection but also cultural and social evolution through the same mechanisms of reproduction, competition, mutation, and chance in an external (and changing) environment.

The first theme then is that British sociology is rooted in the consequences of Darwin's theory of evolution by natural selection. Admittedly, it was initially given a powerful twist by Spencer's individualistic sociology and developed, especially in the United States, as Social Darwinism—the survival of the fittest. The opposite consequence was also generated. Durkheim formulated an anti-Spencerian collectivism. Hobhouse too developed an English type of anti-Spencerian theory linked closely to the doctrine of progress perpetuated by the Whig version of history (Butterfield, 1963). It was Social Darwinism that gave rise to the academic separation and ideological hostility which subsequently developed between sociology and biology. Even today, some sociologists repudiate the Darwinian legacy, asserting that sociology begins where biology leaves off, and that Social Darwinism and social biology were always contaminated by racism, Spencerian individualism, and hereditarian prejudice. We shall see in Chapter 3 how an experiment took place at LSE with Beveridge's conviction that the social sciences had their roots in the biological sciences. The experiment with Hogben's chair of social biology failed but its legacy was a strengthened interest in demography.

Between the First and Second World Wars, methodological advances were made in the understanding of regression and the use of multivariate analysis to aid pluralistic explanations. In consequence, interactionist theories replaced the older simplistic binary debates between Nature and Nurture. Accordingly since the Second World War, neo-Darwinisms in the hands of modern sociologists like W. G. Runciman incorporated the advances of microbiology (the genome, the DNA, and the meme) and reinterpreted the evolution of societies as a process of 'descent with modifications' free from the former preoccupation with moral progress of Hobhouse and Ginsberg. The genetic ideas of replication and mutation have been extended to cultural and social (organizational) evolution through interactions with the particular environment in which they occur. For Hobhouse and Ginsberg the teleological temptations of belief in progress were compelling. For Runciman and many contemporary British researchers they are temptations no more.

Explanation and Interpretation

The second theme is the age-old division between explanation and interpretation, between science and literature, between objective behaviour and subjective meaning. The extension of Newtonian science from inanimate bodies to sentient human beings was the mark of the European movement of Enlightenment and the centre of the search for a science of society in which early nineteenth-century Britons joined. Civil servants, statisticians, political arithmeticians, urban reformers, and economists were all involved. We focus in Chapter 1 on the battle for ownership of the new territory between science and literature. The final outcome has been a schism between cultural studies and scientific sociology, between quantified explanation and qualitative description. British sociology has traditionally ignored the sociology of knowledge, though Karl Mannheim took refuge in England in the 1930s for a few years. Only with Giddens have elements of ethnomethodology, so vigorously developed by Garfinkel and his American colleagues in the 1950s and 1960s, become incorporated into British social theory. The fundamental distinction is between action and behaviour where the latter, as in the knee jerk, is of minor biological interest while the former connotes subjective meaning which, in the context of social relations, has major sociological interest. Max Weber, the most influential of the early sociologists, elaborated the notion to distinguish especially between value-oriented and instrumental actions. There thus developed a social scientific approach to the study of society—action theory— that focuses on sociology as human action and which divides further into phenomenological and hermeneutic sociology, symbolic interactionism, ethnomethodology, and structuration theory. The natural sciences make no such assumption about the objects of their enquiries. Nevertheless, despite the protests of novelists like H. G. Wells, sociology has persisted in its claim to scientific status, offering a rational and coherent account of human action. But what then is to be made of the claims of literature or cultural studies in this regard? We shall tackle this question in Chapter 1.

Methods

And what, it may be added, are the methods to be used in developing a science of society? This is the third theme and one which involves the teaching as well as the research aspects of the subject. The answer, though scattered throughout the following narrative, appears mainly in Chapter 2, where we note the British tradition of empirical study handed down from its origins in the political arithmetic of the seventeenth century and from the flourishing of Scottish enlightenment in the eighteenth century. Mention of either William Petty or Adam Smith is sufficient to dispose of the still widespread judgement that British sociology is a history of mindless collection of 'hard facts'. Indeed, if we look at the tradition from Adam Smith through Spencer and the Webbs, not excluding Hobhouse, and on to Giddens, Goldthorpe, and Lockwood, it is clear that social research in the United Kingdom has been addicted neither to 'abstracted empiricism' nor to 'grand theory'. The country, to be sure, has never produced a Weber or a Durkheim, but, especially since the Second World War, it has produced a solid body of theoretically sophisticated empirical studies such as the *Affluent Worker* series, G. Brown and T. Harris, *The Social Origins of Depression*, or J. Rex and R. Moore, *Race, Community and Conflict*.

Quarrels over deductivism or inductivism, historicism or lawless trends, universal generalizations or *post hoc* particularities, have certainly occurred and the disputes are as yet unsettled. But advances in understanding how and how far scientific method can be used to study society are part of the proven record and more are promised for the future. We review the history of the social survey in Chapter 2, attempting to unravel the claims of various people to statistical originality and tracing the biography of Booth as a controversial contributor.

Surveys have gradually become more sophisticated, especially in building up a more comprehensive picture of the patterns of social interaction. Government has taken more and more responsibility for the collection of data, covering not only the basic facts of economy and demography, but also the accompanying social patterns of family, leisure, housing, transport, education, and, in general, the distribution of resources in an advanced industrial society. What is less developed but gaining ground is the secondary analysis of large data sets about fact and opinion, especially the use of cohort studies. What remains unsolved is the puzzle discussed by Goldthorpe (2000) of the British failure earlier in the twentieth century to adopt the 'new English statistics' and to use them in sociological analysis.

Social Policy

There are intimations throughout this book that sociology, certainly in Britain but also in the United States, has been bound closely to reactions to modern social change. Sociology, whether as science or as literature, has been part of the movement to deal with problems thrown up by the industrial revolution. The search for a 'science of society' in the earlier decades of the nineteenth century is described in Chapter 2 as 'political arithmetic', as the formation of statistical societies in provincial industrial cities, as Florence Nightingale's campaign for hospital reform, as the development of the Register Office, as the poverty surveys of Booth and Rowntree, and as the emergence of a Royal Statistical Society.

When all this led to demand for a national Sociological Society in 1903 and to the foundation of academic sociology with the first chair at LSE (in the wake of Victorian developments in France, Germany, Belgium, Italy, and the United States), there was much uncertainty and argument over the definition of the subject. The factions came together in London in response to a circular by Victor Branford (Collini, 1979: 198), formed the Society, and gathered for its first meeting in 1904. Most historians (Abrams, Bulmer, Kent, Soffer, Studholme) have simplified the conflicts into three parties. The Eugenicists, the Town Planners, and the Ethical Evolutionists—all with policy aims but different political commitments.

All three contending schools began from biology, that is from Darwin's theory of evolution by natural selection. In the intellectual world of late Victorian and Edwardian England, this was the main key to the problems of what, some fifty years later, came to be called social policy. In those days, it was usually referred to as 'the social question' of why poverty persisted in a time of growing prosperity.

The Eugenicists, led by Francis Galton (a cousin of Charles Darwin), wanted to define sociology as the science of good breeding. They preferred hereditarian to environmental explanations, giving priority to nature over nurture. They wanted to encourage fertility among the educated and sober sections of society and to discourage it among the disorderly urban mob whose violence, crime, drunkenness, profligacy, and lack of discipline threatened potential stability and industrial efficiency.

For Town Planners, led by Patrick Geddes (who was a biologist and therefore aware of the importance of heredity), the improvement of the environment was vital to the advance of civilization. They wanted to educate the citizenry, not to suppress the mob. They encouraged the survey to discover the best and worst in nature. They were supported by Charles Booth, some geographers, and some social reformers such as Ebenezer Howard and Thomas Sharpe.

The Ethical Evolutionists led by L. T. Hobhouse took a more academic approach. Hobhouse accepted Darwin but, like Durkheim, set his face early against Spencer's interpretation of the theory. Instead, he stressed that *homo sapiens* had been rescued from biological evolution by the emergence of the self-conscious *mind* (1901), which made it possible to formulate moral ideals (1906) and to promote them through social reform. Hobhouse wanted sociology to be argumentative and advocatory, not a policy science as Spencer intended. Politically Hobhouse belonged to the New Liberals, who represented a modified individualism, a recognition of the importance of collectivism, and were cautiously willing to use the state to relieve poverty, to deliver generous public services, and thus to make more equal the fate of rich and poor. He was, for example, active in the work of Trades Boards, settling wages for workers where Unions were non-existent or weak.

Thus, the roots of British social policy like those of sociology lie in nineteenth-century efforts to come to terms with the social and economic problems of a developing industrial society, and to explain the persistence of poverty and squalor alongside conspicuous wealth. The challenge was posed by Disraeli's *Sybil*. And, as in sociology more generally, alternative approaches and interpretations lay uneasily together and remain contentious.

The influence of the Eugenicists was immense with their faith in voluntary effort to alleviate distress and encourage social progress. Young men from Oxford went to 'find their friends' in the East End of London and other industrial cities, attempting to bring order and civility into desolate communities. In the 1860s, the Charity Organisation Society (COS) established rules to regulate the multifarious activities of the many philanthropic societies and individuals, reflecting the Society's sharp distinction between the 'deserving' and the 'undeserving' poor. All applicants for relief should be carefully investigated so that the former might receive appropriate help and the latter be referred to the deterrent poor law. Indiscriminate charity, the Society feared, would not meet the needs of the deserving and would encourage dependency among the undeserving. Statutory services too—other than minimal poor relief—were regarded with suspicion as insensitive to individual need and undermining independence.

On the other hand were the environmentalists who advocated state action to tackle squalor and distress and reduce the burden on the poor rates—especially through public health measures. Only the state had the power and resources to provide the basic necessities—the drains, literacy, nutrition—to develop the independence, efficiency, and loyalty to society that could turn people into responsible citizens.

The first approach led to controversy about professional social work throughout the twentieth and into the twenty-first century. The second approach has evolved into the central preoccupations of social policy. These concern the proper role of the state in the distribution of resources and opportunities—between rich and poor, men and women, old and young, workers and dependents, North and South, and so on. They are also about the responsibilities appropriate to government and to other social institutions, the market, the voluntary sector, the family, or the individual—and for most sociologists, about the social and economic consequences of different arrangements.

The first tentative steps towards state welfare were taken early in the twentieth century. Liberal reforms of the first two decades brought old-age pensions, unemployment and health insurance to wage earners, school meals and medical care, and the expansion of maternity and child welfare services with home nursing and health visiting for women with young children. Hospital almoners, probation officers, and child care officers all established themselves as professionals with recognized qualifications during the first half of the century.

To some extent the old hostility of the COS to the state melted away as social workers moved into the public services, allowing (it was hoped) for careful assessment of individual needs by professional people who could judge the most appropriate support, though the exact nature of their responsibilities might be disputed (Wootton, 1959). What is reckoned to be appropriate help is not, of course, always available, so social workers may find themselves torn between their professional activities and political agitation for more generous statutory resources—a far cry from the COS antagonism to state welfare in the nineteenth century.

However, powerful arguments for an independent voluntary sector remained. Beveridge in the 1940s deliberately restricted social security to a minimum level to leave room and incentives for voluntary effort and individual saving, and was at pains to distinguish a range of activities which the state should never attempt to perform. Social policy students are still asked to discuss the advantages and disadvantages of statutory and voluntary action, but the conventional boundaries constantly shift. While the legislation of the 1940s reflected a move to a 'welfare state', the last decades of the twentieth century witnessed a reassertion not only of the voluntary sector but also of the market, as the vociferous opposition of Mrs Thatcher's governments to the 'nanny state' lingered to colour the policies of subsequent, even Labour, administrations. Local authorities were encouraged to reduce the services they supplied directly and to delegate their responsibilities to voluntary and private bodies. But the terms of the debate had changed. The arguments for cutting back state provision were less in terms of the danger of undermining family or individual responsibility—though the fear of inducing dependency still remained—as in claims that public bureaucracies were wasteful and inefficient, and unresponsive to people's needs and wishes. A variety of bodies supplying services and still others to inspect and regulate them would, some supposed, bring the virtues of market arrangements: competition would reduce costs and offer wider choices.

While the questions about the proper place of voluntary action in tackling the social and economic problems of a changing society remain a subject of lively debate in social policy, so equally do the questions of the reformers and the town planners about the appropriate character and objectives of the statutory services. Interest in the living conditions of the 'labouring population' and government attempts to regulate the worst abuses had increased through the nineteenth century as the growth of the industrial towns made poverty and squalor more visible, and aroused fears that disease and political unrest might spread through the population. On the one hand, were the urban, provincial statistical societies, detailing the domestic and working environment of the poor. Later in the century came colourful depictions of metropolitan life from Means and Mayhew. Tales of deprivation and struggle and attacks on corrupt individuals and corrupt institutions were scattered throughout the novels of Dickens and Mrs Gaskell. And descriptions of working-class life continued to attract novelists such as George Orwell, Jack Commons, and John Braine. Then there appeared, at the close of the century, the careful statistical surveys of the rich amateurs, Booth and Rowntree, in London and York aiming at precise measurement of the amount and type and, in

Rowntree's case, the causes of poverty among the working classes. Efforts to define and measure poverty, and criticism and appraisal of the many methods employed, remained fundamental in the academic study of social policy at the beginning of the twenty-first century (Webb, 2003).

Just as important as amateur social investigations and journalists' and novelists' vivid stories was the information accumulating within government about the living conditions of the working population, as new central departments were created permitting the collection of national statistics and initiating legislation relating to factory employment, poor law administration, health, and education. But not only did these developments create a new fund of knowledge about the state of the nation; they also brought into government a new band of independently minded, highly educated, and able civil servants, the Inspectors, in a position to scrutinize and criticize public policies. The result was that powerful pressure for more state intervention to tackle a variety of social ills began to come from within government itself (Chadwick, 1842; Roberts, 1960; Goldman, 2002).

Chadwick's *Report on the Sanitary Conditions of the Labouring Population of Great Britain 1842*, produced while he was secretary to the Poor Law Commission, had detailed the squalid state of the working-class dwellings, the accumulation of refuse, the contaminated water, and the associated mortality statistics. And it was the evidence assembled in Chadwick's report that fuelled the movement for preventive action by government to tackle insanitary living conditions. Not only were there economic costs in loss of working ability and premature death of wage earners, leaving destitute women and children to poor relief, in addition, Chadwick argued, 'noxious influences' also undermined the moral character of the young and tended to produce adults who were 'short-lived, improvident, reckless and intemperate, and with habitual avidity for sensual gratifications.' (Chadwick, 1842: 423).

The Public Health Act that emerged in 1848 embodied the idea of prevention as an aim of legislation that has become a continuing theme in the academic study of social policy. The Poor Law Commissioners of 1909 were unanimous in recommending schemes to prevent and cure the destitution, which the deterrent poor law at best merely relieved, proposals which the Webbs saw as evidence of a shift in public opinion away from the tenets of Darwinism and the Eugenicists who had favoured strict administration of the 1834 Poor Law and limited alms giving (Webb and Webb, 1963: 550).

The 1940s witnessed a move towards specialization with the restructuring of local government and more generous services. Public social care was no longer restricted to the destitute and no longer designed to be deterrent but, in theory at any rate, determined by need and intended to reflect the ordinary experiences of independent family living. Whenever possible, children at risk were to be placed with foster parents, and old people in need, according to the wishes of Bevan and his ministers (Townsend, 1962: 32), in small homes like residential hotels.

Although social policy and social administration only became firmly established in the 1950s, they were beginning to gain a foothold in the universities much earlier in the century—largely under the guise of training courses for social workers. Social workers, almoners, and probation officers had courses offered to them in such provincial red-brick universities as Liverpool, Birmingham, Manchester, Leicester, as well as at Oxford before the Second World War.

How then are we to summarize the historical relations between social policy and sociology in twentieth-century Britain? We shall see in Chapter 10 how social policy established itself as a separate discipline. Both of them have nineteenth-century roots in the problems of a society passing through its industrial revolution. The roots are tangled. Both could and did have their early growth under the LSE logos of *rerum cognoscere causas*,[3] both were influenced by the tradition of individualism that dominated Victorian thought, and both sought a collectivist politics, albeit in its Fabian form. But social policy aspired to action rather than thought. Sociology was inclined more towards the glamorous academic sunlight of theoretical scholarship: it fed more directly on the search for a science of society. In the first half of the century both occupied a tiny place in the neglected garden of the social sciences, overshadowed by economics and politics, and dwarfed by the arts and humanities.

In the immediate post-war decades the social end of the social sciences began, as we shall see, to flourish. Clapham gave initial research funds, the Home Office financed social work training, Robbins expanded social science faculties, the SSRC was formed in 1965, and the Central Council for Education and Training in Social Work (CCETSW) in the 1970s. But meanwhile the May Events of 1968 and 1979 occurred while, within the universities, sociology separated itself from the training of social workers.

The consequences for academic sociology were uncertain after 1975. Departments of sociology teaching the core of the subject became threatened and relied increasingly on service teaching to departments of social policy, health studies, law, and management. The teaching of social work was abandoned in part by the leading universities and 'relegated' to the polytechnics (the post-1992 universities). Departments of social policy prospered throughout the university system and managed to attract much of the research funding previously allocated to sociology. The problems were increasingly tackled by interdisciplinary teams of economists, historians, political scientists, geographers, and statisticians, fewer and fewer of whom were willing to call themselves sociologists. Social policy departments were increasingly linked to specialized research centres, inside or outside university campuses.

LSE, the Provinces, and Oxbridge

Both sociology and social administration, later called social policy, were placed first at LSE, the Fabian institution invented and fostered by Sidney and Beatrice Webb in 1895. There, from unlikely beginnings as a night school for part-time

---

[3] 'To know the causes of things'.

students, eventually evolved not only a flourishing college of the University of London but the principal alternative centre of social science learning in England, challenging the centuries-old dominance of Oxford and Cambridge. This is our final theme and its details run through Chapters 3–5 and into the analytic history presented in Part III of this book.

The history of British sociology before the Second World War is in effect an aspect of the history of LSE as told in Chapter 3 with its small number of Hobhousian devotees, its separate department for the training of social workers, and the underlying but powerful influence of R. H. Tawney, formally a professor of economic history but in practice the carrier of an ethical socialist tradition, which guided much of the research and teaching of 'the School' in its formative years, and which was to spread to provincial universities between 1950 and the end of the century. In Chapter 4, we shall recapture the emergence of a first generation of professional sociologists with Glass, Marshall, and Shils as their mentors. But of equal significance was the appointment of Richard Titmuss to a chair of Social Administration. He, more than any other single individual, not only through his teaching and research but also through his service to government, established social policy as an independent discipline.

1

Literature or Science?

IS SOCIOLOGY a science? Towards the end of the twentieth century, in 1990, Stephen Turner and Jonathan Turner published their perspicacious institutional analysis of American sociology under the title *The Impossible Science* (Turner and Turner, 1990).

Though disagreeing with each other about the possibility of sociology as a science they agreed that its American history had argued its impossibility, essentially because resources had eluded it since its beginnings after the Civil War of the 1860s. By resources they meant primarily not only student demand, but also careers for sociologists in government, civil service, universities, and charitable foundations funding social research. Much of their analysis may be applied cautiously to Britain, if usually at a later date, though the American Sociological Society was founded two years after its British counterpart. The emphasis on student demand in the American case reflected the earlier and faster development of tertiary education and the persistence in Britain of a hierarchy of income and status, which ensured that student demand was restricted to a minority until well after the Second World War. The role of government in the nineteenth century, as Abrams argued (1968), also provided opportunities for people to influence public affairs in ways which inhibited the formation of departments of sociology in the universities. Moreover in both countries the role of the rich philanthropist was a fragile and declining resource for the funding of social research. Nevertheless, there were other common factors identified by the Turners: the rise of reformist sentiment, the search for a substitute for loss of Christian faith, the movement from rural to urban living, competition with other disciplines, bureaucratization, and so on. What the Turners did not deal with directly is the rivalry between science and literature for ownership of the intellectual territory of social criticism and social reform. In Europe, the arts formed a significant barrier to scientific sociology.

Science and Literature

The traditional struggle for possession has not ceased. Science and literature still compete. The last sociologist I knew who was also and probably better known as a poet was Charles Madge. That was in the 1950s at the University of Birmingham. The last poet I ever knew who wrote serious sociology was

T. S. Eliot, whose *Notes Towards a Definition of Culture* were required reading for undergraduates in the 1940s as a measured reply to the then fashionable views of Karl Mannheim on the sociology of knowledge and on planning for post-war social reconstruction. At the end of the twentieth century, W. G. Runciman, a leading British sociologist and President of the British Academy, declared that 'post-modernism has retreated, taking with it those aspects of the study of human social behaviour which properly belong with literature rather than science' (Runciman, 1998: vii.). He goes on to argue that a new evolutionary paradigm is emerging within which historical and cross-cultural hypotheses can be formulated and tested in accordance with standards shared among all the various disciplines involved in explaining why human beings are what they are and do what they do.

This sounds uncannily like an echo of Hobhouse around whom there raged a similar debate in the first decade of the twentieth century. Thus, for example, Frederic Harrison, the positivist, discussing C. F. G. Masterman's *The Condition of England* in the *Sociological Review* (Vol. 2, 1909: 396), dismissed H. G. Wells, Bernard Shaw, G. K. Chesterton, and Hilaire Belloc as 'masters of paradox and burlesque' who could 'hardly be accepted as "the sources" of scientific sociology'. The following year (1910, Vol. 3, No. 2) there appeared in the very same journal— the only official publication of the Sociological Society formed in 1903—a review by S. K. Ratcliffe of 'Sociology in the English Novel' claiming that modern fiction was descriptive sociology in a larger and truer sense than the term possessed when it was used by Herbert Spencer. 'As the sociology of the ancient world is enshrined in the Hebrew Bible and Homer, in the Vedas and the Mahabaharata, in saga, folk-story, or Arthurian legend—so the modern world has its multifarious record in the pages of the novel.' We might now want to add 'in the footage of the film, or the script of a play'.

We must not be misled by Runciman's remark. He also admires the work of Michael Young whose greatest claim to fame was published in fictional form— *The Rise of the Meritocracy*. No, following Krishan Kumar (2001), we must take seriously the thesis of Wolf Lepenies (1988) who sees the rise of sociology in the nineteenth century in Europe as located *Between Literature and Science*. He argues that French and German struggles for possession of the disputed territory led to an earlier formation of sociology departments in the universities of those two countries than in England. In France Balzac in *La Comédie Humaine* laid literary claims to an exhaustive description of French social structure in Comte's time, and later Zola (1840–1902) perhaps as impressively in the Durkheimian climate of the Third Republic. Our task here, however, is to consider the British case. Did Booth or Rowntree, or 'the social accountants,' leave us with a stronger legacy, or is the depiction of industrialization, urban life, and social hierarchy best found in Dickens, George Eliot, Trollope, or H. G. Wells, or in literary criticism or social history? Lepenies sees a 'concealed sociology' in Victorian and Edwardian England, while Kumar uses the alternative phrase 'implicit sociology' to point at the social importance and political acceptability of the novelist or the historian.

Lepenies argues that while in such countries as France and Germany sociology had developed distinct yet varying profiles as a science, both opposing and supporting the Establishment, and had then within each country gone on to splinter into separate schools, in England sociology was simply a constituent of social common sense: it had no need to secure its existence by becoming an independent academic faculty. This argument could be extended. Given the long British tradition of individualism (Macfarlane, 1978), the emergence of political economy as the dominant interpretation of nineteenth-century society was bound to sway governments and the governed against sociology with its insistence on the strength of social forces as determining reality in the shape of '*geist*' or the spirit of the age.

It was in the troubled years between the wars that there lay the seeds of that development which was in the end to create a sociology in England as well, though, to be sure, its institutionalization largely had to wait until after the Second World War, as we shall see in Chapter 4. Compared with the construction of schools of sociology in America, France, and Germany, however, 'English sociology always remained curiously pallid and lacking in distinct identity: the disciplines that came into being in England during the post-war years, and were its essential contribution to intellectual contention both at home and abroad, were so-called "cultural studies"' [as represented by such names as Stuart Hall, Richard Hoggart, Raymond Williams, Terry Eagleton, and Fred Inglis.]. 'A brief characterization of what constitutes "cultural studies" would', writes Lepenies, 'amount to an abstract of English intellectual history since Matthew Arnold: they are a blend of sociology and literary criticism' (Lepenies, 1988: 195).

What then are the claims of science and of literature for sovereignty over what we may provisionally call the third culture of social science in general and sociology in particular? We have seen already that names, especially perhaps that of sociology, change their meanings through time and space. Both the arts and the sciences were once admitted to the French Academy. Buffon, the author of *Histoire Naturelle* (1749), was elected to the *Académie Francaise* in 1753 where he spoke at his first meeting on the subject of style, and, a century later, even Baudelaire was impressed. Today, the division between the Royal Society and the British Academy is rigid; only statisticians and demographers are eligible for election to both.

What happened in between? Kent has told the story of the limited success of science in the nineteenth century as social accountancy, social inquiry, and social survey (Kent, 1981). The claims of science may be briefly put. Reason and calculation are their roots. Karl Popper's *Logic of Scientific Discovery* and *The Poverty of Historicism* and Thomas Kuhn's *The Structure of Scientific Revolutions* are their modern canons. We shall look in detail at various aspects of these claims as our story unfolds. Ernest Gellner argued confidently that the emergence of natural science and its application to material technology has bequeathed to *homo sapiens*, since the Enlightenment, a set of procedural rules, all conquering of local cultures, destructive of revelation, insisting on rationality as the path to successful understanding of any culture. In that sense, the scientific method stands above all particular claims of the relativist for the sacred, special, exceptional character of any given society (Gellner, 1992).

But what of Literature and History?

For an answer we must momentarily return to France where Honoré de Balzac followed Buffon with an announcement of a new and ambitious project, to extend the latter's *Histoire Naturelle* into human life. *La Comédie Humaine*, as finally formulated in 1841, was justified as 'an analogical appeal to the disciplines of history and science' (Prendergast, 1990: x). It was to be a form of social history ('*histoire des moeurs*') to be understood in all its complex diversity by analogy with the taxonomic models of zoology. The animal world had been classified into '*espèces zoologiques*'; now the history of French society was to be portrayed as '*espèces sociales*'.

Eugenie Grandet was the first venture in this huge project. Against a vivid background of French provincial life, Balzac portrays the innocence and subsequent disenchantment of a dutiful daughter in all her provincial religiosity, subject to patriarchal familism and a restricted division of labour between men and women. Her narrow existence is interrupted by a visit from her cousin Charles from metropolitan Paris where styles of life are corrupted by aristocratic manners and plutocratic greed and where marriages of convenience separate sex from love. Yet, she falls in love with the elegant Parisian, and rebels against her miserly and tyrannical father.

These themes of conflict between metropolis and province, parent and child, class and class, man and woman, recur and recur through Balzac's novels and create a comprehensive drama of human life, the panorama of 'espèces sociales'.

The eighteenth-century Enlightenment had brought with it a wave of interest and belief in the power of Newtonian science to explain and predict the physical world. There were at last immutable laws governing the behaviour of bodies (including the heavenly bodies as well as the familiar tides) in an orderly universe. In the nineteenth century, in Europe, this worldview was extended to the behaviour of human kind. Simple principles ruled the diversity of human activity. In England, these principles were formulated as Bentham's utilitarianism. James Mill, a devotee of the philosophy, reared his son John Stuart (born 1806) in strict accordance with a puritanical version of the doctrine. Charles Dickens' Gradgrind in *Hard Times* (1854) is a caricature of the father. No poetry, no idleness. John Stuart Mill's later life was a tormented struggle against paternal teaching; a passage from the culture of science to the culture of feeling, aided especially by the reading of Wordsworth and the love of Mrs Harriet Taylor whom he married in 1851. Auguste Comte in France laid out an elaborate positivist science of society before becoming involved in a similar relation with Clotilde de Vaux and eventually founded a (scientific) religion of humanity. Florence Nightingale (1820–1910) always thought statistics 'more enlivening than a novel'.

Herbert Spencer, who died in 1903, was a similar sage of the Victorian period, carrying the powerful influence of the natural sciences into the study of man. Admired by Andrew Carnegie and later by Chairman Mao in his youth he in J. D. Y. Peel's words 'struck American universities like lightning in the early 1880s and dominated them for thirty years'. His visit to the United States in 1882 was a triumphal progress (Peel, 1971: 2). But in Europe 'his theories were abandoned if they seemed false or irrelevant, and if they were true or useful, like many of his sociological concepts, they were absorbed into a tradition and their author forgotten'. (*Ibid.*, p. 3). Arnold Bennett at the turn of the century saw himself as illustrating Spencer's *First Principles* in every line of the novels he wrote.

Beatrice Webb was also a Victorian child much influenced by her mentor Spencer. She too grew up believing in science, progress, and reason. In her *Diary* on 23 May 1900 (Mackenzie, 1984, Vol. II: 175–6), she wrote 'Our effort is now directed to one end—to establish on a firm basis a Science of Society . . . Partly by our own individual work and partly by the [London] School of Economics . . . We have gained university status, we have secured a building and a site, and we have the prospect of regular income, we have attracted students and we are training teachers. But how far the new activity will prove to be genuine science and not mere culture or shallow technical instruction remains to be seen . . .' But her later life, like J. S. Mill's, was haunted by literary ambitions. She wanted to be both the author of a new science of society and to write a novel, *Sixty Years On*, in which the two major themes were to be the final emancipation of women and the steady advance of state welfare services. In the event, the novel remained a dream, substituted by her diaries and her two volumes of autobiography, *My Apprenticeship* (1926) and *Our Partnership* (1948).

She married Sidney Webb in 1892. The marriage produced 'solid but unreadable books' (Webb and Webb, 1948: 13) but was childless; she thought of herself as having had four children: the London School of Economics (LSE), the Minority Report, *The New Statesman*, and *Soviet Communism* . . . (Lepenies, 1988: 135). Her search for science and for faith led to admiration of Lenin and of the Soviet Union as a 'New Civilization'. She died in 1943 never having resolved her competing impulses towards science and literature nor her perennial attraction to religious ritual.

Malcolm Muggeridge's wickedly satirical account of the Webbs' final internment in Westminster Abbey 'of two distinguished upholders of Soviet Dictatorship' is itself a demonstration of the literary contribution to the description of British customs. Beatrice Webb's dotty sister Rosie (Mrs Dobbs) turned up to make a famous intervention. Identical urns containing Beatrice's and Sidney's ashes were displayed in the Abbey. 'Which', she inquired bemusedly, 'is Sidney and which is Beatrice?' (Muggeridge, 1975, Vol. 2: 302). The question could have been metaphorical or rather metasociological for it still applies in sociology today. The Webbs thought of themselves as sociologists, assembling and·classifying the facts of society as would zoologists with flora and fauna and then applying their results as social engineering in the guidance of social policy towards local government, trade unions, cooperatives, or poverty. These principles were observed in their *Methods Of Social Study* (1932). While insisting on sympathetic understanding in the social sciences (and specifying Shakespeare and Goethe as exemplars of *verstehen*), they nonetheless stuck to their biological conception of the character of sociology.

But he indefatigably led his life from project to project while she gradually allowed her literary dreams to dissipate themselves into her voluminous diary (Norman and Jeanne MacKenzie, 1982, 1983, 1984). 'The model of a philistine' was Virginia Woolf's judgement on Sidney.

The Claims of Literature

The novelist gripped the reading public in Victorian England at least as firmly as in France or Russia. Just as Balzac, Hugo, and Zola were avidly read in France so was the galaxy of novelists in England. Perhaps the most enduring was Charles Dickens (1812–70). Innocence is displayed by his Amy in *Little Dorrit* or by Lizzie Hexham in *Our Mutual Friend*, miserliness by Fagin in *Oliver Twist*, lust for gold by Merdle, again in *Little Dorrit*. Dickens began to parallel Balzac with a no less vast and vivid contemporaneous picture of London and of provincial life in England. And he was followed by an estimable band of novelists, including George Eliot, Thackeray, Trollope, Mrs Humphry Ward, and the Brontës. Together with Cobbett, Carlyle, J. S. Mill, and Ruskin they developed what F. R. Leavis was to call *The Great Tradition* and Raymond Williams *The Long Revolution*—a sustained criticism of the social consequences of the industrial revolution. Writing about the poor began in the eighteenth century, but confused the sober, the riotous, and the n'er-do-wells, as for example in Defoe's *Moll Flanders* (1722). Beatrice Webb complained of this continuing habit among journalists and social investigators in the nineteenth century when she visited her respectable working-class relatives at Bacup in Lancashire.

Among the nineteenth-century novelists, Mary Ann Evans (George Eliot (1819–80)) may be taken as representative. We may treat her here not only because she ironically had a brief intimacy with Herbert Spencer but perhaps more because she was an early example of a person who espoused the cause of literature as the prime vehicle of social criticism, was a woman, a meritocrat, of 'humble origin', a provincial non-conformist, and a moral idealist—all significant roles in the structure of Victorian society.

Among her works, *Silas Marner* (1861) is a tale, in the form of a parable echoing Bunyan's *Pilgrim's Progress* (1678), told to illuminate the central problems of the industrial revolution in Britain—the loss of community and the loss of faith. In a perspicacious introduction to the Penguin edition of *Marner* in 1967, Queenie Leavis writes:

> The book begins by deliberately establishing in 'anthropological'[1] terms the conditions of a poor nineteenth century Christian whose burden is not original sin but loss of faith and of community—in fact what the City [Lantern Yard in Leicester] had given him in the way of a religion was not recognisable as such by the traditions of the countryside, the village life in which the English civilised themselves' (p. 14).

---

[1] Mrs Leavis's use of the term 'anthropological' rather than 'sociological' reflects a hostile Cambridge attitude to the social sciences, including sociology.

Both Mrs Leavis and George Eliot mythologise the 'old fashioned village life', the latter through nostalgia for her rural childhood by contrast with the crowded dirty streets of London, the former for ideological twentieth-century reasons, misrepresenting the village of Raveloe as 'the timeless past of the pack-horse and spinning wheel of the organic community and the unified society' (p. 14). Yet the, possibly vain, search for community has been a preoccupation of sociologists from that time and the secularization thesis is disputed among sociologists of religion into the twenty-first century.

A striking aspect of the *Silas* story is the confrontation of market relations with those of community and the outcome for the care of young children (Young and Halsey, 1995). Young and I ended our, avowedly partisan, pamphlet published by the left-leaning think tank Institute of Public and Policy Research (IPPR) with a reference to her novel, published in 1861, about a time when the nineteenth-century form of child neglect was becoming more and more visible. Silas, unjustly thrown out of the narrow community of his chapel, migrated southwards to live amongst strangers (Raveloe) and set himself to work as a weaver. He was a marginal individual connected to others only through the market for his cloth. His reaction was to hoard gold from his earnings. But, as the tale runs, he was robbed of his gold and left with a golden-haired infant child. He then had his own glimpse of socialism. As Eliot puts it: 'In old days there were angels who came and took men by the hand and led them away from the city of destruction. We see no white winged angels now. But yet men are led away from threatening destruction: a hand is put into theirs which leads them gently towards a calm and bright land so that they look no more backward; and the hand may be a little child's.' The future, we argued, must give us a new child-centredness in a new community.

Mrs Leavis goes further, pointing out that George Eliot demonstrates a sophisticated understanding of the many facets of ideology and inequality, leisure and work, class and status, in the English countryside of the 1820s without idolizing the villagers. 'The coarse repartee and the illiterate arguments in the Rainbow [the local pub], drink and stupid jokes and superstitions are there and coexist with great good sense and kindliness and love of children, and with the hospitality and co-operation that are obligatory in the Raveloe Code' (p. 39). Included among these complex elements of a community life was the class dialect of the people 'whose speech and art of expressing, ... notable for its force and rhythm, and subtlety, had a flavour quite absent from educated English' (p. 41).

Nothing should surprise us in all this; sociologists are interested in the role-playing that makes up a social structure and may be expected to apply their findings to urge or to warn against proposals for social reform. Men and women of letters like Balzac, Dostoevski, Goethe, George Sand, or William Morris may be similarly inclined and perhaps more explicitly passionate about people in society. The surprise is that, as social groups, they have not found ways of living together or side by side in coffee houses, salons, or university departments with less friction than they have exhibited over the past two centuries. And part of the explanation must be the deeply divisive impact of science on culture, on religious beliefs, and on politics in that period.

At all events the war went on. In the end it divided the Webbs from H. G. Wells who had been recruited to the Co-efficients Club of 12 in 1902, but in 1911 published *The New Machiavelli,* a sociological novel in which Sidney and Beatrice, thinly disguised as fictional characters, were both devotees of the uncritical faith in science propounded by Herbert Spencer. Wells had joined the Sociological Society as a founding member in 1903. In 1906, he lectured to it at LSE on 'The So-Called Science Of Sociology', denying the subject's scientific pretensions, demanding the destruction of Comte and Spencer as idols, and insisting that Plato was the original source of sociological thought. He also echoed the familiar dismissal that sociologists could not agree on the definition of their subject, but went on to claim that all procedures founded on mathematics (counting, classifying, computing) led only to error. What was needed for progress was a combination of science and art. In future, there could be no scientific but only a literary sociology (Wells, 1907). Wells, it is said, had wanted the chair of sociology created at LSE in 1907, but it went to Hobhouse.[2] Not until 1950 did a man of letters enter the British sociological professoriate—Charles Madge.

Madge was a rebellious child of empire who turned away from the imperial inheritance of his father, one of 'Milner's young men' who busied themselves with rebuilding the empire after the Boer war. Charles was born in Johannesburg in 1912. When his father was killed in the First World War he was brought to England. He bore the personal marks of a gentle and superior upbringing—a diffident and self-effacing manner that hid his passionate and impulsively radical nature. He was a clever child, entering Winchester as a scholar, and going on with a classical scholarship to Magdalene College, Cambridge where he was determined to read science. He had already begun to write poetry. Could the two interests be combined?

The 1930s were times of turbulence for intellectuals. Not only were the economies of the world in disarray, but Madge's generation was faced with political and moral upheaval. Dictatorship threatened democracy, slump brought the menace of social inequality. Madge struggled to combine science and verse in the service of humanity as did his Cambridge contemporaries like J. D. Bernal with his *The Social Function of Science* (1939), or Lancelot Hogben with his *Science for the Citizen* (1938a) and *Mathematics for the Million* (1937). Madge welcomed news from the East and became an inactive member of the Communist Party. From Paris too he welcomed surrealism (a movement to apply realistically the ideas of psychoanalysis and Marxism in aid of social change). His poems were selected by W. B. Yeats for inclusion in the *Oxford Book of Modern Verse* (1936). And his personal radicalism led to his being 'swept off his feet', as the saying then went, by the glamorous young Kathleen Raine for

---

[2] This may be doubted. There is nothing in the biographies of H. G. Wells to confirm that he ever applied and nothing in the letters or diary of Beatrice Webb (N. J. Mackenzie, 1971 and 1982) to suggest that he wanted to pursue an academic rather than a literary career, though he did play with a political one through his attempted reform of the Fabian Society. In any case the main competition was between Hobhouse and Geddes.

whom he left Cambridge, his degree incomplete, to seek his fortune in London. They married in 1938 but the marriage was dissolved in 1942.[3]

Meanwhile he came under the favourable notice of T. S. Eliot who liked his poetry if not his politics, published his first book of verse in 1937 (*The Disappearing Castle*), and was influential in getting him a job as reporter on the *Daily Mirror* (1935-6). Then came the event for which Madge is properly remembered: he founded Mass Observation with the autodidact anthropologist and entrepreneurial publicizer and self-publicizer Tom Harrisson.

At the *Daily Mirror* Madge became increasingly conscious of the gap between what ordinary people thought and what their leaders thought they thought. So deeply impressed was he by this gulf between popular opinion and its representation by the powerful in press, parliament, and party that, when Edward VIII abdicated, he wrote to the *New Statesman* (2 January 1937) calling for 'mass observation' to create 'mass science'. He knew both the popular Caribbean calypso 'On the 10th of December 1936, the Duke of Windsor went to get his kicks...', and the constitutional opinions of the Queen, Baldwin, and Churchill. He wanted to interpret each to the other and to base democracy on shared scientific fact.

By extraordinary chance Tom Harrisson published his first and only poem in the same issue of *NS&N* as Madge's letter. Harrisson, recently returned from 'living with cannibals' in the New Hebrides in the Pacific, was setting up a study of the English natives of the North in Bolton (Worktown). He wrote to Madge in Blackheath and within a month the national Mass Observation was formed. Two such contrasted personalities could hardly be expected to cooperate permanently and Madge soon drifted away, but not before the enterprise had achieved success and national notice: and not before the Madge/Harrison partnership had produced a Pelican Special, *Britain* (1939), in which their journalistic skills had combined to offer a lively picture of contemporary life through the eyes of 'observers' and voluntary diarists from all over the country.

Mass Observation was as Madge put it 'a science of ourselves'. It sprang, according to Tom Jeffery (1978: 3), 'from a realization that ordinary people were being misled by a complacent press and an indifferent government...'. Current sociology was dismissed as academic. The urgent need was to amass facts and to circulate them. Madge's day reports after a year confronted him with 2,300,000 words. He needed a year to sort them out. T. H. Marshall in *Highway*, December 1937 and Marie Jahoda in *Sociological Review* Vol. XXX, 1938 recognized the sincerity of the intention behind the Bolton survey and the national panel of volunteers' diaries, but denounced the method as unscientific. The total of all respondents ever replying between 1937 and 1945 was 1,894. They were youngish, left-leaning, and preponderantly middle class and therefore not a random sample of the national population. Nevertheless, the archives now deposited at Sussex University (for details see Calder and Sheridan, 1984: 246-59) are an invaluable source to social historians of the war and immediate pre-war period.

---

[3] When he married Inez Pearn. Each wife bore him a son and a daughter.

After Mass Observation, Madge's career became more soberly conventional. He analysed working-class spending habits for J. M. Keynes at the National Institute for Economic and Social Research from 1940 to 1942, worked on the research staff of PEP in 1944 and as director of the Pilot Press in 1944, and became the Social Development Officer at the new town of Stevenage in 1947, before going on to be the first professor of sociology at Birmingham University from 1950 to 1970. His work there was rather scanty, though he was occasionally employed by UNESCO in development projects. His poetry dwindled and his academic reputation did not prosper. His second wife Inez published novels under the name of Elizabeth Lake and they eventually retired to the South of France where she died in 1976. He married for a third time—Evelyn Brown—in 1979 and she died in 1984.[4]

Oddly enough Richard Hoggart, who came to found the Centre for Contemporary Cultural Studies (CCCS) in 1963 at Birmingham University, had little contact with Madge. Perhaps neither of them knew of a relevant historical event: the plea by T. H. Huxley in 1880 in a lecture at Josiah Mason College (from which the university was subsequently developed by Joe Chamberlain) that sociology should be added to a basically scientific and technological curriculum.

While the CCCS developed more or less quietly in Birmingham under Stuart Hall's leadership from 1964,[5] the spectacular drama was staged in Cambridge as an ill-tempered fight between C. P. Snow and F. R. Leavis. The life of F. R. Leavis, his outsidermanship at Cambridge, and his vision through *Scrutiny* of making English studies the focus of a modern university education, has itself accumulated a wide literature (see, for example, Lepenies, 1988: 175–95; Annan, 1990). Snow in his Rede lecture in Cambridge in 1959 confronted and contrasted the two cultures of literature and science. In England especially, their reciprocal hostility and prejudice—the philistinism of the scientist and the indifferent ignorance of the humanist—had dire consequences for a burgeoning scientific civilization. He accused literary circles of harbouring anti-democratic attitudes. Since science and democracy were the bases of future development, he wanted pre-eminence for the culture of science in the education of undergraduates and an end to the traditional dominance of letters. Leavis gave a polemical reply in his Richmond lecture of 1962 (Leavis, 1962).

The dispute has never ended. What is of interest here is not so much that it was a split begun by Matthew Arnold and T. H. Huxley in the last decades of the nineteenth century, but that a third culture, that of social science or social studies, was now beginning to make it a triangular struggle.

---

[4] While he never lost his early enthusiasm for social planning on behalf of humanity, his later years were dogged by ill health until he died in 1996, still the same charming and tentatively friendly man but somehow defeated and self-critical despite his very considerable talents.

[5] This mild assertion is turned into a bald one by Chris Rojek and Bryan Turner in their 'Decorative Sociology: towards a critique of the cultural turn' (*Sociological Review*, 2000, 48/4). But the actual occurrences were more complicated. They are retailed more fully with unequivocal appreciation of Stuart Hall's part by Richard Hoggart in volume 3 of his autobiography *An Imagined Life*, 1993: 89–100.

The sociology department at the University of Birmingham, once the home of such leading sociologists as John Rex or Sheila Allen, the second woman to be elected President of the British Sociological Association (BSA) in 1975, was a conspicuous victim of the ideological disputes and fiscal cuts of the 1970s and early 1980s. It was demolished and the incumbents scattered to other departments. But the chair was resuscitated in 1998 with Frank Webster as the new professor and the department reconstituted as a combination of cultural studies and sociology. Webster's inaugural lecture looked forward to a new period in which the quantitative strengths of Oxford would be united with the qualitative merits of Birmingham's and Stuart Hall's CCCS.[6]

Cultural studies, nevertheless, have come to occupy a large if not dominant place in sociology at the beginning of the twenty-first century. The reference here is to British universities, especially since their expansion and absorption of the polytechnics in 1992. At the end of the twentieth century, science correspondingly occupied a shrinking space as indicated by the minor, voluntary, or absent component of statistics in first degrees or even second degrees (Masters) in sociology. While some introductory texts like W. G. Runciman's *Social Animal* marvelled at the exactitudes of sampling technique and advocated the learning of these elementary mysteries of mathematics as essential equipment for all those who would call themselves sociologists, there were others advertising themselves as introductory text books of sociology in which no numbers, apart from page numbers, were to be found. Of course, there are some sociology degrees, for example, at the University of Surrey, where papers in quantitative analysis cannot be avoided. But from many universities the sociology graduates may emerge with little or indeed none of what others would regard as the *sine qua non* of a professional sociologist. The profession accordingly remains a mixture of people some of whom might be entirely competent in the use of log linear models while others are incapable of defining a chi-square or the difference between absolute and relative rates of mobility. The majority no doubt lie between the extremes of statistical competence and innumeracy (and attitudes towards the importance of scientific and literary approaches to the disciplines are similarly scattered). But it was always so. The division is as old as the discipline. The question now is whether division will or ought to end in schism, and if so in what organizational form(s).

Conclusion on Cultural Studies v. Quantitative Sociology

We have considered the battle for possession of the social studies, which has persisted from the beginning of the nineteenth century. In Popperian terms the strength of modern positivist quantitative sociology lies in the rigorous

[6] Unhappily the marriage ended in divorce. The University of Birmingham again ended its sociology staff in 2002 for 'research failure' (the RAE had ranked it 3A). Webster could have stayed on but bravely chose severance. See Chapter 7, p. 130.

checking of clearly formulated hypotheses against meticulously collected fact. This is where the novel is at its weakest. But in the same Popperian terms, fiction of the Balzacian or Dickensian type is rich as a source of hypotheses as well as providing descriptive material of normally superior subtlety and range.

The inference to be drawn is clear. There is space for both 'the sociological novel' and the statistically sophisticated survey—the one to describe and formulate (Popper's induction), the other to attempt falsification (Popper's deduction and experiment). What is fatal to sociology is antagonism between the two approaches and what is debilitating is the persistence of education in isolation of the two, resulting in mutual incomprehension between scientifically trained sociologists and innumerate products of the schools of cultural studies.

There is here a reflection of the tension between quantitative and qualitative research methods—the one addressing questions of what, where, when, and how, the other exploring why. Taken together such research data can yield results which are accurate, rich, and rounded. If postmodernism has retreated then, it may be argued, these two approaches need no longer condemn each other but instead cooperate so as to give a fuller and truer picture of society.

There can be little doubt that, at the beginning of the twenty-first century, there is a central debate in sociology between cultural studies and quantitative science. But that is not all. We shall see below that the story is also of two escapes—from London and from philosophy. We can adumbrate and anticipate these themes, which will occupy us in detail from Chapter 3, by considering the career of W. J. H. Sprott that illustrates first the role of Cambridge as an originator, second the Abrams pathway to institutionalization by describing a de facto sociologist who never formally held a chair in sociology but in philosophy and psychology, and third the role of the provincial universities, in this case of Nottingham, as a challenge to the LSE.

W. J. H. Sprott

Sprott was born in 1897. His father was a country solicitor. He was sent to Felstead, a private boarding school with a rigorous regime, and then, in 1919, entered Clare College, Cambridge to read the moral sciences in which he took a double first.

This was the central characterization of Edwardian boyhood among the English professional classes. But Sprott was eccentric. Charm, wit, and oratorical skill led him effortlessly into the magic circle of John Maynard Keynes's close friends; he became an intimate of E. M. Forster who eventually made him his literary executor, and of Lytton Strachey. He became 'Sebastian' in the overlapping circles of Cambridge and Bloomsbury. He was elected to the exclusive society of the Apostles in 1920. He regularly went riding with Keynes, accompanied him on a holiday to Algeria and Tunisia in 1921, and was probably his last male lover. This intimacy, though not the friendship, ended with Keynes's marriage to Lydia Lopokova in 1925.

In that year Sprott, who had been a demonstrator in the psychology laboratory at Cambridge since 1922, moved from Cambridge to a lectureship in psychology at Nottingham University, though the habit of frequent, almost daily, letters customary between 'Bloomsberries' continued to include 'Sebastian'. Much of this correspondence was later destroyed. Thus, many of the letters from Sprott were burnt either by Maynard himself or by his brother Geoffrey. However a few survived. One, written in April 1921, after reading Hirschfield's *History of Sex*, reads 'I suspect I am tainted with Transvestitismus, Autonomosexualität, and Hermaphroditismus... to say nothing of Homosexualität and Onanie... My love, Yours ever, Sebastian' (Skidelsky, 1992: 35). That was to Keynes.

The combination of intellect with aestheticism was much admired after the First World War, so much so that 'sprott' was generalized in Cambridge argot as a label for fashionable cleverness. Yet, Sprott made no secret of his sexual tastes. He pioneered the path to the nightclubs of Berlin, subsequently followed by Christopher Isherwood and W. H. Auden. Later, in the period between the Wars, with his friend Joe Ackerley, he sought 'low-life adventure' in the pubs of Dover and Portsmouth. In Nottingham, he lived in a squalid Victorian terrace where academic colleagues and their wives would be served at table by his discharged prisoners. Here the Bloomsbury appellation 'Sebastian' was dropped in favour of the more matey and proletarian first name of Jack.

Nevertheless, this dark side of Sprott's character, throwing a shadow as it undoubtedly did of loneliness and sadness over his personal life, did not darken the charming courtesy or cloud the manners of the old-fashioned don, which he unfailingly presented to the respectable world. Nor did it blight his academic performance. He was applauded on every side as a lecturer of outstanding wit and eloquent exposition. Invitations to give public lectures came in a steady flow throughout his career. Caustic and ruthless demolition of theories, especially those promoting salvation through simplistic politics or the 'quick fix', came readily to his lips, and was appreciated by colleagues or students who relished his private conversation.

Moreover, he ranged freely over a wider intellectual territory than is now attempted by the vast majority of academics. He held chairs in philosophy and in psychology at Nottingham. Above all he held fast to his belief in sociology as an academic discipline throughout the time in which it was resisted by the British establishment, that is, from his translation to a lectureship in psychology at Nottingham in 1925 through his incumbency in the chair of philosophy there from 1948 to 1960. He served Nottingham University with steadfast loyalty and was its Public Orator from 1948 to 1964.

Sprott translated Kretschmer's *Physique and Character* and Freud's *New Introductory Lectures*. But his sociological writings, though little read today, remain important in the history of the subject. He was the first English sociologist to offer an informed, critical, and sympathetic view both of European writing in 'the grand manner' and of the sophisticated functionalism of the American R. K. Merton. There were only three named chairs of sociology in the United Kingdom when he gave the Josiah Mason lectures at the University of

Birmingham in 1953. His *Sociology* (1949), *Science and Social Action* (1954), and *Sociology at the Seven Dials* (1962) form a bridge from Hobhousian evolutionism to functionalism, and they also link Parsonian general theory to more modest theories of the middle ground. So Sprott challenged functionalism by quoting Talcott Parsons, 'the combination of an occupationally differentiated industrial system and a significantly solidary kinship system *must* be a system of stratification in which the children of the more highly placed come to have differential advantages' (*Social System*, p. 161). He thereby showed that the evolution of industrial societies has functional limitations (*Science and Social Action*, p. 139). He was a genial and articulate link between the older founders of sociology in Britain, such as Hobhouse and Ginsberg, and the new professionals of the aftermath of the Second World War. He was hailed (*Times*, 14 September 1971) by Sir Leon Radzinowicz as an influential figure in the development of criminology as an academic subject. And all his works were written with lucid elegance.[7]

Conclusion

We have now summarized the claims and counterclaims of the attempt by novelists and men and women of letters to claim the territory of social criticism and 'espèces sociales' for literature, rather than an explanatory subject. We cannot decide whether science or literature is the true owner. We have hinted that the battle has become triangular rather than binary. We shall later trace the institutional history of schism, collaboration, and the varied attempts of the social sciences to establish themselves as an independent academic force. We turn now to relate the history of the search for a science of society.

---

[7] Sprott died in September 1971 at the age of 74 at his home in Blakeney, Norfolk. He was childless and unmarried, but mourned by many friends.

2

The Rise of Scientific Method

S URVEYS OF one sort or another have been with us at least since the Norman Conquest. The word came into use as a verb in 1467 and, according to the *OED*, means 'the act of viewing, examining or inspecting in detail especially for some specific purpose' or it means 'a written statement or description embodying the results of such examination'. In 2001, the BBC's Radio 4 *Today Programme* undertook a survey on the dating of autumn, designed to test the hypothesis that the growing season in Britain was being elongated by early springs and late autumns, possibly as a consequence of global warming. Listeners who happened to be listening were invited to send in observations of such events as the departure of swallows, the ripening of conkers, or the last cut of the lawn, and a report was promised. Of course, the British are well known as a nation of bird watchers and gardeners, and collective expertise is worth mobilizing; but some, and not only sociologists, meteorologists, or statisticians, might well question both the collection and the report of such a survey, for in its scientific form enquiry of this kind has a history and, before Arthur Bowley introduced probability to sampling, a pre-history. Yet, as the BBC example shows, pre-history and history overlap and as recently as the 1940s, that is, a generation after Bowley, Geoffrey Gorer wrote his *Exploring English Character* (1955) after inviting participation by advertising in a popular daily newspaper. Our purpose here is to outline the origins, antecedents, advances, and vicissitudes of scientific social surveys as a major instrument of empirical sociology. At the outset a distinction may be made between the first half of the *OED* definition (collection) and the second (analysis), though they have interacted in the course of development of the method.

'What's wrong with sociology?' was the title of one of the anxious books that greeted the twenty-first century in Europe and America (Cole, 2001). We have seen the disputatious beginnings of academic sociology—the contest for possession between literature and science, the new gospel of a 'science of society' in the early nineteenth century and its chequered history after the 1840s, the uncertain and minimal, and again contentious, first absorption of it into the universities of London and (though hitherto unmentioned) Liverpool in the early twentieth century, and especially its nervous and philosophical placement at the London

A good introductory text for non-statisticians is Agresti, A. and Finlay, B. (1997) *Statistical Methods for the Social Sciences* (Prentice Hall). The essential terms are explained in the text and in footnotes here.

School of Economics (LSE), which was emerging as an alternative citadel of culture to the established classical and upper-class traditions of education in Oxford and Cambridge.

After the Second World War new enthusiasm for sociology spread to the provincial universities and it expanded rapidly in the 1950s and 1960s only to be doubted, slowed, and arrested in the 1970s and 1980s. The enthusiasm is our theme in Chapters 4 and 5. The pessimism will occupy us in one way or another thereafter. But in this chapter we can ask the opposite question—'what is right with sociology?' Many answers can still be given. It has led the extension of the enlightenment project from the natural into the social world and thus provided, at least for its denizens, an endlessly absorbing set of teaching materials for the education of the young and an exciting set of intellectual problems for its researchers. It was the engine of moral progress for nineteenth-century reformers, the inspiration for the post-war generation of people who had experienced the siege socialism of the Second World War, and a continuing challenge to the contemporary young to understand the changes and the continuities of their world.

No doubt there would be disagreement as to whether sociological theory has advanced since, say, Malthus, but very few would question the assertion that methods of social study have advanced and even cumulated in the past century. Which leads to our topic in this chapter, expressed modestly by an outstanding practitioner, James Davis (Cole, 2001: 106). 'Controlled experimentation is seldom possible in sociology. After a flashy start, mathematical formalisation doesn't seem to be getting anywhere because you can't formalise mush. This leaves the non-experimental analysis of large data sets—OK I'll say it out loud, "survey analysis" as our sharpest tool'. We must now trace the rise of the sample social survey, or 'finite population sampling' as the statisticians have it.

At the end of the twentieth century, a memorial organization devoted to the theory and method of social statistics was instituted by the University of Manchester to commemorate the life and work of Catherine Marsh. It is the Centre for Census and Survey Research, and named after her. Her biography dramatizes the past history and present discontents of quantitative contributions to sociology. She was an undergraduate in Cambridge in the high tide of anti-positivist fervour—an accompaniment of the still unexplained student rebelliousness of the 1960s. Given Cambridge's reluctant and controversial half-acceptance of sociology at that time and its traditional Tripos arrangements, Marsh took Social and Political Sciences as a Part II subject. Though she sat the compulsory research methods paper, she graduated with the conventional conviction 'that survey research was hopelessly empiricist, the product of vulgar American sociology, atheoretical and generally a waste of time' (Marsh, 1982: 1).

Vulgar American? It was ironic that her conversion began in listening to the always amusing and cleverly skilled American Jim Davis, then Director of the National Opinion Research Center (NORC) at Chicago, who came to England to give a course of lectures on survey analysis at a summer school organized by the

Social Science Research Council (SSRC) using Paul Lazarsfeld's method of elabo-rating the variables in a survey. She was, she writes, 'hooked on this method of handling data analysis' (p. 2) while retaining her rather arch views on other aspects of survey research. George Bernard Shaw once narrated the story from the 1870s of the old lady from Colchester, a devout Methodist, who moved to the City Road in London, and, as was her wont, set out the following Sunday and mistook the Hall of Science for the local Methodist Chapel. She there sat at the feet of Charles Bradlaugh for many years entranced by his eloquence, without questioning his orthodoxy or moulting a feather of her faith (*Prefaces*, 1965: 165).

Not so Catherine Marsh. She shortly thereafter moved to a new job in London at the Survey Unit, set up in 1970 and modelled on NORC and the Survey Research Center at Michigan. Apprenticed at the Survey Unit, Marsh painfully learned her survey skills and returned to the academic fold in 1976, convinced that there was no contradiction between good sociology and good science (Marsh, 1982). Her book on the survey method appeared in 1982 as one of Martin Bulmer's series devoted to combining two hitherto stubbornly separ-ated elements of sociology—theory and empirical evidence. Marsh offers in this book a succinct review of the contributions of surveys to sociological explanation, firm replies to the critics, and a brief history beginning with the Domesday Book of 1085.

Yet, two decades later the editors of the *International Journal of Public Opinion Research* (IJPOR) tell us that 'there is a general impression in the social science world that quantitative research approaches have largely been American, while European scholarship has emphasised systematic theory' (*IJPOR*, 2001, 13/3: 225). It is, of course, true that the classical sociological theorists were European—Weber, Durkheim, Pareto, and others among whom Marx has been increasingly recognized since about 1970[1]—but equally true that, at least after the Second World War, American theorists, especially Merton and Parsons, have influenced several generations of students worldwide. What the editors were insisting here was that Paul Lazarsfeld was claimed to be both 'the founder of modern empirical sociology' (Jerebek, 2001: 229-44) and also a European. The same claim has been made for Booth and Rowntree, the English 'chocolate sociologists'[2] of the end of the nineteenth and the beginning of the twentieth centuries (Abrams, 1951; Easthope, 1974). No less an authority than Claus Moser has asserted '. . . it is Booth who should be considered the Father of Scientific Social Surveys' (Moser, 1958: 18). This view is contested by Marsh and by Selvin (1985) who saw Booth's greatest contribution to social science satirically as a mere £30,000.[3] A more plausible claim to innovation perhaps could be made for William Farr (1807–83), or for Quetelet, or for Richard Jones, the political economist (Goldman, 1987) who attacked Ricardian political economy as

---

[1] A new introduction to Marx, especially early Marx, was influential in this regard (Bottomore, T. and M. Rubel, *Karl Marx: Selected Writings in Sociology and Social Philosophy*, 1956).
[2] In fact, Booth was neither a quaker nor connected with the cocoa trade.
[3] £30,000 was what he spent on his Inquiry.

deductionist and advocated a new inductivism to dons in Cambridge among whom Whewell, the leading natural scientist, was a supporter. Quetelet (1796–1874), the contemporaneous Belgian mathematician whose interest in 'social physics' angered Auguste Comte as a theft of his own concept, also made crucial advances in multiple correlation techniques leading towards modern multiple causation (Marsh, 1982; Goldthorpe, 2000). Farr, as a prominent civil servant and devotee of the new science of society, was at the Register Office from 1837. Quetelet is described by Goldman as 'the dominant statist of the period' who influenced the statistical movement in Britain more than anyone.

Anyone? It depends on the exact question. Are we speaking of statistics, of political arithmetic, of social causation, of demography, or of sample surveys? John Graunt (1620–70) is arguably the father of statistics. He worked out the first life table[4] in his *Natural and Political Observations on the London Bills of Mortality* (1662). Together with William Petty he launched an 'invisible college', the political arithmeticians of the seventeenth century. But probability underlies all these phrases.

The traditional survey was descriptive, designed to set out its findings in relatively simple tabulations. Analytic surveys are, mathematically, an application of the general theory of probability with respect to both the representativeness of the sample and the measurement of associated factors through multivariate analysis.[5] Risk and uncertainty are universal concerns for human beings. The need for probability solutions is accordingly a normal demand of every day life. Magic, spells, and tokens have supplied the traditional answers, but mathematicians supply modern answers. Pascal and Fermat in their correspondence of 1654 are commonly held to be the originators, though medieval sources, notably the Pardoner's story in Chaucer's *Canterbury Tales*, are also cited. However Karl Pearson (1837–1936) named Blaire Pascal (1623–62) as introducing modern probability theory. Here then is yet another claim. Certainly Pascal suggested the notion of mathematical expectation to solve the 'Problem of Points' (how to allocate gains and losses in an unfinished game of chance) and, also certainly, in his correspondence with Fermat in 1654, he set a problem about the duration of play, which later became known as the 'gambler's ruin'.[6] It is true that he 'solved' the problem of belief in his 'Pascal's Wager'. He used his concept of expectation to argue that one must assume the existence of God because however small the probability, the value of eternal salvation was infinite and it is essential to 'consider mathematically the magnitudes when these things are multiplied together'.

---

[4] A table which shows the number of persons who, of a given number living at a specified age, live to successive higher ages, together with the number who die meanwhile.

[5] Just as univariate analysis describes variation in a single variable and bivariate analysis does so for two variables, so multivariate analysis examines the simultaneous effects of many variables taken together. Algebraically this takes the form of a set of linear equations which specify how the variables combine with each other to affect the dependent variable.

[6] A game in which a gambler wins a certain predetermined sum of money for every success and loses a second sum for every failure. The play may go on until his initial capital is exhausted and he is ruined.

Perhaps a case could even be made for Florence Nightingale, 'the Passionate Statistician' who, after the Crimean War, used her popularity, family connections, and wealth to do battle with officialdom in the cause of sanitary reform in Army hospitals and more generally in public health. She was a competent statistician determined to discover and to disseminate knowledge of the causes of sickness. She worked closely with Farr and much admired Quetelet. Her resolve was to win over the politicians and their bureaucrats to the view that the main cause of the devastating death rates among Crimean soldiers was not their half-starved and feeble condition at admission, but the filthy state of the hospital itself. Farr both helped and hindered her. He shared her enthusiasm for the ascertainment of 'hard fact' but he cautioned against her over-dramatic presentation. The statistician, he wrote to her, 'has nothing to do with causation; he is almost certain in the present state of knowledge to err' (Heyde and Seneta, 2001: 173, essay by M. Stone).

R. A. Fisher (1890–1962), the English statistician, working at the Rothamsted Experimental Station in the 1920s and 1930s, made major advances in statistical theory and method and advanced regression analysis.[7] He worked mainly in the biological sciences but excited the world of social survey by showing how all but one factor could be held constant by the now familiar device of creating control and experimental groups by random allocation. In Marsh's judgement however the innovative prize has to go to the Scotsman George Udny Yule, 'in many ways the real founding father of survey analysis' (Marsh, 1982: 42).

These various claims are complicated and verge on the meaningless except as the customarily required assertions in *elogues*, the celebration of the illustrious dead. More intriguing than the search for originators of ideas or theories is the explanation of how, why, and why not crucial advances are or are not made by particular virtuosi under particular circumstances. A case in especial point for this history is that of probabilistic statistics. Why did sociologists and especially English sociologists not apply the methods of the 'new English statistics' to their own problems of multiple correlation with social factors earlier than they did? We shall come to the mystifying cases of Hogben and Glass below. At this point the more general point that modern sociology was born out of political prejudice in the wake of Spencerian, individualistic interpretations of Darwinian evolution may be emphasized. Sociology, it was strongly held and aggressively taught in the English universities before 1950, began where biology left off.

---

[7] The simplest case is that of bivariate linear regression. A line is fitted to the plot of data from two variables so as to represent the trend between them. If we assume that the dependent variable (Y) is determined by the independent variable (X), and that the fit is less than perfect then

$$Y_i = a + Bx_i + E_i$$

that is, the value of Y for the individual is determined by X together with an individual error term, E. The slope of the line is the regression coefficient, B, and a constant a which represents the intercept or point at which the regression line crosses the Y axis.

In a multiple linear regression the equation [$Y = f(X) + E$] remains valid if X, instead of being a single variable, refers to a set of variables $X_1, X_2, \ldots$.

Diverse explanations are offered for the failure of sociology to embrace the probabilistic revolution in statistics. Among these, and covering France and Germany, though not the United States, Goldthorpe's is the most elaborate and most recent (Goldthorpe, 2000). However, these accounts sometimes illustrate the fact of uncertain cumulation. Cumulation is the mark of science but it is by no means automatic, as is shown by the famous case of Mendel's long neglected genetic experiments in a monastery garden. In sociological surveys the degree of uncertainty tends to be greater than in the laboratory sciences, where information retrieval techniques are more highly organized and consequently arguments about origins and priorities more rare.

Nevertheless, it is worth setting some of the competitors for originality prizes in their historical place. The first British survey is probably that of the Norman Conquerors in the eleventh century, which illustrates an ancient tradition, at least among numerate governing classes, of assessing their empires for taxation and military purposes. Social changes and challenges are not, however, confined to conquest. They can also arise from environmental or demographic or technical transformation. In Britain, such transformations have been exemplified by the bubonic plagues of the fourteenth century, the London plagues of the seventeenth century, the industrialization and urbanization of the nineteenth century, and the rise of state interventions with their accompanying bureaucracies of health, education, and welfare—the welfare state of the twentieth century.

Historical authorities like Lawrence Goldman, Philip Abrams, Martin Bulmer, Krishan Kumar, and Perry Anderson differ in their interpretations of the history of sociology. This partly reflects the different meanings of crucial words and phrases like 'theory', 'social science(s)', 'social physics', 'social theory', 'social policy', 'empirical sociology', and sociology itself. Our central concern in this chapter is with the social survey—a method that evolved from its origins in political control (the Domesday Book) through administrative convenience (the Census) to its modern forms of sophisticated sociological explanation through birth cohort studies, analyses of voting behaviour, mobility studies, distribution of income statistics, etc.

Goldman, in a series of essays from 1983 to 2002,[8] is concerned with writing the history of social statistics from the point of view of the intentions of the principal actors at the time. Thus, in discussing W. Farr and W. A. Guy he quotes the third annual report of the British Association to the effect that these early Victorian British statists sought 'facts relating to communities of men which are capable of being expressed by numbers, and which promise when sufficiently multiplied, to indicate general laws'. Thus, the statistical movement 'developed a certain self-consciousness in the 1830s as explicit efforts were made to constitute this new science, to define its range and disciplinary boundaries....No single work did more to give shape and order to the new science than Adolphe Quetelet's pioneering social statistical treatise of 1835, *Sur L'Homme*...It was

---

[8] Collected together as a book (Goldman, 2002).

his presence in Cambridge in 1833 that provoked the foundation of the Statistical Section of the British Association and it was Quetelet who then suggested to [Charles] Babbage, that a metropolitan statistical society was needed' (Goldman, 1991: 426). So the London Statistical Society (LSS) was founded in 1834. The Manchester Statistical Society had been formed before the London one—appropriately in the city which was then seen as the centre of the new industrialism. Both were intended as fact-collecting agents of social reform but London saw itself also as, in effect, an arm of government. It evolved in 1887 into the Royal Statistical Society with its own journal.

Quetelet, born in Ghent in 1796 (Hankins, 1908), was educated in mathematics and physics, but during the 1820s turned his prodigious energies to social phenomena. By 1829, he was director of the Belgian census. His aggressive and brilliant positivism caught a European-wide taste for scientific approaches to society in the 1830s and 1840s and was especially well received in England where active social reformers included Chadwick, Farr, Guy, Florence Nightingale, and the Prince Consort, Albert (to whom he was tutor in 1836). Quetelet noticed that the regularity of social phenomena was demonstrable by statistical analysis and that even 'moral' regularities (i.e. rates of crime, divorce, and suicide) displayed the physical regularities already uncovered by natural scientists. Their pattern followed that of the normal distribution of observations of a given phenomenon—an error curve as it was then known. Only later, in the 1870s, did doubts begin when it was further noticed that moral statistics showed greater variation about the mean than would be expected on the theory of random or accidental error. Quetelet himself had noticed this phenomenon, which had led him to early experiments in multivariate analysis. There followed, as Goldthorpe expresses it, quoting the French statistician Desrosières, a movement away from the statistics of the average and towards the statistics of variations (Goldthorpe, 2000: 265). In the meantime, however, Quetelet and his followers had inferred that the social uniformities were caused by social circumstances rather than by individual choice and were accordingly a proper object of social or political action. In that way Quetelet offered powerful intellectual reinforcement to the moral fervour of would-be reformers. As Goldman put it (1991: 428), 'ameliorative reform was now sanctioned by "science", the most potent of Victorian ideologies'.

Thus, the history of the survey may be written from several points of view, none of which has a priori superiority, all of which throw light on the subject. Marsh wants to expound the merits of the survey and to answer its critics. Goldthorpe insists powerfully on the absence, especially in Britain, of recognition by sociologists of the probabilistic revolution in statistics. Both therefore focus on intellectual factors in the cumulation (Marsh) or lack of it (Goldthorpe) in the articulation of theory and method. Kent, Abrams, and Bulmer are also interested in linking theory to method but refer more widely to the non-intellectual components of the absence of synergy. For Abrams the key is a failure of institutionalization. For Goldman the intellectual currents are contained within a broader stream of social changes, especially conflicts over power and influence in

Westminster and Whitehall between the older established land-owning aristocracy (increasingly prone to incompetence and nepotism in early Victorian
England) and the rising power of a new administrative class bent on establishing
meritocracy (Goldman, 1986, 1991). As he sees it, 'Social investigation in the
nineteenth century was something more than those few celebrated poverty
surveys that periodically captured public attention. In the mid-Victorian period
social investigation became part of a bureaucratic routine that was integral to the
processes of constructing, implementing, and regulating social policy, and a
continuing obligation on the state if legislation was to keep pace with changing
social conditions'. Thus, the 'revolution' in government was led by such influential civil servants as Edwin Chadwick, John Simon, William Farr, and James
Kay-Shuttleworth, backed by middle-class professionals in Whitehall and by the
factory inspectors, medical officers of health, inspectors of schools, and chief
constables in the provinces drawn from the class of lawyers, doctors, journalists,
and professors—the experts of Victorian society (Perkin, 1989: 252).

Take, for example, beliefs even among the educated classes about size of
population, its rise and fall, and its causes and consequences. In the seventeenth and eighteenth centuries, mercantilism had held, as a central doctrine,
that a rising population was a major cause of national wealth. Yet strife,
disease, and urban fire in Europe, and especially the plague in England in the
1660s, aroused fears of depopulation and awareness of the absence or unrelia-
bility of public records of birth, fertility, morbidity, and death. There followed
a movement of political arithmetic in the seventeenth century. The fear of
depopulation persisted through the eighteenth century and was accompanied
by exchanges between 'optimists' and 'pessimists' but remained unsettled
until parliament was eventually persuaded to institute a Census in 1801, the
dispute having been turned on its intellectual head by Thomas Malthus in his
Essay on Population (1798).

Up to that historical moment, though influenced by the deep divide of
Christian religion, the unconscious beginning of empire, and the slow advance
in wealth and literacy, Britain remained an essentially rural society, familistic,
localized, governed by aristocracy and gentry in a pre-industrial village culture
of status inequality. Some, and Catherine Marsh is one, describe the changing
social structure of nineteenth-century Britain in a Marxist fashion. Exploitation
was intensified and the emerging classes sealed off from each other, especially in
the northern cities. The rising bourgeoisie feared above all the violence of the
mob as the market displaced divinity in ordaining inequalities of health, housing, income, and living and working conditions. While united in individualistic
belief in free enterprise there was a simultaneous growth of belief among the
middle classes in firm administrative control through measures such as punitive
poor laws and factory reform. These forces were contradictory and ensuing
battles were therefore broad and long. Public record keeping accordingly
developed slowly; necessarily so before the age of the telephone, the aeroplane,
the telegraph, and the computer. The main drive was reform allied to and
supported by the intellectual resolve to develop a science of society in which the

interests of the emerging administrative class, the professional experts of medicine, law, and the civil service, were pitted against a traditional but increasingly incompetent aristocracy (Goldman, 1991) and a newly created ignorant and powerless proletariat (Marsh, 1982). Poverty in the midst of plenty was 'the problem of all problems' for the Victorian era.

Government was dominated by the non-interventionist doctrine of political economy. In the private or civil sphere there were, of course, the Chartists, the riots, the trade unions, and other forms of revolt and protest. But the political agitation that took the form of exposure and scandalizing left a voluminous inheritance to the sociology and history of the nineteenth and early twentieth centuries, from Engels' *Condition of the Working Class in England in 1844* and Henry Mayhew's *London Labour and the London Poor* (1861), through Andrew Mearn's pamphlet *The Bitter Cry of Out Cast London* (1883), the novels of Jack London, and later those of George Orwell, especially his essays on the spike, *Down and Out in Paris and London* (1933) and *The Road to Wigan Pier* (1937). And later, a more scholarly Marxisant study of the relations between classes in Victorian society was Gareth Stedman-Jones' *Outcast London* (1971).

All this literature reflects the shifting class struggles of the nineteenth and twentieth centuries and is of great importance to social history if marginal to the development of the survey method. This may surprise those who see the main origins of the survey in the classical tradition created by Booth and Rowntree and the later studies in London and Merseyside by Llewelyn Smith and Caradog Jones between the Wars. We must therefore look more closely at Charles Booth.

The phrase 'problem of all problems' is associated with him, though coined by his wife Mary. He occupies a disputed position in the history of sociology in Britain. His Inquiry into the London working class, which after seventeen years produced the seventeen volumes of *The Life and Labour of the People of London* (1902–3), was one of several possible beginnings of the development of empirical sociology in Britain because it combined the older customs of social accountancy with those of social investigation described by Kent. The Simeys' biography of Booth offers a vivid description of the social history of Liverpool and tells in detail the story of the Booth family. Charles was born in 1840, brought up in the prosperous home of a corn merchant, and taught the Unitarian version of Christian principles. However, like many members of his class and his own as well as the following generation including Hobhouse, he suffered a catastrophic loss of faith as he contemplated the life of the poor in Toxteth through which he walked daily to the offices of the new family shipping business. What caused poverty and what would cure it? His protestant Unitarian background had given him an answer to both questions: God and Nothing. The collapse of the one and the tragic urgency of the other alienated him from his family and from the way of life of the non-conformist bourgeoisie in Liverpool. His was the moral dilemma of a rich man whose prosperity seemed to be tied inexorably to the poverty he saw all around him. To be sure, Booth always regarded himself as primarily a merchant and a financier. Moreover, his belief in individualism sustained a lifelong detestation of socialism.

What could he do? After eleven years, developing his shipping business from the age of twenty-two, vigorously overworking on both sides of the Atlantic, he left for Switzerland in December 1873 'in so low a state of mental and physical health that doubt was entertained as to whether he would be able to make a full recovery' (Simey and Simey, 1960: 32). Though the Swiss holiday was a failure, leaving his health and the ideological conflict within him (between science and religion) unresolved, Booth returned to London where his wife, a daughter of the Macaulay family, introduced him into a circle of family and friends—'the new intellectual aristocracy' (Noel Annan, 1955)—very different from his Liverpool milieu. Among them was the Potter family. Among the Potter daughters Beatrice took to him and drew a compelling impression of him in her first volume of autobiography '. . . one was left in doubt whether the striking unconventionality betokened an initiating brain or a futile eccentricity' (B. Webb, 1929: 219). Booth's spirits gradually revived. He went back to his exhausting business and practical affairs, deciding that 'the eternal mysteries must remain unsolved' (Simey, 1960: 60). He was able to rest content with the 'reverent unbelief'—to use a phrase of his own—which sustained him until his death. But he also practised the Unitarian doctrine that wealth brought social responsibility. He was personally ascetic but spent his income freely on whatever he deemed desirable including his famous Inquiry.

'Half a century after the Inquiry', wrote the Simeys in 1960, 'it has become plain that it represents one of the first attempts to apply the methods of the natural sciences to the solution of the social problems of an industrial society' (p. 242). 'In fact, he was not merely a successful statistician but a great sociologist even though the standard textbooks of sociology give him virtually no mention at all' (p. 247). Simey footnotes several American textbooks. Since 1960, the modern American view has been expressed most clearly by James Coleman. In 1979 he wrote 'The modern period in the history of social policy research began with the development of systematic sample survey research in the late 1930s and the 1940s. The creation of this instrument allowed what had been an art in the hands of Charles Booth in London to become a technical skill based on codified methods with which ordinary social researchers could provide policy-relevant information' (Coleman in Bottomore and Nisbet, 1978: 694).

Even Coleman's is a pious judgement. First, Booth did not use sampling which is owed to Arthur Bowley, though probably the first example of it was a study by the Manchester Statistical Society in 1833 (Kent, 1981: 17). Bowley, a Cambridge mathematics graduate of 1891, addressed the Royal Statistical Society in 1912 with an account of the technique using a sample of one in twenty households in Reading. When the first Chair of statistics was created at LSE in 1919, Bowley was elected to it. Second, policy-relevant information from survey presupposes the testing of theory. Booth nowhere explicates such a theory: this had to await the development of correlation, regression, and multivariate analysis by the statisticians Galton, Pearson, and Yule. As to sampling it must be noted that Quetelet was opposed, preferring to base his studies on complete enumeration. Booth followed suit. The idea of basing studies of large populations on sampling seems to have come from A. N. Kiaer, the Director of the Norwegian Central Bureau of Statistics who, in the 1890s, used sampling in enquiries into old age and sickness benefits. Kiaer presented ideas about what he called 'representative sampling' at the International Statistical Institute (ISI) in 1895. They were opposed, but Kiaer persisted in his advocacy. In the end he won. Bowley later presented a theoretical discussion of sampling (including random sampling, both stratified and unrestricted) at the ISI meeting in 1925. Similar developments, starting before the First World War, took place in Russia and a treatise entitled *Basic Theory of Sampling Methods* was published by Kowalsky in 1924 (Chatterjee, 2002: 509). Finally the Polish statistician Neyman established, in 1934, that 'in the case of a finite population the only rational way to sample would be to adopt some form of probability selection' (Chatterjee, 2002). From that point the sample survey developed rapidly.

What Booth had accomplished over and above the meticulous presentation of fact (an immense labour on a huge metropolitan population collected by house-to-house visiting, the witness of informants, and governmental statistics) was a detailed chronicle of the life, the work, the housing, and the leisure of the working class in late Victorian London. Moreover, he built into his work *implicitly* many sociological insights which, had they been made explicit, would be recognized as among the theoretical concepts of today's sociology including urban ecology, social stratification, and the sociologies of industry, religion, education, and leisure. As Kent (1981: 62) puts it, he fashioned 'a very sophisticated sociological eye and a scientific attitude towards social facts'.

Perhaps Booth's greatest failure lay in his rejection of Yule's application of correlation techniques to the relation between total pauperism and outdoor relief with its implications for solving the problems of the causes of poverty from Booth's laboriously collected data. The explanation in general for the separation of sociology from the advancing capacity of statistics to throw light on social causation by the use of probabilistic methods remains something of a mystery, especially perhaps in Britain where the 'new English statistics' might have been embraced as a new sociometry, as indeed they were in other subjects so as to develop econometrics, psychometrics, and biometrics (Goldthorpe, 2000). Little can be added to the existing British literature. Selvin has demonstrated that Durkheim in France was 'protected' from enlightenment by his personal domination of a close (almost closed) institutional circle. Perhaps Spencer, Hobhouse, and Ginsberg were too philosophically inclined. Perhaps, too, Goldthorpe is right in suggesting that Booth was intellectually 'out of his depth' vis à vis Yule. Certainly he was no Cambridge mathematician and the affinity between double-entry bookkeeping and odds ratios is relatively remote. On the other hand, there are compelling sociological explanations as well as intellectual ones (Goldman, 1991).

Kent's discussion of Booth's failure here is also worth reading along with Marsh's chapter 2 and Goldthorpe's chapter 12 (Kent, 1981: 195–9). It is put forward as an illustration of barriers to the diffusion of innovations and combines the observation of relative scarcity of networks of communication with the subjective awareness of relevance. Booth was a member of the Royal Statistical Society and was its President from 1892 to 1894. Yet, Booth showed no awareness of the innovations made by Kiaer, Galton, Pearson, or Yule in the 1890s. (Nor did Rowntree or Bowley.) In 1895, Yule actually criticized Booth's use of his own findings on poverty. Booth responded (1896) in a way that showed he did not grasp the concept of correlation. He saw only a dichotomy: perfect association or none at all. Selvin (1976) suggests that Booth was alienated by the right-wing politics of Galton and the Eugenicists, but he fails to point out that Yule was agnostic or neutral on hereditarian issues. As Kent suggests, it is possible that Booth 'just did not see the potential in using correlation coefficients to measure the degree of relationship between poverty and other variables' (p. 197). Anyway, the techniques of statistical correlation were never applied to the analysis of survey data until over half a century later. There was, to quote Kent again, 'no sociological community at the time in which new ways of doing things could be discussed or even passed on from individual to individual' (p. 199).

So Booth was not the founder of a new British empirical sociology for the twentieth century. He died in 1916. The tradition of local social surveys continued and is summarized by A. F. Wells (1935). Some advances had been made on the survey methods used by the early nineteenth-century statistical societies. There was certainly a trend towards the use of *respondents* rather than knowledgeable *informants* such as school attendance officers, sanitary inspectors, and the like (to give the economy of what Beatrice Webb labelled as 'wholesale interviewing') which had earlier replaced the unreliable working-class witness by the 'responsible' judgement of the expert. The repeat or revisit study, for example in London, or Merseyside, or in Northampton, became routine. Standardized questions and trained interviewers came in, and Bowley certainly instituted sampling to make surveys immensely cheaper. The gap between theory and research remained wide, though Catherine Marsh was wrong to assert that 'by the beginning of the Second World War no major methodological advances had been made for two decades' (Marsh, 1982: 32). The basic principles of modern sampling were, in fact, developed between 1930 and 1940.

There were also significant institutional advances in the administration of the British state and in the world of commerce. The Second World War was a total war to an extent only foreshadowed by the First World War. Civilian morale was tested by aerial bombardment, food and clothing had to be rationed, the munitions industry had to be mobilized for maximum output. In 1940, the Wartime Social Survey was founded by the Home Intelligence Division of the Ministry of Information. Louis Moss, a survey researcher from the Gallup Poll, was later recruited to lead it. After the War, having served government well, the Social Survey was attached to the Central Office of Information. The Labour government used it increasingly up to 1951 and, after some Conservative vicissitudes, it was merged with the Registrar-General's Office under Claus Moser's leadership, and finally by the end of the century became the Office for National Statistics (ONS). Celebrating thirty years of its existence *Social Trends* 2000 began with an editorial policy statement: 'the Office for National Statistics works in partnership with others in the Government Statistical Service to provide Parliament, Government, and the wider community with the statistical information, analysis, and advice needed to improve decision making, stimulate research and inform debate. It also registers key life events. It aims to provide an authoritative and impartial picture of society and a window on the work and performance of government, allowing the impact of governmental policies and actions to be assessed'.

This is a far cry from the nineteenth-century days when state interference was so strongly opposed by classical liberalism, or from the 1860s when the Charity Organisation Society tried to become an alternative to the state, or even from late Victorian times when a search was made for a charitable substitute of wealthy amateurs like Charles Booth or Seebohm Rowntree. Reinforced after the Second World War by the growth of market research in the private sector through readership and audience surveys, consumer surveys, and political opinion polls, the survey is now part of the stock in trade of industrial society, a property of both the public and private sectors of the economy.

Links to academic sociology, especially in the United States, have been provided by Stouffer, Likert, Guttman, and above all Paul Lazarsfeld, the Austrian/American (1901–76). Though born in Vienna and trained in mathematics at the University of that city, Lazarsfeld spent most of his life at Columbia having been admitted first as a Rockefeller fellow in 1933 and pushed out of Austria by the Dollfuss regime of clerical fascists who took over that country in 1933/34. He did however exercise a great deal of influence in Europe through such social scientists as Raymond Boudon in France, Hynek Jerabek in Czechoslovakia, Elihu Katz in Israel, and Elizabeth Noelle-Neumann in Germany. He survived the criticisms of Theodore Adorno for his 'administrative research', of C. Wright. Mills's charge of 'abstract empiricism' (Mills, 1959), and of Terry Clark's 'Columbia Sociology machine'. His methodological innovations included reason analysis, the programme analyser, the panel study, the elaboration formula, latent-structure analysis, and contextual analysis—all now part of the equipment of survey specialists and so much taken for granted that their authorship has been forgotten.

The significance of the survey for social planning was noted in 1951 by Mark Abrams (Abrams, 1951: 124–5). Recognizing that this was a period of high optimism in the development of a British welfare system balanced between state control and market forces, Abrams saw a threefold revolution since 1800. First, a sparsely populated agrarian country became a densely occupied industrial one. Second, the laissez-faire political philosophy declined and was replaced by a collectivist programme to provide minimum standards for all citizens. Third, eighteenth-century oligarchy was reformed gradually into democracy. 'Social surveys', he writes (p. 124), 'have been used as a method by which society could obtain precise information about itself and thus achieve social change in a peaceful and coherent manner'. He looked forward to an extensive use of the survey for a democratic welfare state: '... the modern community needs social engineering—the planning and building of physical environmental conditions which aim to maintain human welfare—... in such engineering the social survey is a necessary and valuable preliminary to planning'. The post-war years were indeed cheerful. The survey was seen as an instrument for promoting citizenship and even as a partial substitute for the price mechanism of a free, but historically cruel, market.

But Abrams' optimism of the 1950s has to be contrasted with the pessimism of the 1980s when the survey was seen, for example, by Burawoy (1989, 1998), as an instrument of power used by the authorities to control the masses.

The distinction between collection and analysis is both historically and logically important. Historically, it is in part straightforward: there was, in the Civil Service, a split between collection and analysis, and probabilistic methods were readily applied to the former, resulting in highly sophisticated sampling on a random basis with stratification (e.g. by class or region or age or gender) to ensure sufficient numbers of significant categories for the purposes of description or analysis. This process began at the end of the nineteenth century and was pretty well perfected by the 1930s. But Civil Servants left the analysis side to their academic counterparts who ran into opposition in the social studies including, according to Goldthorpe, clever resistance from Keynes. Herein lies the mystery of why English sociologists failed to adopt the new English statistics. The case of Hogben and Glass in the 1930s at LSE, described in Chapters 3 and 4, is especially puzzling. Hogben was after all a populist writer about mathematics and Glass a sophisticated statistician. But both placed themselves firmly in the contingency table tradition of analysis refusing to go much beyond percentages (Goldthorpe, 2000). Neither could be suspected along with Booth of being statistically incapable. Both detested deductionism of which they accused their fellow economists at LSE in much the same way that Richard Jones had attacked Ricardian political economy in the 1830s. Both were 'men of the left' passionately committed to improving the lot of the poor among their compatriots; both may have associated correlation and regression techniques with the hereditarianism of Galton and Pearson (though a declared socialist) at University College, London (UCL) and more generally, in the climate of the times, the reactionary and racist politics so vigorously pursued in Germany and the United States (Kevles, 1985). In fact, out of this ideological evil was to come the statistical good of multivariate analysis and log linear modelling (aided by the development of much more powerful computers in the 1960s).

Part of the ethnomethodological reaction against 'positivism' in the 1970s was grounded in the rediscovery that 'facts' are socially created. Thus Jack Douglas, Max Atkinson, and Hindess, writing from an Althusserian Marxist point of view (which he abandoned soon after), launched a ferocious onslaught on official statistics. Suicide in particular, they pointed out, was socially defined—the outcome of relations between coroners, police, the families involved, priests, and doctors—a complex and veritable chain of events. But instead of denouncing all empirical use of official records of unemployment, crime, and indices of human development, such sociologists might have been expected to put forward their own alternative concepts, to spell out their methods of measurement, and thus enrich debate across the whole discipline of sociology.

Goldthorpe ends his history neatly with the observation that the question of why sociology was not responsive to the probabilistic revolution in statistics much earlier has itself to be answered probabilistically. The level of probability of a response by sociology to the 'new English statistics' was low in the nineteenth century but never zero. For the twenty-first century there are some 'encouraging signs that such a sociology is at last beginning to take recognizable shape [but] its eventual success is still by no means guaranteed' (2000: 294).

The twentieth century ended with the establishment of the ONS which strengthened the publication of *Social Trends*, an increasingly valuable annual first launched in 1970. Meanwhile Claus Moser and David Cox were elected to be Wardens of Wadham and Nuffield at Oxford, respectively. The Royal Statistical Society (*RSS News* 29/8, April 2002) launched a consultation about redesigning itself for the twenty-first century. It was however highly self-satisfied and perhaps even complacent, but justly so, about the overall performance of statistics and operational research in the 2001 research assessment exercise. Performance was described as 'an overwhelming success' and confirmed the position of the United Kingdom as 'one of the world's foremost research nations'. The last claim is dubious. When expressed in per capita terms, the United Kingdom slips from third to tenth place in statistical performance among nations. Nevertheless Social and Community Planning Research (SCPR) had a record of providing first-class service to survey research, had been drawn into the university system through integration with City University, had developed firm links with Anthony Heath and his colleagues at Oxford, and had pioneered regular surveys of British social attitudes since 1984 in collaboration with Whitehall departments. It was now renamed and reorganized as the National Centre for Social Research. The Economic and Social Research Council (ESRC) was an active supporter with its Survey Archive and its new Research Methods Programme—a £4 million venture for the twenty-first century, beginning in 2002. The new programme is intended to link quantitative to qualitative methods. Perhaps there will be a new rapprochement?

Conclusion

This has been a somewhat complicated chapter. It has been an attempt to trace the context of the search for a science of society. The primary impulse to the scientific movement, it was emphasized, lay in the human consequences of nineteenth-century industrialization. There was a challenge to both the government and voluntary civil institutions to deal with the problems of poverty, disease, and disorder that arose. Part of the intellectual response, as we saw in

Chapter 1, was literary—the emergence of a vigorous literature of prose and poetry and a didactic drama of exposure in novels, pamphlets, magazines, and plays. A second culture also arose in the form of applications of Newtonion science to social affairs. Government, national and local, became the focus of a scientific revolution with heroes like Farr and heroines like Florence Nightingale devoted to developing and disseminating clear record keeping and scientific statistics as bases of reform. Statistical societies sprang up in urban Britain. Expertise rose in public life. The survey began to emerge as an instrument of social policy.

At the same time there was an anguished response by charitable, religious, and reformist voluntary bodies and individuals. Booth and Rowntree could have been the originators of a modern British sociology. Certainly they influenced public opinion and government. But advances in the theory of probability and their application to social problems were slow to develop, especially in the universities, where only LSE and UCL fostered social statistics. A network of sociology departments was particularly slow to emerge. Only after the Second World War did expansion penetrate the provincial universities to offer the possibility of a national flourishing of a sociology firmly connected to the methodological advances made by statistics in the previous century and a half.

So much for the context. We now turn to a narrative of the institutional development of sociology.

Part II

Narrative

3

Sociology Before 1950

WHENCE CAME SOCIOLOGY? We have asserted in Chapter 1 that the history of sociology, or at least modern British academic sociology, was for long the history of a great institution—the London School of Economics and Political Science (LSE). The LSE, founded in 1895, exercised a virtual monopoly over the subject between the two World Wars, and was restored to new vigour in 1945 on its return from wartime evacuation. Institutions are organizations of people and their ideas. Let us therefore begin with people.

It is worth remembering, at the beginning of the twenty-first century, that sociological writing is perhaps more subject to fashion than literature and certainly more so than the natural sciences. A minority of the professors of sociology who took part in my survey in 2001 declined for one reason or another to answer the question of who had contributed most to the subject in the twentieth century. One respondent was explicit. 'I would not', he wrote, 'pick out any specific figure. I think that sociology has been developed by the sociological community, generally impeded by the fetishism of great men'. We have already had occasion to question the assumption of a sociological community. The survey shows, however, that 'great men' succeed one another with alarming rapidity and it is this, with its warning against hubris and encouragement of humility, that is the point here.

Early in our period Max Beerbohm span a salutary yarn about a minor poet with whom he dined weekly at a restaurant in Soho. Enoch Soames was a dispirited writer, a Catholic diabolist, who complained bitterly of the lack of appreciation he received from his contemporaries and longed to be translated by a time-machine to visit the Reading Room of the British Museum at the end of the twentieth century to see whether posterity would be a better judge of his merit. The Devil, a vulgar and villainous fellow in a scarlet waistcoat, interrupted from the next table and offered Soames a Faustian bargain. Soames accepted; here then is his account later that evening. (I should explain that many of the intelligentsia in the 1890s firmly believed that their successors would phoneticize the language.) He had ransacked the library of the British Museum in vain except for the following:-

From p. 234 of 'Inglish Littracher 1890–1900,' bi T. K. Nupton, published bi th Stait, 1992:
'Fr egzampl, a riter ov th time, naimd Max Beerbohm, hoo woz stil alive in th twentieth senchri, rote a stauri in wich e pautraid an immajnari karrakter kauld "Enoch Soames"—a

thurd-rait poit hoo beleevz imself a grate jeneus an maix a bargin with th Devvl in auder ter no wot posterriti thinx ov im! It iz a sumwot labud satire but not without vallu as showing how seriusli the yung men ov the aiteen-ninetiz took themselvz. Nou that the littreri profeshn haz bin auganized az a department of publik servis, our riters hav found their levvl and hav lernt ter doo their duti without thort ov th morro. "Th laibrer iz werthi ov hiz hire," an that iz aul. Thank hevvn we hav no Enoch Soameses among us to-dai!' (Beerbohm, 1919: 33).

Soon after the Devil arrived to 'take him home' to eternal hellfire.[1]

From the 1880s to the 1940s, roughly from Hobhouse's youth to the renewal of LSE in Clare Market, there were at least a dozen relevant and recognized names with academic connections. Spencer, Booth, and Rowntree had none but, among those with university affiliations, three were Scots—Patrick Geddes, his follower Victor Branford, and R. M. McIver. Barbara Wootton held a lectureship in Cambridge until she was elected to a sociology post at Bedford College, London. All the rest, Sidney and Beatrice Webb, Edward Westermarck, L. T. Hobhouse, William Beveridge, Morris Ginsberg, T. H. Marshall, David Glass,[2] and Alexander Carr-Saunders in that date order were associated with LSE. All were sociological writers, all thought of themselves as sociologists. Did all share or escape the fate of Enoch Soames?

The fleeting character of fame typifies at least most of the British sociologists of the past and is likely to continue to do so in the future. 'Who reads Spencer now?' was the confident if ill-informed[3] opening to Talcott Parsons' *Structure of Social Action* in 1937. 'Who reads Hobhouse now?' might well have been substituted after the Second World War at least until Stefan Collini published his *Liberalism and Sociology* in 1979, and indeed 'who reads Parsons now?' after Mills' hostile 'translation' in *The Sociological Imagination* in 1959. None of the sociology courses in the LSE Calendar for 2001–2 includes a reference to any work by L. T. Hobhouse (though his *Liberalism* is listed in a politics course on British Political Ideas). He has disappeared from the surface of British sociology as completely as Harold Laski from political studies (Shils, 1997: 179).

Though Hobhouse was an important figure at LSE his subject did not prosper. Urwick ran a more successful department of social science, T. H. Marshall was recruited to teach sociology in it, and there were but a handful of sociologists around Hobhouse after the First World War and around Ginsberg from 1930. Karl Mannheim was marginally connected in the last few inter-war years and during the evacuation to Cambridge. Nothing happened elsewhere except for the founding of a social science department at Liverpool in 1909 with a social research appendage of modest dimension. Caradog Jones directed the Merseyside Survey in the 1930s. Carr-Saunders was appointed to succeed

---

[1] The story also illustrates the fatuity of historical prophecy. Beerbohm was wrong about phoneticization and about the socialization of writing. Nor could he have anticipated that the library might move to Kings Cross.   [2] See later, Chapter 4.

[3] Ill-informed in the sense that the language of sociology was bequeathed by Spencer to the English-speaking world and remains with us in the twenty-first century. Parsons' remark was, incidentally, first offered by Crane Brinton.

Beveridge as the Director of LSE in 1937, leaving the Charles Booth Chair at Liverpool which he had occupied since 1923. His background was in the natural sciences at Magdalen College, Oxford out of which he moved gradually to the social sciences via Toynbee Hall[4] and the Eugenics Society as well as war service in the Royal Army Service Corps. He established his academic reputation with a book on *The Population Problem* in 1922 and by subsequent direct contributions to sociology—*The Social Structure of England and Wales* in 1927 (with D. Caradog Jones) and *The Professions* in 1933. His sociological interests were centred on population studies and he defined demography very widely to include the empirical study of family and class. In 1938, he replaced Hogben's department of social biology with a readership in demography for Robert Kuczynski, an event of which more is told below (in Chapter 4) in connection with David Glass.

The Scots have left little trace. McIver was born a Hebredian (at Stornoway) (McIver, 1968). He moved from this fishing community by scholarship to read classics at Edinburgh and 'Greats' at Oxford and to teach politics and sociology at Aberdeen, quarrelled with his first professor, and migrated to Canada in 1915 and later (1929) to Columbia in New York. His career led him increasingly and successfully into sociology and he was known in Britain after the Second World War as the author of a textbook—*Society* (1937 and 1949)—and as an eager if uninspiring lecturer. Geddes became famous before the First World War as a vigorous, enthusiastic proponent of Le Play's sociology, a brilliant lecturer, an energetic member of the Sociological Society (1903), and a playful inventor of sociologese. He competed unsuccessfully for the LSE chair in 1907 and founded Outlook Tower in Edinburgh, the first sociological laboratory, and an empiricist renewal of the social survey which had more influence in town planning than in academic sociology (Mairet, 1957). Branford (1864–1930) was a Scottish businessman who had known Geddes in his undergraduate days at Edinburgh. An amateur enthusiast, he championed Geddes' cause and identified himself with the Sociological Society. He served on the editorial committee of its *Sociological Papers* and also as Honorary Secretary to the Society from which he resigned in 1911. He was an embarrassment to Hobhouse with what Hawthorn (1976: 167) dubbed his 'romantic effusions'.

Had Geddes, who died in 1932, been elected to the first British chair the course of sociology in Britain could arguably have been different. Much greater emphasis might have been given to environmental forces in the shaping of society. Martin White and Victor Branford certainly favoured Geddes.

---

[4] Toynbee Hall was founded in 1884 in Whitechapel in the East End of London as the Universities' Settlement with Samuel Barnett as its first Warden. It was surrounded by poverty, destitution, and squalor. But its connections were to the liberal intelligentsia of the day, especially to Balliol College, Oxford, and further to the powerful politicians and concerned upper-class establishment. Named after Arnold Toynbee, a Balliol Don and Christian socialist, it later attracted William Beveridge, Clement Attlee, and R. H. Tawney to its visitors and residents. L. T. Hobhouse was among its early supporters. A centenary account by Asa Briggs and Anne Macartney was published in 1984 under the title *Toynbee Hall: The First Hundred Years* (Routledge and Kegan Paul).

Why Hobhouse was preferred remains something of a puzzle. Geddes was an outspoken Scot, sarcastic in the face of established authority, formally without relevant educational qualifications, and given to loquacious *impromptu* outbursts when criticized. Hobhouse by contrast was a public school and Oxford classical scholar with acceptable family connections and manners. They did not get on with each other but they might easily have collaborated professionally for both held to theories of nurture as determining social institutions as against the nature theories of Galton and his followers in eugenics.

Beatrice and Sidney Webb both thought of themselves as sociologists, but are seldom read today except by historians. Their biographies are carefully and exhaustively assembled by Norman and Jeanette Mackenzie (1978: 84) and by Royden Harrison (2000) who was officially appointed by the Passfield Trustees as the Webbs' biographer.[5] William Beveridge is the most doubtful inclusion in our list. He is there because he had a huge influence on the LSE between the Wars—'the heroic days of the school', as Dahrendorf (1995) describes them. He is there too because of his even greater influence on social policy—his 1942 report being the first HMSO best seller. But he retreated in some bitterness from LSE to University College, Oxford in the face of professorial antagonism. José Harris has written a celebrated life (Harris, 1977).

The pre-war history of sociology has been analysed by others. What is common ground in an otherwise contentious literature is the failure of nineteenth-century Britain to institutionalize the sociological imagination. Not that there was any lack of distinguished political arithmeticians, social philosophers, and social anthropologists. As Philip Abrams has described it (1968), the failure of sociology to develop in Victorian Britain was not a consequence of inadequate intellectual resources. The difficulty was to find recognized sociological posts for able people in a society which

provided numerous outlets for social concern of a legitimate, satisfying, and indeed, seductive nature; all these were disincentives to role-innovation. Above all it provided, for a large and apparently open class of 'public persons', access to government. Use what indicators you will, it is clear that, whatever happened to the British economy, British government, both amateur and professional, grew continuously and faster than any other throughout the nineteenth century. The political system was growing and malleable. Performing administrative and intelligence functions for government soaked up energies which might have gone towards sociology had such opportunities not been there (Abrams, 1968: 4).

Even when sociology began at last to be institutionalized in the Edwardian period (with social anthropology already securely established), the men who took the decisive part—Victor Branford and J. Martin White, Geddes and Hobhouse, Francis Galton and Frederic Harrison—'were one of three

[5] Royden J. Harrison (2000), *The Life and Times of Beatrice and Sidney Webb 1858–1905, The Formative Years*. This was published as Vol. 1 and was hailed by the *Times* obituary of Harrison (22 July 2002) as 'an undoubted masterpiece'. The author died in June 2002 but left behind the result of completed research and a writing plan for a second, final volume to be completed by others.

things: wealthy amateurs with careers elsewhere, academic deviants, or very old men' (Abrams, 1968).

The Abrams thesis of failure to institutionalize sociology should be modified. He concentrated on the openness of the political system; the expansion of opportunities in government for civil servants, inspectors, social administrators, and the like, creating a new class of professional experts. But there also developed new institutions for the training of these social professionals and for research into the burgeoning problems of industrial society. Thus, late Victorian times witnessed the birth of the LSE, the development of provincial statistical societies, the Registrar-General, local social surveys, new departments for training social workers in new universities like Liverpool and elsewhere.

Throughout this network of nascent teaching and research centres the issue arose of the introduction of sociology into curricula aimed at the growing class of social experts and of social research aimed at developing the knowledge base of the new professionals. Among its many difficulties the rise of sociology, both its teaching and its research, was opposed by established academic opinion, with its centuries-old citadels in the Oxford and Cambridge colleges and its ramifications in schools, in government, and in learned societies.

An early example is provided by Sir James Bryce, the first president of the British Sociological Society and later of the British Academy. He addressed the first meeting of the Sociological Society in 1904 with confident claims for the future of the subject. The nineteenth century had seen the transformation of physical and biological sciences; the human sciences had made strong recent strides in Germany, France, and America. It was now time for their advance in Britain and it was the task of sociology to bring them up to date and to use the new society as a means for promoting their communication and coordination. Yet, thirteen years later, in 1917, he gave a lecture to the academic establishment from its headquarters at the British Academy on 'The Next Thirty Years'. And he failed to mention sociology! (Brock, 2002). We shall return to this topic in Chapter 5. Meanwhile we may note that everything claimed for sociology was widely held to be covered already by history, anthropology, economics, and political science.

Hobhouse

The first half of the twentieth century brought little institutional change. Between the Wars, the British universities continued to ignore the academic claims of sociology, and it was virtually confined to London. Hobhouse was an academic deviant who left an Oxford career as a college tutor in philosophy to work as a journalist for the *Manchester Guardian* before going to London where he took the LSE chair in 1907. Moreover, Abrams went on (in Bulmer, 1985: 182) in a subsequent essay to elaborate Morris Janowitz's distinction (1970: 243–59) between 'enlightenment' and 'engineering' methods and 'models' of sociology and to argue that a strong trend from 'policy science' to 'advocacy' had informed British sociology since 1831. Some would agree with an elaborated version of this proposition and concur with his judgement that Hobhouse was the first British sociologist to deploy an enlightenment (clarification) model 'as an adequate and proper conception of the use of sociology' (p. 193).

Spencer by contrast had intended sociology to be a policy science. Hobhouse's own series of books 'was addressed to the business of unmasking the Policy-science ambitions of Spencer, Galton, and the Eugenicists and Social-Biologists who followed them'. Hobhouse saw that the subject had to be argumentative. It had to comprise scientifically collected evidence in a framework of values. Like so many other sociologists, he wanted the subject to be useful as a guide to action, but evidence had to be grounded in scientific method: values had to be validated by moral philosophy. The two, methods and values, combined to make up a general 'science of society'. Application was then possible through reasoned advocacy, in his case and time through the political movement of New Liberalism.

The daunting task of establishing sociology as a bridge between the worlds of ought and is, between theory and action, is a feat as little accomplished today as it was a hundred years ago. But at least Hobhouse could look back to a time when sociology had been without an academic institution. He had his place in the LSE, already a decade established. He also had a thirty-year-old mood and sense of purpose among the educated classes—the desperate need to find a substitute for religious faith. As Beatrice Webb put it, for some who in an increasingly rational and scientific age had lost their evangelical religious faith, the 'impulse of self-subordinating service was transferred consciously and overtly from God to man' (Webb, 1926). Mrs Humphry Ward had written a fictional account of this subjective loneliness in her *Robert Elsmere* (1888), in which an Oxford graduate of the 1870s who was ordained into the Church of England lost his faith and went to seek a substitute in adult education in the East End of London. Hobhouse himself was born in 1864, the son of a Cornish Vicar, gave up Christianity while at school at Marlborough (though retaining Christian morals), became alienated from his father, was oppressed by never-ending guilt in the face of his life of privilege as an Oxford don, and sought a gentlemanly collectivist solution at Toynbee Hall and the *Manchester Guardian*. As a political and social moralist he anticipated much of the ethical socialism later to be expounded by R. H. Tawney (Dennis and Halsey, 1988). He was an unhappy radical. This personal and moral travail contributed no doubt to his recurrent bouts of depression and pessimism. The First World War dealt a crushing blow to any theory of progress. *Homo homine lupus est* was Freud's judgement. Wilfred Owen wrote a savage poetical satire on his experiences in the Flanders trenches:

> My friend you would not tell with such high zest
> To children ardent for some desperate glory
> The old Lie: *Dulce et decorum est*
> *Pro patria mori.*

Nevertheless, for all that, Hobhouse was prolific in his academic writing, and well aware of the difficulties of winning a place for sociology as a science. The atmosphere of the first decade of the twentieth century is well, if unconsciously, caught by Hobhouse himself in 1909 in Volume Two of the *Sociological Review* (p. 402), where he reviews *The Origins and Development of the Moral Ideas* (1908) saying 'Professor Westermarck's book as a whole is a contribution of first importance to the work of removing sociology from the regions of more or less plausible theorizing and establishing it once for all as an inductive science'.

Edward Westermarck was a close colleague of Hobhouse at LSE. Born in Finland in 1862, he was exposed to but rejected the influence of German culture where he thought that metaphysics appeared to be profound only because of its obscurity of argument. He turned instead to English culture, and soon came to admire its dominant empiricism and readiness to test all hypotheses in the light of experience (Ginsberg, 1940: 1). He learnt English and began to visit the country in 1887, was introduced to Martin White by Victor Branford, and was appointed to a three-year university lectureship in sociology in 1903. When Hobhouse was given the chair in 1907 Westermarck's lectureship was renewed and he eventually divided his time between Helsingfors where he held the chair of moral philosophy, the LSE where he lectured on sociology, and Morocco where he did field work—a peripatetic pattern that he maintained for many years. He died in September 1939. Within the Hobhousian context of orthogenic evolution he was outstanding in his relentless pursuit of truth. Eing Kaila, his colleague at Helsingfors, said of him that 'he opened up the world of English thought. For three centuries our [Finnish] scientific life has been overwhelmingly under German influence. Westermarck was the first to make himself decidedly at home in the English language' (Ginsberg, 1940).

The question of 'who reads Hobhouse now?' might just as easily be put by contemporary physicists about Isaac Newton. But the answer, some would maintain, has a different meaning in that the natural sciences have, historically, cumulated. Since Auguste Comte the 'science of society' has had devotees of similar aspiration. Hobhouse along with Westermarck and many others was a believer in the scientific method. Essentially a disciple of T. H. Green but, self-confusedly, not an idealist, he substituted Progress for the Anglican God of his childhood and sought through prodigious labour to establish his own version of evolution, 'orthogenic evolution'. 'Orthogenic evolution' means true evolution and refers to the emergence in *homo sapiens* of a self-conscious mind. This was the key departure from Darwin, the point at which ethical development becomes possible, the reason why mankind becomes liberated from the mindless bonds of 'natural' evolution and begins to shape its own destiny (Hobhouse, 1901). This modified Darwinian theory had, of course, to be placed on a firm empirical basis. Hence, *The Material Culture of the Simpler Peoples* with M. Ginsberg and C. Wheeler (1915), *Morals in Evolution* (1906) (required reading for sociology undergraduates until 1960), and *Development and Purpose: An Essay Towards a Philosophy of Evolution* (1913).

How important was Hobhouse to sociology? He has no entry in the Name Index of Bottomore and Nisbett's *History of Sociological Theory*. A chapter by Kenneth Bock (included by Bottomore and Nisbett), on Development and Evolution, has no text reference to Hobhouse and mentions him only in the last (97th) footnote. On the other hand, Albion Small in his *AJS* review of *Social Development* (1924–5) wrote in high approval 'It is doubtful if all the living philosophers and sociologists combined command among American sociologists a reputation equal to that of Professor Hobhouse' (p. 216).

Ginsberg, who succeeded Hobhouse after he died in 1929, became his disciple, perhaps as Collini suggests his only disciple, though he too was followed by a few adherents including R. Fletcher (1974). Both Hobhouse and Ginsberg began as philosophers and later wished they had remained in their original discipline. Sociology has a persistent history of reluctant recruits, and also deserters, as well as of administrative, social, or political climbers. Hobhouse's fame was, as Collini (1979) put it, 'thrust upon him'. He hesitated over accepting the LSE chair in 1907 and the American chairs later offered him were mostly in moral or social philosophy.

Maggie Studholme argues that Hobhouse's influence on British sociology persisted into the twenty-first century. He held sway over the subject even into the work of Giddens and despite many efforts to dethrone him in the name of Geddes, Durkheim, or Weber. Collini takes an opposing view. At the beginning of his impressive book on L. T. Hobhouse and political argument in England from 1880 to 1914, he writes, 'Liberalism and sociology are not obviously compatible theoretically . . .'. Indeed the relation has been antagonistic with liberalism the political voice of individualism and sociology the theology of collectivism or, as he put it, 'its origins are usually traced to the social theorists of the late eighteenth and early nineteenth centuries' (Collini, 1979: 1), when understandings of society were first developed in criticism of idealism, materialism, and utilitarianism. In fact, the four way box of liberalism, individualism, sociology, and collectivism is too crude, too abstract to fit the history of Europe and Britain at the turn of the nineteenth and twentieth centuries. Durkheim and Weber were never neatly and completely encased in any of these four conceptual categories. Nor was Hobhouse. What was interesting to Collini was the British background of social thought and political dispute which attracted young men and women in the 1880s into collectivism and the new sociology and into liberalism, or rather New Liberalism, redefined as essentially social. It was an age of transformation, a reaction to the social consequences of the first industrial revolution and perhaps also to the rise of rationalism and the fall of Christian belief.

In *English Ethical Socialism* (1988), Dennis and Halsey treated Hobhouse as a characteristic Edwardian representative of the tradition descending from Thomas More in the early sixteenth century to the greatest of all Christian Socialists, R. H. Tawney. The purpose there was to trace and illustrate a collectivist ethic running through English politics from More to Tawney. The purpose here is to describe the opposition to, followed by the rise of, sociology in the twentieth century, though two people (Hobhouse and T. H. Marshall), and one institution (the LSE), figure largely in both stories.

The first English sociologists, Spencer and Hobhouse, were nineteenth-century post-Darwinians and curiously associated with liberalism—the one with traditional liberalism, individualistic and anti-state,[6] and the other with New[7] Liberalism (favouring certain kinds of governmental intervention on behalf of positive freedom and against poverty and inequality[8]). There had been great sociological contributions from the Scottish Enlightenment of the eighteenth century,[9] but our story begins when Hobhouse took up the first British chair of sociology at LSE in 1907.[10] In addition, of course, Max Weber[11] in Germany and Emile Durkheim[12] in France are traditionally labelled liberals, though both were also nationalists.

At the beginning of the twenty-first century we are prone to discuss sociology—the science of society—in methodological terms, a tendency reflecting the very real advances in method and measurement since the First World War. Nevertheless, Hobhouse was originally a philosopher of the nineteenth century when the new science was criticized and widely rejected by moral philosophers. His contemporaries are described by Collini in a way that fits Hobhouse well: 'Sons of the genteel but not rich middle and professional classes, from religious homes (Anglican clergymen predominate among the fathers) set in the country or smaller provincial towns, they most commonly went to Public schools and then read Greats at Oxford, losing their faith and gaining a sense of guilt about their social advantages in the process, and then came to London to do social or journalistic work of some kind' (Collini, p. 51). Andrew Abbott and Edward Shils, both of Chicago, describe the first generation of American sociologists as religious and rural. Was it the same in the United Kingdom, only with a further emphasis on the loss of faith? We offer an answer in Chapter 8.

Hobhouse was something of an outsider at Oxford, poor by comparison with his noble and rich fellow undergraduates, and with a sense of guilt at departure from his father's orthodoxy. So he delighted in his own radical opinions, supporting abolition of the House of Lords, for example, to challenge the Tory orthodoxy of the Oxford of his day.

His sociology, says Collini, can only be understood in the context of 'the pivotal role of the belief in Progress' (p. 148) which informed late nineteenth-century

---

[6] Spencer (1884), *The Man Versus the State*. See also J.D.Y. Peel (1971), *Herbert Spencer: The Evolution of a Sociologist*.

[7] 'New' like 'post' is always historically doomed. Such propositions as 'New Labour' quickly acquire anachronistic flavour: they are, like the New Testament, or New College, or New York, the *nouvelles* of the time.

[8] L. T. Hobhouse (1911), *Liberalism*; and (1918), *The Metaphysical Theory of the State: A Criticism*. See also P. Abrams (1968) and G. Hawthorn (1976).

[9] David Hume, Adam Ferguson, Adam Smith and John Millar are all among the founding fathers of sociology.

[10] There was also a second position occupied part-time by Edward Westermarck.

[11] A. Abbott (1999), *Department and Discipline*. See also R. Bendix (1960), *Max Weber: An Intellectual Portrait*.

[12] S. Lukes (1973), *Emile Durkheim: His Life and Work: A Historical and Critical Study*.

social thought. 'Collectivism needed its own Spencer' (p. 149). He offered through *Mind in Evolution* and *Morals in Evolution* an optimistic and teleological review of historical development. Orthogenic Evolution was inspired by a conception of the self-realization of rational humanity (p. 216). Dennis ends his essay on Hobhouse with A. E. Housman's lament for lost labour, while Collini (p. 253) ends with a disavowed intention to evaluate his reputation which is in fact a shattering denunciation of his work: 'his thinking was embedded in a set of assumptions which no longer demands our allegiance . . . a range of problems which no longer commands our attention'. This is a contentious assertion. Is 'development' a pre-occupation which no longer concerns us? Was it not a concern of Parsons in his later work? Is modern evolutionary psychology irrelevant? And, if not, is the question of moral progress a dead issue? In a twenty-first century of 'ethnic cleansing' and genetic manipulation, these are live issues.

Outside the LSE sociology never came to much.[13] Even Parsons' functional-ism and his claim to detect a European tradition moving through Alfred Marshall, Max Weber, and Emile Durkheim towards his own unified theory (Parsons, 1937), which challenged Hobhousian theory in the 1940s and 1950s, was only temporarily triumphant and was itself based on Parsons's visit to the School in 1924–5 on his way to Heidelberg. Indeed the hegemony of LSE was at first only reinforced by the system of London external degrees which carried the LSE definition of the sociology syllabus to the dependent provincial university colleges of Southampton, Nottingham, Leicester, Exeter, and Hull. Candidates at these institutions were taught, in effect, by Hobhousian mis-sionaries for the London examinations until after 1950 when these colleges were granted independent charters. Distinctive approaches begin to appear only during the 1950s, influenced by anthropology at Hull, social psychology at Nottingham, and European theory at Leicester, where Norbert Elias was appointed in 1956.

Ginsberg

The most outstanding carrier of the Hobhousian banner was Morris Ginsberg who was born in Lithuania in 1889. He migrated to England where he attracted attention as a talented undergraduate while reading philosophy at University College, London (UCL), which he entered in 1910. Such a migration was com-mon enough at that time but, as Maurice Freedman (his junior colleague, friend, and admirer as joint editor of the *Jewish Journal of Sociology*) remarked, 'there can have been few Talmudic scholars, entirely Yiddish-speaking until their adolescence, who transformed themselves into members of the austere English middle-class' (Fletcher, 1974: 269). Part of the interest of Ginsberg's life and an

---

[13] Tom Simey was given the Charles Booth chair at Liverpool in 1939 as a PPE graduate from Balliol and a lecturer in public administration at Liverpool. But research had to wait for its main development from the 'Clapham money' at the end of the forties (Clapham, 1946).

essential key to his character lies in the long bridge he successfully crossed from an obscure Lithuanian Jewish community and a childhood education in classical Hebrew to a prominent position in British social studies at LSE. Much of his early life will probably remain obscure: for he was determinedly reticent about his youth, refused to record his personal memories, and clearly wished to be remembered mainly, even exclusively, through his writing and teaching.

Ginsberg's unusual quickness of mind and lucidity of expression earned his recognition at UCL before the First World War, when he was a Martin White and John Stuart Mill scholar. While the connection with UCL and the grounding of his life's work in philosophy was maintained, it is with sociology and the LSE that Ginsberg is mainly associated from 1914, when he was first invited to be a part-time assistant to Hobhouse. Permanent tenure did not come to him until 1922, but his service to the school continued for more than forty years as reader (1924), successor to Hobhouse in the Martin White chair of sociology (1929), and as an emeritus professor (1954) who undertook part-time teaching well into the 1960s. He was prevented from active service by poor eyesight in the First World War, but the legend and indeed truth is that he stood in for four of the regular teaching staff, including Major Attlee and Sergeant Tawney.

Ginsberg's association with and devotion to Hobhouse began while he was at UCL, where he collaborated in a comparative anthropological study which became a classic (Hobhouse *et al.*, 1915). Not that Ginsberg's Hobhousianism was parochial. It was after all embedded in a wider conception of the social sciences dominated by economics and buttressed by elements of economic history, psychology, and statistical demography. The B.Sc. Econ. degree also assumed that a mastery of the Western European languages was necessary in order to read social scientific works in French, German, and Italian. The early numbers of the *Sociological Review* took it for granted that its readers would understand German and French as well as Latin, though from 1927 candidates for the language papers were allowed to use dictionaries and the language requirement had disappeared by 1960. Ginsberg himself was at ease with the European tongues and, for example, was the first to introduce Pareto's *Mind and Society* to English readers. He was prepared to lecture too on Weber and Durkheim, but generally managed either not to do so or gave them a subsidiary place in his lectures on sociological theory. Hobhouse dominated the theory syllabus even after he died in 1929 and Ginsberg, who succeeded him, never mentioned either Geddes or Parsons in his lectures.

Subsequently and throughout his working life Hobhouse was the dominant influence and he devoted himself to the same essential problems of the liberal tradition, the understanding of the evolution of mankind, materially, socially, culturally, and morally. At the centre of this tradition was a preoccupation with the idea of moral progress and its economic and social correlates: and around that central problem Ginsberg undertook wide exploration of how variations in social structure were related to moral belief and behaviour, steadily searching for the basis of a rational ethic and for ways to build social institutions expressing reason and justice.

The pursuit of these intellectual concerns required philosophical sophistication and an immense knowledge of social history. Ginsberg acquired both and demonstrated them in a long series of books, essays, and lectures. His prose style was economical and unpretentious, carrying lightly a vast erudition. The titles convey the theme of these sustained interests—*Moral Progress* (1944), *The Idea of Progress: A Revaluation* (1953*a*), *On the Diversity of Morals* (1953*b*), and *Reason and Unreason in Society* (1947). His last published work, *On Justice in Society*, which appeared in 1965, is a characteristic analysis of the concepts of justice, equality, rights, and duties and their application in criminal law, contract, and international relations.

Ginsberg's contribution to these difficult and enduring problems of ethics in society gives him a permanent place in twentieth-century scholarship. Dahrendorf called him 'the wise social philosopher' (Dahrendorf, 1995: 204). His reputation as a sociologist is, however, less secure. After Hobhouse he was the major British sociologist between the Wars. But the rapid development of the subject after the Second World War passed him by and he was absent from the reading lists of the LSE calendar by 1996-7.

A rapidly expanding profession of sociology with diverse methods and theories replaced the coherent blend of moral philosophy and social enquiry in which Ginsberg had followed Hobhouse as the leading scholar. The question of the relation between moral and social evolution, which they both examined with painstaking scholarship, remained important but no longer occupied the centre of the subject.

On a personal level, Ginsberg won and kept strong affection from colleagues and students: but he also had enemies, notably Karl Mannheim. Fletcher affects to know nothing of this animosity which the director of LSE described as the Mannheim–Ginsberg problem[14,15] (Fletcher, 1974: 6; Dahrendorf, 1995: 295), but both Dahrendorf (1995) and Shils (1997: 215-6) offer objective accounts of it. Ginsberg's humility and academic assurance were often remarked. Both were real in him but appeared to others as paradoxical—a kind of self-effacing arrogance. Although his chair was in a subject held suspect by many scholars, his own standards were of the highest demanded by academic tradition. His contemporaries remembered him professionally through his writing and personally as 'a small, quiet, serious yet friendly man, curled up in an old armchair, surrounded by walls of books, looking as if he had grown out of them' (Fletcher, 1974: 265).

---

[14] Mannheim took a chair at the Institute of Education in London in 1946. Geoff Whitty, one of his successors, wrote (1997): 'not one of the 28 copies of the nine books by Mannheim held in the Institute library had been checked out on loan [since the 1970s] and even what is generally regarded as his most important work, *Ideology and Utopia* (1936) had been borrowed from the library only a handful of times'. Is this another case of Enoch Soames? Possibly not: it may be attributable to the analphabetic state of teacher training at that time. And the Enoch Soames syndrome is not to be confused with the cycles of fashion. Thus, Mannheim may be due for a period of revival; for example, see Jane Pilcher, 'Mannheim's Sociology of Generations: An Undervalued Legacy', *British Journal of Sociology*, 1994, 45/3.

[15] For a more extended appreciation of Ginsberg by his admirers (especially Professor Maurice Freedman and Professor Ronald Fletcher), see R. Fletcher (ed.), *The Science of Society and the Unity of Mankind* (1974).

T. H. Marshall

The third figure at LSE between the Wars was Thomas Humphrey Marshall (1893–1981) who was born in fashionable Bloomsbury, in London. His Anglicanism was strongly reinforced at Rugby School, but he subsequently lost his faith at Trinity College, Cambridge, where he gained a first in part one of the history tripos in 1914. That summer, destined for a career in the foreign service, he went to Germany to learn German, only to be interned in a prisoner of war camp at Ruhleban, near Berlin.

Ruhleban was an enforced escape for Marshall from the narrow social confines of his background in the English bourgeois intelligentsia. A prison camp, being non-producing, cannot be a class society in the Marxist sense. But the merchant seamen and fishermen, the 'camp proletariat', introduced Marshall to an unfamiliar subculture of class: 'without its seafarers Ruhleben would have been a very different camp, softer, less virile, top-heavy with intellectuals' (Ketchum, 1965: 126). In a formal academic sense, it was an unknowing introduction to his future profession. The experience of Ruhleban was morally and intellectually crucial: it generated in Marshall a new dimension of social sensibility reaching well beyond Victorian London and Edwardian Cambridge. Superficially and initially, however, it was not so. Marshall returned to Cambridge after the First World War to compete successfully for a fellowship at Trinity College on the basis of a dissertation on seventeenth-century guilds, a topic suggested by J. H. Clapham.

But Marshall soon made a diversion, at least temporarily, from the normal path of the don into another encounter with working-class people. He stood as a Labour candidate for Farnham, a safe Conservative constituency in Surrey, at the general election of 1922. He was beaten, and returned to Cambridge knowing that he was not suited to a career as a politician. Campaigning did not fit his temperament. Though politics engaged his deep interest, he decided at that point that the academic cloister must be his base. He went on with his historical studies, revisiting G. T. Warner's *Landmarks in Industrial History* (1924) and writing a short life of James Watt (1925). But here too was a limitation of personal character, for he also knew that it was not in his nature to spend his working life poring over original documents to the extent demanded by reputable historical research. As the end of his fellowship approached he realized that he must get away from Cambridge and, accordingly, he applied for the first post he saw advertised, that for a tutor to students of social work at LSE. Beveridge appointed him in 1925. Thus, his formal journey into sociology began; it was soon confirmed by his promotion to a readership in 1930.

During the 1930s, Marshall came to identify himself wholeheartedly as a professional sociologist. He was to help to launch the *British Journal of Sociology* in 1950 and meanwhile developed interests in social stratification and social policy, editing studies such as *Class Conflict and Social Stratification* (1938a) and *The Population Problem* (1938b). In neither of these fields, however, did he equip himself with the statistical skills which might have been available to him from his colleagues A. L. Bowley or, later, D. V. Glass. Such expertise would have been well within his competence. It is clear from his essays and reviews that he thoroughly understood methods of survey, the powers and limits of social measurement, and the logic of multivariate analysis. But he remained a sophisticated consumer and did not become a professional practitioner of these statistical techniques; for this he advanced the dubious rationalization, by analogy with his experience as a skilled if amateur violinist, that a sociologist must not only learn to use instruments but also 'learn to grow them on the tips of his fingers'. This also, some believe, was a mistake by the man and a lost opportunity for his subject.

For better or worse Marshall never acquired the driving puritanical dedication to research and writing which might have been possible in the ethos of Houghton Street. His professionalism was never so narrow. Teaching was at least as important as research. Administration at the LSE, burdensome as he found it, was a compelling duty, especially as professor of social institutions and head of the social work department (1944–9) and later (1954–6) as Martin White professor of sociology, succeeding Ginsberg. Public service, though never sought, was always felt as a call to be unstintingly answered. He served in the Foreign Office research department from 1939 to 1944, with the British Control Commission in Germany 1949–50, and as director of the social sciences division of UNESCO from 1956 to 1960. And beyond both professional and public duty there remained the constant pull of a highly civilized private life of music and friendship where he expressed perhaps his greatest gifts of character.

In his extra-academic excursions from 1939, and during his retirement to Cambridge from 1960, Marshall applied his sociology. He did so in the analysis of German war propaganda, in planning the post-war reconstruction of German education, and in directing the UNESCO effort towards applying the social sciences to the problems of development. In his retirement he devoted himself to social policy and administration, writing and revising the standard text on that subject as well as a series of occasional papers which Robert Pinker persuaded him to put together and publish. We shall return to his work on social policy in Chapter 10. Again the work is applied sociology, indebted to, yet independent of, the definition of social policy and social administration which was so strongly advanced after 1950 by Richard Titmuss and the productive group of academically passionate advocates of welfare at the LSE. Marshall's definition was wider, and more securely grounded in history, though it lacked the detailed empirical foundation of much of Titmuss's work. It was also less sharply egalitarian, and more an advocacy of the 'Butskellite'[16] welfare state.

Apart from his seminal Cambridge lectures on Citizenship and Class, Marshall's definitive studies in social policy were not written until after his retirement. In particular, *Social Policy in the Twentieth Century* (1967) and the last collection of essays, *The Right to Welfare* (1981), demonstrate his unique ability to relate the sociological aspects of social institutions to issues of social policy. Marshall believed that the value conflicts generated by the interaction of

---

[16] A widely used journalistic reference of the time to the combination of R. A. Butler and Hugh Gaitskell who both advocated the Welfare State from Conservative and Labour positions.

competitive economic markets, representative democracy, and statutory social services indicate the resilience rather than the weakness of democratic welfare capitalism in the context of social change. He also challenged the convention that the abolition of poverty requires strictly egalitarian policies, arguing that certain inequalities that facilitate economic growth are a precondition of the elimination of poverty, provided that the state guarantees the right to a basic level of social services.

Marshall's writing is elegant and economical: sociological jargon is avoided and meticulous citation shunned. In his teaching there was a personal style of clear, cool analysis dominating an easily borne but wide scholarship. In his public and administrative work the rigorous honesty of a Leonard Woolf was combined with no less rigorous standards of professional skill. Courtesy and competence, diffidence and dedication marked all his activities. Marshall's qualities of mind have been described by Lockwood as 'a finely balanced tension of opposites'.

How is it possible to explain the transition from the Victorian order of class inequality, evangelical religion, and social deference, to the consensus which produced the welfare state and the Butskellism that Marshall spent his life in analysing? His answer was to emerge as sociology. Yet, it was rooted in the intellectual culture of Cambridge. First, it was an extension of Maitland's view of history to take in the development of civil, political, and social rights in the twentieth century. Second, it represented the further development of a corpus of work in the 'moral sciences' in Cambridge from the middle of the nineteenth century—with Henry Sidgwick, Alfred Marshall, and Leslie Stephen as the founding fathers—which aimed to produce a secular substitute for the traditional theological justifications of social morality and explanations of social integration.

Marshall absorbed these ideas and preferences into his personal life. They also later appeared in his writing and most cogently when he revisited Cambridge in 1949 to deliver the Marshall lectures, published in the following year as *Citizenship and Social Class*. By that time a mature sociologist, he found it natural to expound his theme from Alfred Marshall's equally characteristic phrasing in 1873 of the question 'whether progress may not go on steadily, if slowly, till, by occupation at least, every man is a gentleman' (Marshall, 1950: 4). Alfred Marshall had held that it would. T. H. Marshall was to go on to show how, and to what extent, it actually did—through the development of citizenship. His method was that of the detached and civilized observer from the study and the library, rather than the party activist on the hustings. Tawney (his senior by thirteen years) had gone from Balliol to Toynbee Hall in the East End of London and to the Workers' Educational Association in Rochdale. George Orwell (ten years his junior) went to the slums of Paris, the spike, and Wigan Pier. Marshall never moved far from the Cambridge and Bloomsbury connection. Except that he went to Houghton Street.

Marshall went to LSE stamped with the personal and professional morals and manners of the Cambridge elite. But he was not merely a representative of that high culture. His assured gentlemanliness was more than convention: it was expressed exquisitely by a shy and handsome man of critical but generous sympathy towards others. His austere blend of irony, diffidence, and duty made him a delightful colleague and a punctilious public servant. His quiet passion for justice took him momentarily to the hustings, made him a co-signatory of the memorial to the master of Trinity College in favour of reinstating Bertrand Russell to a lectureship (Hardy, 1917), and impelled him to a lifetime's study of class inequality and social policy. His awareness of his own limitations tended to draw a modest veil over what we can now see as a genuinely original sociological mind.

For Marshall, civil rights are the bulwark of a free democracy. Legal rights as rights of citizenship are dispersed through many institutions: they are intrinsic to all social relations, not simply to the polity; and they refer to citizens as political actors not merely, as with social rights, to people as consumers. They are more than an institution: they are a culture. The rights to freedom of thought, speech, and assembly, and the right to justice and the rule of law, are externalized expressions of principles internalized by upbringing.

'They thus become part of the individual's personality, a pervasive element in his daily life, an intrinsic component of his culture, the foundation of his capacity to act socially and the creator of the environmental conditions which make social action possible in a democratic civilisation' (Marshall, 1981: 141). Marshall, the inheritor of high civility and the scholar of high sensibility, was here describing his own best self, his ideal for his country, and the ultimate hope of ethical socialists for all societies.

Marshall's relevance outlived him, and formed the title, *Citizenship Today*, of the twelve T. H. Marshall lectures delivered since their inauguration at the University of Southampton in 1983. The lecturers, all leading British social scientists, agreed that Marshall was a highly significant figure in sociology after the Second World War. His analysis of citizenship and social class with its historical framework of evolving civil, political, and social rights and its contention that citizenship and social class 'have been at war in the twentieth century' (Marshall; 1947: 115) were both applauded and attacked. Raymond Aron detected *histoire raisonneé*. Giddens blamed Marshall for leaning towards the ethical evolutionism of Hobhouse and his neglect of Marx. Dennis and Halsey argued that Marshall's was a crucial contribution to the sociology of ethical socialism. For Mann the thesis was too English. For Giddens it omitted women. All these matters are controversial. What is beyond dispute is that Marshall set the stage on which argument about citizenship will continue for the foreseeable future. He was no Soames.

Barbara Wootton

There was a fourth inter-war figure, at Bedford College, London. Barbara Wootton (1897–1988) was one of the most illustrious daughters of late Victorian England. She was born in Cambridge, the third child of two Cambridge dons. But two circumstances marred what would otherwise have been as privileged a start in life as Edwardian England had to offer: death and gender. Her father died when she was ten and he only forty-seven. Her best schoolfriend died at school and her brother Arthur in war. Then she endured the fate of so many of her contemporaries. She was widowed by war. Her husband, Jack Wootton, from a non-conformist manufacturing family in Nottingham, was a friend of her elder brother Neil, a promising Cambridge research student, and a handsome young man whom she married on 5 September 1917. He was twenty-six and she twenty. They had thirty-six married hours together before she saw him off to France at Victoria station. Five weeks later the War Office 'regrets to inform you' and in due course punctiliously returned to her his blood-stained uniform. Thus, before she came of age she knew more of death than of life. We can reasonably speculate that the phobias and obsessions which plagued her had their origins in these adversities. Yet, she herself remained resolutely pre-Freudian in her attitudes towards responsibility in the face of disaster. Utter self-reliance was the creed of a quietly courageous and spectacularly formidable person. 'We would do better', she thought, 'to encourage children from the earliest possible age, however wretched their backgrounds, to believe that they are, or at least soon will be, masters of their fates'.

The other circumstance—that she was born a woman—was no less powerful in shaping her character. For girls of her class were expected to acquire honour and distinction in competition with their brothers but without the normal male opportunities. Though she prayed earnestly to be sent away to school like her brothers, she did not in fact escape the home nursery until at thirteen she was allowed to enter the Perse High School in Cambridge as a day pupil. Her mother's will and ambition was that she should follow the same scholarship path to classical erudition at Girton. She was aware that at this point in her life her brothers would move from prep to public school and the vast majority of her compatriots would leave school altogether for a life of wage earning in field or factory. Barbara was dutifully successful in the entrance examinations and became a candidate for the first part of the tripos even though her strong personal inclination was to abandon dead languages for Alfred Marshall and modern economics, in pursuit of understanding of the contemporary civilization which she saw as collapsing all around her. The war went on and she went on with her studies until the examination approached and she succumbed, apparently psychosomatically, to virulent tonsillitis, resulting, so to say, in an aegrotat degree. She later confessed in her autobiography to an act of conscious and deliberate revolt—'revenge for the Greek verbs on my lovely summer holidays, revenge for years of being exhibited as the clever daughter, revenge for a world which could value my distinction as a classical scholar above the extra hours that Jack and I might have had together'. Her autobiography, *In a World I Never Made* (1967), took its title from A. E. Housman. She dwelt like him as a stranger and laconically recalled the highlights of a sexual travail that never ended.

Liberation from the well-intentioned matriarchal dominion of her childhood began with Part II of the tripos. She put aside the Greek and Latin texts and turned to read economics with determined enthusiasm and was placed not merely in the first class but with a mark of distinction never awarded to anyone else, male or female, before or since. Yet, ironically, as a woman she was prevented from appending B.A. to her name. Girton recalled her from her research studentship at the LSE to a fellowship and the directorship of social studies in the college a year after graduation, and the Board of Economics invited her to lecture on Economics and the State. The University of Cambridge at this time had still not legislated the admission of women and therefore could not licence lectures by a non-member. Hubert Henderson intervened gallantly, offering himself as the advertising lecturer but on the understanding that the university would add in brackets that the lectures would be delivered by Mrs Wootton.

Cheerfulness often triumphed over irony. She married again in 1935—to George Wright, her colleague in adult education and London government, who was temporarily a cab driver—but there was no permanent peace. He turned out to be a 'natural polygamist' who kept a succession of 'secondary wives' round the corner, though making it clear to each one that his loyalty to Barbara was paramount. She nursed him through a long illness till he died of cancer in 1964.

Liberation went further. She not only forsook the classics but also conventional scholarship and institutional religion. Her circumstances and temperament gradually formed her into a rationalist, an agnostic, and a socialist—a method, a philosophy, and a commitment which gave steady consistency to a long professional and public life. Her rationalism evolved, no doubt, in part not only from sheer intellectual prowess, but also from the experience of bereavement and the illogicality of a gifted woman's place in her society. Her agnosticism was nurtured from deep scepticism about the benevolence of any conceivable deity or principle of cosmic order in the Great War. And her socialism was rooted in the same experiences, which convinced her that, given sympathy for others, critical reason was the only road to salvation on this earth. At all events these were the lights by which she lived and for her they burnt brightly. Ivory towers could offer no resting place so she worked for the research department of the Labour Party and the Trades Union Conference from 1922, as Principal of Morley College from 1926, and as Director of Studies for Tutorial Classes in London from 1938, until she took up a readership in the sociology department at Bedford College in 1944. In 1946, she was disappointed at the LSE in a competition for the chair and headship of the department of Social Administration which went to T. H. Marshall. Within academe her preoccupation was always with practical problems. She became an acknowledged expert in criminology, penology, and social work, and her *Social Science and Social Pathology* (1959) remains a classic in the application of utilitarian philosophy and empirical sociology to the enlightened management of society.

Above all she became an outstandingly vigorous public figure. She was a governor of the BBC from 1950 to 1956 and served on four royal commissions (workmen's compensation 1938-44, the press 1947-9, the Civil Service 1953-5, and the penal system 1964-6). She was also Chairman of the Countryside Commission (1968-70) and the first woman to be elected President of the BSA (1959-64). Created a life peer in 1958, she was also the first woman to sit on the woolsack in the House of Lords. Her ambivalence to the Upper Chamber surprised some democratic socialists. She recognized that it was 'totally indefensible in a democracy'. 'No one in his senses would invent the present house if it did not already exist...but...Ancient monuments are not light-heartedly to be destroyed.' More generally she made the best of the institutions she found and was unwilling to see her country pay the price in misery to ordinary people that revolution along Stalinist lines would entail. She preferred to work piecemeal and her service as a justice of the peace in London, from the age of 29, that is, before she was entitled as a woman to vote, is a long record of humane public effort. She died in 1988, admired by those who knew her, honoured by a festschrift,[17] a woman whose steadfast faith was in argument and persuasion towards a socialist commonwealth.

Social Anthropology

So far in this account of the history of sociology in Britain we have scarcely mentioned social anthropology. We must now do so. For the single institution, LSE, which nurtured sociology was also the home of Malinowski and his seminar as well as earlier that of Westermarck and later of Firth and Gellner. Social anthropology in Britain was established earlier and held in higher esteem not only in academe, but also in the wider circles of the elites in the colonial administrative, political, and literary worlds.

The boundaries without and the divisions within sociology were defined more fluidly in the early part of the twentieth century. Thus, Westermarck, though formally a sociologist, asserted in his Huxley memorial lecture of 1936 'that there is no country in the world that can rival in its achievements in social anthropology, whether pursued in the study or in the field, largely owing to its sterling qualities of lucidity and good sense' (Ginsberg, 1940: 28). Was Hobhouse's *Material Culture* a work of sociology or social anthropology? 'Pursued in the study' rather than in the field, no doubt, and it was also engaged in the search for principles of social evolution which ruled the social sciences from Comte and Spencer until Malinowski changed the agenda to seek functionalist explanations. Nevertheless, social anthropologists responded to the new enthusiasms after 1950 by following exclusionary strategies in the Association of Social Anthropologists (ASA) founded in 1946, neglecting undergraduate studies and fostering the research seminar as the socializing instrument in forming collective identity (Spencer, 2000). Sociology, by contrast, welcomed its sudden post-war popularity with an inclusive strategy, hospitable to undergraduate courses, and giving membership in its professional association, the BSA founded in 1951, to anyone interested in belonging (Platt, 2003) We shall examine the consequences in Chapter 5.

---

[17] There is a full bibliography of her writings in Bean, P. and Whynes, D., *Barbara Wootton: Essays in her Honour* (1986). A movingly informative essay on her has been written by Terence Morris, 'In Memoriam: Barbara Wootton 1897–1988', *British Journal of Sociology*, June 1989, 40/2: 310–18.

Social Administration

Although social policy and administration (the second preceded the first, though they are closely bound together) only became firmly established in the 1950s, they were beginning to gain a foothold in universities much earlier in the century—largely under the guise of training courses for social workers in such provincial red-brick universities as Liverpool (from 1909), Birmingham, Manchester, and Leicester, as well as at Oxford, before the Second World War.

Most important were developments at LSE where a Department of Social Science and Social Administration was established in 1912. The new department absorbed the School of Sociology set up by the Charity Organisation Society (COS) seven years earlier to train social workers and which had previously guarded its independence from LSE, mistrusting the collectivist tendencies of an institution created by the Webbs (Harris, in Bulmer *et al.* (1989)). The department, a product of the intellectual and political climate induced by the Poor Law minority report, Dahrendorf suggests, was in fact about social policy (Dahrendorf, 1995: 197). Supported by money from the Ratan Tata Foundation, its aims were to develop empirical research and to professionalize the social services. But the two activities of social enquiry in the tradition of Booth and Rowntree and social work training did not lie easily together. Friction persisted between theoretical and applied subjects; between sociology and social administration; between a discipline which aspired to be value-free and one which aimed to reform the world. There remained, Dahrendorf remarks, an ever-present tension at LSE between the desire to know the causes of things and the desire to change them.

Matters developed in a similar way, though on a much smaller scale, in Oxford. There, in 1914, Barnett House was established as a memorial to Samuel Barnett, founder in 1884 and then warden of Toynbee Hall, the first university settlement in London's East End. For Barnett the problems confronting society at the end of the nineteenth century were similar to those identified by Dahrendorf a hundred years later (Dahrendorf, 1988); they were about finding ways of extending to everyone 'entitlements' to a common culture and a common way of life (Parker, 1998: 29–49). Originally a supporter of the COS, by the end of the century Barnett had come to reject some of its most fundamental principles. Independence of state relief and saving, he claimed, had become ideologies, defended by the COS as an icon defended by its priest. But it had lost touch with the problems of the times. 'Abuses increase, beggars parade the streets, indiscriminate giving demoralises whole neighbourhoods, and the Society's voice is hardly heard. Working men can find no work, striving homes are broken by want, and the Society suggests no remedy' (Barnett, 1887; quoted in Parker, 1998).

The new institution in Oxford was to be a centre for the study of social and economic problems and the education and preparation of young men and women for social work or social research. Initially Barnett House, like LSE, was not formally attached to the university, but close association was guaranteed by the heads of houses and college fellows among its founder members and who continued to be strongly represented on its governing body. In 1946, the university became responsible for the Social Training Course, appointing a delegacy to supervise it. By 1961, Barnett House had become fully absorbed into the university as the Department of Social and Administrative Studies.

In the early years, it pursued its aims of research and education by maintaining a library, arranging lectures and conferences, publishing papers, running various training courses, and conducting local surveys of social conditions. A major research venture was a survey of social services in the Oxford district, a joint effort of dons and local government officers aided by a Rockefeller grant. Two volumes emerged from this enquiry, published by the University Press, but further work was interrupted by the Second World War. A later study of London children evacuated to Oxford was directed from Barnett House and published by the Press in 1947.

After 1946, when the university became responsible for the Social Training Course, other activities at Barnett House slackened and in 1954 Hebdominal Council decided to end its existence as a corporate body, transferring its assets to the university to be administered as the Barnett Fund. Barnett House has remained the familiar name of the department, its official title changing eventually to the Department of Social Policy and Social Work. Sociology was split off in 1998 to form a separate department.

London School of Economics

Coming back finally to LSE as an institution, it is hard for a former student to be objective about a history of 'the School'. Ralf Dahrendorf came there first as a graduate from Hamburg in 1952 and returned from West Germany and Brussels to take up the directorship in 1975: he saw his task as a crusade. The LSE had been like that from its inception, attracting defensive affection and serving too as the cockpit or reflection of the great issues of the day, expounded in lectures and fiercely argued in seminars by both cognoscenti and enthusiasts. Dahrendorf's is among the best modern essays in institutional history. Most such histories are ruined by nostalgia. Perhaps this one has to be compared with the two essays by S. M. Lipset and David Riesman on Politics and Education at Harvard (1975): both have a firm sociological grasp of place and period.

If fault is to be found with Dahrendorf's account it is that he sees the whole century of the School too much from the Director's chair. Presidents rarely make, though they may sometime break, colleges, despite the contrary instances of Aydelott at Swarthmore, Bullock at St Catherine's, Jowett at Balliol, or Morris at Leeds. It is doubtful whether Beveridge or Carr-Saunders seriously altered the fate of the LSE. Indeed, as Dahrendorf himself argues (p. 488), a university does not need to be run. The essential job of the director is to ensure the survival of the institution. Financially for the LSE this is a story of crises, miracles, and negotiated settlements with the state, great philanthropists, and foreign foundations, as well as the University of London. Politically it was always a matter of balancing enthusiasms and intellectual virtuosity against external, including state, pressure and prejudice—again a delicate operation. So at the beginning in Victorian London, the problem was whether the LSE was properly defined as a university college, with its evening students and its allegedly narrow curriculum. Now it is no longer Fabian, no longer dominated by famous professors. Some will regret the demise of the evening lectures and the decline of the teaching ethos. There are many clamorous voices: the eager undergraduate deplores preoccupation with prices rather than values, rationalists vie with traditionalists, wealthy accountants jostle with out-at-elbow political visionaries. The director must watch an alchemy which has nurtured and still aspires to find space for all these constituents.

For students, and certainly for undergraduates, the magical character of the place was that great scholars carried on the Scottish tradition of professorial lectures and taught both earnestly and brilliantly on both sides of Houghton Street. It was the home of Laski, Robbins, Tawney, Malinowski, Popper, Plant, Meade, and Gellner. It drew visitors from all over the world. It welcomed the Treasury and Transport House, the Lords and the Commons. Collectively it constituted the major alternative British Establishment nursery, from before the First until after the Second World War. In London, yet not metropolitan, it rose with the Labour Party but was neither engulfed by its decline nor revived by its resurgence in the 1960s. The trick of living dangerously with political conflict has been a fact of the LSE and is a theory applauded by Dahrendorf. Suspicion of bias was never very far from the official mind and was, of course, a more notable feature of universities in other countries which lacked the pragmatic restraint of British institutions. The School was, after all, founded by the Webbs, Bernard Shaw, Graham Wallas, and the Fabians, and recruited the perennially adolescent Harold Laski among the first generation of professors. Dahrendorf relates all this fairly despite the obvious difficulty that much of it remains within living memory. Moreover, the sustained quarrel between Robbins and Hayek at the LSE and the Keynesians in Cambridge remains largely unsettled.

There is an ill-understood strand in LSE history which Dahrendorf skilfully unravels. This is the search for an ethically neutral, politically unbiased social science. Beveridge imagined he had found it in biology. A beneficent result was the development of demography. But a less happy outcome, involving complications in the relations between Beveridge, the LSE professoriate and the governors, and the Rockefeller Foundation, was the appointment of Lancelot Hogben to a chair of social biology. There can be little if any doubt that Hogben was a spectacularly quarrelsome colleague. He resigned in 1937. But he left behind *Political Arithmetic* (1938*b*) which, not so much because of his own arguments against the deductivist methods of his economist colleagues but because of his grasp of the tradition which came down from the early days of the Royal Society in the seventeenth century, offers a permanent base for the social sciences. Passionate commitment to ends is accepted. Social science is then concerned with rational means towards the attainment of these ends. The hard labour of empirical enquiry thus becomes the business of the social sciences. On those terms the LSE should run for at least another millennium.

Conclusion

What then, before we turn to an account of the post-1950 professionals, are we to make of our past leaders? I have considered the Soames label. In fact, there seem to be three possible categories: those, mostly foreign, who have left a permanent mark on sociology, those who unhappily deserve the label if not the fate of Enoch Soames, and those who, reflecting a marked feature of the culture of social sciences, come into and fall out of fashion. In the third category we might place Hobhouse, Mannheim, and Parsons. Parsons was undoubtedly the dominant world figure in sociology in the mid-century, decades before his theories were eclipsed by more radical ones in the 1960s. There followed 'a lengthy period of visceral hostility toward, indeed, of outright dismissal of [his] work but it is today enjoying a revival in the world of sociology' (Trevino, 2001: xv).

No equivalent to the Parsonian school of standard American structural functionalism developed in Britain around any of the leaders so far discussed either before or after 1950. No Weber circle, no Durkheim school, no Chicago school. The LSE was no challenge to any of the three dominant American centres of sociology, Chicago, Columbia, and Harvard, before the end of the Second World War.

4

British Post-war Sociologists

SUPPOSE AN American social scientist, say Flexner, had visited Britain after the Second World War. He would have noticed the secure establishment of Economics in Cambridge and Political Studies in Oxford. These subjects also enjoyed a sturdy, if modest, existence in other universities such as Manchester and Glasgow. And there was the distinctive London School of Economics and Political Science (LSE) where the visitor's eye might have been caught by about a dozen students of sociology, similar in age but of a style and outlook very different from that of their Oxford contemporaries. They took their degrees, and busied themselves around Houghton Street with a novel aspiration. They wanted to become professional sociologists.

Fifteen years later Raymond Aron was visiting Oxford from Paris and some of them were gossiping in Halsey's room at Nuffield College about the state of the British sociological art. Aron suddenly cut in to exclaim, 'The trouble is that British sociology is essentially an attempt to make intellectual sense of the political problems of the Labour Party.' Fifteen more years later Ernest Gellner suggested to Halsey that he write an essay on what turned out to be the first group of career sociologists in Britain. What had been their political and intellectual concerns? What formed their unprecedented and unlikely occupational ambition? And what happened to them and their intentions?

Halsey promised to write the essay[1] knowing that the reference was to those who graduated with him in sociology at 'the School' in the early 1950s, together with one or two, notably Ralf Dahrendorf, who came from elsewhere to join them as graduate students. A handful of predecessors were known to them, but like John Porter or Anthony Richmond, had gone abroad to seek their fortunes in Canadian, Australian, or US universities.

To be more precise by enumeration, the group consisted of:

	Then	Now
J. A. Banks	LSE Graduate 1950	Emeritus Professor of Sociology, University of Leicester
Olive Banks	LSE Graduate 1950	Emeritus Professor of Sociology, University of Leicester
Michael Banton	LSE Graduate 1950	Emeritus Professor of Sociology, University of Bristol

---

[1] A first version of the essay appeared in the *European Journal of Sociology*, 1982: 23: 150–75.

	Then	Now
Basil Bernstein	LSE Graduate 1952	Emeritus Professor of Sociology of Education, University of London (Died 2000)
Percy Cohen	LSE Graduate 1951	Emeritus Professor of Sociology, LSE (Died 1999)
Norman Dennis	LSE Graduate 1952	Reader in Sociology, University of Newcastle
Ralf Dahrendorf	LSE Graduate 1952	Former Director, LSE & Warden of St Antony's College, Oxford
A. H. Halsey	LSE Graduate 1950	Emeritus Professor of Social and Administrative Studies, University of Oxford
David Lockwood	LSE Graduate 1952	Emeritus Professor of Sociology, University of Essex
Cyril Smith	LSE Graduate 1950	Former Secretary, Social Science Research Council
J. H. Smith	LSE Graduate 1950	Emeritus Professor of Sociology University of Southampton (Died 2002)
Asher Tropp	LSE Graduate 1950	Emeritus Professor of Sociology University of Surrey
John Westergaard	LSE Graduate 1951	Emeritus Professor of Sociology University of Sheffield

This chapter, in other words, is about an LSE group that became a significant part of the sociological establishment by the mid-1960s. They did not monopolize sociological development between 1950 and 1965: their immediate predecessors remained active—Jean Floud, Michael Young, Donald MacRae, Tom Bottomore, Tom Burns, Duncan Mitchell, and Ilya Neustadt. Contemporaries from elsewhere followed similar careers towards the British professoriate— Peter Worsley and John Barnes from Cambridge anthropology, Joan Woodward from Oxford, John Rex from South Africa, Stanislav Andreski from Poland, and John Jackson from Ireland. And the School continued to send graduate students to join them—Bryan Wilson, John Goldthorpe, Frank Parkin. But they began as a more or less self-conscious group, and ended as more or less prominent individuals in the British sociological professoriate, scattered about the country as the heads of newly created university departments. Such group identity as they had in the 1950s was lost in the 1970s, its boundaries engulfed by the tide of new recruits to the profession for which they had clamoured.

The story is, therefore, restricted to a time when sociology was becoming recognized and established in Britain; not a complete account but an answer to particular questions about those who graduated from LSE in the early fifties to be dispersed by professional success during the sixties.

Who were they? A short answer is that most were provincials: provincial in social origin, provincial in political preoccupation, and provincial in their early jobs. A longer and more adequate answer would recognize the provincial as only one kind of outsider and so would take account of the three others who were foreigners, Cohen, Westergaard, and Dahrendorf. Native or migrant, they were all initially sleep-walkers, but their education and profession led them towards metropolitan and cosmopolitan recognition, which was scarcely attained before their subject and their academic calling had again been transformed. In the 1960s, twenty-eight new university departments of sociology were created. A rapid expansion of staffing went on throughout the decade from each year's new graduates against a background of student radicalisms in America and Europe. By the 1970s, the LSE pioneers had become a middle-aged minority so small as to be barely noticeable among the diverse armies of their younger colleagues.

Yet, before their time, sociology as an academic profession hardly existed. Its British origins as a mode of thought can, as we have seen, be traced back to the nineteenth century and beyond. The post-war group was the first to find adequate institutional support. It was the first set of individuals to be absorbed into the university senior common rooms by the normal processes of undergraduate and graduate education in their own subject.

But what subject, some may still ask, is that? Sociology in the now received view is continental in origin. It had been the European reply to Marxism. Is that the subject which was taught to undergraduates at LSE in the late 1940s? Certainly not directly. On the contrary, the LSE syllabus still rehearsed the nineteenth-century battles between the statistical empiricism of the London Statistical Society and the synthetic or orthogenic evolutionism espoused by Hobhouse. 'Classical sociology' as developed on the continent by Weber, Durkheim, and Pareto was imported into LSE for the most part by Edward Shils in the form of Parsons' *Structure of Social Action*. An assessment of the 1950 graduates' response to the confused sociological inheritance offered to them is therefore an essential part of the description of their intellectual preoccupations. First, however, we must look at their social and cultural origins.

The Path to LSE

The ten natives were born in the slump years between the Wars on the periphery of English society, not in its central circle of the well born and well connected. By no means all of their parents were working class, but none of them, gentile or Jew, sprang from the metropolitan professional or administrative families or from the class of big business. Some were of wholly uncomplicated provincial proletarian origin. Halsey was the son of a railway porter in Kentish Town, Norman Dennis of a tram driver in Sunderland. Others had their childhood in families on the margin of the working class, their fathers in petty trade or clerical work. Almost all looked back on a home dominated by political radicalism and awareness of 'the Labour movement'. All, as Wyndham Lewis would have put it in those days, were 'branded on the tongue'. Short of strenuously sustained efforts of elocution, their class and province would henceforth claim ownership of them.

Most, if not all, had 'won the scholarship'. There was only one woman (Olive Banks).[2] There were no 'public' school boys among them. They went to their grammar schools and absorbed the curious provincial patriotism that that experience afforded in the 1930s—a national and nationalistic history and literature which, with science and mathematics, was taught, often with high skill and devotion, in a refined version of the local dialect. 'My country right or left' (Orwell, 1970) was as much a principal component of the hidden agenda of the provincial grammar school as it was of Orwell's Eton. And, combined with education in the kitchen from fathers who had served in the First World War, it was effective. J. A. Banks was exceptionally a conscientious objector, but the rest completed their pre-university schooling in the armed services. Banton had been a naval officer, Bernstein had been a bombardier in the Royal Air Force. More than one came across the word sociology reading H. G. Wells in a Nissen hut. Most of them argued themselves into democratic socialism and enthusiastic support for Attlee's government on His Majesty's ships, airfields, and army camps. They acquired the resolve which Orwell had formulated for them during the War:

they will have to take their destiny into their own hands. England can only fulfil its special mission if the ordinary English in the street can somehow get their hands on power. We have been told very frequently during this war that this time, when the danger is over, there should be no lost opportunities, no recurrence of the past. No more stagnation punctuated by wars, no more Rolls-Royces gliding past dole queues, no return to the England of the Distressed Areas, the endlessly stewing teapot, the empty pram, and the Giant Panda. We cannot be sure that this promise will be kept. Only we ourselves can make certain that it will come true, and if we do not, no further chance may be given us. The past thirty years have been a long series of cheques drawn upon the accumulated goodwill of the English people. That reserve may not be inexhaustible. By the end of another decade it will be finally clear whether England is to survive as a great nation or not. And if the answer is to be "yes", it is the common people who must make it so.[3]

Few, if any, of them had any notion while at school of going on to a university. That aspiration was a product of war service and the FET grant.[4] They chose to come to LSE. They carried a picture of their country as a status hierarchy still strongly entrenched but now outmoded by the social democratic revolution which the War and a Labour government promised, and for which Laski's LSE was an intellectual instrument. They came to study at a place which, though physically in London, they knew to be outside what Edward Shils later depicted as the 'Oxford–London–Cambridge axis', knowing that sociology had no place in, and was indeed rejected by, the cognoscenti of that golden triangle of politics, power, and letters.

[2] The social historian Leonora Davidoff (1987) was also to write in a distinctly sociological style and was a regular attender at the Thursday evening seminar referred to by Dahrendorf (1995).
[3] George Orwell (1970 vol. III p. 55).
[4] A British scheme similar to the American GI Bill which gave studentships to servicemen who had, or were willing to say they had, university intentions frustrated by the War.

Their LSE

Social attitudes, antecedents, and responses are a necessary background, but cannot explain the desire for academic careers in sociology. Obviously the experience of the School was crucial despite some important limitations and discouragements. In the first place, though provincial to the Oxford–London–Cambridge axis, the LSE was an intellectual-cum-political Mecca. Its buildings sprawled in grimy vitality on the East and West sides of Houghton Street off the Aldwych. Demob suits and battle jackets, incongruously adorned by the college scarf, thronged the street between the two main lecture theatres. The library was heavily used, assailing the nostrils with the mustiness of books and the sickliness of human sweat. The students' refectory was a clutter of cheap and unappetizing snacks, and the Students' Union pub, The Three Tuns, normally permitted no more than standing in discomfort. But the aspiring sociologists were indifferent to the chaotic ugliness of the architecture. The inconveniences of a human ant heap were of no significance by comparison with the conversation and the visibility and audibility of great scholars. The tradition of first-year undergraduate lectures by the most eminent professors was fully and conscientiously practised. So they listened to Robbins, Popper, Tawney, Laski, and Ginsberg, and absorbed the excitement of the social sciences.

Of course, the intellectual encounters were inextricably interwoven with the social experience of getting to know each other and their tutors. They developed their awareness of establishment attitudes towards the modern universities in general and sociology in particular, and of the contrast between their own biographies and those of the typical pre-war English don. A few years later, Kenneth Tynan, with characteristic histrionics, dramatized the same conception of establishment attitudes in an epigrammatically angry letter to a young man about to graduate in 1956. He spoke to and for the whole class of rising 1944 Act (Hoggart, 1957) meritocrats or, rather, the stratum of the more successful successors to Richard Hoggart's scholarship boy. 'You are', he wrote, 'among the sixty per cent of undergraduates who are receiving financial aid from the state and your position as such is defined, fearlessly and without equivocation, by Somerset Maugham in his Christmas 1955 message to *The Sunday Times*. "They are scum".'

Tynan thought that Maugham had been a bit harsh, but what they lacked, he added, was a rallying point, social and political. 'They are classless, or rather, they are drawn from every class except the top one. They need a platform to articulate their impatience with convention, with "good taste", with "British prestige"'. Tynan offered one platform—his own dramatic criticism, John Osborne's plays, and Kingsley Amis's early novels. The 'sociological scum' at the LSE sought and offered an alternative sociological analysis and criticism. It was less brilliant and more conventional in its conscious continuity from the traditions of 'social investigation' into poverty and inequality. But it was less conventional in avoiding the use of the academy as a point of entry into a political career. None of the group was active in the student union or LSE Labour Club politics—organizations fairly or unfairly dismissed as the property of political careerists like John Stonehouse, a notorious LSE Labour Club activist who later became a Labour MP, was involved in spectacular scandal, and was finally jailed. They all read Max Weber's two essays on Science and Politics as vocations and chose the former for themselves while in no way abandoning their political enthusiasms.

The Formation of Ambition

But was professional ambition socially possible? The dilemma was one of personal style as well as institutional place. From this point of view the biography of the man among their English mentors who eventually gained their greatest respect for his intellectual stature stood in illuminating contrast to any of theirs. T. H. Marshall was, at least by the external marks of origin and personality, typical of the social stratum and culture to which they were outsiders. As he describes himself, Marshall was born in 1893, the son of a successful London architect.

Our home was, I suppose, typical of the higher professional classes of the period—intellectually and artistically cultured, and financially well endowed...Add to this my conventional schooling, first in a very select preparatory boarding school, and then at Rugby, a solidly bourgeois but not particularly snobbish "Public School", and it is easy to understand how limited, and how naively unsociological was my youthful view of society. I knew nothing of working-class life, and the great industrial north was a nightmare land of smoke and grime through which one had to travel to get from London to the Lake District (Marshall, 1973).

Neither Marshall nor the citing of him should be misread. His sympathy for working-class people, if not for 'the working class', was absolutely genuine. His eyes had been opened to the realities of class prejudice when he took temporary leave from his fellowship at Trinity College, Cambridge, to campaign in the general election of 1922 as a Labour candidate in a Tory constituency in Surrey. He had been jolted into sociological awareness by internment in the prisoner of war camp at Ruhleban in 1914. There he shared the roughest kind of collegiate *gemeinschaft* with untutored seamen as well as intellectuals and musicians. And his *Citizenship and Social Class* (Marshall, 1950), an elegant interpretation of the history of social inequality in Britain, disguises a passionate advocacy of the rights of ordinary people. The significance for the LSE sociologists in the early 1950s was that Marshall's world—the Cambridge voice, the shy self-assurance, the faint air of *ennui*—was no longer to be joined but to be transformed.

It had been different before the War, when the handful of English recruits to sociology were isolated individuals such as Tom Simey or Dennis Chapman at Liverpool. The possibility of academic expansion and cultural openness was virtually inconceivable. If, like David Glass or Jean Floud, they came from the working or lower-middle classes, they were under strong pressure to assimilate in dress and speech to the culture of the higher metropolitan professionals, and so to be heard by the post-war students as people who used 'telephone' and 'motor' as verbs. Again the continuity of social outlook in the sense of opposition to ancient social hierarchy and inequality was no less important and taken for granted as the ethos of 'the School', at least on the East side of Houghton Street where the sociologists were mainly to be found. Moreover, the newcomers were more impressed by Glass's suave erudition and Jean Floud's vivacious intelligence than by their socially elevated appearance. And these two seniors were after all of 'humble origin'. But they were assimilators, perforce or by choice, in ways which seemed less compelling to the post-war group.[5]

In any case the social character of their predecessors and teachers, though important to the 'definition of the situation' (a much contemplated jargon phrase of the time), was not crucial to the outcome. The intended journey was an intellectual and professional one: the vehicle and travelling clothes were secondary. No doubt those of the new group who were gentile and low born were sensitive or over-sensitive to the surface *son et lumière* of English gentlemanliness. But some were Jews, some foreign, and one both. The same was true of the tutors and authors who fashioned their intellectual outlook. And these exotic influences were essential signposts to the journey out of provincial obscurity. Among the students, Cohen came from South Africa, Westergaard from Denmark, and Dahrendorf from Germany. Among the tutors Donald MacRae was a Scot (only a little older but with a longer academic biography reaching back to schoolboy precociousness), Ernest Gellner was a Prague Jew, and Edward Shils an American. The head of the department was Morris Ginsberg (see Chapter 3). Socially and culturally he was an ambiguous figure. If he noticed his students' ambition at all, it was with a gentle negative sadness. He gave no encouragement.

For some, perhaps the majority, the assured expositions of the professors gave no more than a glimpse of majestic social scientific scenery. For the minority, two men stood out as guides to further ambition—David Glass and Edward Shils. Both oddly enough were indifferent lecturers, but they were endowed with a compelling charisma (a convenient word avidly acquired especially by those with no religious education). Glass offered a method; Shils a theory. Glass was the active leader of empirical research into the social structure of Britain. Radical in politics, as privately angry as he was publicly knowledgeable about social inequality, precise in research technique, learned in the LSE tradition of demographic and statistical investigation, he was doing what they aspired to do.[6] Ambition seemed therefore to fit both their political outlook and their personal intellectual abilities.

---

[5] Even so, I would not want to over-emphasize the difference. I remember one member astonishing me in the mid-1950s with the confidence that he thought my voice deep and individual, whereas he heard his own as a squeaky Cockney and wanted to modify it! The rise of estuary English was to come much later.

[6] For an appreciation of Glass and his crucial importance in the drive towards meticulous analysis of social inequality, see John Westergaard, 'In Memory of David Glass'. *Sociology*, 1979, 13: 173–8.

David Glass

There is however a special (in the sense of peculiar) story to be added from before the Second World War, related in Dahrendorf's history of LSE (Bulmer, 1985: 16; Dahrendorf, 1995), which involved the connection of sociology to demography as well as the early career of D. V. Glass. Beveridge, the Director, believed that the social sciences had their roots in the natural sciences. After protracted negotiations with the Laura Spelman Rockefeller Memorial Foundation (Beveridge had written a first memo in 1925) and the Professorial Council of LSE, it was agreed to establish a new chair of social biology. Lancelot Hogben, a peripatetic Cambridge biologist, was then professor of zoology in Cape Town. He was offered the new chair and accepted in 1930. The curmudgeonly Hogben spent a stormy period at LSE and retreated in 1937 to a chair at Aberdeen. According to the famous demographer Eugene Grebenik, he made 'little lasting impact on the School' but out of it all LSE demography was born, David Glass was launched on a distinguished career, and *Political Arithmetic* was published in 1938.

David Glass became the dominating figure in British sociology in the 1950s. Born in 1911 into a Jewish tailoring family that had immigrated into the East End of London, he made his way to the School via Raine's Grammar School and graduated in 1931 as a geographer. He was taken on as Beveridge's research assistant. But Hogben interested him in population studies and convinced him of the importance of quantitative research in the social sciences. Glass responded, developing exact and ascetic standards which, while in his case firmly linked to passionate left-wing political principles, must remain the permanent mark of any scholar. He wrote extensively on population problems and became the most learned authority of his day on the history of demography and its social setting. His *Population, Politics and Movements in Europe* (1940) was immediately recognized as a classic and has remained so. After wartime work in the Civil Service he came back to LSE as reader in demography. That was in 1945, but he was promoted to a chair of sociology in 1948. Always busy and imposing, but often to be found chatting to students in Joe's café in Houghton Street, he encouraged the young to his own enthusiastic empiricism. He served the Royal Commission on Population which reported in 1949 as he had the Population Investigation Committee from 1936. Many of his colleagues, like Eugene Grebenik or R. K. Kelsall, were deeply respectful of his broad range of talents and many of his students, like Olive Banks or John Westergaard, revered him as a demigod of the social sciences.

From the chair of sociology he took the lead in promoting one of the most famous empirical studies in sociology—the 1949 survey of social mobility—which he edited and published in 1954. It was a landmark in the history of the subject, not only in Britain but, especially through Glass's influence in the International Sociological Association, in many other European countries and in North America. Yet, this was Glass's first and last excursion into sociology as distinct from demography or social history, though a highly significant one. Thereafter, he retreated more and more into historical demography until an untimely death in 1978.

Why this retreat by a man who was given the Martin White chair of sociology in 1961? In positive part the answer was surely that the population interests of his youth properly never ceased to attract him. He was by nature an indefatigably exact historian and a painstaking statistician. But negatively his immediate surroundings at LSE became increasingly uncongenial to him. An uncharitable and rancorous atmosphere emerged in the 1960s which drove people away from the department.[7] One of the post-1951 cohort of research students remembered the word 'abysmal' as the then typical evaluation of other sociologists and their work. And, as we shall see, opportunities were opening elsewhere, outside LSE. How far Glass himself promoted or opposed this expansion is not known.

Given its intrinsically competitive character, it is hardly surprising that academic life is riddled with malicious gossip or 'character assassination'. Attacks on one's peers are understandable, but slander against juniors is rightly condemned. Yet, Glass often spoke ill of at least some of the juniors in his own department and of rising outsiders such as Michael Young, A. H. Halsey, or Ralf Dahrendorf. He also tried to prevent the Social Science Research Council (SSRC) from funding a new mobility study at Nuffield College and Barnett House in Oxford in the late 1960s on the grounds that he himself was working on the topic with a view to early publication which never materialized. It was a sad end to a career of otherwise admirable scholarly standards. Perhaps he is best remembered as a demographer, rather than as a sociologist.

It would be uncharitable to leave Glass on a sour note. His contribution to both sociological research on class and to demography was immense, and his love for historical demography was expressed in such intellectual gems as his paper on John Graunt (the founder of demography) published in 1963. His obituarist in *The Times* (27 September 1978) wrote a summary which would be difficult to improve: 'Some found David Glass a hermetic person, introvert and ascetic. Others liked to see him thaw when he talked about books or about India ... He will be remembered at LSE as one of the great men who have given distinction to this unique academic institution.'

Edward Shils

Edward Shils was an alternative spur to academic aspiration who presented classical European sociology to his students in an American voice which simply assumed that undergraduates would become graduate students and subsequently professionals. His blend of tutorial ferocity and Olympian erudition challenged their still half-formed ambition to fearful aspiration. His *Present State Of American Sociology* (1948) conveyed the idea that a subject of great difficulty and worth was at once both dignified in its European antiquity and accessible in its American modernity. Sociological research was a living practice as well as a hallowed tradition.

---

[7] See Ernest Gellner's review of Ralph Dahrendorf's *LSE* in the *Times Literary Supplement* (26 May 1995).

Shils was born in 1910 in Philadelphia, followed the normal path through local high school and the University of Pennsylvania, and emerged with a B.A. in 1931 to face the severe conditions of the labour market of that decade. He worked briefly as a social worker but then he gradually found his way as Louis Wirth's research assistant into what he saw as the intellectual heights of the University of Chicago. Unsurprisingly in the 1930s he was a Rooseveltian New Dealer but, as he matured in the Chicago atmosphere, he became a liberal, distrustful of 'the powers', bellicose against state tyranny of the right or the left, and a devotee of freedom. In the 1970s he also became a neo-conservative in the twentieth-century American sense, trustful of tradition, seeing social order as rooted in face-to-face ties, and finding his utopia, as did his Manchester friend Michael Polanyi, in the worldwide networks of scientists and scholars intensively looking for truth and protected by the institutions of free science. Co-founder of the *Bulletin of the Atomic Scientists* and actively opposed to McCarthyism during the 'cold war', he defended democratic pluralism in his *Torment of Secrecy* (1956). He was among the last fervent missionaries of academic freedom, enamoured of German universities in their Humboldtean heyday, always seeking to preserve and to reinvent what he increasingly feared to have been lost by Marxist ideological betrayal and state patronage. Fairly or unfairly, I think unfairly, he saw Glass as an English Stalinist.

At Chicago, Shils was influenced by Robert Park in Chicago empirical sociology, by the economist Frank Knight in the pursuit of a rigorous logic, and by the physicist Leo Szilard in a relentless effort to influence the political authorities. He occupied himself energetically with the associated movements towards international control of nuclear weapons. Yet, he was faithful to his academic calling, reading the European classics and modern American empirical studies, working closely with Talcott Parsons, and publishing widely. Indeed it came to light beyond the circle of his close friends and only on his death that he was engaged on a breathtakingly ambitious, Weber-like project on the Movements of Knowledge down the ages and across cultures and religions—an unfinished and probably unfinishable programme of scholarly research. Such was the grandeur of his reading and his knowledge of disciplines, languages, and history.

When the United States entered the Second World War, Shils seized the opportunity of coming to England where he worked jointly for the British government and for the US Office of Strategic Services interviewing German prisoners. His conclusion, confirmed by later research, was that the influence of primary group loyalties rather than the Nazi ideology sustained the fighting power of the Wehrmacht.[8]

Meanwhile, he soon penetrated and enjoyed the London circle of European intellectuals, including Raymond Aron (then a member of the Free French

---

[8] Shils' original insights (with Morris Janowitz, in 'Cohesion and Disintegration in the Wehrmacht in World War II', *Public Opinion Quarterly*, 1948, XII: 280–315) have survived in a considerable literature during the following half century. There is a more measured study of 1982 by Martin L. Van Creveld, *Fighting Power: German and US Army Performance 1939–1945*, in which Van Creveld refers to the contribution made by Shils and Janowitz.

Forces). After the War he became one of the first transatlantic academics with a joint post at LSE and Chicago. Later (1961) he went to Kings College Cambridge and later still (1970) to Peterhouse to escape the influence of Edmund Leach, the famous social anthropologist, who was later referred to by Lord Dacre as 'the swinging provost'.[9] He, meanwhile, retained his connection to Chicago where he joined the Committee on Social Thought which John Nef had founded. He knew an extraordinary number of intellectuals in Europe, North America, and Africa, as well as in India where he made a special study of their place in society and wrote a much discussed monograph—*The Intellectual Between Tradition and Modernity* (1961). He seemed to be in perpetual motion, arriving everywhere at congresses, conferences, and conversations. Yet, he was an essentially private man. He was also a busy man, aggressive and either scowling in the face of an enemy or smiling at the sight of a friend. 'Nor', as Noel Annan has written, was he 'afraid to bludgeon with his erudition those who did not realise sociology was a subject that rested on a great European intellectual tradition' (Annan, 1990).

For Shils the structural connection between centre and periphery was crucial to sociological analysis. In it lay the key to understanding society as a complexity of collective self-consciousness. A development of Durkheim's organic division of labour, Shils' notion of centre and periphery was a more inclusive concept than Marx's class consciousness, filling the gap into which feelings, perceptions, and ideas were shunted by Marxists as 'false consciousness'. So, for example in his appreciative but critical essay on Robert E. Park, he notices Park's failure to 'respond to the challenge of analyzing that assimilating society [i.e. the United States in general and Chicago in particular]: the society which assimilates into itself the peripheral minorities (ethnic, religious, national etc.) and which *thereby diminishes the distance between center and periphery, which is one of the major features as it is one of the great moral achievements of modern liberal democratic societies*, (Shils, 1992). I italicize in order to emphasize the ambitiousness of Shils' challenge to Marxism.

Perhaps Shils' most enduring interest was in the university as an organization for the creation and preservation of important knowledge. To this end he founded *Minerva* in 1962 and was its active, some thought over-active, editor until the end of his life. Many contributors would have their scripts returned and find them cascaded in showers of green ink by the editor's comments and suggestions—in effect rewritten. Lord Ashby thought Shils the outstanding editor of the century (Shils, 1997). Certainly no editor put a firmer stamp on his journal in our time.

He was a Jew who neither believed nor practised, but was nevertheless proud of his ancestry and deeply if sceptically pious, knowing, and deploring the secular tendency among his colleagues to believe that reason could put religion to flight. For him the unsolved mystery of life was in the origins of social consensus and

---

[9] At a memorial service in Cambridge at the Church of St Mary the Less, 10 June 1995. See *Minerva*, XXXIV (Spring 1996), p. 92.

that, in all their paradoxical complexity, the roots of rationality remained in human emotions. Thus, a man may be dominated by the love of God or a woman by the need to impress her lover either by admiration or envy of their predecessors. But their success in science or scholarship requires them to harness their emotions to the institution in which rationality rules through the developed customs of exact reference, open publication, and peer review.

One confusing aspect of Shils' reputation and his period of great if declining influence is that it happened to coincide with the cold war. He was decidedly a warrior on the American side of that protracted struggle which began after the Second World War and which changed its form but did not end even when the Berlin Wall fell in 1989.

Shils' service to the OSS was, it turned out, to the precursor of the Central Intelligence Agency (CIA) which subsequently funded the Congress for Cultural Freedom (CCF) and therefore the journal *Encounter* with which he was closely associated. When all these connections were exposed in the mid-1960s not only did the CCF lose influence (Coleman, 1989), but Shils' reputation was damaged among the socialists who dominated the European universities at that time. His move from Kings to Peterhouse in Cambridge and his continuing intense loyalty to the University of Chicago further reinforced his reputation as a right-wing intellectual and thus weakened the persuasiveness of his persistent adherence to conservation and tradition in respect of university affairs.

Moreover, the 1960s and 1970s were a time of ready translation of academic into political attitudes. The campus was even likened by the Parisian Professor Touraine to the early industrial town as portrayed by Marx and Engels. Shils was accordingly a victim of the same over-simplified interpretation. Subsequent events have taught us painfully that the university is not a microcosm of society, that its ethical problems, its principles of admission, exclusion, and internal governance, its *eidos* and its *ethos*, rest on contingencies that differ from as well as reflect the political order surrounding it. Of course there was always a correlation between support for the Welfare State and the expansion of educational opportunity for the hitherto excluded or disadvantaged sections of society (ethnic, sexual, or class). But correlations between categories are not to be turned into predictions about individuals. Every undergraduate is taught to avoid the ecological fallacy. Shils remorselessly insisted on freedom as the *sine qua non* of research and teaching. He further insisted on loyalty to the university to which a teacher or a student was attached. Equality was for him a more complicated matter, always to be subordinated to intellectual merit.

Portraits of Social Scientists

A life and career may be mirrored and possibly distorted in sketches of the lives of contemporaries. Shils offers in *Portraits* vivid pictures of the luminaries who made up his intellectual and social environment at the University of Chicago in the 1930s and later at the LSE. The portraits show Shils to be a deft wielder of words in presenting an economical sketch of his colleagues, whether in Chicago or London. He shows respectful affection for his heroes (there are no heroines here but see his *Cambridge Women*) (Shils and Blacker, 1996) but also a fair-minded weighing of virtue and vice in those of whom he disapproves. For example, in the sad story of Harold Laski, Shils points devastatingly to the substitution of slogans learnt early ('very vague Marxist clichés') for scholarship maintained, and observes that a fabulous memory and a quick facility of utterance can be immediate gains but long-term losses. Student audiences at LSE were enthralled by Laski's wit and rhetoric. Shils notices his bold departure from the Weber ideal that politics has no place at the scholarly lectern. He fails to notice, however, that Laski would invariably and meticulously add to his biased diatribe a short bibliography of the best works opposing his own position.

Shils' academic utopia is composed of people of independent mind, immensely learned, and above all resolute in seeking truth and devoted to the tradition and the institutions that enable them to do so. Nor is this a pantisocracy entirely of the intellect. Individuals with their personal eccentricities are exactly observed at all points of the gallery. Thus 'Robert Park was like a bear—built like a bear, hunched over like a bear, putting his nose into everything like a bear, and grumbling and grunting like a bear' (p. 32). Arguing with Frank Knight 'was like wrestling with an intellectual porcupine'. Shils remembers Raymond Aron on a street corner in Paris after lunch: 'In response to a remark of my own, he said laughingly, "C'est un pessimiste jovial". I now return the compliment by saying "C'était un optimiste triste". With that I take my unhappy leave of Raymond Aron'(p. 75). Tawney 'looked and spoke like an untidy angel who had learned English from the Authorised Version . . .' (p. 192).

Stepping back, Shils observes that 'Most sociologists looked very ill-assorted. They were no longer clergymen; they were not businessmen; they were gawky, awkward country boys, however old they were. Parsons looked a little like a genteel Easterner, although like many sociologists, he too came from the Middle West, having been born in Ohio' (p. 41). 'He was a saint of sociology: his life was consecrated to it' (p. 47).

Ginsberg offered a stark contrast to both Glass and Shils. The weight of his teaching continued to rest on the interests he inherited from Hobhouse and conceded little or nothing to the eagerness of his post-war students to come to grips with the topical issues of social reconstruction, the growing volume of American empirical sociology, or the development of quantitative methods and, later, of Marxist and phenomenological approaches to sociological theory.

The idea of progress that Ginsberg accepted had been maimed in Flanders in the First World War and finally destroyed in Auschwitz in the Second. His post-war audience heard him as a nostalgic rationalist humanitarian. It seemed as arid as Durkheimianism seemed to Aron between the Wars. Vigorous young men and women wanted a future as well as a past. Their politics assumed the practice of progress, and they were ready to believe in some English, Fabian, Labour-movement version of the idea of progress. Ginsberg's version would not do. They looked elsewhere in sociology for a theoretical answer.

Marxism

It was not clear whether the LSE graduates of around 1950 ever found it. Classical sociology may perhaps be best thought of as the liberal reply to Marxism. If so it was a central feature of their provincialism that they were unschooled in, and conditioned to be resistant to, both the Marxist thesis and the liberal sociological antithesis. Both were historicist. John Westergaard was the exception. He was an avowed Marxist whose early work was with Ruth Glass in urban sociology. Nevertheless, the aspects of his Marxism which were most apparent were also characteristic of the group as a whole: hostility to social inequality and commitment to empirical research. His greatest work (with H. Resler), *Class in a Capitalist Society*, appeared in 1975. Tom Bottomore, who had graduated from LSE in 1949, was also a Marxist, but it is significant that after '1968' he came to be seen as tainted with the reformist empiricism of the group discussed here. Thus, Martin Shaw (*Sociology*, September 1976, 10/3: 519) disparages his 'neutral commentary' style and the use of sources 'rather tilted in the direction of early twentieth-century reformism'. Shaw is shocked to find that 'Bottomore is also capable of statements such as "Marxism has brought into existence political oppression and cultural impoverishment—which might have come straight out of [Karl Popper's] *The Open Society and Its Enemies*. He obviously feels that Marxism would be better off without its socialist political commitment." ' Some of the others of this generation have spent their later sociological careers in an at least partially successful search for a viable synthesis.

Perry Anderson, the Marxist theoritician, made an astonishing volte-face in 1990[10] in which he 'discovers' Giddens, Mann, Runciman, and Gellner as the great leaders of a systematic sociology in Britain. He fails to recognize Lockwood, Bernstein, Dahrendorf, or any of my thirteen, not to mention Glass, Bauman, Goldthorpe, Heath, or John Scott. It is all rather arbitrary and, most sociologists would say, eccentric. But, be that as it may, his judgement in 1968 on the group of sociologists I am discussing had been unequivocal: 'To this day, despite the recent belated growth of sociology as a formal discipline in England, the record of listless mediocrity and wizened provincialism is unrelieved. The subject is still largely a poor cousin of social work and "social administration", the dispirited descendants of Victorian charity' (Anderson, 1968).

The point about such a sneering dismissal was not so much the view of social theory that lay behind it as its rage against any sociology which was not subordinate to revolutionary politics as defined by Marxists. It is a judgement narrowed by the blinkers of 1968, by which time, after a quinquennium in

---

[10] In *New Left Review* 180 and 182, 'A Culture in Contraflow', Anderson apparently found a home at UCLA in Los Angeles in the 1990s. His essays (gathered together under the title *English Questions* and published by Verso in 1992) demonstrate a virtuosity and erudition of gargantuan sweep through philosophy, economics, history, anthropology, and politics, as well as sociology. His dazzling scholarship is, however, underlain by a tenacious adherence to anti-capitalism through a modern Marxism with all its weaknesses and, especially since 1989, its neglected strengths as a basis for criticism of capitalist institutions.

which the number of social scientists in British universities had tripled, the character of sociology had shifted decisively towards a chaos of conflicting ideologies. Anderson's prejudice prevented him from appreciating the radicalism of post-war British sociologists. Theirs was indeed a provincial radicalism, but nonetheless passionate for all that, and nonetheless powerful in its impact on the ruling academic and political elite. The ex-service students had grown up in committed Labour families to which was added the experience of the War with its siege socialism, the sense of a just cause against Fascism, and the promise of a planned and open society without the unfreedom of a communist state. With these social experiences they had no need of Marx to support a radical fervour.

As an interpretation of their experience as working-class children and patriotic soldiers, Marxism in practice was read and heard more as the shifting propaganda of the Russian foreign ministry than as an analysis of the social structure of their own country. The polarization thesis they knew to be as much rhetoric as reality. It was only after the end of the post-war years in 1974 and the regime of a new economic liberalism that they had to recognize the return of polarizing tendencies. In the 1950s, they could come from Holborn Tube station to Houghton Street without passing a beggar. By the mid-1980s they could not avoid this reminder of a world they assumed had disappeared. Meanwhile the polarization phenomenon had been a useful rhetoric in the debate with their political opponents, but one for which they had viable and powerful alternatives whether from the *Magnificat* or from Tawney or William Morris or Orwell. Marxism was for middle-class pre-war intellectuals. Russia was for the Webbs. Such events as the Hitler–Stalin Pact of 1939, Czechoslovakia in 1948, the Twentieth Congress, and the Hungarian Revolution of 1956 only confirmed that Marxist-Communism had nothing to do with the socialism to which they were committed—a democratic socialism without secret police and the suppression of free speech.

They did not hate or reject their country. For all its persistent inequality, the social hierarchy which branded the tongue of every British child, the incompetence of the slump Tories, and the stuffy closeness of the culture, nevertheless they knew Britain as a relatively decent society. They were confident that the democratic institutions invented by the Victorian and Edwardian working class, the Unions, the Co-operative Societies, and the Labour Party were the foundations of a New Jerusalem, a free and socialist Britain. If their Party and the Attlee government lagged behind, their idealistic impatience called for renewed radical persuasion. It did not require a total therapy of revolution and the massacre of people by their own countrymen. Resolve, pressure, argument, and firm insistence on democratic action would be repeatedly necessary over a long haul. But democracy and decency need never be abandoned.

In short, the LSE post-war sociologists were committed to a socialism that had no need for Marxism and no time for communism precisely because it was so deeply rooted in working-class provincialism. Then the intellectual experience of sociology added a further vocabulary which, *inter alia*, led to a confrontation with Marxist theory. The confrontation was not at first direct. Though Ginsberg's synthesis of rational ethics and the evolution of social institutions

[handwritten: it did not happen according to Hamish Fraser 1999]

was remote and limp, it was, however vaguely, consistent with the Labour programme of radical institutional reform. The National Health Service was citizenship, triumphant nationalization of industry was an institutional step towards justice for workers, and the expansion of free grammar-school places promised parallel justice to workers' children. Glass's direct application of the method of political arithmetic to expose inequality strongly reinforced the bridge from social theory to political reform. Still more important was the impact of Karl Popper's justification of 'piecemeal social engineering'. While they may have chafed under its implications of extreme caution, they were comforted and encouraged by a theory which simultaneously offered reassurance that reform rather than revolutionary change was likely to be most effective and (what they ardently wanted to believe) that the logic of discovery permitted an important role to the social scientist in the process of social reform. Sociology could be seen as an intellectual trade union to solve problems by the hypothetico-deductive method. There was a logically justified place in the syllogism for theory (ideals), method (research), and substance (political action).

It was an elaboration of Popper's view in *The Open Society* (1945) and *The Poverty of Historicism* (1957) which gave most of the young LSE sociologists the first theoretical as distinct from political engagement with Marxism. Then came Parsons. *The Structure of Social Action* gave a first synopsis of the sociological tradition. But they were uneasy with *The Social System,* not because of its weirdly unwieldy and polysyllabic prose (that was attributed to nationality), nor because Glass dismissed it without argument (that was opaque political prejudice), nor because it revolved around norms and values (for their essential politics was ethical socialism), but precisely for the reason that Anderson was later to admire it.

Sociology, in this sense, came into existence as a science which aspired to a global reconstruction of social formations. This was its *differentia specifica*. It is no accident that it later developed into the monumental architectonic of Parsonian action theory, embracing every dimension of social existence in a single schedule of classificatory concepts. Whatever the concrete outcome of this enterprise, the ambition to provide such a master synthesis was inscribed in its vocation from the start (Anderson, 1968).

But not for the 1950 graduates. Both Parsons and Marx offered theories of society as a totality in terms of categories which were surely too arbitrary to carry the empirical weight of social analysis of a particular country in a particular historical period.

Functionalism

Functionalism, it should be added, later ritually slaughtered before first year undergraduates every Michaelmas, was not the undisputed sociological piety of the 1950s which the fashion of the 1970s made it out to be (Martins and Rex, 1974). True, it was rescued 'politically' for the LSE group by R. K. Merton's ingenious defence of its analytical neutrality in *Social Theory and Social Structure*

(1949, among the two or three most exciting publications of their student years). But they were no more reconciled to the functionalism of Parsons than to the Hobhousian harmony offered by Ginsberg. Nevertheless, suspicion of a theory which turned on consensus did not mean accepting Marxist contradiction. Their general inclination was to reject the totality of both systems, and then to seek a combination of Parsons' abstractions of value with Marx's abstractions of material circumstances.

The most remarkable early expression of this idea, and one which deeply impressed the group as a whole, was David Lockwood's review of Parsons' *Social System* in the *British Journal of Sociology* (1956) adumbrating his monumental *Solidarity and Schism* (1992). Lockwood placed both Parsons and Marx in the tradition of social theory on social order descending from Hobbes. For Lockwood, as for Parsons, Marx's fundamental insight was that the transition from the state of nature (with its endemic and fractionalized conflict) to the state of civil society was one in which conflict became systematic, between the interests of groups through the social relations of production. Conflict was non-normative as well as non-random. The two systems thus appeared in almost polar opposition. A Parsonian social structure is based on dominant value patterns; a Marxist one on forms of ownership and control of the means of production. Socialization in the one is set against exploitation in the other.

The theoretical question is whether a sociologist had to take the two sets of abstractions as exclusive choices. Lockwood refused, seeing both as particular sociologies. On the one hand, he suggested that society is unthinkable without some degree of integration through common norms and that sociological theory should deal with the processes whereby this order is maintained. On the other hand, society is unthinkable without some degree of conflict over the allocation of scarce resources in the division of labour, and sociological analysis has been given the task of discovering how divisions of interest are structured and expressed. The latter view, which seems to be the general import of the Marxian sociology, does not necessarily imply that resources refer only to productive means, or that conflict is necessary and not contingent. Thus, it can be argued that there is no real rivalry between the two sociological systems, but that they are, on the contrary, complementary in their emphases (Lockwood, 1956).

Lockwood's theoretical development of this position occupied him throughout his career in Cambridge and Essex, issuing finally as *Solidarity and Schism*. His doctoral thesis on the *Black Coated Worker* (1958) and his later books on *The Affluent Worker* (1968/9), with Goldthorpe and their Cambridge colleagues, were important empirical studies of British class structure within the theoretical framework of non-Marxist radicalism. Dahrendorf's graduate studies yielded *Class and Class Conflict in an Industrial Society* (1959) and bore the stamp of a similar theoretical origin. It included a brilliantly argued and empirically based demonstration of the failure of the polarization thesis. Marshall's subtle account of citizenship as a principle of social change cutting across class and status conflict had also been assimilated. And Dahrendorf's first book already pointed the way towards the liberal (rather than the egalitarian) political position that he eventually took (Hall, 1981). He too delivered a summary judgement in 1988—*The Modern Social Conflict*.

Halsey's doctorate was an empirical study of the implications of the 1944 Education Act for social mobility. Jean Floud and he collaborated in the 1950s to give the sociology of education a place in the general development of sociological theory and research. The emphasis was again on egalitarian analysis of social inequality, but in their case consciously carrying on the tradition of political arithmetic—marrying a value-laden choice of issue with objective methods of data collection and analysis (Free Press, 1961). The influence of Glass was plain, and his programme of research into the modern history of the British occupational hierarchy also covered Tropp's thesis on *The School Teachers* (1956) and Olive Banks's *Parity and Prestige in English Secondary Education* (1955). J. A. Banks was also supervised by Glass in preparing a much applauded study of the decline in fertility among the Victorian upper-middle classes (Banks, 1954), launching a series of enquiries by the Bankses on that remarkable shift in the behaviour of a key status group. Meanwhile, Bernstein began the explorations of class, language, and school performance which were to be so celebrated in later decades. And Dennis began his empirical studies of modern urban democracy with a period of fieldwork in a mining community near Leeds (Dennis, 1956).

Taken together, the work of the LSE group in the 1950s added significantly to knowledge of the changing social structure of Britain. In one important sense it was a sociological expression of autobiographical experience—a projection of the country they had learned in their families, schools, work places, and local communities. In another sense it was, as Aron suggested, a sociology of the programme of Labour Party reform. But in its most fundamental sense it was the assimilation of international sociology and its application to the understanding of British society. Percy Cohen's theoretical work, Lockwood's awareness of both Marx and Parsons, Dahrendorf's linking of Weber to T. H. Marshall, and Bernstein's appreciation of Durkheim's legacy in the sociology of education, all bound British sociology to its origins in European and American thought. In its labours, the group made obeisance to a powerful Pantheon. It was neither a pantisocracy nor a shrine to any particular theoretical orthodoxy. Marx, like Parsons, held an honoured, but by no means dominant, place.

Altogether, and without intending it, the work of the group, especially its equivocal attitude to functionalism, its promotion of conflict theory, and its generally sceptical radicalism, provided some of the foundations for the more strident rebelliousness associated with the 1968 events to which we turn in Chapter 6.

Conclusion

We have described in this chapter the dramatic transformation of sociology at its headquarters, LSE. The circumstances were remarkable; a post-war assembly of ex-servicemen taught by brilliant teachers, including David Glass and

Edward Shils whose biographies are told in some detail, at a rejuvenated metropolitan place of challenge to the traditional supremacy of Oxford and Cambridge. A dozen of the LSE students were intent on becoming the first generation of professional sociologists. Their implausible dream was to be realized through an expansion of the universities and within them of the social sciences in general and sociology in particular.

Between them, these aspirant LSE sociologists provided a comprehensive description of British society, its demography, its ethnic composition, its education, its religion, industry, crime, and its class structure. They also joined enthusiastically the international progress of the subject in America and Europe. And finally they engaged, in an empiricist and largely non-Marxist fashion, with the New Left movement that led to the student rebellions at the end of the 1960s.

5

Expansion 1950–67

SUDDENLY AN implausible dream became a reality and by 1960 the London School of Economics and Political Science 1950 graduates found themselves launched into permanent academic careers. For some life became 'Christmas every day', for others the anxiety had to be faced of a real if implicit demand for personal productivity in research as well as the more or less private torment of teaching. These are, of course, the age-old challenges of academic work which are met with varying success by high honours graduates selected for university life. But soon the system of higher education began to be transformed. The first generation of LSE professional sociologists were described in Chapter 4 as sleepwalkers. They had no idea as undergraduates or indeed as graduate students in the 1950s that they were riding the first tide of an influx of sociology into the life of the universities and still less of the press, radio, and television (later to be called the media). They had no idea that they were destined to become leading members of a new, much sought after if also much abused, profession. They were enthusiasts for a discipline which was at the same time uncertain in the minds of its practitioners, encouraged by an alliance of liberal dons and eager students, and regarded with suspicion or hostility by those who saw themselves as guardians of traditional scholarship. Whereas in the 1940s there cannot have been more than 200 undergraduates studying sociology, and these largely concentrated at LSE, by 1966/7 there were nearly 3,000, and by 1970/1 nearly 4,000 in the UK universities, not counting students in the then polytechnics or The Open University.[1]

What lay behind this abrupt expansion? Some sociologists would invoke their own persuasiveness, others would point, perhaps more plausibly, to the eagerness of the young for new, more modern, more relevant studies. Most compelling, perhaps, were the social and economic circumstances. In the advanced industrial world, out of the wreckage of war there had emerged an economic boom in 1945, which was to be sustained until the oil crises of the mid-1970s. The American advance into a new age of affluence had begun with Roosevelt, accelerated during the war, and carried on in the post-war years with Marshall Aid to revive the economies of Western Europe. There was an increasingly felt prosperity, especially among the young.

---

[1] Appendix 2 gives details of the number of students from official records between 1950 and 2000.

The Organisation for Economic Cooperation and Development (OECD) had been set up in Paris to encourage and monitor economic growth. The effects in Britain were initially muted. Victory had been won at the price of economic exhaustion. Loss of Empire and accommodation to a reduced international status also diverted attention from celebration of the heroic achievements of Attlee socialism and from the pursuit of economic growth to match the remarkable pace of German and Japanese recovery. Expansion in education had been similarly held back and perhaps also hindered by reformist movements to reduce pre-war inequalities, for example, by building new primary schools and developing comprehensive secondary schooling. The slogan adopted by the OECD for higher education in Europe in the 1950s was 'doubling in a decade', whereas the Robbins Report of 1963 was a more cautious British response to a rising middle-class demand for university places.

A general expansion of student numbers, admittedly on a gentle scale, was however in the university air from the end of the Second World War. The then existing universities, either ancient, like Oxford or Cambridge and the four-centuries-old Scottish universities, or modern, like the Victorian/Edwardian products of the industrial revolution in the provincial cities, were bulging with ex-servicemen returning from the War to begin or resume their studies, aided in many cases by state grants. Before the Robbins Report pressure was contained by the near universal assumption that universities were restricted to a tiny minority who would follow professional and managerial careers. Oliver Franks gives some idea of the contrast between the years between the Wars and the period after Robbins when he describes his 1920 undergraduate admission to the Queen's College, Oxford (Danchev, 1993: 15). He was asked three questions: which school, which religious denomination, and whether he owned a horse. Replying no to the third question, he was told that he ought to acquire one; the next three or four years would be a crucial part of his gentlemanly education in which character formation would be a prominent component and by learning to sit in the saddle he would become equipped to take his place as a governor of the Empire ruling a fifth of the world!

One obvious consequence of expansion was that the number of sociologists employed in universities mounted rapidly. Another less obvious result was that they were continually on the move not only in and out of LSE to the other London colleges and the provincial universities but also across the Atlantic and to international conferences. Visits to America in the 1950s already echoed the traffic of scientists to German universities before the First World War. Money began to flow from the United States along with courteous welcome from sociology departments at Harvard, Columbia, and Chicago. The dazzling rise of Clark Kerr's Berkeley and the prestigious attraction of fellowship at the Centre for Advanced Study of the Behavioural Sciences at Palo Alto in California were also features of the 1950s.

None of the LSE group described in Chapter 4 stood still. By 1960, all had taken advantage of the widening horizons to move out of the sociology department at LSE, though Westergaard had moved back in 1956 after spells at UCL and Nottingham, and Asher Tropp, after Princeton, held a lectureship at the School from 1954. Bernstein was about to move to the Institute of Education in London, Banton was in Edinburgh, Jo and Olive Banks in Liverpool, Dennis and Halsey in Birmingham, Cyril Smith in Manchester, Percy Cohen in Leicester, Lockwood in Cambridge, John Smith in Southampton, and Ralf Dahrendorf in Germany.

Moreover all these movements of individuals in the 1950s and 1960s had their impact both on the character of their institutions (mostly new university departments of sociology) and on the collective state of mind, especially the development of an international, as well as national, provincial, and metropolitan, outlook. Thus, the International Sociological Association was formed and in 1953 Tom Bottomore took over as its secretary, and there were well attended World Congresses of Sociology, the second in 1956 in Amsterdam where a Russian delegation (the males of which appeared in proletarian Sunday suits, trousers at half mast, and hair cut to short back and sides) was faced by the young, eagerly aggressive, and sociologically challenging Marty Lipset from New York. The third was bigger and held in Stresa in Italy in 1959, again attended by Europeans and Americans including Talcott Parsons. The fourth was a huge gathering in Washington, DC in 1962 and was still more elaborately sectioned. Sociology by that time seemed to be a powerful growing force in the international world.

In the process, the 1950 group became merged, perhaps better to say engulfed, by its predecessors and its successors. Yet, if we consider the larger picture then social scientists, and professorial sociologists in particular, stand out as a group in flux against wider norms of persistent institutional immobility. The wider scene has to be explained by a national pay scale imposed after the War by the University Grants Committee (UGC), virtually automatic tenure, and the custom of largely internal markets for promotion to a readership or senior lectureship. Only at the point of first appointment and promotion into the professoriate was movement between universities a normal part of the academic career. Consequently, the rate of movement of individuals between British universities for all ranks and disciplines barely altered between 1938 and 1967, rising only from 1.3 to 1.7 per cent. The difference is not statistically significant even though the 1930s were a time of very modest growth while the post-Robbins 1960s were a time of marked expansion. For later years the figures,[2] again for all ranks and disciplines, show a marginal fall from 2.8 per cent in 1975/76 to 2.6 per cent in 1988/9, including and therefore inflated by counting movement between the different colleges of the University of London.

By contrast and on average, no fewer than 10 per cent of this group had moved from place to place in any year from 1950. In other words, these sociologists on the way to their chairs had moved between institutions at a rate of

[2] For more detail see Halsey, A. H., *Decline of Donnish Dominion* 2nd edn, 1995a, pp. 142–5. The first figures were calculated from the Commonwealth Universities Year Books and the second from the Universities Statistical Record (a data bank on all senior members of universities).

at least four times that of their colleagues in the second half of the twentieth century. Does it matter? On the one hand, it can be argued that the movement of ideas is more important than that of people, and that information flowed more freely year by year as information technology was refined and journals, conferences, and international contacts proliferated. On the other hand creativity, though we do not know precisely its defining circumstances, may continue to depend on the intensity of face-to-face contact with colleagues and students in a department, college, or research centre. There are probably both upper and lower limits to the turnover of staff in an optimally creative milieu. Similarly, what sociologists have come to recognize as the balance between 'locals' and 'cosmopolitans' often influences attitudes to the internal allocation of resources in a university. It is possible that the difference in rates of institutional mobility influenced both creativity and decisions about how to distribute the sudden and severe financial cuts of the 1980s between disciplines. Indeed, if locals support institutions while cosmopolitans favour disciplines, the decisions may have gone systematically against sociology even where its defensive strength had not been weakened by intra-disciplinary conflict.

Communication, even community, among the LSE 1950s group was not, of course, entirely lost. As they entered into the leadership of a burgeoning international profession of sociology, they were in touch with each other through the British Sociological Association (BSA), formed in 1951, by occasional seminars at Birmingham University and elsewhere, by meetings of the Teachers' section of the BSA, and by the 'Thursday evening seminar' at LSE.

A more confident professionalism was in any case developing in the 1950s, and America played an even more important part than the English and Scottish provinces. The process had begun in the late 1940s with Edward Shils' influence on the LSE undergraduates. It was continued by the visits to a Cambridge Visiting Professorship of such distinguished Americans as W. L. Warner, Talcott Parsons, and George Homans, as well as by the young Norman Birnbaum from Harvard who came first to the LSE in 1953 and thence to Nuffield College, Oxford. He returned to America in 1962 to follow a successful career as a radical sociologist who spoke frequently, eccentrically, and with egotistic brilliance for his version of sociology and socialism. His most recent book, *After Progress*, appeared in 2001 (Birnbaum, 2001).

The young British sociologists meanwhile began to be invited westwards and were welcomed into the flourishing and expanding world of American sociology. Lockwood was at Berkeley in 1958; Halsey held a fellowship at the Center for Advanced Study in the Behavioural Sciences at Palo Alto in 1956, as did Dahrendorf the following year. By the end of the 1950s, most if not all of the LSE group had become connected to the American and European network of a now expanding international academic profession. In America, they met the New York sociologists. Bell, Lipset, Glazer, Moynihan, Coleman, and Trow were rising stars, anglophile and academically adventurous, but culturally unthreatening because deaf to the subtleties of English status snobbery. They possessed intellectual excellence without social condescension. Most had Jewish fathers who had been subjected to quota, so their's was ethnic, not class, resentment: and they were already learning to be grateful to the America of expanding opportunity. Mingling with them, Halsey guessed for others as for himself, was to set free a new sense of Englishness which the alien culture of the metropolitan class had stifled. 'They too became grateful to America and returned to England with twice the patriotism if half the salary' (Halsey, 1995*a*).

The LSE itself, as we have noted, though holding its position as a leading competitor, was passing through one of its phases of institutional self-doubt, and the sociology department was somewhat fragmented. Shils had gone back to Chicago, and was in Manchester in 1952–3. Ginsberg retired in 1954, Jean Floud moved in 1953 to the London Institute of Education, and the unifying and civilizing influence of T. H. Marshall was absent from 1956 to 1960. The atmosphere of the department was clouded with obscure hostilities between individuals and small groups with negative attitudes to each other's work. It is doubtful whether any clear principles of theory or method were involved, though passions could flare occasionally over the value of empirical enquiry. In 1970 (*New Society* no. 387) Donald Macrae asserted 'Empirical research is easy, as well as quite often being genuinely useful. Most of it, like most natural science, could be done by well-designed mechanical mice.' Peter Marris at the Institute of Community Studies replied satirically. Geoffrey Hawthorn (then of the University of Essex) provided the candid and crushing riposte that 'only someone who has never done any can think that empirical research is easy'.

The contrast with provincial university life was marked. Leicester, under the leadership of Neustadt and Elias, became a highly successful teaching department, attracting creative young lecturers like John Goldthorpe, R. K. Brown, Percy Cohen, and Anthony Giddens, and producing a stream of graduates like Bryan Wilson to challenge the previous monopoly of the LSE. Research in the, new departments in other universities was pursued with cheerful enthusiasm perhaps by people with opportunities beyond their expectations, nervously resentful of the continuing resistance to sociology of the high establishment.

Though by no means an exceptional place, something of the liberating influence of provincial experience pervaded the University of Birmingham[3] between 1954 and 1962, during which period the total number of full-time students grew from just over 3,000 to over 4,000. It was an optimal rate of growth. The academic staff were aware of the probability that an extra (lecturer) in the same or a nearby subject would probably be appointed next year or the year after, and it was all very buoyant but of human scale and easily manageable. Social scientists were incorporated into the Faculty of Commerce, a phrase resonant with Joe Chamberlain's sturdy conception of a civic university relevant to a great industrial town. There were about twenty-three people in the faculty. Mainly by accident, though the half-dozen professors were understandably prone to be self-congratulatory about it, there had gathered in

---

[3] Taken from a letter by Halsey to the then leader of the Liberal Party, Jo Grimond, who was chairing a committee of self-appraisal.

the faculty a quite unusually brilliant group of young people including the econometricians Hahn and Gorman and the social historian David Eversley, as well as economists like Alan Walters, Michael Beesley, and Ezra Bennathan. There was an intense intellectual life. There were no departmental barriers. Even the 'Russians', who lived under the benign czardom of Alexei Baykov, were part of the mainstream of life in the faculty. Staff rooms were scattered and their doors open to conversation and dispute on all matters concerned with the social sciences. Most people were either unmarried or newly married. There was something of the same intellectual excitement characteristic of the University of Chicago and something of the same reason for it in an environment suggesting the beleaguered garrison. The Jewish element in the culture was important. The doyen was Sargant Florence who had continued a kind of respectable radical tradition that presumably began with Sir William Ashley in the early Chamberlain days. The young men and women were too young to worry very much about individual careers and the excitement of developing the social sciences in those days was more than sufficient to concentrate most people's attention most of the time on the intellectual life of the faculty.

Another example is the University of Sheffield. There the department of sociological studies had its origins in 1949 when Ellinor Black was recruited from Liverpool to direct a new school for training social workers. At first, the courses contained no formal sociology. Then, in 1951, Peter Mann was appointed as the first lecturer in sociology. Black died in 1956 and Keith Kelsall came to a newly established chair of sociology. By 1961, a Faculty of Social Sciences had been formed with the department running a new single honours degree in sociology and an expanding staff including David Martin, Trevor Noble, and John Jackson. The separation of sociology from social work within the department proceeded during the 1960s, the focus of sociology shifted to graduate studies, and the non-graduate social work courses were phased out.

This division between sociology and social work was typical of many departments in UK universities such as Leeds, Newcastle, Exeter, or Reading. But within sociology Sheffield again illustrates what the head of the department in 2002, Professor Richard Jenkins, described[4] as 'a ferment of intellectual and ideological conflict' which continued into the early 1970s 'about the undergraduate curriculum—the opposition between theory and empiricism seems to have been a particularly hot topic—and how it should be delivered'.

Jenkins then offers two accounts of two differently remembered eras of Sheffield experience—the early 1960s and the turn of the 1970s. First, Trevor Noble's recollection of the early 1960s:

In the first few years, Professor Kelsall was Dean of Social Sciences and the running of the Department was largely in the hands of Peter Mann. With the increase in numbers and some relaxation in the workload, we campaigned for and succeeded in bringing about a large measure of democracy in the running of Departmental administration and the determination of Departmental policy. In those days these matters were almost entirely

---

[4] In a memo sent to the author in early April 2001.

academic and pedagogic, with little of the preoccupation with financial control, income generation and budgeting which came to preoccupy us in the 1980s. Resources were scarce and facilities poor. We lacked secretarial support, teaching assistance with the large first-year numbers, we had only a Departmental telephone line, and teaching material could be produced only on a stencil/duplicator or Banda machine . . . I was in no way exceptionally burdened but in my first year in the Department, I was required to present a 48 lecture main undergraduate course, a 22 lecture Applied Sociology option, plus seminars for both, to tutor four first-year tutorial groups fortnightly (two each week), supervise six undergraduate dissertations and an M.Sc. research student.

By 1970—and even allowing for nostalgia, and for differences in personality between informants—although there were still pressures, life seemed to have become somewhat different. This is as Ankie Hoogvelt remembers it:

Being very green and young and uncertain of my facts, I was bowled over by the self-confident militancy and political stridency of the students, many of whom seemed to know the difference between, say, Trotskyism, Maoism, Leninism, and who made a point of testing me on my credentials. I specifically remember one incident involving a class of some twenty plus students. There was this big bloke, with open shirt, hairy chest, and a copy of Marx, *Das Kapital*, on his desk, who began to interrogate me, wanting to find out how much I knew, or was I just bluffing. Phew! A passionately revolutionary bloke, who wanted to become a tax inspector. . . .

On the other hand, pressures had eased with respect to curriculum:

the un-pressured academic life is one of the more abiding memories. Everybody seemed to have aeons of time for socialising. Every day, that first year, a group of us from the Department who were housed in a small annexe building, would drift down to the secretaries' office around 3.30 in the afternoon to lengthy tea sessions. We very nearly always had lunch together and with other University academics in the SCR, lunches that lasted a good two hours. . . .

But in between and interwoven with this gentle academic conviviality, there were many filthy, bruising, ideological arguments that were always out there in the open, brought out at every opportunity, in staff meetings and even on one occasion in my own house, at my own birthday party. On that occasion it ended in something close to a fist fight. And always about some obscure (so it now seems) difference between one left position and another. . . .

One way or the other, Theory, and the Truth were central to our working lives. Because that's what it was all about.

Sociology then was finding a bracing but invigorating climate in provincial England in the later 1950s and 1960s. Before the Robbinsian boom it was a smaller and more dispersed enterprise than social anthropology. By 1981, it was to acquire more than 1,000 government funded posts and was growing at ten times the rate of social anthropology (Spencer, 2000: 4). Hence, migration made it possible for new academic structures to emerge. Peter Worsley, Ronnie Frankenberg, Max Marwick, Paul Stirling, Clyde Mitchell, and John Barnes had begun their careers as anthropologists but took chairs in sociology departments. Some sociologists like Banton crossed temporarily into social anthropology on their way to sociology chairs. The influence of Max Gluckman, the great

Manchester social anthropologist was considerable. Cleverer than any 'cartload of monkeys'[5] and as benignly authoritarian as any traditional Jewish matriarch, he was a tall athletic man of vast energy, confident that anthropological method could be used to examine the problems of modern industrial society, and outstandingly persuasive in university politics. He cared little about academic trade-union labels. Accordingly, he set Tom Lupton to work in a factory, Colin Lacey and David Hargreaves in schools, and Ronnie Frankenberg in a Welsh village. He even persuaded Cambridge to offer its new chair of sociology to John Barnes in 1969.

In Wales, Rosser and Harris began to develop research on the sociology of the family and, from Swansea, Margaret Stacey began her famous community study of Banbury which launched Colin Bell onto his career in sociology and university administration. Banbury was also where Michael Mann began his graduate work, studying from Barnett House, Oxford, the movement of Birds' custard factory from Birmingham. At Leeds in the early 1950s Norman Dennis collaborated with the anthropologists C. Slaughter and F. Henriques to study at the nearby mining town of Featherstone to produce *Coal is Our Life*. Exeter and Durham, which recruited John Rex from South Africa and Richard Brown from Leicester, were strong teaching departments and Edinburgh was developing vigorously under the direction of Tom Burns, as was research in the sociology of medicine at Aberdeen under Raymond Illsley.

Meanwhile, post-war British society was changing. The remodelling of public services, representing a huge extension of state power and bureaucracy as well as something of a triumph for collectivist ideology, provided the impetus for the academic study of social policy and administration. The universal services were in one sense the embodiment of the idea of prevention. Free secondary education for all children, a guaranteed minimum income, medical and social care to be available according to need, and full employment policies were all means towards minimizing social and economic risks and enabling people to become independent, secure, and law-abiding citizens in a solidary society. But the proliferation of government activity also invited evaluation and scrutiny of its effects—not least among those who were fearful of the threat to individual freedom and responsibility (Hayek, 1945). In the immediate post-war years interest tended to be focused on the structure and history of the new services but attention soon began to shift to wider questions of cost and equity and social need—the problems of a welfare society rather than the administration of a welfare state. Initially, however, interest was centred on British health and welfare services and social security, and the most widely read text was written at Liverpool University by Penelope Hall, *The Social Services of Modern England*, in 1952.

Concern for equity provided a major incentive for investigation into the NHS. It led to questions about how far the private sector undermines the ideal of a universal service; to criticism of gross inequalities in the geographical

---

[5] From the title of one of his early papers.

distribution of doctors and hospital beds leaving some of the poorest and most unhealthy areas with the poorest provision; to noting the scarcity of resources for certain kinds of illness or disability; and to enquiries into class-related inequalities in the use of and benefit from health services (Townsend and Davidson, eds., 1982).

The Conservative governments from 1951 to 1964 which succeeded Attlee's Labour administration reflected a political climate more critical of state welfare; more alarmed by the public costs and by the supposed excessive redistribution entailed. Within the universities the fledgling social policy and administration departments fell under the influence of other more established related disciplines—economics, sociology, politics, and psychology as well as history (Birrell *et al.*, 1973), and further research questions began to be raised.

Growing awareness of the similar interests and of the research methods of allied subjects stimulated new forms of appraisal of state welfare. Attention shifted from the structure of services to their success in achieving their ends. Studies investigating the quality and effectiveness of particular British social services were appearing in greater numbers through the 1960s. Some came from LSE, but some from elsewhere in Britain including government departments, and some from scholars in Europe and America. Townsend wrote a particularly damaging report on public institutions for old people (Townsend, 1962) and there were many other studies of residential and community services for the old, for children, for the mentally ill, and for other vulnerable groups (Jones and Sidebotham, 1962; Davies, 1968; Packman, 1968). The findings were highly critical: of provision that was inappropriate for needs, of the lack of qualified staff, and of failures in coordination and cooperation between different agencies and different workers involved in the same problems (Donnison, 1954; Rodgers and Dixon, 1960). Suitable dwellings at prices that people can afford are, of course, a fundamental element in community services, and housing policy—the role of the private sector and of the local authorities—was the subject of careful scrutiny (Cullingworth, 1965; Nevitt, 1966; Dennis, 1970; Stone, 1970).

But, perhaps more importantly, came the recognition that the success of public services lay not only in themselves but in the attributes of the people for whom they were intended. The significance of class, of family, of sex, of ethnicity in the use made of and benefit received from schools and hospitals and the National Assistance Board (NAB) became increasingly clear. Thus, the development of academic social policy was heavily influenced by sociology. The focus of research shifted to individuals and families and local communities in efforts to understand how readiness and ability to use public services reflected personal aspirations and social and economic circumstances.

Poverty and inequality were among the most important areas of research. Different definitions of poverty were developed relating the living standards of the poor to the rest of society; and its prevalence, severity, and the people most vulnerable were meticulously investigated (Cole and Utting, 1962; Abel-Smith and Townsend, 1965; Townsend and Wedderburn, 1965; Townsend, 1979).

Sociologists and economists joined the debate. Among the most notable contributions to the social policy literature, W. G. Runciman gave a finer meaning to the concept of relative deprivation (Runciman, 1972), Amartya Sen argued that poverty must be understood in absolute as well as relative terms (Sen, 1983) and A. B. Atkinson examined the evidence about poverty in Britain and evaluated various proposals for reforming the social security system (Atkinson, 1969).

One outcome was the debate about 'cycles of disadvantage'; the idea that predispositions to poverty, delinquency, and anti-social behaviour were passed through the generations from parents to their children echoing the nineteenth-century controversies about the deserving and undeserving poor. Sir Keith Joseph had put forward a subcultural version of genetic inheritance theory, but the environmentalists' emphasis on social conditions proved more convincing (Rutter and Madge, 1976).

While studies of poverty, the distribution of income, and of the costs of public services owed much to the economists, enquiries into education were similarly indebted to sociologists, and reflected interest in the distribution of opportunities and 'life chances'. The welfare services associated with education, school meals, and medical services and provision for handicapped children have always had their place, albeit a small one, in studies of social administration and the welfare state. But analysis of the total education system, of how many children from what sort of background have what sort of education and for how long, was a relatively new interest generated directly by sociologists.

Social policy as a subject, originally mainly concerned with the relief of destitution and the care of people with physical or mental disabilities, was now also concerned with questions of social justice and equality, and with those institutions, public and private, that influence opportunities and standards of living. Here, the importance of education is obvious. The effects of different kinds of school on different children, the relative significance of schools, families, and wider social background in educational achievement, and the advantages enjoyed by children from middle-class families or particular geographical areas become apparent. For education can be shown to be systematically related to social structure; it both influences and is influenced by social, economic, and political position (Halsey *et al.*, 1980; Simon, 1991). But the search for equal opportunities in education is not without its risks. Michael Young had warned in the 1950s of a society bitterly divided between those able to use their opportunities and those less well endowed if the rewards for educational achievement remained widely inequitable (Young, 1958).

In London, sociology was also beginning to make headway outside LSE. At Bedford College, George Brown began his classic studies of psychiatric medicine while Barbara Wootton and Oliver McGregor the social historian were busy in research on the sociology of crime and of the family. Ron Dore from SOAS and LSE began his notable studies of Japan, and he later developed a sophisticated comparative method, especially in his studies of Italian society.

Social medicine was developed under Margot Jefferys and Jerry Morris at the London School of Hygiene and Tropical Medicine.

Max Gluckman continued a vigorous programme of applied anthropological research at Manchester, which attracted Peter Worsley and Clyde Mitchell to a strengthened sociology, and that added Colin Lacey's and David Hargreaves' studies to the sociology of education.

Thus sociology, many faceted, was beginning in the 1950s to occupy a prominent place on the national stage, and we have not so far mentioned the arrival of Titmuss at LSE as the new professor of social administration in 1950 nor the setting up of a new independent Institute of Community Studies in Bethnal Green by Michael Young, nor the new journal *New Society* begun in 1962 under the editorship of Tim Raison and later carried on as a lively weekly by Paul Barker. Sociology was not only being taught in a widening range of universities but also being reported to a widening readership. Circulation of *New Society* attained 37,000 by 1972 and was probably read by 200,000 people every week (Barker, 1991).

The story of innovation in sociological research could go on at the risk of failing the first of Kelsall's tests, that of listing without discussing a large number of sociologists.[6] From the 1950s and 1960s such a list would have to cover the sociologists of industry, of community, of race and ethnicity, of politics, of education, and of religion. People would then emerge in particular places in and out of London, on and off university campuses. W. H. Scott on industry at Liverpool, Banton and Alan Little on race at Bristol and in London, Rex on ethnicity at Birmingham, Aston and later Warwick, Wilson, and Martin on religion at Leeds and LSE, Laurie Taylor and Stan Cohen on crime and deviance, and so on.

Sociology professors came from almost everywhere in the spectrum of disciplines. Only in the exceptionally brilliant case of Ernest Gellner was a chair in anthropology (at Cambridge in 1984) offered to a disciplinary outsider.[7] From the publication of his *Words and Things* in 1959, Gellner continued to relate sociology to many philosophies by a continual stream of critical writing until his death (at Prague airport) in 1997. Rosaire Langlois aptly observed that 'his mischievous wit may be the closest thing to a naughty pleasure that sociology affords'.

Oxford and Cambridge Reluctance

Meanwhile, however, George Homans, visiting Cambridge from Harvard in 1955–6, remarked the continuing frostiness of the older culture towards the subject.

---

[6] See Preface.
[7] Though a philosopher, he had more than served his apprenticeship to anthropology through resident study of the Berbers in North Africa.

My friends in Cambridge are apt to say to me: 'You used to be an historian. What'd you get into *that* for?' But when I ask: 'Why, what's the matter with sociology?' the replies tend to trail off: 'Well, you know, old boy, it isn't quite ... Well ...', and heads shake. One feels the lack of a phrase, at once comprehensive and precise, like the one sometimes overheard at American cocktail parties: 'She isn't quite our class, dear' (Homans, 1962).

Nevertheless, Homans was cautiously cheerful about a British future for sociology, which fairly accurately described and predicted its fate.

In spite of all objections, a great and increasing amount of sociology is being done in Britain. But it tends to be done in research institutions, not as part of a regular university programme; or, if in universities, then in London and the provinces, not in Oxford or Cambridge; or if in Oxford and Cambridge, not under the name of sociology. There is a Professorship of Race Relations at Oxford and one of Industrial Relations at Cambridge.... That is, the British will do sociology, but will withhold, in a carefully graded fashion, like negative knighthoods, recognition that they are doing it. As the British Commonwealth grew great on the principle, at once moral and practical, "let not thy left hand know what thy right hand doeth", this may do no harm except to the sociologists themselves, for it is a Lucky Jim that does not need to be loved. Some sociologists say that every attitude has its function in maintaining society. If this is the case, the function of the British objection to sociology is to produce sociologists who can be objected to.

Yet, there was also ambivalence and anxiety about the social and personal implications of becoming a career sociologist. Edward Shils noted that the heroes of contemporary novelists lauding the vitality and humanity of provincial life tended to end up in Oxford or London. This was a dilemma for the aspiring sociologists. It was not so much that the post-war recruits wanted a totally different culture from that of the metropolitan class. But they did want to widen its compass, to give it more catholic sympathies, to include both its provincial and international sources, and, above all, to have an acknowledged and equal right to participate in that which their experience of grammar school, the Nissen hut, and LSE had shown them to be their birthright and their competence.

On the narrower issues of institutional opportunity, when a vacant assistant lectureship at the School was announced in 1951, the suspicions of the LSE graduates were expressed in ready acceptance of the rumour that Morris Ginsberg had remarked that 'they (the graduate students) can't be any good or they wouldn't be here'. Perhaps the moment of highest resentment was reached in 1959 when Halsey wrote:

The social and academic status of sociology was dramatised by a recent decision of the Fellows of King's College, Cambridge. These gentlemen proposed to elect a research fellow in the subject *from among the graduates of Oxford and Cambridge*, i.e. a first degree in sociology automatically disqualifies its holder from consideration. The Fellows of King's have since reduced their restrictions to include any male member of any university in the United Kingdom. But similar attitudes fortify some of the Oxbridge expatriates in the Arts faculties of the modern universities.... our knowledge of the tendencies in working class culture, for all *U.L.R.*'s discussion of it, is hopelessly meagre and must remain so while direct study organised through the universities is left to a handful of research workers. It is significant that the most widely acclaimed contribution to the discussion,

Richard Hoggart's *Uses of Literacy*, has come from an Arts tutor in an Extra Mural Department, and is based on autobiographical reminiscence and the study of reading matter in mass circulation.

Future recruitment is fraught with uncertainty. Educational selection through the schools directs the most able students towards Oxbridge, or if to Redbrick, to the Science faculties: and there is much in the content of English secondary and higher education to induce trained incapacity for the exercise of the sociological imagination (Halsey, 1959).[8]

The conquest of Cambridge and Oxford was in fact already in train and slowly advanced in the 1960s. Goldthorpe was elected to the King's College fellowship, Lockwood and Michael Young followed to lectureships in 1960. Sociology was introduced into the Cambridge economics tripos in 1961, and into Oxford Philosophy, Politics, and Economics (PPE) in 1962. Martin Bulmer has put together a summary account of the Cambridge story (Bulmer, 1985) up to the mid-1980s, underlining the relative strength of Cambridge sociology in research as distinct from teaching.

But that is not the whole story. There is also the counter-factual proposition that the progress of British sociology would have been earlier and faster if Oxbridge support had been unequivocal. In fact, it was not and the story of the Cambridge chair confirms and illustrates the reluctance of the university establishment to accept this disciplinary newcomer. As Bulmer has argued, it was the indifference of Cambridge and Oxford to the study of the subject that deprived sociology of a solid base and of crucial support for the development of social research. In 1925, the Laura Spelman Rockefeller Memorial offered to endow a chair of sociology at Cambridge. In reply the Vice Chancellor wrote politely:

At present the University does not possess any Professorship, Readership, or Lectureship in Sociology. As long ago as 1899 Professor Henry Sidgwick, in a statement of the needs of the University in his department, concluded with the words: 'I have said nothing of Anthropology, Ethnology, or Sociology, partly because they are not at present included in any branch of our curriculum, partly because their boundaries, relations and methods are still rather indeterminate. But the scientific study of social man, however defined and denominated, is of growing importance: and I expect that the absence of any representation of it in our staff of Professors and Readers will before long be regarded as a serious and palpable deficiency' (quoted in Bulmer, 1985: 158).

However, no professorial appointment was made until 1969 and it was 1983 before a sociologist occupied it—Anthony Giddens. The electoral committee in 1983 included Bernard Williams (Provost of Kings), Barry Supple, (the economic historian), and three sociologists: Lockwood (Essex), Dore (LSE), and Halsey (Oxford).

In the intervening half-century, Cambridge sociology advanced at a snail's pace. During the 1930s, a committee was set up to explore sociology teaching, but without result. The LSE was a presence in Cambridge during the War. In 1946, as a result of the Clapham Report, the university received money including

---

[8] In a review of C. Wright Mills' *Sociological Imagination* for the *Universities And Left Review (ULR)* (to be merged later with the *New Reasoner* into the *New Left Review*).

nment gift for establishing a chair of sociology, but again without result. d, Cambridge devised a scheme for distinguished Visiting Professors in ι Theory beginning with Talcott Parsons in 1953–4. Some said and still say tɪɪaι he put back the cause by a decade. Homans, the Boston Brahmin, was slightly more successful.

Then came the introduction of two papers in sociology into economics undergraduate teaching, followed by the creation in 1968 under Philip Abrams' chairmanship of a separate Part II Tripos in Social and Political Sciences. Again there was heated public debate before Regent House (the assembly of Cambridge dons) finally approved with a narrow majority, and sociology was at last firmly established in the teaching arrangements.

Oxford has a longer if more obscure history of relations to sociology than has Cambridge or even LSE. The first director and the first professor of sociology at the School were drawn from Oxford. This is not to deny that Oxford opinion, especially among senior members, has always been suspicious and often hostile to the introduction of the subject, particularly in the undergraduate curriculum.[9] How was this possible in the modern and modernizing twentieth century? The brief answer is twofold. First, Oxford originated in medieval Catholic times as a *studium generale* for celibate monks. It therefore developed a collegiate organization, partly to discipline its novitiates, partly to defend itself from the laity. Second, this collegiate university incorporated an education for the ruling classes and their amanuenses (in church and state). It was an education for gentlemen rooted in the governmental problems and, therefore, the language of the ancient Romans and Greeks. 'Greats', that is, two years of Latin and Greek followed by two years of history and philosophy, led the intellectual life of the colleges. Then, in the nineteenth century, there were two developments of importance: first, the rise of the science departments which fitted less and less easily into the collegiate pattern, and second, the move towards meritocracy in the admission of students and the election of college fellows.

Science and the Arts emerged as the two giants of decision making with the former based on the university and the latter based on the colleges. Social studies were a junior partner of the Arts, dependent largely on collegiate decisions, which had created the PPE degree in the 1920s but until 1962 had excluded sociology from undergraduate teaching. An institute of social anthropology, led with distinction by E. E. Evans-Pritchard, was founded in the 1930s, but also barred from undergraduate teaching. Against a background of pressure on the colleges to absorb a growing number of students and tutors, the outlook for sociology in the 1950s was bleak.

Four forces, however, transformed the prospect. First sociological research as distinct from teaching was already practised. Earlier Violet Butler of St Anne's

[9] It was explained to me in 1960 that Hugh Trevor-Roper (later to become the Regius Professor of Modern History, Lord Dacre, and the Master of Peterhouse, Cambridge) had announced that sociology would be introduced to Oxford only over his dead body. The friends of the subject then looked forward with keen anticipation to an early date for the coincidence of these two dramatic events.

conducted a social survey of Oxford (Butler, 1912). Sidney Ball of St John's and A. L. Smith of Balliol were signatories of the *Report on Oxford and Working-Class Education* in 1908. And later G. D. H. Cole, 'throughout his influential years in Oxford . . . was one of the pillars of Barnett House' (Asa Briggs, in Halsey, 1976) and did an exemplary sociological class analysis based on the British Census of 1951. Cole was also influential as the acting Warden of Nuffield College in generating ideas and research papers during the Second World War on post-war reconstruction. Nevertheless 'amateurish, fumbling, embryonic' were the words used by John Redcliffe-Maud to describe the ten years of social research in Oxford before the Second World War (Halsey, 1976: 75).

Second was Barnett House. Founded in 1913 as a reciprocal to Toynbee Hall, it was the marginal centre for social studies in inter-war Oxford and a place for social work training, which also included some sociology in a diploma for students who were increasingly graduates from other disciplines, arts or sciences. In 1958, Barnett House became a recognized department of the university, but neither the director nor the tutor held college fellowships and only one, Peter Collison, was a sociologist, though Joan Woodward the industrial sociologist had a part-time appointment in the early 1960s.

Third was Nuffield College, formed with a benefaction by Lord Nuffield in the 1930s, built immediately after the War, and developed as the first graduate and co-educational college in Oxford focused on the social studies. It began to be a novel influence in the 1950s, quickly demonstrating the superior power of a college compared with a department of the kind exemplified by the Department of Applied Economics in Cambridge. But again it was not constituted as an undergraduate teaching body.

Then fourth came the crucial decision. Prompted by discontent with PPE, the Social Studies Board proposed and the University decreed that two papers in sociology be introduced into the degree. Halsey was elected to direct Barnett House and Bryan Wilson from Leeds was elected to a new readership in sociology. They collaborated in teaching the two papers. A B.Phil. (later M.Phil.) was instituted in sociology alongside an M.Sc. in Social Policy and Administration. John Pringle, the Linacre professor of zoology, newly arrived from Cambridge, went to see Halsey in 1965 and proposed a new first degree in Human Sciences (which took six years to find its way into the Examination Statutes). It included papers in sociology and social anthropology. Meanwhile two politics fellows, Steven Lukes at Balliol and John Torrance at Hertford, signalled willingness to tutor candidates in sociology, and Frank Parkin came to a similar post at Magdalen.

Halsey took the lead in developing sociology with the advantage of having been elected a fellow of Nuffield. A lectureship in industrial sociology went to Alan Fox[10] in 1963; one in demography with a fellowship at Nuffield went to Michael Teitlebaum. Four other lectureships with fellowships were added and

---

[10] Alan Fox (1920–2002) wrote voluminously: his *History and Heritage: The Social Origins of Britain's Industrial Relations System* (1990) is recognized by the cognoscenti as among the best of Oxford's post-war contributions to the understanding of reform in economic and social affairs.

later, in 1971, Anthony Heath came to Barnett House with a fellowship at Jesus. Thus, by the end of the 1960s the Barnett House department of social and administrative studies had grown to accommodate most Oxford sociologists with manifold connections to the colleges. Research staff were recruited to support the considerable programme of research in sociology and social policy of a now fully fledged Oxford department.

Meanwhile sociology was also developing at Nuffield College. Added to the fellowships already mentioned as adjacent to university posts at Barnett House, the College also spent its endowment on 'official' fellowships, in effect research chairs, with no obligations to university teaching. First came Jean Floud in 1962/3 to replace the Africanist Margery Perham. Then in 1969 John Goldthorpe joined from Cambridge, then Clyde Mitchell from Manchester and later Duncan Gallie from Warwick. These sociology fellows of Nuffield formed a third group to match the college economists and political studies groups. They were not formally composed but sufficiently powerful in the college, the social studies faculty, and the university to attract attention and allegiance from such distinguished non-sociologists as Brian Barry, the professor of politics (Hayward *et al.*, 1999: 426). Yet, undergraduate teaching faltered while research flourished. Indeed, all but two of the sixteen sociologists appointed in the 1960s met the most exacting modern standards of publication. Oxford, through Nuffield College and Barnett House, was becoming famous as a centre for empirical study of social institutions: the British place where theory and method were 'positivistically' combined to advance the subject of sociology.

LSE, Oxford, and Cambridge did not however complete the picture. Essex developed a large department of sociology in the 1960s. Albert Sloman, the founding Vice Chancellor, began with ambitious plans for the social sciences. In sociology he recruited such stars as Lockwood and Stanley Cohen. Alasdair McIntyre and Peter Townsend were also attracted to chairs. Readerships were occupied by Marsden, Rudd, Sinfield and P. R. Thompson and the staff was expanded to number twenty-four lectureships including such future notables as Newby, Craib, Gallie, Gordon Marshall, David Rose, Leonora Davidoff, and A. B. Woodiwiss. Colin Bell had already left the leadership of the department in 1975 for a chair in sociology in the University of New South Wales. The Essex record in sociology was to be remarkable, in attracting talent, in launching new research projects in new areas, in supporting a new centre for the storage of data and preparing individuals like Bell, Newby or Gordon Marshall for distinguished careers in university administration. Durham, Sheffield, Manchester, Warwick, York, Lancaster, Sussex, Brunel, Aston, East Anglia, Salford, Keele, Bradford, Edinburgh, and Glasgow also provided new opportunities in that frantic decade.

The SSRC

Another aspect of expansion, part cause, part consequence, was the creation of the Social Science Research Council. The Clapham Committee which reported in 1946 (Cmnd. 6868) was in favour of more resources for social research but against the introduction of an SSRC on the grounds that social scientists in the universities were too few and too busy. In fact, there were thirty-five professors of the social sciences in 1945 (including economics, economic history, anthropology, industrial relations, social science, social psychology, demography, economic statistics, commerce, and political science, as well as sociology which accounted for only two chairs). By 1965, the comparable figure for the social sciences was around 200 within which sociology itself was rising rapidly.

Any remaining 'Clapham' objections were thereby removed and a small committee under the chairmanship of Lord Heyworth had been set up by the Conservative government with all-party support to set up a new SSRC. In 1964, Wilson's Labour Party took office. Crosland was appointed Secretary of State for Education and his friend Michael Young was installed as the first chairman of the new council to develop the social sciences with governmental backing in Britain. He was supported in the role of secretary by Albert Cherns who had become well informed about social research through acting as secretary to the Heyworth Committee and as head of the human sciences division of the government's Department of Scientific and Industrial Research. He left the SSRC in 1969 to take the chair of sociology at Loughborough University. Heyworth had been chairman of Unilever from 1942 to 1960 and was a keen supporter of research in the social sciences through the Leverhulme Trust which he chaired for twenty-one years.

He was a practical man who rose to eminence in Unilever between the Wars before the social sciences became established and when knowledge of both government and the governed was essentially amateur, a wisdom ascribed to politicians and civil servants. Only occasionally would some academic mandarin such as Keynes, or Beveridge, influence Westminster, Whitehall, and public opinion. For the most part practical men picked up their sociology, economics, and politics from experience, the Bible, and classical allusion. Business experience allowed Heyworth, for example, to induce the generalization that the per capita sale of soap was a reliable indicator of a country's level of civilization. But he was thoughtfully practical, came to appreciate the need for systematic and sustained study of an increasingly complex and unstable society, and was aware that freedom was threatened if people did not have access to collective self-knowledge independently of government. Accordingly, he proposed to set up another buffer organization, following British custom with respect to the public financing of activities which were to be controlled in practice by the beneficiaries—in this case the academic social scientists.

The upshot in 1965 was the formation of a Council designed to sustain social research, especially in the universities where the teaching of economics, politics, and sociology was expanding to meet unprecedented student demand. The SSRC budget was tiny by comparison with those of the already established Councils for research in Science and Medicine: but it existed, and was insulated from political control in the traditional British manner. Then came the May events. The first, in 1968, demonstrated that the social sciences had entered the culture of many countries, including Britain, as a vocabulary of challenge to the social order of at least irritating and potentially destructive power. Students, largely at the expense of the taxpayer, suddenly appeared, armed with sociological jargon, not as aspirants to but as subverters of suburban respectability. The revolt is described in Chapter 6.

Social Science and Government

Traditionally the scientific community had had access to government through largely informal connections and advisory policy. But, in the twentieth century, these relationships were transformed by war and advancing military technology, by governmental concern with the efficiency of industrial techniques and the supply of scientists and technologists, and later by concern with ecology and the 'environment'. Official arrangements developed *pari passu* with these changing military and political preoccupations. Thus, in the 1950s, a Science Advisory Committee was established in the United States, concerned mainly with the meaning and implications of recurrent revolution in military technology and with the increasingly recognized need to strengthen basic scientific research in the universities. The United Kingdom set up an Advisory Council on Scientific Policy in 1947 and appointed its first Minister for Science in 1959. In France, an Inter-ministerial Committee and also a Consultative Committee for Science and Technology date from 1958. Thus, in Britain, the trend was away from advisory virtuosos like Professor Lindemann towards councils and committees, which fused advice with participation in decision making, and further towards something that came to be called science policy or 'une politique scientifique'. In the meantime governmental expenditure on scientific research and development had multiplied until outlays of 3–4 per cent of GNP were common in the richer countries.

After the Second World War the social sciences were caught up in a similar process of incorporation, partly through the concomitant development of an economics of science, partly in their own right as the disciplinary bases of economic and social planning and, in the 1960s, through the emergence of a new style of administration which was of immense potential importance—experimental public policy formation. The trail leading to incorporation was blazed by American economists in the Roosevelt administration. After the Second World War, governments everywhere increasingly and explicitly accepted responsibility for the management of economic growth. The assimilation of economists into government was brought about by the capacity of professional economists to generate agreement on the means to that end and the measurement of progress towards it. The subsequent arrival of the sociologists reflected a shift in emphasis on the part of governments towards concern with distribution as well as production, with social order as much as economic progress.

These expressions of the social science interest, albeit assuming a politics aimed at social change, even radical reform, still retain the fundamental assumptions of a social science in service to an established political consensus. Thus, action research became fashionable in the 1960s. It was immensely difficult. The laboratory is, by definition, natural and not experimental. There were political as well as scientific determinants of the areas chosen for the projects. The desired outcomes of action were often imprecisely defined and in any case resistant to clear measurement. The inputs were not completely controlled and the relation between input and output was to that extent uncertain. It is doubtful whether the intellectual tools or the numbers of qualified social scientists were adequate to the task. Nevertheless, the challenge was irresistible. It was for the social scientist to become involved in the development of social policy, its definition of ends, its planning and allocation of means, and its measurement of result. The task in the case of the Educational Priority Area (EPA) and Community Development Projects (CDP) was to produce a theory of poverty and to test it in the very real world of the urban twilight zones.

But compared with the intellectual problems the political difficulties were even more daunting. Almost by definition, an action-research project is one in which things will happen that cannot be foreseen. And the unforeseen can be politically dangerous. Innovation in social services and schools may not serve to gentle the masses and action may not confine itself to the schoolroom, the clinic, or the probation office. A developing community under these circumstances may sweep the social scientists along with it in a march on the town hall and thence to Whitehall. The theory of poverty to which social scientists were led through their service to a governmentally financed experiment might call for political action which was unacceptable to their political masters. In other words, experimental social administration is likely to test the assumption that the welfare society may be attained through the legitimate use of the existing political structure.

Nevertheless, within the limits of this assumption, a new relation between social science and social policy was postulated. It asserted that political ends might be seriously pursued through social science experiment. The traditional political mode of reform had been to announce a nostrum which was held to be certain in its cure of the social ills to which it was addressed. The new idea acknowledged ignorance. The politician commits himself to trying to plan in an experimentally devised situation, but at the same time commits himself to abandoning it for another scheme if evaluation by valid social science techniques shows that it does not work.

The emancipation for administrative civil servants implied by this idea can scarcely be exaggerated. It could mean for them a quite new relationship with ministers, a substitution of positive for negative responsibility of a kind which they had seldom been challenged to exercise in the past. It also implies a strengthening partnership with social scientists in the universities—a development of intellectual exchange from which both might hugely profit.

Yet, the fundamental problem remains. Such exchanges may well reveal that there are 'social problems' which cannot be adequately formulated in terms similar to those describing medical problems where a social scientist would be defined, by analogy, as the skilled diagnostician. Such a model, apart from assuming that there is a social science theory to be applied in the same way that doctors may draw on medical science, also takes it for granted that there is agreement about social ends just as there is consensus about the nature and desirability of good health. If all social problems were like that, there would be no need for politicians. In fact, the language of 'social problems' may all too often disguise an underlying conflict of political and social interests. The historic role of the social scientist as critic of the social order must set limits to her or his incorporation into administration just as the maintenance of political democracy must set limits to his or her participation in the making of decisions.

Policy Research and University Expansion

In the period after the Second World War, the place of the academic social scientist in Britain seemed to have been transformed. Between 1919 and its demise in 1989, the UGC acted as bridge and buffer between the universities and the state, carrying the academic interest and protecting it against governmental control. The two academic 'products' of teaching and research were funded as if, like wool and mutton, they were delivered in harmonious joint supply. Half of a don's time was assumed to be devoted to research while money for libraries and laboratories flowed in proportion to the number of students, geared to a tenaciously defended 8:1 ratio. This arrangement served the academic interest. In the 1950s and 1960s, at least until the May Events of 1968, it was the privileged foundation of a period which Noel Annan (1990: 337) labelled 'the golden age of the don'. Much admired and envied in other countries, its attractive logic could never have survived expansion at the rate of 'doubling in a decade' nor persisted from the sunlit post-war years through the inception of the polytechnics to the clouded new conditions of faltering economic growth after 1973.

The 1950s and 1960s were indeed a golden age. Scientists had little difficulty in convincing society and its political leaders that there should be a substantial national commitment to research, including fundamental research. Technological (and thence economic) development was coming to be seen as dependent on a stock of basic discoveries that needed continuous replenishment. The university system had to train the large number of research scientists who would be needed by what was to be an increasingly research-based industrial system. 1963 was the year of Harold Wilson's famous speech 'Labour and the Scientific Revolution', heralding the beginning of a 'white-hot technological revolution' in British industry. Research was seen as essential to national prosperity as well as an indispensable adjunct of university teaching.

Full-time teaching and research staff in the universities doubled between 1960 and 1970, not counting the Open University nor the growing numbers of staff paid from non-university funds. Between 1955/6 and 1972/3 this central core of academic men and women increased by about 10 per cent each year. In the decade of the 1960s, funding fully met the aspiration of the expanding university professions to maintain the traditional balance of teaching and research activities. Research money made available through the research councils (reorganized, and confirmed in their independence of government following the Trend Report of 1963) also grew at an average rate of 10 per cent in real terms (Blume, 1982: 11). Furthermore the belief that science had an intrinsic need for continuous growth (more funds for achieving the same rate of discovery), expressed by the term 'sophistication', was widely accepted and embodied in governmental science policy. What then was the fate of sociology in this new phase of expanding scientific research?

Michael Young: First Chairman of SSRC

Michael Young, author of *The Rise of the Meritocracy* (1958), was an inspired choice by Crosland as the first chairman of the SSRC. He had a fabulous reputation as social entrepreneur, prolific writer, and successful fund raiser. *Let us Face the Future* was always Young's message. It was the title of the manifesto he wrote for the Labour Party at the general election of 1945 and he went on to become the outstanding practical sociologist of twentieth-century Britain. In 2002, at age eighty-six, he died. A festschrift for his remarkable career appeared in 1995 as *Young at Eighty* edited by Geoff Dench *et al.*, and there followed a biography by Asa Briggs in 2002 in which Young is convincingly portrayed as a traveller in search of utopia and, on his travels, finding Dartington School, the Elmhirsts, Political and Economic Planning (PEP), the Labour Party, the Institute of Community Studies (ICS), The Open University, and the SSRC as means to further exploration.

Briggs' record of Young's innovations or organization-building adds valediction to a multifacetted life of super-human energy. The reader may well come away bewildered and incredulous from a tale which is at once rambling and fascinating, and may also notice that, like George Orwell, Michael Young kept his friends apart or at least did not encourage the potential network. And, consequently, the biography must have been difficult to write for there is little evidence that Briggs talked directly to Young, who was notoriously reticent about his personal life.

Young could be dubbed 'the last Victorian', at least in the sense of being possessed by a conscience, suspicious of the state, and dedicated to the study of urban conditions under modern industrialism. Be that as it may, the reader of Briggs' book is likely to want to know how Young became a sociologist and how he fitted or did not fit into the world of professional sociology, which emerged so explosively after 1950, when he was already in his thirties. One answer lies in Young's political career. He was a liberal at school, became a communist of the bohemian kind before the Second World War, and then took to Labour

Party socialism, like Titmuss, as a close witness of London under bombardment. He was most forcibly struck by the cohesion of the cockneys and wanted to discover its roots. The quest for an answer led him to found ICS in Bethnal Green and to write with Peter Willmott his first classic of sociology, *Family and Kinship in East London* (1957).

Briggs quotes Raymond Aron's remark that British sociology was preoccupied with the intellectual problems of the Labour Party.[11] Young was the prototype. He was interested, among many other things, in Labour's housing policy, and was convinced that the family was or ought to be the key institutional focus of social policy. He wrote in 1951 that neighbourly socialism could become the core of a Third Force in ideas, a faith free from the materialism of the United States and the tyranny of the Soviet Union. He saw in Bethnal Green the traditional mechanisms of conviviality and sharing in the face of adversity—the extended family and the demeter tie between mothers and daughters.

Three Peters (Willmott, Marris, and Townsend) followed him to produce the famous and controversial ICS studies. None of them knew much about sociological theory or survey method in the early 1950s. They were all inspired by Titmuss and encouraged by Shils who taught them the approach of the Chicago School of Park and Burgess. Accordingly they incurred the suspicion and hostility of academic sociologists. They were extra-curricular researchers, amateur anthropologists: their quotable writing suggested journalism, they were untrained in sample design or in multivariate analysis (Platt, 1971). Townsend referred to the 'absurd mathematics of the survey exponents'—not a remark likely to win friends on the statistical wing of academic sociology. Thus, debate over the mathematical character of the social sciences was rekindled and still rages.

A summary word could be added to Michael Young's life as a sociologist. He was an instinctive follower of David Hume—an optimist who thought that fellow feeling was the ultimate motive of human life. His sociology and his social action were conceived in that frame and he was a man of his time. We now need a book comparing Young's utopia with Durkheim's dream for France: to be written by a student of Lockwood, Giddens, or Bourdieu? What would be the shape of post-meritocratic society?

In the universities he was known best as a sociologist of education and community. He always sought the educational dimension of life in the family, ·
the neighbourhood, the school, and the college. He saw the process of learning, moral as well as cognitive, as taking place in work and leisure and retirement—literally from the cradle to the grave, and literally as the totality of experience. Thus pubs, street corners, theatres, and holidays are always schools. Even Robben Island has to be counted, and it is entirely characteristic

---

[11] See Chapter 4.

that he focused on it as a potential site for the Open University of Southern Africa when he visited Cape Town in 1994. And mothers, mates, companions, and social workers are all part of the network of potential educators as well as formal lecturers and teachers. Hence, his outlook was as broad as it is possible to be. Perhaps in his early days he neglected the educative possibilities of church, chapel, and voluntary associations (scouts, trades unions, co-ops, cycling clubs, etc.). But he neglected little else. He thought of a manifold ensemble and he had immense faith in it as the origin of human achievement and therefore of the virtually unlimited power of people to invent, to create, and to cooperate, everywhere.

His ingenuity as a social engineer was fabulous. But he was no philosopher and no mathematician—which makes his story more interesting in that had he been a philosopher he would have seen himself as dedicated to optimizing the balance between liberty, equality, and fraternity (which today for obvious reasons we call community). He was a Rawlsian before Rawls. This was, after all, the project of the post-war Labour Party. Instead, he guided policy by instinct, avoiding too complete a victory for liberty, or for equality, or for fraternity. And if he had been a mathematician, he might have followed up his invention of the idea of meritocracy to produce a sophisticated genetic/psychological/social theory of selection in human society. There had been a debate since Cyril Burt and the eugenics movement about the multiple determinants of intelligence, the role of intelligence in shaping patterns and pathways of mobility, and the significance of work as well as education in approximating modern countries to a meritocracy rather than to the caste or estate rigidities of medieval societies. Michael Young was content to leave his readers with a now famous formula: $IQ + E = M$, where IQ is measured intelligence, E is effort, and M is merit. Sociologically this is a good frame. Unfortunately, none of these variables could be measured in ways from which policy could be unequivocally inferred: but that only deepened and widened the discussion. Part of the thesis, after all, was that revolution as well as the counter-revolution was dependent on advances in psychometrics and the application of the findings beyond the education system to the entry of recruits to industry and their subsequent career progress. Young in his *Meritocracy* envisaged the development of Regional Adult Education Centres where records of retesting were kept and the lazy genius eliminated while the second or third chance was perennially on offer to the diligent student. A simple formula was sufficient to start a complex debate over policy—a debate which still goes on (Halsey, in Dench *et al.*, 1995).

So the rising tide of sociology carried with it a new SSRC with its emphasis on the training of graduate students (901 new postgraduate awards in 1968) and the support of research held to be important for central policy formation. Thus, Young initiated the Educational Priority Area projects (Halsey, 1972) and the Data Bank at the University of Essex. Young retired from the SSRC in 1969. He was followed by Andrew Shonfield and, in 1971, by Robin Mathews who saw the end of the glory days, as we shall see in Chapter 7.

Conclusion

There were twenty-five years of unprecedented expansion for the British universities with the social sciences accorded priority and among them sociology especially privileged in student places, research grants, and permanent staff appointments. It was a golden age.

New departments of sociology were established throughout the university system in England, Scotland, and Wales. Inroads were made even into the resistant redoubts of Oxford and Cambridge, though in both places a stubborn suspicion lingered. Britain began to make a significant contribution to both teaching and research. Tensions emerged between theory and empirical research. Campus confrontations eventually broke out at LSE, Essex, and elsewhere, in which sociology was implicated. Graduates multiplied to fill not only vacancies in the universities but also the civil service, the welfare services, and industry, though social administration and social policy gradually became separated from sociology as academic disciplines.

Finally, from 1965 government started a Research Council for the social sciences. Thus, sociology was expanded, established, and funded in its research. It faced the 1970s in good heart before the disturbances of the late 1960s and early 1970s in the universities, and the economy, began to threaten its future.

6

Revolt 1968–75

YOUTH RESPONDS eagerly to new ideals and innovations, often with violent emotion. In every generation, young men and women are socially selected for their superior capacities, mental or physical, by tests of past privilege and, especially lately, of cognitive merit, and increasing proportions of them are segregated in universities or other institutions of higher education. Accordingly, the history of universities is also the history of rebellion. Violence is by no means confined to the political left. German universities in the inter-war period suffered the Nazis' anti-semitic brutality. And commenting on Bakunin's report in 1870 of 40,000 revolutionary students in Russia, Engels wrote in alarm to Marx 'How awful for the world....If there is anything which might ruin the western European movement, then it would have been this import of 40,000 more or less educated, ambitious, hungry Russian nihilists; all of them officer candidates without an army' (Avineri, 1967: 154).

This chapter is concerned with the causes and consequences of the events usually labelled 'the May Events' of 1968, though in reality they began in Berkeley in 1964 and were continued spasmodically into the 1970s. But the story will be short on causes and long on consequences. Second, it must be remarked that though our account is of Britain, 1968 was international and very largely imported, especially from Berkeley and Nanterre. Third, we shall consider in Chapter 7 how far the causes lay with sociology and how the consequences shaped the subject in the later twentieth century.

In Britain, student life has been relatively peaceable from the twelfth to the twenty-first century. This is not to ignore the frequent clashes between the 'nationalities' at the University of Paris in the twelfth century, nor the massacre of students by townsmen in Oxford on St Scholastica's Day in 1341, nor the fact that disputes between undergraduates in the sixteenth century were often resolved by the sword rather than by reasoned argument, nor McConica's judgement that the streets of Tudor Oxford were far from tranquil. One might imagine that undergraduates at least were protected from scenes of violence within the walls of colleges, but the records do not confirm this sentimental assumption: '[R]ecourse to violence was common throughout the social strata, for the conduct of the Oxford scholars resembles that of the more wealthy and prominent in the country villages' (McConica, 1986: 660). More recently the antics of undergraduates before the First World War called forth an acid comment from Hilaire Belloc: 'For tis distinctive of the upper class, To like the sound of broken glass.'

Nevertheless, 'peaceable' student life best describes the emergence of the 'English Idea of the University' in the nineteenth and early twentieth centuries. This notion combined medieval commensality (the college) with the humanistic education of the governing classes. This traditional educational institution provided for maximum solidarity between teachers and taught through the absence of a separate administration and an emphasis on close personal relations through tutorial teaching, high staff/student ratios, and shared domestic life. The ideal of university life embodied in this form of higher education preceded the rise of specialized scholarship, the widened social recruitment to new professions, the management of advanced industrial society, and the abandonment of the traditional responsibilities of those *in loco parentis* or *in statu pupillari* along with the lowering of the voting age from twenty-one to eighteen years. By the 1960s, it was clear that adaptation to advanced industrialism in the United Kingdom was modifying the character of the universities. It brought expansion, specialization, a trend towards science, wider social recruitment, and less collegiate social life. At the same time, the older traditions resisted modernity, most successfully at Oxford and Cambridge, less so in the red-brick universities described by Bruce Truscot (1945) as imitative of the ancient colleges, and least so in the Colleges of Advanced Technology or Polytechnics which, though invented by Anthony Crosland as 'public sector' alternatives to the 'independent' degree-granting bodies, were to become universities in 1992. Whereas in the older tradition the university was defined as a preparation for entry into the Anglican church or the professional and managerial occupations, as a nursery of the governing classes or a finishing school of the upper classes, it was now increasingly seen as training for the occupational needs of an internationally competitive economy, the sorting house of a perpetual process of producing a 'world class' workforce and, in its laboratories, as the source of industrially valuable innovations. Skilled manpower was the scarcest resource of modern society.

In this context, the university was becoming a representative institution to the student. It represented 'the system' as an opportunity structure and along with it the medley of conflicting values in politics, religion, and sex from which the young had somehow to choose a way of life and livelihood. The organizational changes associated with mass higher education—the 'multiversity' described by Clark Kerr (1963)—were not yet in evidence in Britain and least of all the pervasive bureaucracy, which induced so many Berkeley students to see themselves resentfully as 'an IBM card'. Only London approached the scale of Michigan or the University of Moscow or the Sorbonne.

The week of 3 February 1967 saw three events: the founding conference of the Radical Student Alliance, a demonstration at the London School of Economics (LSE) against a decision by the principal to ban a meeting to consider means of direct action against the appointment of Dr Walter Adams as the new principal (in the course of which a porter died of a heart attack), and a lobby of Parliament by 4,000 students in protest against a government decision to raise the fees charged to overseas students in universities and colleges.

In subsequent press comment, the first of these events was widely linked with the other two.

The events at the LSE were at least partly due to factors peculiar to that institution. The LSE is unique in England. Before the founding of The Open University it was perhaps the only significantly 'new' university of the post-Victorian period. It has always attracted a minority of left-wing students with serious political and intellectual preoccupations, anxious to translate political ideas into immediate action and therefore peculiarly vulnerable to disappointment with their environment and their seniors. These young people were especially proud of the multiracial traditions of the School. Whatever the facts, they were prone to interpret the appointment of anyone but the most extreme and militant opponent of racial discrimination to be director of the School as a betrayal of their conception of LSE's values. At the same time, however, the LSE was a college that approached more nearly to the anonymity of the American 'multiversity' than most other English institutions.

The connections between the issue of raising overseas students' fees and the central 'student syndicalist' concerns of RSA were closer than may appear at first. Many senior members of universities were concerned by the method of implementing the increase, which they saw as an interference with university autonomy, while many students saw it as a dress rehearsal for the introduction of loans as a partial substitute for, or alternative to, grants. The justification of the increase in terms of the need to give priority to British students was rejected not only because more British students were studying in foreign universities than foreigners in British ones, not only on international principle, and not only as a concealed cut in overseas aid, but also as a sign of an increasingly vocational spirit in the government's rationalization and expansion of higher education.

The binary system of non-university as well as university institutions of higher education was attacked as if Crosland had invented it to replace those invidious distinctions between types of secondary school that the progressive supporters of expansion were determined to eradicate. All these developments were seen as symptoms of a trend to subject traditional university freedoms to the needs of a more complex, more technological, and increasingly planned and integrated society, in terms very similar to American criticisms of the integration of the 'multiversity' into the industrial system.

Broad aims were agreed upon. The argument between the RSA and the National Union of Students (NUS) was about method—with the former concerned more with the 'grass-roots' and the mobilization of mass student support through demonstrations and petitions. The NUS executive preferred personal approaches to policymakers.

The rise in the number of students after the Robbins Report reflected also a change in their social situation. Before the Second World War, 2.7 per cent of their age group were in higher education. By 1967, this had risen to 11 per cent. Students were still an elite group, but their social destinations had shifted. The university no longer provided almost automatic entrance into an elite professional class. Now a much larger and less exclusive social group demanded degree qualifications. The pre-war university prepared its members mainly for law, medicine, the church, or civil service. In the modern university, the predominant goals of students were industry and further academic research. This changing social function of the university was partly reflected in the growth of new subjects—in particular sociology, a discipline still socially disconnected from professional needs. It is significant that much of the leadership in the LSE revolt came from students in the sociology department.[1]

These changes in the origins and destinations of the students would by themselves have been sufficient to pose a profound challenge to the traditional 'English idea' of a university. They were interpreted by the radicals as a sign that higher education was becoming subordinate to the manpower needs of industrial development and provoked conflict both locally and nationally.

The most widely publicized of these local conflicts, that at the LSE, shows a widening of the original demands and grievances of a limited and 'liberal' kind (the alleged undesirability of a proposed principal, the question of student freedom of speech, and the victimization of elected representatives). A feeling grew among the students involved that what was at stake was the whole structure of the administration of the School, the composition of its syllabi, and the relationship between these and wider political and social trends. The exact form of the disturbances was affected by a number of factors highly specific to the LSE, which might suggest that the events, however spectacular, would remain unique. These factors, some of which were seized on by the press as the 'causes' of the events, included the special character of the LSE's students. They also included the peculiarities of the administrative structure, which gave full power to governors who were not fully engaged in the work of the School and many of whom had outside contacts in industry and commerce, which lent particular force to the view of the social function of the School put forward by the radicals. Other matters affecting the disturbances were the physical layout of the School, overcrowding, some lack of student–staff contact, and various tactical mistakes of the authorities.

But while all these factors were peculiar to the LSE, the events there had wider relevance. Radical students both at the LSE and at other colleges and universities interpreted these special circumstances not as 'causes' but as common conditions clearly visible within LSE, if less immediately perceived elsewhere. A noticeable feature of the LSE sit-in was the participation by

---

[1] T. Blackstone *et al.* (1970) contains a thorough analysis of the events at LSE with a survey of the composition of students and their political opinions. See also G. Stedman-Jones *et al.* "Student Power: What is to be Done?", *New Left Review*, 43 (May–June 1967). For the British universities as a whole, no exact analysis exists of the composition of political activists by social, ethnic, or religious background, or by disciplinary attachment, year and type of course, and so forth. That activism was centred in the social studies faculties needs no special explanation. It is partly a matter of self-selection among school children and is reinforced by the political outlook of the typical university teacher in the social sciences. Sociology was, however, particularly interesting in Britain as the most recent vehicle of political awareness for the young. Another possible source of radical recruits is from experience of marginalism and mobility. But the patterns are undoubtedly complex.

delegations from other universities and colleges, which also sent larger contingents to a protest march. Definitions of the situation 'imported' by foreign students, especially Americans, were only acceptable because they reflected existing fears as to the future development of policy towards higher education in Britain, and with the unease underlying the conflict at LSE. For example, the project for a 'free university' in the LSE buildings during the vacation was organized and advocated initially by a group of American graduates. But it was taken up at a later stage in policy discussions in the Union meetings, countering the extreme demand to continue the sit-in through the vacation without advocating what seemed like a retreat. It also reflected earlier student dissatisfaction with control over the content of the syllabus. Before the Adams question was raised, the Union had challenged the dismissal of an economics lecturer in circumstances apparently connected with conflicting views on what should be taught.

The precise forms of student rebellion were largely determined by the 'political culture' shared by student radicals in institutions of differing kinds and by the organizational links between them. There was no sign of any tendency for the attitudes of radicals in any of the constituent groupings of the RSA to be differentiated by type of institution. This may be explained by a common political background in CND, Young Socialists, or Young Liberals shared by many activists before they arrived in their respective institutions. As one member of the RSA Council said at the founding convention: 'We all cut our political teeth in the New Left'.

While changes in higher education had begun to undermine the traditional English notion of the university and its normative hold over student conduct, no clearly stated alternative concept of the status and purpose of higher education had taken its place. There was a tendency for the traditional idea to be defended along left-elitist lines against the impact of 'technocratic' reform, but the political and organizational consequences of such a view could vary between the 'American model' and the 'French model' of an 'official' students' union captured by the Left, based on a more or less explicit Marxism and seeing itself as a Trade Union. Trends were present in both directions, and the future was uncertain.

After Robbins's recommendations had been accepted university academic opinion about expansion was divided (Halsey and Trow, 1971) but youthful impatience was insistent and, during the late 1960s, sociology found itself at the centre of campus struggles. In positive part, and led from the left by newcomers like John Rex, Stuart Hall, and Robin Blackburn, there was a reinvigorated iconoclastic sociological interest in power, the sociology of conflict rather than Parsonian consensus, the hegemony of class-based authority, the excitement of a Millsian critical social imagination, and the inclusion of a feminist view. In negative part, sociology became a carrier if not the cause of the disturbances associated with the Parisian May Events of 1968, and the eruption of Marxism and feminism (sometimes combined) in the following years.

How can we account for this emerging state of affairs? Perhaps sociology had grown too quickly in the 1960s and externally an image similar to 'folk devil' in political culture produced something like 'moral panic' among the conviction politicians of economic liberalism in the 1980s. University expansion in the 1960s coincided with unanticipated (though not at all unprecedented) student disorder. Sociology and sociologists were identified with disruption and dissent, by some as cause and by others as effect. In either case, hostility was most intense among the supporters of neo-conservative politics. Malcolm Bradbury's *The History Man* (1975) continued to exact a heavy bill long after its characters among tutors and taught had disappeared from the campus.

Sociology as the cause of conflict was an implausible explanation. Consequences do not precede their causes. Student protest and turbulence is spasmodically as old as the European university. Moreover, other powerful forces were at work. In the United States, there was the Vietnam War and widespread racial tension. In Europe, there was impatience with the feeble achievements of social democratic politics, disillusion from the increased visibility of the chasm between international ideals and the inhumanity of war, guilt over First World plenitude and Third World penury, and frustration among a uniquely indulged generation struggling to come to terms with the gap between the romantic expectations of undergraduate life and the boring, competitive realities of preparation for professional and managerial careers. Sociologists were twice unblessed. They were urgently invited to forsake the vocation of sociology for the avocation of politics and they were simultaneously blamed for their incapacity to explain the changing world which had itself created their profession. Add to these troubles the logistic difficulty of staffing the rapid increase in university posts—at least twenty chairs were created in Britain during the 1962–7 quinquennium—and a parvenu profession, at once passionate in its mission and tenuous in its tenure, was suddenly instated and simultaneously ridiculed.

It was a moment of classic Durkheimian *anomie*. Some Marxists even spread the doctrine that students could take over the historic mission of the working class as successful agents of total revolution. Tempers ran high as dons tried to cope with unexpectedly 'revolting' students and students with their unrehearsed escape from the restrictions of *statu pupillari*. On neither side was the reaction sober. It is difficult now to recapture the level of passion then displayed at LSE, Cambridge, or Essex both for and against Malcolm Bradbury's fictional portrait: perhaps a more reasonable description of students in the social sciences may be had, for example in Tessa Blackstone *et al.* (1970) or Colin Crouch's *The Student Revolt* (1970).[2] Second, in sociology itself, the sudden enlargement of youthful opportunity was chaotic, chronic, and comic. Thus, Peter Worsley, newly elected to the Manchester chair of sociology, has recorded

---

[2] Crouch subsequently had a distinguished career at LSE, Oxford, and Florence. His book on the social structure of European countries (2000) took the empirical and comparative study of advanced industrial society to unprecedented heights. Blackstone eventually became Blair's minister for higher education.

'ringing Chelly [Halsey] and saying "have you got any human body capable of teaching sociology" and he replied "There is this fellow who's just come back from Chicago who's very good," and he turned out to be' (Mullen, 1987: 62). That was how the market stood in the mid-sixties. Demand absurdly outran supply.

The research and teaching of the 1950s LSE group were significant in these events. It was among them that the democratic, egalitarian impulse was most manifest and was expressed most clearly in Lockwood's rejection of Parsonian functionalism and by Dahrendorf's championing of conflict theory. The LSE group in the 1950s and 1960s were a rising radical influence in university politics and policy to expand numbers and reform the curriculum.

The Onslaught of Anti-positivism

In ways and places mentioned in Chapter 5, the graduates of the 1950s found their improbable aspirations fulfilled. The LSE and the Attlee government had been their institutional parents, and they emerged from their provincialism, intellectually and culturally compounded, in search of a way of linking social thought to political action. They sought their metropolis in the academy, but it was never clearly defined. Perhaps the search was futile then: it was to become more difficult. There was no acknowledged metropolis in the 1970s either of institution or of doctrine. Voyaging was much simpler in the 1950s. The centre lay westwards to Harvard, Columbia, and Chicago from which radiated an orthodoxy of theory expounded by Parsons, Merton, Shils, and Riesman, with a litany on quantitative method by Lazarsfeld and Stouffer.

By the 1970s the simplicities of an organized orthodoxy and structured opposition were gone. Berkeley rose and fell. Factions fought for dominance and the sociological empire had no capital. It retreated in disorder, though it left indelible marks on social history, linguistics, political science, and social anthropology, which it briefly threatened to annex. Meanwhile, the critical sociology of the Frankfurt school systematically undermined the idea of rational academic contributions to social reform which the 1950 group assumed in its choice of an academic rather than a political role. Piecemeal social engineering was anathema to the new neo-Marxist radicals. Positivism and its patient counting of heads became for some a term of abuse, relieving students of the obligation to read the books so labelled[3] or to learn the methods which, in the experience of the 1950 group, were indispensable to professional competence. For these ultras epistemological nihilism and moral relativism removed respectability from all but the totally committed opponents of capitalist society.

---

[3] M. F. D. Young came to Nuffield College to give a seminar on the 'new sociology of education' in 1975. Questioned about Halsey and Trow's *The British Academics*, he asserted that this was 'too positivistic' to be included in the new syllabus.

To survive the assaults of the newer radicalisms was to be the travail of the 1970s for a beleaguered minority in the sprawling profession they had done so much to create. Some retreated into inactivity or administrative busy-work. Others went on with their research and teaching, persisting in their belief in the possibility of exploring social facts 'as things'.

When confronted with things, therefore, every effort must be made to remove the influence of one's own fears of what the facts may show, and the influence of one's own desires about what the facts ought to show if the world were benign and just. Science is a set of procedures which, over a range of activities and practitioners, has been shown to have been effective in diminishing subjectivity. It is impossible to diminish subjectivity to zero anywhere. It is extremely difficult to get it below a very high level in the study of social affairs. Some researchers pretend to follow the protocols of science but do not. ... To say that a social science, again to use Weber's term, is value-free—*Wertfrei*—is never, therefore, to describe what has been achieved. It only indicates the direction of endeavour. (Dennis, 1980).

If this was the outlook—commitment to social ideals disciplined by a scientific method—that had made the LSE group successful in securing professional standing, how were they to ensure their own academic succession? As they pursued their careers and built up their departments, the university offered two rather different models.

In the natural sciences there is at best an ideal blend of the authority of the senior with the apt learning of the junior, buttressed by an efficient system of communication about the structure of knowledge in the relevant specialisms. These arrangements ensure a research-minded academic succession and guarantee that innovation by the young is constrained by the experienced wisdom of the old. That is what we mean by a discipline. Science is a permanent but controlled revolution. And at worst the situation ensures that the young recruit, though tyrannized by the prejudices of some powerful senior, has only to bide his or her time before having the chance to break out in a new direction, meanwhile establishing his or her credentials for doing so by learning existing methods, theories, and skills. Their world is one of public knowledge, accepted canons of truth and falsity, and recognized, impersonal evaluations of individual worth.

The alternative academic model comes from the arts where it is much more a matter of providing places for outstanding students whose claim is a previously demonstrated capacity to honour the 2000-year old conversation in which it is a privilege to join. Part of the difference is that of cumulative as distinct from critical contributions to theory. But another part depends upon methods. The arts technology is essentially medieval—the library, paper, and pen—and is adapted to individual work, private knowledge, and the related subtleties of personal evaluation. Science as an institution generates a different and changing technology. Obsolescence of skill is a constant and often catastrophic threat to a scholar's research capacity in a way which is virtually impossible in the arts.

The social sciences tend to be caught between these two worlds which together encompass two definitions of knowledge—the one akin to natural science and the other to the long humanistic conversation. The victory of either would be disastrous precisely because the social sciences deal simultaneously with human values and the explanation of human behaviour. For example, we argue about the relative emphasis to be put upon intellectual history as distinct from cumulated (in the scientific sense) theory. We know how to say 'the science which hesitates to forget its founders is lost' and also how to impress our students and each other with knowledge of the doctrines of the founding fathers.

By 1975, sociology and its neighbouring subjects were in disarray of both theories and methods. Sociology was no longer one subject. Those who defined it as cumulative and explanatory in its aspirations, with due respect for natural science models and attempts at quantification and comparison, had one credible answer. Similarly, those who assimilated the subject to the arts as intellectual history and theoretical interpretation had a related, but different and also credible, solution. So graduate studies in the social sciences were riven, and the battle for student allegiance was also the struggle for an academic succession, which would define the nature and significance of the social sciences for the future. The tendencies of the late 1960s and early 1970s towards the use of the campus either as a base for direct political action, or as a protection for non-communicating worlds of private knowledge in which excellence is a function of fashion and amnesia a virtue, were equally inimical to the idea of sociology as an academic discipline.

What then was the fate of sociology after 1975?

7

Years of Uncertainty 1976–2000

THE INSTITUTIONAL story of sociology in the third quarter of the twentieth century was, on the whole, one of great success. In substance too, both teaching and research flourished. True, towards the end, there were campus confrontations; but our earlier chapters nevertheless tell a cheerful story of the establishment of a new discipline with increasing numbers of staff, students, and research projects throughout the growing university system. Then came the student troubles described in Chapter 6.

Must we now tell a different tale for the last quarter of the century? Yes and no. Traditionalists and conservatives would be strongly inclined to see these twenty-five years as a period of decline towards the impending collapse of sociology both intellectually and institutionally. They might well allow that in the post-war years sociologists were asking pertinent and penetrating questions about modern societies only to find them answered more powerfully by sociologically stimulated philosophers or historians or evolutionary psychologists. The sceptics would emphasize the fragmentation of the subject, its too frequent descent into a fog of unstylish imprecision, its failure to attract students of high quality, its politicization first by Marxists and then by feminists, and its suicidal tendencies towards various forms of relativism, which in the end make nonsense of any claim to offer explanations of the social world.

Another, also radical interpretation is far removed from such total pessimism. Past presidents of the British Sociological Association (BSA) have leaned towards optimism (*Network*, 2001: 80) about 'highlights and low points in the intellectual development of British sociology over the past half century'. The annual meeting at Aberdeen in 1974 is commonly regarded as a crucial turning point. David Morgan (BSA President 1997–9, chairman of the Manchester department) has a typical retrospect on the meeting and its theme 'Sexual Divisions and Society' as 'something of a paradigm shift rather than simply the raising of a set of equal opportunities issues'.

Shortly afterwards there was a low point in the 'Gould Report' of 1977. Julius Gould of Nottingham wrote a scholarly but denunciatory analysis on behalf of the Institute for the Study of Conflict (ISC) (1977), criticizing Marxist infiltration of sociology as a threat to established customs of research and teaching.[1] The BSA

---

[1] For a hostile review, see Chris Husbands, 'Sociologies and Marxisms: The Odd Couples', in Abrams *et al.* (eds.) *Practice and Progress: British Sociology 1950–1980*, pp. 163–7.

responded angrily, and Gould refused to appear before what he doubtless thought was a kangaroo court of Comrades. That the outcome was indecisive is not important. The significant underlying fact was that sociology, an increasingly powerful force in both university and society, was simultaneously derided and attacked by both academic and political interests. The 1980s dealt severe blows to the subject. Posts were abolished, postgraduate scholarships were reduced, research resources impoverished, departments were closed, and the Social Science Research Council (SSRC) was wounded and banished to Swindon under a new name. Yet, later in that decade the demand for student places revived, there was some institutional recovery, some reinvigoration of funded research, and then, in 1992, ironically from a Conservative government, there came the admission of polytechnics and colleges of higher education into the university system, doubling the number of sociology students and staff. It was almost as if adversity had never struck.

By the end of the twentieth century, a huge expansion of the British university system had taken place with the additions of the 1990s dwarfing all previous extensions and converting the university from the restrictive experience of a highly privileged minority into the normal expectation of a near majority. This new mass higher education began at last to acquire some of the characteristics of the American system, with over a hundred tertiary institutions arranged in a roughly inflexible hierarchy of prestige whose zenith resembled that of half a century before with Oxford, Cambridge, and Imperial College at the top and the converted polytechnics of East London, London Guildhall, and Thames Valley at the bottom. *The Times* survey of 2002 ranked them all using nine measures of university quality:

(1) Teaching, using the results of recent official assessment of each department's teaching quality, aggregated for the university as a whole and weighted 2.5 in the integrated score;
(2) Research, graded from the 2001 Research Assessment Exercise, undertaken by the Funding Councils. The weighting is 1.5;
(3) Entry standards. The Average A-Level score of new students under the age of twenty-one in 1999–2000;
(4) Staffing levels. Higher Education Statistical Agency (HESA) figures for the number of students divided by the number of staff;
(5) Library and Computer spending. 1997–2000 compiled by HESA;
(6) Facilities, spending. Per student expenditure over three years including sport, health, counselling;
(7) Degree classifications. The proportion of graduates awarded firsts and upper seconds in 1999–2000;
(8) Graduate destinations;
(9) Completion: the proportion of students completing their course in the expected time.

No doubt a hundred particular objections may be made to the nine assessment criteria and their weighting. A single index made up of several indicators is always open to criticism. Nevertheless, something may be learnt from a study of the details. What is striking is that 'the university experience' is so varied today, whereas before Robbins strenuous efforts were made through the system of external examination and the channelling of funds through the University Grants Committee (UGC) to ensure that a British degree in any subject and from any campus was of comparable quality.

The top twenty places are shown in Table 7.1. The ordering of universities now follows a predictable pattern. No post-1992 university appears in the top half. The first newcomer, Oxford Brookes, is 51st in the rank order. The pre-1992 places are above and the later places are below, though this is not inconsistent with considerable overlap in particular subjects. The old order of privileged equality in a restricted system of higher education has passed into history.

Where then does sociology fit into the new arrangement?

For intending undergraduates *The Times* (7 May 2002) has devised a ranking of universities by combining three indicators: teaching quality assessment (weighted at 2.5), research assessment (1.5), and the average A-Level score of entrants in 2000 (unweighted). The outcome for sociology is shown in Table 7.2.

This ranking from *The Times* is unofficial, though based on official figures, and is offered as advice to entering undergraduates. Oxford is excluded and so

TABLE 7.1 *The general hierarchy of universities in 2002*

Rank	University
1	Oxford
2	Cambridge
3	Imperial College
4	Bath
5	LSE
6	Warwick
7	Bristol
8	York
9	Nottingham
10	St Andrews
11	UCL
12	Manchester
13	Durham
14	Loughborough
15	Edinburgh
16	Newcastle
17	Birmingham
18	Sheffield
19	Aberdeen
20	Kings, London

Note: Only the top 20 of over 100 universities are listed here.
Source: *Times*, Survey 9 May 2002.

TABLE 7.2 *Sociology: the institutional hierarchy in 2002*

Rank	University	Rating
1	Warwick	100.0
2	Cambridge	98.2
3	Sussex	96.5
4	Edinburgh	95.8
5	Loughborough	95.7
6	Aberdeen	93.2
7	York	92.5
8	Sheffield	90.4
9	Glasgow	89.7
10	Stirling	88.7
11	Essex	88.2
12	Brunel	87.3
13	Manchester	85.4
14	Birmingham	85.1
15	Surrey	83.0
16	Keele	82.9
17	Kent	82.9
18	Lancaster	82.4
19	West of England	81.7
=20	Bristol	81.4
=20	Aston	81.4

is the London School of Economics (LSE).[2] Both of these leading competitors offer more general degrees though both also offer sociology at the undergraduate level. Also, despite their larger numbers of sociology undergraduates, the post-1992 universities do not appear until the 19th place, occupied by the West of England University.

Sociology, however contentiously, can justifiably be said to have arrived in the British universities before the Robbins Report. It was being taught in some fashion in most institutions: it entered the Advanced (A) and Ordinary (O) levels of the General Certification of Education (GCE) in 1972 and was increasingly regarded as a necessary element in the training of teachers, doctors, lawyers, town planners, and nurses, as well as in courses for an increasingly professionalized body of social workers.

Universities played an essential part in all this, not only as the gateways to the key profession (Perkin, 1969), but also as the source of knowledge through social research and of qualified teachers. In Britain at least, it is the university which nourishes the disciplines. Establishment within the

[2] This is odd and seems to be a mistake. It is possible to read a first degree in sociology at LSE, the B.Sc. Soc. Moreover, Oxford undergraduates in PPE or Human Sciences may read sociology as a component of their first degree.

universities is therefore essential for sociology or any other aspirant subject. Yet, in fact, the university is the academic tip of an iceberg. A discipline is placed in society also by its submerged bulk—its diffusion throughout the life of a country's people and institutions, its government, its media, its professions. But even thinking only of educational institutions the metaphor of an iceberg still fits. The university remained the tip and the bulk was made up, especially after Robbins, by the departments in polytechnics, teacher training colleges, and so on for which statistics were separately collected by local authorities.[3]

The Robbins Committee was the first to treat further and higher education as one tertiary system. But it centred on the universities which fell under the control and protection of the UGC, and the plan was to expand and to keep the university as the main provider of places in higher education. The same quality of teaching with its 1 : 8 ratio was to be kept. The same high quality of working conditions and research support was to be maintained, the same differential salaries and the same social prestige were assumed.

However, at the same time, a binary system was brought in, sanctioned by Crosland as the Secretary of State. Thirty polytechnics were created which granted degrees under the control of the Council for National Academic Awards (CNAA) and the local authorities. Growing out of the tradition of technical education they were, from the outset, given poorer material conditions, poorer staff/student ratios, lower salary scales, and they were not expected to match the research standards of the universities on the other side of the binary divide.

Sociology went through remarkable growth under these circumstances. Before 1975, the number of departments labelled as sociology rose from seven in 1961 to thirty-five in 1974. The seven new universities were especially hospitable as was The Open University (chartered in 1969). Sociology outstripped the rate of expansion of the university system as a whole. Between 1961/2 and 1975 the number of university degrees awarded in sociology rose from 130 to 1,255 (an advance from less than 1 to nearly 3 per cent of all degrees). In consequence the number of academic staff in sociology departments also rose from 40 in 1960 to 613 in 1975.[4]

Nevertheless, the years after 1975 held many challenges for the autonomy and health of the discipline. Thatcherism brought with it a fundamental rupture of the trust that had traditionally informed the life of the universities and of the professions more generally, while most directly vilifying sociology. Thus, the subject had a troubled time associated with a faltering economy in the 1970s, political attacks in the 1980s, and internal disputes in both decades. But the following decade saw a tentative revival, associated with renewed student and social demand and an uneasy fragmented truce between factions within the profession.

---

[3] Until HESA became responsible, these non-university statistics were not collated. We include them here only after the 1992 incorporation of them as universities.

[4] It should be noted that this expansion, already dominantly female, was accompanied by trends towards a decreasing share of sociology degrees for women. Thus, in 1961/2 women took 97 out of the 130 degrees (75 per cent) awarded and by 1975 they secured 730 out of 1,225 (60 per cent). (The trend was, however, later reversed.) The proportion of academic staff who were women on the other hand rose from 15.9 per cent in 1961 to 19.8 per cent in 1975.

Feminism

We have raised the question of how university sociology was checked after its meteoric rise in the 1960s and early 1970s. One part of the explanation was discord within the profession and one element was renewed dispute over feminism, the second wave of which was strongly felt by sociologists in the 1970s. In the first wave, dating from the eighteenth and nineteenth centuries, agitation involved women's property rights and political enfranchisement. The vote was finally won in 1928. We noted however in Chapter 3 how female educational disadvantages were vividly illustrated in the life of Barbara Wootton. Here was a person of exceptional gifts who spent an Edwardian childhood in educationally privileged circumstances, gained a most distinguished commendation in her Cambridge degree, yet was not allowed to lecture in that university without the rescue of the 'gallant' Hubert Henderson. By the end of the twentieth century, women had secured their fair share of undergraduate places and were advancing rapidly at the graduate student level. For example, at Nuffield College in Oxford women made up 5 per cent of the admissions in 1945–50, 14 per cent in 1971–5, and 41 per cent in 1996–2000 in a severe competition. Liberal masculine guilt responded to a just claim for more equality. Some feminists continue to argue perfectly reasonably that they do not yet have their fair share of university chairs but there can be little doubt about the progress of sexual, political, educational, and occupational opportunity. This is not to contend that complete gender equality was attained and, still less, that a utopia of human society was established. It is rather to put into historical context the modern course of *'la lutte éternelle'*,[5] especially in relation to the inequalities of class, of ethnicity, of age, and of geography, all of which have arguably made slower progress and with which sociology has been concerned since the first British chair was founded in 1907.

This is no place to offer a complete account of feminism which is amply treated elsewhere (Delamont, 1980; Banks, 1981; Mitchell and Oakley, 1981; Walby, 1988*b*; Oakley 1989; Wallace, 1989). It must however be noted that, like sociology more generally, by the 1980s it had fragmented into its radical, socialist, Marxist, and lesbian strands, including a backlash involving former spokeswomen like Betty Friedan and Germaine Greer apparently performing a *volte-face* in abandoning sexual politics and turning to conservative forms of feminism in defence of the family, what Mitchell and Oakley called 'an unsatisfactory but alluring institution' (1986: 5). By the end of the century academic feminism had 'come of age' (Roseneil, 1995). Marxism had given way to post-structuralism and postmodernism with their emphasis on culture 'discourse' rather than 'material' conditions. An internal debate as to whether 'agency' rather than 'structure' should be the focus of feminist sociology in the future was also beginning.

Meanwhile, there was much theoretical borrowing between feminism and other ideologies or 'isms', and debate leading to some intellectual advance and

---

[5] This was Baudelaire's phrase.

institutional change. Intellectually the traditional treatment of women as an ahistorical or biological 'given' (Beauvoir, 1949) was overturned in a series of discussions on the division between sex and gender initiated by Ann Oakley. This dichotomy added to the language of sociology, taking its place alongside the established distinctions such as status and contract (Maine), class and status (Weber), ascription and achievement (Parsons), and many others. It also led to new research on patriarchy, male hegemony, and the history of women as social beings, including Leonora Davidoff's celebrated reconstruction of the role of the wife in the course of industrialization. Institutionally, it led to the conquest of the British Sociological Association (BSA) and the famous conferences of 1974 and 1982 (Platt, 2003).

Perhaps the most important if unanticipated consequence was that feminism became the prime recent example of a movement combining ideas with action— a search for truth allied to a struggle for political advantage. Feminism, like Marxism, seeks to change as well as to understand the world. Past struggles for the vote or for a wife's right to her property were absorbed into renewed women's militancy. Thus, the ancient medieval problem was again raised of the seminar and the pulpit, the rostrum and the hustings, the laboratory and the enterprise. In that sense women's studies are inheritors of an age-old tension of the European university and for sociologists the latest replay of the Weberian drama.

Substantively the changes in family life to which we referred in Chapter 5 mean, among other things, that family care for old people and for children is less secure, and gives greater credence to the view that public services, far from undermining family responsibilities, are essential for preserving them. Many studies have tried to assess the effects on children of their mothers' employment and of parental divorce or separation, and there have been corresponding proposals for public measures to safeguard children's welfare. Jane Lewis detects an 'explosion' in literature on the family in the 1980s, suggesting that feminist writers 'brought the family back to life' and offers examples (Lewis, 1989). But interest in family matters did not either begin or end with the feminists. Questions as to whether any coherent family policy existed in Britain and what its aims should be were widely discussed before the second wave of feminism, as well as in the 1990s in government enquiries, by academics working independently, by bodies such as the Child Poverty Action Group (CPAG), the National Children's Bureau (NCB), and the Family Policy Studies Centre (FPSC), and by research institutes as far apart in their political leanings as the Institute of Economic Affairs (IEA) and the Institute of Public and Policy Research (IPPR).

The 'explosion' of literature on the family did not in any case extend to old people. Feminist writers were naturally enough more concerned with the position of younger women in changing social and economic circumstances, and discussion of family policy tended to focus on the small group of parents and children. Sociologists and demographers were more interested in old age (Shanas *et al.*, 1968). In 1957, Peter Townsend painted a vivid picture of the close kinship networks within which old people lived in Bethnal Green (Townsend, 1957), and thirty years later Peter Laslett told a similarly arresting though very different story of a 'third age' in which old people, freed from employment, might energetically pursue educational, cultural, and social interests and actively participate in public life (Laslett, 1989).

Social policy writers were more concerned with the public costs of an ageing population and the nature of the 'burden' that the growing number and proportion of older people imposed on the younger generation. Studies proliferated of employment and retirement practices and policies, of the health and activities and social and economic circumstances of old people, of their contribution to public well-being through voluntary work, and of their services to children and grandchildren within community and kinship networks (Phillipson and Walker, 1986; Carnegie, 1993).

Also during these years there developed a strong interest, particularly in America, in the idea of the 'underclass'—a phenomenon closely linked to the feminist struggle, to urban deprivation and resurrecting the old spectre of the 'undeserving poor' (Wilson, 1987; Murray, 1990; Smith, 1992; Morris, 1994; Lister, 1996).

Events from 1975

The sequence of events began within the framework of relations between social science and government, focusing especially on the transformation of the SSRC into the Economic and Social Research Council (ESRC). This shift of research policy was followed in 1989 by an inquiry into sociology by the UGC (UGC, 1989; Westergaard and Pahl, 1989). It was not the only subject to be reviewed. The sub-committee, made up of and chaired by non-sociologists as well as sociologists, produced a sturdy and, on the whole, an optimistic defence of the subject at a moment when lay disapprobation and internal dispute over Althusserian (structuralist) Marxism, symbolic interactionism, and ethnomethodology were subsiding but still raging over feminism, quantification, and cultural studies. The report was pragmatic, surveying recent trends, calling attention to the urgent need to attract more academic sociologists, welcoming the growth of combined studies and specialisms, but insisting on the need to maintain some departments where the 'core' of the discipline would be taught. The fashion at the political centre was to follow a policy of 'cut and concentrate' but the sub-committee resisted such a convenient solution (Westergaard and Pahl, 1989). Then came the sudden 'pen-stroke' explosion of 1992 when the polytechnics were admitted into the university system.

The post-war years had come to an end in the mid-1970s. With them ended the long economic boom and the political era of 'Butskellism'. Years of uncertainty were ushered in under the premiership of Wilson, replaced by Callaghan in 1976, the Thatcherite governments of 1979 and Major in 1990, until New Labour took office in 1997. Linked to these economic and political changes was a set of social attitudes towards higher education. There was a switch from confident expansion to puzzled adversity from around the middle of the 1970s which may be partly explained perhaps by folk memory of the events that had taken place at the end of the 1960s. At what was then seen as the high tide of unprecedented growth, the image of the university student changed. Popular respect for the student as either a playful young aristocrat or an earnest young man or woman who would advance social progress through economic productivity gave way to widespread suspicion of an irresponsible juvenile subversive, who imagined that revolution could be effectively conducted by persons aged 18–21. Was it right that such campus privilege should be subsidized by the taxpayer?

Expansion had taken universities beyond their previous marginal condition as nurseries for the elite. The emerging system of higher education was becoming a nationalized industry, big business, an economic human-capital machine in the service of competition between nations. The 'golden age' of the don and his privileged pupils was ending. Universities were emerging as central institutions, the gateway to the growing professions, the lifeblood of scientific research and industrial development.

All this was widely accepted at the end of the 1960s. Crosland's recognition of the polytechnics in 1964 as necessary for a competitive economy was approved by a majority of the left as well as the right. Only diehard traditionalists resisted the substitution of technical efficiency for established scholarship, though a larger minority opposed Martin Weiner and Corelli Barnett in their view that the Oxbridge tradition had robbed Britain of the entrepreneurial spirit[6] (Weiner, 1985; Barnett, 1986). Yet, the search for a cure for the national economy divided the right from the left and a new wave of Conservatism, devoted to the market and monetarism, was led by Keith Joseph politically and by the IEA ideologically.

The transformation of tertiary education, in which 1992 was a huge landmark, is illustrated in the career of Frank Webster, professor of sociology at Birmingham University from 1999 to 2000,[7] who had served at Oxford Brookes University (before 1992 the Oxford polytechnic) for twenty years. He came there from Enfield polytechnic, now Thames Valley University, as a recent Ph.D. in 1979 aged twenty-seven and left for Birmingham aged forty-seven.[8]

Webster's account of a post-1992 university and a post-Robbins polytechnic brings to life three notable features of the binary system. First, the modular structure of degrees as characteristic of the polytechnic tradition. Second, the trend towards priority for the research side of the life of a college that accelerated sharply after 1992 and led to the formal expansion of the professoriate (in sociology to 200 by the end of the century). Third, the struggle over feminism which turned so sharply over the question of the sexual composition of the teaching staff.

---

[6] For a short demolition of the Weiner argument, see Soares (1999).

[7] Birmingham closed down its sociology department for the second time as a result of 'research failure'. The RAE exercise had classified the department as 3A. But compare this with the *Times* hierarchy in Table 7.2.

[8] Webster's account of life and work at Oxford Brookes was sent in a letter to me of 9 November 2000 as part of his response to my questionnaire survey of 2001.

The modular system used in the polytechnics was a great success. It 'cheered on the troops'; it permitted novel combinations of sociology with, for example, planning or computing or music; and it allowed a core staff of four or five to collaborate with sociologists numbering about fifteen in the other departments of the polytechnic. But, Webster points out, the core staff was overladen with teaching duties. While government denied staff expansion, the student/ staff ratios rose to over 20 : 1 during the 1980s and 1990s from a traditional 12 : 1. After the transformation to university status in 1992 the 'teacherly' tradition was undermined, doctorates were expected among new staff, and research began to reign. In the older regime the staff were widely read but wrote little.

In consequence, new strains were imposed on the ageing staff. Webster's belief was that 'a good deal of research which took place and still takes place at Oxford Brookes in areas such as Business, Nursing, and Hotel Management, need not have been located at a university since it was very basic market research, assessment of policy implementation and the like... Yet whisper the word research pretty well anywhere and the teacher knows his or her place [is] on the lower levels'. There was 'a remarkable reduction in class contact with students'. The Research Assessment Exercises assumed high significance. So did the professorial title which had been absent in the polytechnic days.

Webster also comments on the sexual composition of the staff at Oxford polytechnic. When he joined in 1979 there were four and they were all male. By the time he left there was only one man left. 'On balance', he writes, 'this was a good thing, since the gender imbalance that we started with was unjust... However it also led to some sharp confrontations and rather unpleasant disputes which could have been handled better with more good will'.

Sociology and Society

Sociology has, of course, significant relations with government and with civil society. A commentator on social science and government is David Coleman, a professor of demography who has been both a parliamentary candidate for the Conservative Party and a special adviser to the Home Secretary, the Minister for Housing, and the Minister for the Environment. His judgement, written in 1991, on the impact of sociologists on governmental policy is unequivocal.

Most British sociologists are not supporters of the present [Conservative] Government. . . . Many eminent British social scientists have served Labour Governments as advisers in various areas, notably in the 1964–1970 government, helping to form its policy on schools, welfare, rent control and race relations. This was the Golden Age of the research-policy link and of the standing of researchers as advisers; the ideal is the example most commonly cited. But this commitment is double-edged. The present government sees little point in turning for advice to specialists who have been their unrelenting critics. It effectively ignores British sociology (Coleman, 1991).

Coleman's description would command the assent of most commentators. The history of sociology in relation to government fluctuates. A full history would go back at least to Comte and the French philosophers who asked what could be the basis of social order after the collapse of the *ancien régime*. The British story would emerge as a particular European variant. It might start from the Domesday Book of 1085; it would have to consider the origins of political arithmetic in the seventeenth century. Victorian antecedents would loom large, covering sociologically minded reformers in public administration like Chadwick or Simon, private philanthropic evangelists like Booth, and political protagonists like the Webbs. American connections would appear, crossing the Atlantic both ways with Spencer westwards and the Chicago developments eastwards.

In the period 1976–2000 an observer was confronted by two contradictory images. One view, repeated endlessly by Conservative politicians and the media, is that sociology is a polysyllabic plague promoting the subversion of the political order. On another and less fashionable view, it is an intellectual organization of thought with powerful potential for the reform of an imperfect society. The history of the relation of sociology to civic responsibility is the history of the fluctuating fortunes of these two opposed views as expressed in power and influence on state action and social opinion. Of course, this is a crude binary depiction but it serves to point to a central problem. How far can sociology be harnessed to the refinement of political democracy—a means of elevating social consciousness, elaborating consensus, and conflict between group interests, measuring the consequences of purposive action, monitoring unanticipated consequences—in short an apparatus of accountability in a society committed to political action based on rational argument between free citizens? There are, doubtless, limits to the power of sociology as social accountant. And there are conditions, political, professional, and financial, which have to be met. But that is the ideal to cherish while appreciating that it must depend on a culture of citizenship, political support for an open society, and professional commitment to a difficult intellectual discipline.

There is here a sanguine, perhaps starry-eyed, but reasonable interpretation of the twentieth century and a continuing ambition for the twenty-first century, especially after the western half of what had been labelled the 'second world' was abruptly drawn into the 'first world' of parliamentary democratic states. It is incidentally a notable correlate of this interpretation that the relation between Marxism and sociology is being recast for the twenty-first century. In the earlier years sociology was a reply to Marxism, but now sociology is a challenge to incorporate those elements of Marxist thought which criticized and protested against the conflicts generated by free-market capitalism. Civically responsible sociology must continue to resist historicism in either its Marxist or its liberal forms; but the balance of intellectual conflict, with sociology pushed into more 'left-wing' positions while remaining anti-Marxist, seems to portend a future still more difficult than the past.

Social Forms of Accountability

Can sociology be conceived as an intellectually advanced apparatus of account-ability? It is by no means the only instrument of democratic accountability. What, then, is its place in the wider array of accounting institutions? A total-itarian system is instructive. Solzhenitsyn in volume III of his *Gulag Archipelago* remarks that 'the special camps must have been among the best-loved brain children of Stalin's old age. After so many experiments in punishment and re-education this ripe perfection was finally born. A compact, faceless organisa-tion of numbers, not people, psychologically divorced from the motherland that bore it, having an entrance but no exit, devouring only enemies and producing only industrial goods and corpses.' We have here, perhaps, both a perfect definition and a warning against perfectibility in any system of control. The Gulag system was one of costless inputs and valuable outputs, carefully controlled by, and answerable to, the will of one man.

Of course, the totalitarian concentration camp does not represent the polit-ical and social context that most people have in mind in the contemporary search for improved accountability. Current European and American discussion derives more or less self-consciously from the world of innocence in which the welfare state was born after the Second World War. It was a world of common consensual goals: public health, education, and welfare were agreed aims, and the means, it was thought, were possible. In Britain, this meant a benign state, an uncorrupt bureaucracy, and public-spirited professions. Government enjoyed remarkable credence. Political democracy rested on enthusiastic sup-port, and belief was widespread that the will of the majority, expressed through a democratic electorate, would inform Parliament, instruct the executive, and finally shape political action. Moreover, the immediate post-war years had added cheerfulness to innocence despite the fact that, objectively, resources were meagre by the standards of the twenty-first century. For example, the National Health Service (NHS) was predicated on the belief that a backlog of unattended medical ailments would shortly be put right, and that demand could be met without insupportable strain on national resources. There was, in short, social accord, political confidence, and economic optimism.

Unhappily, however, discussion of accountability after the end of the post-war period around 1974 could no longer proceed from any of these three amiable assumptions. On the contrary, the grimmer realities of social conflict, distrust of politics, and relatively declining economic fortunes were the bases on which new forms of accountability had to be built. Such contrasting sets of circumstances illustrate two paradoxes of human nature. The first is an original fusion of egotism and altruism. The second is that men and women are purpos-ive in the pursuit of goals, but they are also irascible and idle. They thus face scarcity of means with a mixture, again irretrievably fused, of rationality and irrationality. In consequence two problems arise; first that of how to arrange public life to stimulate private altruism into public good, and second that of efficiency, that is, how to ensure maximum return for minimum effort.

Sociology can contribute to the answers. The development of rational choice theory since the Second World War is in part a response to the two paradoxes—applied by writers such as Jon Elster to the question of effective collective action by individual actors. Thus, the prisoner's dilemma can be represented as the paradigm of socialist politics (Barry, 1988: 147)—'where what is most in the interest of each prisoner individually, to confess, is contrary to both of them together'. The solution, as sociology, is procedural, not moral. Put another way, the sociology that would serve socialism is one which educates people about the connection between individual choice and collective welfare rather than a quasi-religious movement of mass conversion to altruism. The free-rider problem has to be solved by sophisticated organization. The two paradoxes and inferences from them are nevertheless helpful because they distinguish between moral accountability (referring to the first paradox, i.e. to ends or goals) and instrumental accountability (a reference to the second paradox, i.e. to accountability as a test of efficiency). The accumulation of evidence from public opinion polls since 1960 compels us to abandon the idea of a binary political establishment. Though still essentially class based, electorates have become increasingly volatile and increasingly sceptical of appeals to former collective loyalties. And behind the surface phenomena of the electoral process lies a society in an advanced state of transition from reliance on sources of social authority which were given or prescribed into a world in which all social relations are increasingly open to negotiation.

In the 1970s, there appeared a bizarre manifestation of this transition in the social sciences themselves—the emergence of one kind or another of phenomenology or ethnomethodology maintaining what to an earlier generation would have been totally absurd, that is that every social encounter is negotiated, that nothing comes from the past, that nothing is given. Ethnomethodology[9] was born of the collapse of the orthodox consensus of the 1950s in America led by Harold Garfinkel, who denounced all conventional sociology and substituted close study of the methods used by ordinary people to make sense of their activities (Garfinkel, 1967). A wave of enthusiastic support carried the approach to Britain and Europe, but it met fierce opposition (Goldthorpe, 1973) and is now followed by a minority, though incorporated into the theoretical work of Anthony Giddens with its associated terminology. Indexicality and reflexivity (Giddens, 1976, 1984) are key words in this attempt to bring action and structure together in one sociological scheme. In this movement towards relativism so characteristic of the 1970s, the social sciences were, as always, a mirror of underlying social trends. The drift towards the negotiation of all things and the ascription of nothing, which releases women from femininity, children from childhood, ethnics from ethnicity, and so on, was the expression of a search for new sources of moral authority. At the same time there was a parallel increase

---

[9] The origin of this term is that 'ethno' refers to the knowledge available to ordinary members of a society. Ethnomethodology is therefore the study of the commonsense methods of dealing with social relations.

in the demand for instrumental accountability urged on by the daily message of the newspapers that Britain was going through a period of either low or no growth which made efficiency ever more urgent.

The Governmental Interest

It is in the interests of government to define political and organized social science as, in effect, an extension of the civil service. On such a view the problems are essentially technical. Short-term policy enquiries should always be done within the government and basic or fundamental research outside. An intermediate range of problem-orientated and applied research could be done inside or outside, to be decided pragmatically according to available funds and the location of qualified individuals and whether the subject matter is confidential. There could be a free movement of researchers to and fro between government research establishments and the universities and institutes. There are problems too about defining what is researchable, about clear definitions of the questions to be answered, about the time required to produce usable answers, and about the meaning and interpretation of the answers after the research project has been completed. Thus, technical questions arise about organization and communication between the ministers and their civil servants and the researchers. The underlying assumption is of the social scientist as handmaiden. Research strategies and priorities are finally left in the hands of the government. The claim of the social sciences to independence must be made elsewhere. Reliance has to be placed on enlightened politicians and administrators to see to it that public funds are also made available which are not related to governmental preoccupation with policy.

In any case, as David Coleman has argued, limits to cooperation between politicians and social scientists are inevitable. Politicians and parliaments are pressed for time. Political and administrative interests and priorities do not coincide with social scientific research cycles. Politicians have many and wider channels of information than those supplied by the formal research process. Politicians themselves experiment and their activities are difficult to evaluate. It may well be that, highly consensual periods and problems apart, 'the only decisions which are made primarily on the basis of research findings are politically unimportant ones' (Coleman, 1991: 420).

The Social Science Interest

At its humblest level the social science interest is in careers for its graduates, and in research opportunities and resources for social scientists. In the 1960s, this view led to vociferous criticism of the pattern of recruitment to the administrative class of the Civil Service. The great majority of graduates in the administrative class held degrees in the arts or humanities and barely more than a quarter had read social science or law. Only one in ten of the administrative class who were appointed before the War possessed a social science degree. For those appointed immediately after the War this proportion rose to over a third but fell again in the 1950s. In the 1960s, the long-run trend was resumed and 27 per cent of those directly recruited after 1961 were social scientists. Nevertheless, invidious comparisons continued to be made with France where graduates of the Ecole Nationale d'Administration, who go into the French Civil Service with functions similar to those of the British administrative class, have a general education in the social sciences (economics, law, public administration, finance, statistics, etc.). Moreover, it was pointed out, the representation of the social sciences other than economics was no more than a small minority of a minority.

The interests of government and social science rarely coincide. They appeared to do so briefly in the post-war years of social accord and economic growth. But that favourable period soon came to an end. The values which had sustained governmental policies for higher education and for science were undermined in the 1970s and 1980s. The potential conflict between aspirations and restraints, ideas and realities, became clear only after the post-war period ended. When the polytechnics were recognized in 1964 it was as institutions particularly responsive to the needs of local industry and government for applied research, despite the fact that most of their new recruits would inevitably have been nurtured in the traditional conceptions of research and teaching. The demand for a share in the research funding system was equally inevitable but was unrequited even though Britain legislated no institutional division of labour like that decreed by the California Legislature when implementing its Master Plan for higher education in 1960, which reserved to the university the granting of doctorates and direct recruitment from the top one-eighth of high school leavers.

More generally the end of the post-war period in Britain was also the end of the earlier conditions of reasonably assured financial planning under buoyant economic conditions. Inflation rose steeply in the 1970s. Five-year planning—the quinquennium—was destroyed in 1972–7 and the universities as well as the polytechnics have lived ever since under conditions of chronic financial uncertainty as well as straitened funding.

In December 1973, Research Council funds were abruptly cut and in 1974–5 the Advisory Board for the Research Councils had to face a science budget which was reduced by 4 per cent in real terms. Given that the Research Councils for Agriculture, Medicine, and the Environment had significant commitments to their own tenured staff, the consequences included reduced grants to academic researchers and the alpha-rated but unfunded project application became a notable feature of the British science scene. The same underlying financial stringency—issuing in the 1970s from faltering economic growth, and later from the determination of the Thatcher government to reduce public expenditure—eroded the 'dual support' system of university research. The Research Councils now found themselves increasingly pressed to provide basic equipment and other support previously made available from UGC funds. Thus, the administrative frame within which teaching and research funds had been channelled to higher education was changed fundamentally and overall resources had dropped below pre-Robbins standards.

SSRC to ESRC

The tension between the political and the academic domain went beyond financial questions. The relation between the Conservative government and the university was dramatized in the early 1980s by the case of the SSRC.[10] Sir Keith Joseph, convinced that the social sciences were not sciences, persuaded Lord Rothschild to subject the SSRC to an official enquiry (Rothschild, Cmnd 8554, 1982). There was uproar. Lord Heyworth had invented the SSRC in 1965. Now, in 1981, Lord Rothschild was invited to abolish it. It is doubtful whether the invention had ever been fully accepted by the political right. Rothschild could have replied to Sir Keith Joseph in one short dismissive sentence. Instead, characteristically and in the public interest, he presented the Secretary of State for Education with a vigorously argued rejection of the dismemberment and liquidation of the SSRC. It would be an act of 'intellectual vandalism' (Professor Barry Supple's phrase) and would have 'damaging consequences for the whole country—and ones from which it would take a long time to recover'.

The second dramatic May, of 1979, had carried into Downing Street a group of Conservatives armed with stern nineteenth-century theories of society—pro-market and anti-state—determined to restore a manageable order, based on faith in the market. Among them Sir Keith Joseph was convinced that low productivity, as well as antipathy towards business enterprise, patriotism, and familial piety, had been irresponsibly taught to students by left-wing dons. The SSRC was surely a most vulnerable quango. Could it survive the passing of consensus politics?

The incoming 1979 government had other and larger problems. Legislation to abolish the SSRC could not be high on the agenda—but it was subjected to a sharp reduction in the flow of cash. The real resources of the Council both for research projects and postgraduate studentships were cut step by step. In 1979 (at 1980 survey prices) the SSRC received just over £20 million: by 1982 it was down by a quarter to £15.2 millions. In that year, the number of postgraduate student awards for the main social science disciplines was less than one half of what it had been in the mid-1970s. During the 1980s, the SSRC (later ESRC) research budget was halved and the number of doctoral students supported by it fell by 75 per cent. The Council was also urged to direct its activities to problems of the national interest as understood in Whitehall and Westminster.

---

[10] For the latest account, see Claire Donovan's D.Phil. thesis *Government Policy and the Direction of Social Science Research*, Sussex University, 2002.

Esoteric study of remote places and alien cultures must give way to urgent practicalities in a new age of austerity. The Council's Chairman, Michael Posner, took this all extremely seriously. His critics thought that the definition of problems was shifted too far out of the hands of the academic researchers and into the hands of the lay establishment. By 1982, only nine of the nineteen Council members were academics.

Then, with the translation of Sir Keith Joseph to the Department of Education and Science, the solution came into view. Lord Rothschild was the author of something called the 'customer-contractor principle' in his 1971 report 'The Organisation and Management of Government Research and Development' (Cmnd 4814). Surely he could now serve as the agent of abolition. Joseph wrote to Sir Geoffrey Howe suggesting that a report from Lord Rothschild could 'provide us with an effective basis for action—possibly action opposed by articulate and influential sectors of academic and political opinion'. Rothschild agreed 'to conduct urgently an independent review of the scale and nature of the Council's work, both in research and postgraduate training, having regard to the principles he enunciated in his Report . . .' and in particular to advise (the Secretary of State for Education and Science):

(i) Which areas, if any, of the SSRC's work should be done at the expense of the ultimate customer rather than the Exchequer;

(ii) Which areas, rightly supported by the Exchequer, could be done at least as well and as economically by other bodies, and would receive payment from the public purse either on a once-and-for-all or recurrent basis. The bodies concerned should be identified; and

(iii) Which areas, if any, at present supported by the Exchequer through other bodies could better be covered by the SSRC.

The trial began. Social scientists up and down the country bombarded Rothschild with encouragement to resist this destructive commission and braced themselves against a severe sentence. But no, Joseph had made a politically inspired mistake. Rothschild recommended that the SSRC be left in peace for at least three years with no reduction in its money and no more enquiries. He also wanted it sent to Swindon (which it was) and to a school of plain English (which it was not), and to undergo several other treatments for internal maladies of organization which were of no great public interest. But the main point was that he rejected Sir Keith's invitation to hostility. The first question and the one that mattered related to the original Rothschild formula (Cmnd 4814), and a simplistic customer–contractor answer could have obliterated the SSRC. To be sure, government departments could replace the Council if they were given the funds: bureaucrats could play customer to the social science professors as competing contractors. What is wrong with such a sturdy market solution to rationing scarce resources? The answer is that the ultimate consumers are our grandchildren. In any case Rothschild's principle had been misunderstood. He had never supposed that the customer–contract arrangement could be applied to the social sciences. 'There is . . . no doubt of the need for an independent body, such as the SSRC, to fund research, whether "pure" or "applied", for which no suitable "customer" exists'.[11]

Could it then be some other body than the SSRC? The British Academy, the DES, and the UGC were canvassed, and Rothschild again came back with a firm rejection. 'Neither the British Academy nor the University Grants Committee have any money for this purpose; nor . . . would they be willing to undertake the task even if they had the money . . . It is highly likely, therefore, that if the SSRC were not to receive its grant, the research would not be done'.

These recommendations were reached by page four, at the bottom of which Rothschild wrote that 'the rest of this report develops these conclusions'. He meant, it may be presumed, that the further 109 pages were really padding to make up a document of the weight appropriate to the desk of a Secretary of State.[12] Most of the rest was harmless superfluity. The discussion of the nature and significance of social science was praiseworthy. Even such a distinguished scientist as Rothschild faced a tall order in securing a firm grip on so vast a subject so quickly. The social sciences are centuries old, and he had three months, but the sense and lucidity of his general remarks are admirable. Nevertheless, some professional social scientists found it too long to ignore, and too short to be definitive. Of the subjects listed in the SSRC's official catalogue, though social anthropology received handsome and favourable treatment, little or nothing was said about, for example, politics, geography, education, or linguistics.

Worse, there was a whole chapter purportedly about sociology as well as scattered remarks, and they were mostly unfriendly in the received establishment style. The lay reader would gain the impression that sociology was a pretentious mistake now discredited and replaced by more sensible, 'less ambitious and better established disciplines which are the heirs to the grander claims of

---

[11] In a letter to Halsey (18 February 1982) Rothschild wrote: 'In retrospect I wish I had not been so brief in the famous Rothschild Report on Government R&D; and I should probably not have used the phrase "customer–contractor", because so many people think of a woman buying a pair of tights at Marks & Spencer and of someone in overalls with a spanner in his pocket and a ladder on his shoulder. By the same token, although I did not say it explicitly, I did not believe the principle was likely to be applicable to the SSRC, for a variety of reasons with which you are familiar; but I saw no reason—and still do not—why scientists should be better qualified to assess national agricultural priorities than the ministry if the ministry backs up its economic data by having really good scientists in house. They did for a brief period but then gave it up. The good scientists are needed, of course, to stop people asking scientists to make perpetual motion machines.

Unpopular as it is to say so, the same applies to medical research. But in both cases it only applies to a limited extent. One needs a mix of short, medium and long term studies, something I found also to be the case in the Government's Think Tank. The three parties interact with and stimulate each other'.

[12] Chapter 8, however, on postgraduate training must be exempted from this criticism. Here a suggestion was made (p. 41) about the method of allocating students which usefully sharpened an issue much discussed by the universities and in a Working Party led by Sir Peter Swinnerton-Dyer (*New Society*, 8 April 1982). In brief, it was that chosen degree courses organized along the lines of American-style Ph.D.s (one year of courses plus two years on a dissertation) should be given a quota of awards. Then there should also be a separate competition for a pool of awards to be given to individuals in subjects not appropriately catered for by the American system. It was an excellent proposal on behalf of better research training and higher rates of completion.

sociology—for example, human geography, social psychology, and social anthropology'. This was a highly tendentious and ill-informed judgement. Far from inheriting, sub-disciplines like human geography are almost entirely debtors of sociology, borrowing ideas to enliven themselves. Indeed, a knowledgeable and dispassionate historian of the modern social sciences would describe sociology as the major source of ideas about social relations—so much so that neighbouring subjects, including history, geography, and psychology, and not excluding economics, have absorbed sociological ideas to an extent which has transformed them.

Of course, there were and are incompetent sociologists. A subject excited about important matters, and which was in rapid expansion after long neglect, inevitably attracted some charlatans. But the remedy lay in the maintenance of academic standards universally applied. It was gratuitous to recommend that the SSRC should withhold support for new or sub-standard sociology departments. The Council was not in that line of business, and did not have the money if it had the inclination. It was therefore to be hoped that Rothschild's concession to fashionable philistinism would not obscure his more general, more cogent, and more generous message that the case for fundamental or 'useless' science is, in the end, the faith of civilized people that they should expand rational enquiry to their own association, combined with the belief that this association is unable to express itself sufficiently through the market and must rely on a benign state. That some utility sometimes results in the short run is desirable and encouraging, but not essential to the case. To be sure, the SSRC, its officials, and the researchers and students it supports could all be improved. But had Britain done away with them, she would afterwards have had somehow and painfully to reinvent them.

Rothschild also recommended that the Industrial Relations Research Unit at the University of Warwick be investigated as 'unfairly biased in favour of the unions'. The investigation was carried out in 1982 and the accusation, made by Lord Beloff, was repudiated. Beloff had also made similar remarks about the SSRC's Race Relations Research Unit at Aston University, including a personal condemnation of its director John Rex.[13] But this too came to nothing and Rex and Moore's study of ethnicity and housing in Birmingham has remained a classic work (Rex and Moore, 1967).

In its submission to Rothschild (19 May 1982) the doomed SSRC pointed to the hundreds of research projects which it had funded and used as one example 'Halsey and Goldthorpe's research at Oxford on mobility between social classes which (had) recently led to the publication of *Social Mobility and Class Structure* (Goldthorpe, 1980) and *Origins and Destinations* (Halsey et al., 1980) and was the first attempt to link British concepts and measures of mobility and class, to more sophisticated French and American quantitative research techniques. This combination raised these studies to a new level of analysis and technical competence. Moreover, these studies were a major test of a large and

[13] For a much better informed account of John Rex, see Martins (1993).

compelling hypothesis that, by expanding the public supply of a good, e.g. education, you equalise its distribution'.

Sociological Research and its Audiences

In their insouciance and innocence, and the year before, Goldthorpe and Halsey had discussed but never published their reaction to the immediate response to their reported research in the media. Their argument went roughly as follows.

Social research quite often starts from political debate. But when this happens the questions are translated into the theories and methods of an intellectual discipline: and there they ideally dwell in a world of hypothesis, deduction, and observation, judged, not by votes, but by logic and evidence. The first constituency of sociology must always be itself. Eventually the book is written up to the last chapter for fellow social scientists. The 'last chapter', however, is given over to 'implications' and thus invites retranslation back to the political domain.

So the personal excitement of 'being talked about' beyond the circle of professional colleagues takes its place in an ideal recurrent cycle of the research life. The political responses of the media and the brief emergence from the library and the computing room into the radio interview and the political conference is, in a disciplinary sense, an interval of carnival. Soon, the hope is, the argument will take its serious (major or minor) place in both political debate and sociological knowledge, and a new round will begin of renewed affirmation of the worth of social research for the polity and in itself, and sociologists will return, funded and refreshed, to the travail of another project.

Did experience with these two books from the Oxford Mobility survey confirm this happy oscillation between the worlds of thought and action? The reaction was lively but raised some anxiety, which may be summarized by dividing the commentators into four kinds: the populist, the protestor, the party politician, and the pontificator. All were essentially political in character. This may be inevitable, that is, until the more reflective reviews appear in the academic journals, but it is worrying. For such heavy concentration on the 'last chapter' focuses on the political issues arising out of the research rather than on the research itself. The greater part of both books was taken up with arguments closely related to the analysis of empirical data and resting on assumptions and judgements that could be legitimately challenged. It is of the essence of (social) scientific arguments that they offer themselves for critical examination and evaluation, not that they serve to demonstrate 'facts' conclusively. But what was notable about much of the reaction to the books, whether favourable or unfavourable, was its unargumentative style. There was disinclination to engage with the arguments, as distinct from simply expressing agreement or disagreement with them. Or sometimes the books were taken merely as the occasion for expressing views on arguments with which they were little, if at all, concerned.

The populist response demoted the need for social research as a basis for appraising the world. It either agreed with the research findings only to dismiss them as the discovery of what everybody knows; or disagreed with them, drawing on a rich fund of popular knowledge to tell us that it was nonsense to say that class origins impede individual achievement when we had Mrs Thatcher at Number 10.

The protester also ignored the research argument. He protested either about the research having been undertaken at all or, on the other hand, about its unduly limited nature—there should be none of it, or there is not enough of it. The most remarkable basis for the former claim was the view that in so far as class differences and inequalities exist in modern Britain, they are the result of people talking about class; if sociologists, who do most of this talking, would only be silent, then class and its associated problems would largely disappear. This view has its populist expression; but, elevated to the level of a radical phenomenology, it is to be found in high academic places often in happy coexistence with Hayekian economics. The latter kind of protest is best exemplified in objections to the fact that the 1972 enquiry did not cover women. It was assumed that simply to remark this fact is to make a valid criticism of the research without need for further argument; and the language in which the omission of women was condemned—'incredible', 'monstrous'—suggests that this was seen as an aggressively sexist act requiring a response in terms of sexual politics. Even generally sympathetic academic commentators were little concerned to consider the relevant arguments advanced in the books for the research design that was adopted, under the constraints that existed and in relation to the sociological issues that were defined for study.

Not surprisingly, perhaps, spokesmen for established 'party-political' positions drew on the research in a highly selective way in search of support for their own positions. Typically, they emphasized the authoritative nature of those findings that appeared convenient to them, and then ignored, rather than challenged, other less congenial aspects of the enquiry. Thus, the mainstream Conservative response highlighted the increase in upward mobility as evidence that ample opportunity exists for people of ability to rise in the world, and ignored the extreme and persisting inequality in class chances of access to higher class positions, together with its implications for the Conservative assumption that a high degree of equality of opportunity can coexist with a high degree of inequality of condition. The mainstream Labour response, in contrast, stressed the finding that inequalities of opportunity were little, if at all, diminished over recent decades, but then largely avoided discussion of the implications of this finding for the style and content of the egalitarian programme that Labour had, supposedly, pursued since 1945.

Finally, but fortunately not often, there was the 'pontification' review, the characteristic response of the academic who ought to be, but is not, competent to discuss arguments in relation to research findings. His or her solution to this problem is to adopt a proper air of intense melancholy and to pronounce seemingly magisterial judgements of what is good and what is bad but without elaborating the reasons.

The pontificator is a threat to the ideal research cycle. If he or she were the authentic representative of social science there would be no justification for the funding of research or research training. The populist unknowingly threatens to rob politics of a crucial form of intelligence. The protester essentially tries to enslave that intelligence to a particular political cause. The party politician can be forgiven for honest leanings in the same direction. But, would-be dictators apart, it is in the political interest that argument based on social science is continually offered for debate. And to that end, politicians need adequate translations from the language of social science. The twenty-first century has much work to do in both politics and academia before a creative democracy becomes linked to knowledge through a disciplined sociology.

Conclusion

The last quarter of the twentieth century was a period of complicated uncertainty. From 1900 to 1950 there had been a sluggish response from the universities to agitation for the development of sociology among Fabian politicians, visionary town-planners, research-minded criminologists, and social demographers. The Webbs had founded LSE and fostered a chair in the subject which was philosophical rather than active, and habitually opposed by the traditional cognoscenti of Oxford and Cambridge. The War and post-war reconstruction changed the climate of both lay and academic opinion, but slowly until the Robbins Report of 1963. Then a mild expansion began with an enthusiastic boost for sociological studies in London and the provincial universities supported by some university teachers and eager students. The enthusiasm was channelled dominantly through the red-brick and especially the new universities until the late 1960s when doubts developed among the older disciplines, in 'middle-England', and in right-wing political circles. Then came the student troubles, the faltering of the economy in the 1970s, and the election of the Thatcher Conservative government in 1979.

It was the combination of these social, political, and economic forces which in the 1980s spelt at least temporary disaster for sociology. Thatcher's government sought economy in public spending and put pressure on the UGC and on the research councils. From 1981, the universities themselves were required to administer cuts and these fell heavily on the sociology departments: some were closed, some posts were left unfilled, and all were constricted with fewer grants from the ESRC and fewer grant-aided students. Sociology and sociologists were condemned, the one as pretentious and subversive, the other as the bearers of left-wing ideology and anti-entrepreneurial sentiment. The outlook was grim and made worse by divisions within the subject. Marxism, ethnomethodology, and feminism split and weakened the collective ranks of sociologists. These internal, added to the external, forces made the 1980s years of acute anxiety and unease.

Yet, paradoxically under a Conservative administration, the system of tertiary education was expanded in the 1990s. The number of students of sociology more than doubled and some staff in the ex-polytechnics were awarded the prized title of professor. Putting it all together, sociology occupied more space than it had under the previous regime.

The internal forces of centrifugal movement had not, however, disappeared, and disharmony had to be recognized as a continuing problem for the twenty-first century. In this chapter we have outlined both the external and internal conflicts. We have tried to explain the opposing views of sociology as at once a critic of the established social system and a potential social accounting instrument in a free society. We have recognized that Conservative governments have turned elsewhere for guidance and we have sketched the characteristic reception of social research in modern society. We can now turn to analysing our professorial survey and the content of British sociological journals.

Part III

Analysis

8

The Professors

THE LATE Pierre Bourdieu, writing his account of *Homo Academicus* (1984*b*) as an *espèce sociale*, began by reminding his readers of a tale by David Garnett in which a man is exhibited in a zoo with a notice attached to the cage warning visitors not to make personal remarks. My survey below is intended to offer only objective, impersonal, or collective remarks. But, even so, history tends to be written by the victors. So why should professors be taken as representative of anybody but themselves? They are not, but there are two mitigating considerations (apart, that is, from cheapness and convenience in funding a survey): first, a recently and rapidly expanding profession has, in our time, raised the probability of election to a chair for a bigger minority of recruits; and, second, the organization of academic life is such that leadership crucially counts for the quality and direction of intellectual achievement. This question is a vital part of the more general issue of whether sociology, its teachers, its researchers, and its students is in decline. The evidence on student quality for the United States clearly demonstrates a decline in SAT scores. Also, from 1968, there is evidence of a fatal politicization of both teachers and taught (Horowitz, 2001), of fading excitement in sociology (Abbott, 1999), and of fragmentation. Has British sociology suffered in the same way? Hence, this chapter, in which the aim is to look at the British sociological professoriate as a whole, describing its changing composition and the origins, career patterns, productivity, attitudes, specialisms, and exits of its members in successive cohorts. Then, finally, we can turn to the question of whether sociology is in decline.

The UK Professoriate as a Whole

The ingredients of academic success are not mysterious, but neither this nor any previous survey has included them all. We collected information on sex, social origin, schooling, qualifications, attitudes to research and teaching, publication record, and subject area. But, as is usual in enquiry into social phenomena, the 'variance explained', that is, the statistical measurement of the influence of identified independent variables on the variation (yes or no) of the dependent variable (holding or not holding a chair), falls far short of total explanation. We did not attempt to measure, for example, such important contributory qualities as energy, charm, luck, intelligence, or the chance of network connections,

TABLE 8.1 *Correlates of career success 1976–89. UK universities; all subjects*

	Professoriate	Others	Odds ratio[a]
Service of intermediate class origin	86.7	82.8	1.36[b]
Manual class origin	13.3	17.2	0.73[b]
Private secondary schooling	39.2	36.5	1.10
State secondary schooling	60.8	63.5	0.90
Class of degree			
First	57.5	37.0	2.29[b]
Other	42.5	63.0	0.43[b]
Graduation			
Oxbridge	34.6	24.0	1.67[b]
Other	65.4	76.0	0.59[b]
Doctorate	60.3	57.9	1.06
Oxbridge doctorate	19.1	11.9	1.77[b]
Research orientation			
Research mainly	32.1	21.6	2.19[b]
Both teaching and research	32.5	25.0	1.94[b]
Teaching mainly	35.4	53.4	0.46[b]
Publications			
Articles: more that 20	68.4	24.9	6.54[b]
Articles: less than 20	31.6	75.1	0.15[b]
Books (mean)	3.13	0.87	1.43
Sex			
Male	97.6	88.1	5.25[b]
Female	2.4	11.9	0.19[b]
Age (mean)	51.16	41.36	1.12
Subject area			
Arts	20.4	19.0	1.04
Social sciences	27.0	28.5	0.90
Natural sciences	31.1	30.3	1.05
Engineering/technology	12.9	14.4	0.86
Medicine/health	6.9	6.3	0.96
Agriculture/forestry/veterinary science	1.7	1.5	1.11

Notes:
[a] These odds ratios are not controlled for the effects of other variables.
[b] Statistically significant at less than 0.05 level.

Source: A. H. Halsey, 1976 and 1989 surveys.

which a knowledgeable observer of any actual professorial election would look for. Nevertheless, some enlightenment filters through the data we do have. To set the context we begin with past studies of all UK professors, irrespective of subject (Halsey, 1995*a*).

This first set of studies began with a follow-up of the Robbins sample in 1964 and then proceeded with a sample of nearly 6,000 (4,226 university and 1,414 polytechnic) academic staff, taken at two points in time—1976 and 1989. The samples were divided between the professoriate and other academic staff. For each person we noted:

- Class of origin
- Type of secondary schooling
- Class of first degree and whether holding a higher degree
- University group of graduation
- Faculty or subject
- Research and teaching orientation
- Number of academic books and articles published
- Sex
- Age

Our model of the selection process assumed that class origin and schooling influence qualifications and thus indirectly the chances of promotion to professorial rank.

The percentages of the whole professoriate and of other academic staff in each of the relevant categories (independent variables) are set out in Table 8.1; columns 1 and 2 and give a first rough indication of the importance of the variable in question in discriminating between those who do and those who do not take the professorial path. The difference between the percentages in each row indicates how much the variable matters by showing the relative concentration of people with the characteristics specified who are found in the two groups. However, this is a very rough approximation because in real life the characteristics are linked: they 'interact' with each other. The next step is to use the odds ratios shown in column 3. It must be remembered, of course, that even at this stage interactions between the purported causative variables are still not being taken into account. The odds ratio is, nevertheless, an advance on the simple difference between the percentages in columns 1 and 2. We express the results in terms of odds ratios, which are explained for the non-statistical reader in the first example below.

Class of origin has some predictive value in identifying those who are promoted into the professoriate. One way of showing the relationship is to distribute each of the two academic ranks by class of origin. These are the column percentages shown below and in Table 8.1.

Class origin	Academic rank (%)	
	Professors	Other ranks
Service/intermediate	f_{11} 86.7	f_{12} 82.8
Manual	f_{21} 13.3	f_{22} 17.2
Total	100.0	100.0

We can now think of the association between the two variables in terms of odds instead of proportions. Odds are familiar in racing or other gambling circles. An odds is the ratio between the frequency (f) of being in one category and the frequency of not being in that category. It may be interpreted as the chance that an individual selected at random will be observed to fall into the category in question rather than into any other category. We can first calculate the odds, called conditional odds, corresponding to a traditional percentage. Conditional odds are, in this case, the chances of coming from middle-class origins relative to working-class origins for professors or for other ranks. In Table 8.1 the odds on middle-class origin for professors is $f_{11}/f_{21} = 86.7/13.3 = 6.52$ and for other academic staff $f_{12}/f_{22} = 82.8/17.2 = 4.813$. Thus, the odds on coming from a middle-class family are between one-and-a-quarter and one-and-a-half times greater among the professors than among the other academic ranks. In a traditional percentage table, two variables are unrelated if the percentages are identical or close for each of the rows. Similarly, in an odds table, the variables are not associated if all the conditional odds are equal or close to one another.

We can take a second step to compare directly two conditional odds, a single summary statistic being calculated by dividing the first conditional odds by the second. This forms an odds ratio $(f_{11}/f_{21})/(f_{12}/f_{22})$. The odds ratio in this case is 1.36. Thus, a professor is significantly more likely to have sprung from the middle classes. Or, to put it the other way round, a manual-class origin is less likely to lead to a professorial position, the odds ratio on this formulation being 0.73. It should moreover be remembered here that academics generally are heavily recruited from the roughly one-fifth of the population who make up the service class (75.8 per cent), less so from the intermediate class (25.4 per cent), and least from the manual working class (16.7 per cent). But the odds ratio tells us that the dice are loaded still further against those of manual-class origin after they enter the academic profession and compete for promotion to chairs in universities.

Given this explanation of the first association of academic rank in general with class origin, it may be seen from Table 8.1 that there are significant associations with all of our independent variables except for secondary schooling and the possession of a doctorate. It also appears that the stronger associations are with publications record, research orientation, and class of first degree. But again it is to be remembered that these measures are for each of the independent variables separately and do not take account of the obvious fact that these forces are interactive. Some sense of the pattern of interaction may be gathered from the following remarks, beginning with those factors which operate before entry into the academic professions.

The outcome so far in the selection process is that professors were more than twice as likely (2.29) to have first-class degrees as those in the other academic ranks. They were also two-thirds more likely (1.67) to have graduated through Oxbridge. And people graduating through Oxbridge were one-third more likely (1.33) to gain a first-class degree than people who graduated elsewhere.

It turned out that holding a doctorate is not associated with admission to the professoriate, though we should also note that professors were three-quarters more likely (1.77) to have their doctorates from Oxford or Cambridge than were the other academic ranks. Doctorates from Oxbridge made up 22 per cent of all the doctorates held by academic people. Those who held a first-class degree had more than treble the chance (3.12) of doing their doctoral work in Oxford or Cambridge, and this was especially so for those who had taken their first degree in either place. By doing so they increased the likelihood of going on to an Oxbridge D.Phil. or Ph.D. by fourteen times (13.69) compared to graduates from other universities.

So a picture begins to emerge of the effects of class, schooling, and qualifications on success in the academic career. It is a complex picture but focused around education at Oxford or Cambridge. Recruitment seems to pass through two stages. At the stage of undergraduate entry, pupils from private schools are at an advantage over pupils from state schools, and therefore over pupils born into the manual working class. However, pupils from private schools do relatively less well in their degree results compared with the selected pupils from state schools. Students with first-class degrees who did not study at Oxbridge tend to migrate to the ancient universities at the Ph.D. stage, where they join the considerable numbers of Oxbridge graduates with first-class degrees. Among students who got Firsts from a working-class background, 16.3 per cent graduated at Oxbridge and a further 5 per cent did a Ph.D there. Of other students getting Firsts, 31.7 per cent graduated at Oxbridge and a further 6 per cent went on to a doctorate in the same university group. In short, Oxford and Cambridge have played an important but not an especially meritocratic role in the recruitment of academics who finished their education before 1989. The effects of class and schooling can be put diagrammatically, as in Fig. 8.1.

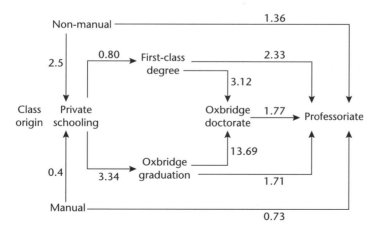

FIG. 8.1 Paths to the professoriate (with odds ratios): UK
universities, all subjects, 1989
Source: A. H. Halsey (1995: 201).

The pathways are clearly differentiated as we have described them and much more could be said about so complicated a web of social relationships. But all of these determinants of career success in the upbringing, education, and training of entrants to the academic professions are relatively weak compared with the determining characteristics that revolve around research interests and performance to which we now turn.

It was found in these previous studies that research attitudes and performance are strongly associated with entering the professoriate. Professors are more than twice as likely (odds ratio 2.19) as other academics to give priority to research; and are also almost twice as likely (1.94) to value both teaching and research as distinct from being oriented towards teaching. Publication records tell a similar story. A person who has published over twenty articles is eight times more likely (8.36) to be found among the professors than a person who has published less than ten articles. Between ten and twenty articles gives twice the chance of becoming a professor as publishing less than ten. Each book increases the odds on being a professor by 0.43 (1.43); thus, three books more than doubles the odds.

None of these estimates, to repeat, take into account any connection with the other factors we have been considering or age or sex. Some of these associations deserve remark. Research interest is linked to publication record. Research-oriented people are twelve times (12.23) more likely to have published twenty or more articles than their teaching-oriented colleagues. People who are equally inclined to teaching and research are approximately eight times (7.74) more likely to have published twenty or more articles than those who prefer teaching. Again, research-oriented people will have published on average 2.3 times more books than those who lean towards teaching.

Returning to the earlier factors, it is noticeable that qualifications are associated with variations in published work. People with first-class degrees are 1.74 times more likely than those without to have published more than ten articles, and 1.64 times more likely to have published more than five books. Oxbridge graduates are 1.36 times more likely to have published more than ten articles than non-Oxbridge graduates. People who have obtained their doctorate at Oxbridge are twice (1.94) as likely to have published more than ten articles and twice as likely to have published more than five books (2.05).

These findings for the whole of the UK professoriate are sufficient to demonstrate the great importance of research success in determining who is promoted to a chair.[1]

The Professors of Sociology

So much for UK professorial and non-professorial academics from Robbins to 1990. We can now turn to the sociologists through a survey of the professors of sociology in British universities in 2001, covering the serving, the retired, and

[1] The next step is to explore the effect of the variables we have mentioned net of their effect on each other. The analysis appears in appendix 2 of Halsey (1995).

the dead. Based on entries in the *Commonwealth Universities Handbook*, it turned out to be a near census.[2] But the definitional difficulty remains and can always be disputed. In this case we included professors of social policy and excluded social philosophers, social anthropologists, social psychologists, and those who emigrated to chairs overseas. The total on this definition came to 296 of whom 256 replied. The dead made up forty and in these cases factual information was recorded from public records, but opinion (e.g. that Ginsberg would have named Hobhouse among the top contributors to sociology in the twentieth century) was eschewed to avoid unwarranted inference. Thus, the attitu-dinal results are biased towards the living and those more recently appointed.

Individuals, especially older people, have entered the foregoing text as illustrations or participants in the story of institutional events. We shall also draw on the survey in Chapter 9 to discuss 'mentors and models' noting that many, indeed most, of the latter are or were sociologists from other countries.

The professors can be divided into four groups by birth. At 2001, the birth cohorts were as follows, with the typical date of entry to the first chair appended in brackets:

	Birth		First chair
1	up to 1930	69	(up to 1970)
2	1931–44	78	(1971–84)
3	1945–9	68	(1985–9)
4	1950 on	41	(1990 on)
	Total	256	

As already described, the background is a cycle of restricted growth, expansion after the Second World War and the Robbins Report, a temporary halt in the 1970s, a decline in the early 1980s, and an explosion in 1992. The foundation of chairs in sociology echoed the background and is shown in Table 8.2. By 1980 there were forty professors compared with two in 1940. Before 1950, only two British universities housed such chairs—London School of Economics (LSE) and Liverpool. During the 1950s, Bedford College London, Birmingham, and Sheffield joined the list. Then, in the 1960s, there was a rush led by the new universities of East Anglia, Essex, Kent, and York, and by the Celtic fringe of Aberdeen, Cardiff, Edinburgh, and Swansea followed by Bangor, Belfast, Stirling, and Strathclyde. Eight more were created in the first half of the 1970s.

Institutional expansion slowed in the mid-1970s and especially under the militant stringency of government in the 1980s, when chairs in sociology were left unfilled or their incumbents encouraged to retire while recruitment virtually came to a halt. Then again after 1992 the old pattern was abruptly restored and

[2] The survey details are at Appendix 1 below. It includes the list of people contacted and their responses and identifies the dead.

TABLE 8.2 *First chairs in sociology in UK universities by year of foundation*

Pre-1950	1950–61	1962–5	1966–9	1970–4	1978–2000
Liverpool	Bedford	Aberdeen	Bangor[a]	Aston	Oxford
LSE	Birmingham	Bristol	Bath	Brunel	and some
	Sheffield	Cardiff	Bradford	City	post-1992
		Durham[a]	Cambridge	Glasgow	universities
		East Anglia	Keele	Hull	
		Edinburgh	Loughborough	Lancaster	
		Essex	Queens Belfast	Leeds	
		Exeter	Stirling	Warwick	
		Kent	Strathclyde		
		Leicester	Surrey		
		Manchester	Sussex		
		Newcastle[a]			
		Reading			
		Salford			
		Southampton			
		Swansea			
		York			

Note: [a] Chair of social studies, social institutions, or similar title.

Source: Correspondence of UGC Sub-committee with Heads of Departments, 1988.

the shortage of professors temporarily echoed the conditions of the 1960s. By 2001, the number of chairs in sociology and social policy had risen to over 200.

The births of the first cohort are chronologically more scattered than any of its successors. Ten were born in the nineteenth century, eleven before the First World War, and nine in the year of the Wall Street stock market crash (1929) and its aftermath (1930). The second cohort were slump and War babies, the third were the most concentrated group of post-war children, and the fourth were born over a decade from 1950.

Those who graduated before 1918 included three from the nineteenth century, Geddes, Hobhouse, and Westermarck, followed by four others who took their degrees early in the twentieth century, McIver (1902), Ginsberg (1913), and T. H. Marshall and K. Mannheim in 1914. None had read sociology and of the eighteen who graduated between the Wars only two could claim sociology degrees, Michael Young and Jean Floud, both from LSE in 1938. Four were women, Joan Woodward, Barbara Wootton, Jean Floud, and Ruth Glass. All were famous.

All except two of the LSE graduate students in the early 1950s discussed in Chapter 4 went on to chairs. Of the two, Norman Dennis turned down offers, preferring to live in his native Sunderland and to work at the then sociology department of the University of Newcastle where he became the Reader in Sociology. The other, Cyril Smith, followed an ordinary academic career but then eventually became the Secretary of the Social Science Research Council. The remaining eleven were typically promoted to professorships in the expansive 1960s and thus, with their predecessors, came to dominate the profession, though they never constituted a professorial monopoly given the rapid rise of demand in that whirlwind decade.

Most of the first group (Group 1 of the Birth Cohorts) took their first degrees in the 1940s, including two women, Margaret Stacey and Dorothy Wedderburn, both of whom had distinguished careers. Ernest Gellner and David Lockwood were perhaps the most outstanding, but the cohort also included Donald Macrae, who eventually held the Martin White chair after David Glass. John Rex, the leading ethnic and conflict theorist, Tom Bottomore the Marxist who went to his final chair at Sussex, Ron Dore, the eminent expert on Japan, and Stanislaw Andreski, the Pole who became the professor of sociology at Reading, were other notable members. And there was the LSE group described in Chapter 4.

All of Cohort 1 grew up before the age of affluence in the period when access to universities was severely restricted. They were mostly children of the 1920s, which saw the rise of authoritarianism of the right and the left in Europe. Theirs was also a childhood of near universal belief in the potency of politics and yet for most of them a world without sociology. It was a time of tension between democracy and dictatorship, between a rich minority and a mass of manual factory workers. Yet also, at least in Britain where most of them dwelt, theirs was a period of widespread popular belief in progress, both material and mental— rising standards of living, advancing medicine, the beginnings of secondary education for the brightest, and the promise of secondary education for all.

There were also many famous names among the second birth cohort, the children of the 1930s and the Second World War. Giddens has become 'globally' known and leads the British sociologists in reputation. Runciman, through his many writings including a three-volume *Treatise on Social Theory* (1983–97) and his earlier *Relative Deprivation and Social Justice* (1972), is also a formidable figure, as is Goldthorpe who has had one of the Modgil consensus and controversy books written about him (1990). He thinks of himself as European rather than British among whom he often courts controversy on the grounds that, following Popper, his ideal world of social science is one in which ideas rather than people are always engaged in mortal combat (i.e. he 'takes no prisoners'). In the public academic arena his weapons are exact, statistical, and clearly related to current theory. Yet, it is doubtful whether sociologists, even in public, really inhabit a world of civil debate among contrary contentions. In fact, and especially in private, it is an unstructured domain in which what really counts is not money nor power, but reputation—that fugitive, frail, and fragile entity. In that world, Goldthorpe is an aggressive and controversial figure. There are others. Pahl is both influential and productive and his *Divisions of Labour* (1984) is widely recognized as an elegant achievement; Albrow and Sheila Allen have been presidents of the British Sociological Association (BSA); and other distinguished scholars include Heath, Gallie, Crouch, Beckford, Bulmer, and Abercrombie. The group was the last wave of entrants to a traditional academic elite.

In Scotland Andrew Macpherson led a reinvigoration of the tradition of empirical research and was recognised by the award of an FBA. Stan Cohen also deserves special mention. He was born in the second cohort in 1942, took an Essex chair in 1974, and went to a chair of criminology at the Hebrew University in Jerusalem in 1981, from which he was recalled to the Martin White chair at LSE in 1995. His book, *States of Denial* (2001), was much applauded. The third and fourth cohorts were born after the War. Cohort three, includes the first large entry of women (11) among whom Barker (LSE), Finch (Keele), Dale (Manchester), Westwood (Manchester), and Oakley (London) are outstanding. The fourth cohort is made up of the young professors born from 1950 onwards.

Most of the two groups of recruits born after the Second World War were natives and fewer were Jews than their pre-war predecessors. Some, like John Urry in the third Cohort, have already established national if not international reputations: others like Howard Newby, Geoff Whitty, or Janet Finch have escaped into administration, though in Newby's case the success of so doing is attributed partly to reading the fashionable sociology of their youth— Goffman's *Presentation of Self in Everyday Life* (1971). Bryan Turner has succeeded Giddens to the Cambridge chair. Jay Gershuny is a leading figure at Essex, Susan Macrae at Oxford Brookes, and William Outhwaite at Sussex. John Ermisch (Essex), Duncan Gallie (Oxford), and Jay Gershuny (Essex) have been elected to Fellowships of the British Academy (FBA).

Nor are the distinguished missing from the fourth Cohort—the post-1950 births. Gordon Marshall was appointed as the Chief Executive of Economic and Social Research Council (ESRC) and then as the Vice Chancellor of Reading University. Other examples are Paul Edward's (Warwick) and John Hills' (LSE) election to the British Academy, John Scott's election to the chair of the BSA, Diego Gambetta's and Richard Breen's FBA and elections to official fellowships at Nuffield College. Yet, other examples from third and fourth cohorts are John Gray at Cambridge, Phil Brown at Cardiff, Hugh Lauder at Bath along with David Raffe, and Lindsay Paterson at Edinburgh who are broadening the bounds of the sociology of education so as to link it to the other social sciences and statistics. These achievements confute any impression that the glory days of the subject and its leadership ended with the first or second cohort.

As to country of birth it should be noted that a significant minority (one-third) of the pre-1930 birth group were born abroad, whereas in the later cohorts there was a sharp switch to native births (87 per cent) rising further to 93 per cent among those born after 1950 (Fig. 8.2). A reduction in Jewish entry into the sociology profession lies behind this trend (Fig. 8.3). Before the Second World War there was a notable recruitment of Jews migrating from the European continent, a tragedy for Europe mitigated to some small extent by academic triumph for the British universities. Though the mainstream of this modern exodus flowed to enrich American institutions, Britain also gained, and in professions beyond sociology—Peierles in mathematics, Gombrich in the history of art, Eysenck in psychology, Frank Hahn in economics, and many others of comparable fame decorated British cultural life after the War. Within sociology we have noted such outstanding individuals as Mannheim, Gellner, Elias, and Neustadt. These Jewish refugees from Fascism were physically the

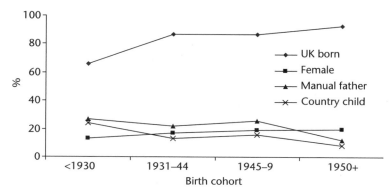

FIG. 8.2 Social origin of sociology professors
Source: Halsey survey (2001).

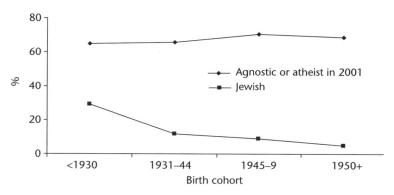

FIG. 8.3 Religion of sociology professors
Source: Halsey survey, 2001.

carriers of an essentially imported culture of social science, which had already established itself in European countries outside Britain.

It is noticeable too that, though we earlier emphasized the link between sociology and the loss of Christian faith in the 1870s and 1880s, secularization still goes on. When they were questioned in 2001, a majority of the sociology professors declared themselves as agnostics or atheists compared with the religious outlook of the family into which they were born (Fig. 8.3). Movement from faith to doubt or disbelief amounts to two-thirds of them in all four cohorts. The End, one may reasonably surmise from the statistics, must be Nigh. Enlightenment, others may conclude, has made steady if slow progress.

There is a significant continuity in the class origins of these professors of sociology. The reference here (Fig. 8.2) is to a first glance at the proportions born in the managerial and professional classes (44 per cent before 1930, 42 per cent after 1950) and to the proportions with working-class antecedents (30 per cent before 1930, 20 per cent after 1950). A second glance however would take into account the wider trend in society towards the enlargement of the middle classes at the expense of the working class and towards a social widening of opportunities for university education. The proportion of the workforce who were manual workers in the years before 1930 was at least 80 per cent while after 1950 it fell below 50 per cent. The cards of educational opportunity were stacked against working-class recruitment to the universities, especially Oxford and Cambridge, in both the early- and the middle-twentieth century with, if anything, a tendency towards decreasing *relative* chances over time (Halsey *et al.*, 1980). Relative class chances of a chair in sociology, in fact, worsened over the period in question.

Not so with sex or gender. Here the trend is steadily if slowly in the opposite direction (Fig. 8.2). In the pre-1930 birth cohort 13 per cent of sociology professors were women and that proportion climbed to 20 per cent for those born after 1950. But here again it must be remembered that the number of undergraduates has increased with a drift towards female recruitment such that women outnumbered men from the late 1990s. Of course, a selection process along the path to the chair still operates, but it is complicated and disputed (see Halsey 1995*a*, ch. 10).

There was once an element of truth in the description of the older generations of sociology professors as 'country boys' (Collini, 1979; Shils, 1997; Abbott, 1999). It was true for a quarter of those born before 1930; but now the percentage has dwindled to 8. This may be a reflection of the urbanizing and suburbanizing tendencies of the late-nineteenth and early-twentieth centuries in both the United States and Britain. McIver, for example, was a child of the Hebrides, and Geddes too grew up in Scotland in a cottage on a hill a mile or so outside Perth. Both were of proletarian origin, though Geddes's father had risen from the ranks to become a captain in the Perthshire Rifles. The biographies of others like Hobhouse, Sprott, Madge, or T. H. Marshall suggest an element of the rural gentry or the liberal professions or at least a childhood in a boarding school in rural surroundings.

At all events by comparison with the general population sociology professors are relatively privileged and tend to be male. Yet, compared with professors in other subjects, they are of more balanced composition with respect to both class and gender (Fig. 8.2) and increasingly so for the more recent cohorts. Collini described the Hobhouse generation as having attended 'public' (i.e. private) schools. But while this was true for over a quarter of them, the proportion is now down to 7 per cent (Fig. 8.4). The family, school, and class background of Victorian graduates used to be stereotyped as a professional, male, boarding school upbringing leading to an Oxford or Cambridge college and admission to clerical orders or to the home or foreign civil service. A modern measure of respondents' educational connection to higher education is whether their fathers and their spouses were graduates. The highest proportion of graduate fathers (27 per cent) was among the pre-1930 birth cohort, falling to the remarkably low level of 12 per cent among the fourth cohort. A similar if less marked trend applies in the case of wives or partners: higher proportions of university attendance were recorded for spouses—78 per cent in the first compared with 69 per cent among those born after 1950 (the fourth cohort).

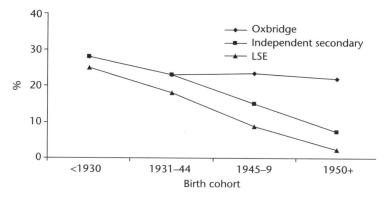

FIG. 8.4 Education of sociology professors
Source: Halsey survey, 2001.

Graduation from Oxford or Cambridge is less common among sociology professors than for the British professoriate in general, but has been maintained at a quarter of the whole through all the cohorts. What comes as somewhat surprising is the decline of LSE as an undergraduate nursery of sociology professors—attracting 25 per cent in the first cohort but only 2 per cent in the fourth (Fig. 8.4). The gainers here have been the red-brick and the 'new', including the post-1992, universities where the greatest expansion in sociology teaching has also taken place.

One of those who gave written evidence to the Rothschild enquiry into the Social Science Research Council (SSRC) in 1982, in answer to the question of what was wrong with sociology, affirmed that it was 'the sociologists'. 'I believe', it was alleged, 'that its practitioners comprise a higher proportion of second and even third raters than any other social science'. The witness provided no evidence. In fact, the professorial evidence is inconclusive as may be seen from Figs 8.5 and 8.6. At first glance the case for declining quality is strong. There was a fall from 60 to 30 per cent in first-class graduates between the oldest and the youngest birth cohort of professors of sociology, and this despite the record of increasing proportions granted first-class honours in universities generally. It appears still more generally that talented young people may have moved away from academic and civil service careers to other parts of the economy. On the other hand, the proportion gaining doctorates rose from the first to the fourth cohort from 60 to 95 per cent.

The Ph.D., since the Second World War, has become a kind of trade union ticket of entry for academics though there are conspicuous exceptions like John Goldthorpe to match the older people like Edward Shils or Richard Titmuss. However, previous study (Halsey, 1995) has shown that the doctorate is but a small determinant among many of a successful academic career. Unfortunately, there is still insufficient evidence to decide on the truth of Rothschild's Cambridge witness. The survey of 2001 is confined to the professors of sociology. The Higher Education Statistical Agency (HESA) are unable

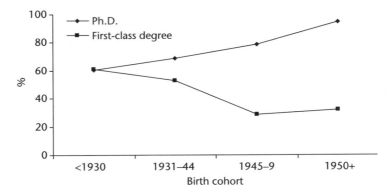

FIG. 8.5 Qualifications of sociology professors
Source: Halsey survey, 2001.

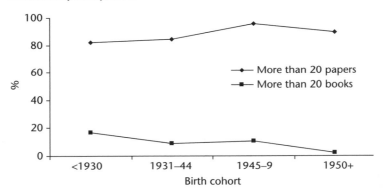

FIG. 8.6 Publications of sociology professors
Source: Halsey survey, 2001.

to provide strictly comparable information before 1994 either about the class of degree of university staff or about their research activity. We are therefore forced back to the other variables listed in Table 8.1 which will provide an incomplete explanation of selection as a professor and an incomplete test of the accuracy of our witness's assertion. The comparisons appear in Table 8.3 for the HESA data. They show the proportions holding doctorates in various categories in 1994/5 and 2000/1: the categories are professors and all academic staff in the social sciences and in sociology in the UK system as a whole.

It is clear that professors of sociology since 1994 held more Ph.D.s than did other professors of the social sciences but slightly less than all professors in the United Kingdom in any subject, but the percentage score is rising among the holders of sociology chairs (Table 8.3).

The evidence from the 2001 survey directly from the professors of sociology is again equivocal and indecisive as to trends in the quality of leadership. Three-quarters of them prefer research to teaching, with a further 17 per cent equally

TABLE 8.3 *Proportions holding doctorates 1994–2001*

Year	Sociology professors	Other sociologists	Professors of social sciences	Other social scientists	All professors	All others
			%			
1994/5	68	33	65	36	72	37
1997/8	70	31	67	36	74	38
2000/1	72	35	69	38	73	38

Source: HESA, by request.

TABLE 8.4 *Preferences for research 2001*

Birth cohorts	Actual	Preference
	%	
<1930	59	58
1931–44	51	72
1945–9	62	86
1950+	65	80

Source: Halsey survey, 2001.

balanced between the two (Table 8.4). These proportions indicate a much stronger leaning towards research than is signalled by any of the previous surveys of professors or of academics generally. Moreover, it appears that the oldest birth cohort (born before 1930) had a lower research inclination then either of the two post-war birth cohorts (86 and 80 per cent). The trend among professorial recruits is generally towards an emphasis on research rather than teaching, though the post-war cohorts are much more inclined than their elders to believe that actual standards of teaching rose rather than fell during the 1990s.

On publications, the evidence is again incomplete. Figure 8.5 shows a continuous rise in the proportion who had published twenty or more papers but a fall in the number of published books. But the two post-war cohorts are mostly still serving while the pre-war cohorts are mostly retired or dead. The oldest people obviously had more time to publish; the younger therefore tend to be underestimated.[3] On the other hand, there are strong rumours that one of the consequences of the recent period of Research Assessment Exercises has been to press academics into immediate *article* publication.

In summary then, and leaving aside politicization and ideological distortion, we cannot conclude that the quality of leadership in the British profession of sociology has either risen or fallen. Pessimistic pronouncement may well be a case of Cambridge snobbery.[4]

[3] Not to anticipate this was an elementary error on my part in conducting the survey.
[4] For further discussion see Appendix 2.

Political Attitudes (Tables 8.5 and 8.6)

Academic opinion is both stereotypically and in fact leftist, and this is markedly so among British sociology professors. The clear majority (over 60 per cent) supports the Labour Party, the Liberal Democrats come second with just over 10 per cent, and the Conservatives third with 2 or 3 per cent. But the details are more interesting. Young chair holders in sociology are more likely to reply that they do not feel close to any party than are the general run of academics or their own disciplinary predecessors. And, with regard to the conventional political spectrum, 16 per cent of the young professors of sociology place themselves on the far left, a score which easily outdistances that of any other disciplinary group. The answers on political affiliation are a strong indication though not conclusive proof that the sociology profession has become politicized. British sociology has always been associated with one form or another of radicalism. But has politicization meant bias, whether in the selection of research problems, the teaching curriculum, service on grant-giving bodies, or on editing or refereeing submissions to journals? We cannot know. Certainly Glass or Titmuss have been passionate supporters of the left. But equally

TABLE 8.5 *Which political party do you feel closest to?*

| | Birth cohort | | | |
	<1930 (%)	1931–44 (%)	1945–9 (%)	1950+ (%)
Conservative	3	3	0	3
Labour	60	64	67	59
Liberal Democrat	13	14	9	5
None	21	16	16	26

Source: As for Table 8.4.

TABLE 8.6 *Where would you place yourself in the following political spectrum?*

| | Birth cohort | | | |
	<1930 (%)	1931–44 (%)	1945–9 (%)	1950+ (%)
Far left	10	8	12	16
Mod. left	67	75	75	74
Centre	20	15	11	11
Mod. right	3	3	2	0

Source: As for Table 8.4.

Spencer, Fletcher, Saunders, and Marsland have been outspoken supporters of the right. Halsey and Heath have advocated political arithmetic as the study of controversial problems, but they have linked their belief in passionate problem selection to rigorous methods of evidence gathering; the meticulous testing of hypotheses. Seekers after the science of society must applaud this stance. They can, however, sincerely regret that recruits to the profession are not more evenly spread across the political spectrum.

Attitudes towards the Career

A handsome majority of professors of sociology think of themselves as primarily sociologists (Table 8.7). A fair majority (over 60 per cent) of professorial British sociologists would not wish to hold or have held their chair at any other university, and this opinion must be seen against the fact that the subject has become predominantly one supported by the new (including the post-1992) universities. Figure 8.7 shows that these institutions have become places for

TABLE 8.7 *Do you think of yourself primarily as a sociologist?*

Birth cohorts	%
<1930	75
1931–44	87
1945–9	81.5
1950+	80

Source: As for Table 8.4.

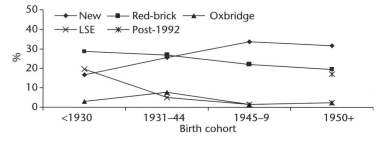

FIG. 8.7 University of first chair

holding the first chair of the career. Of the rising minority (just over a third) of the would-be movers, a quarter would choose Oxford or Cambridge and 17 per cent would like to go or to have been to LSE.

When asked to explain the apparent decline of the subject, the suggested trend is increasingly questioned by the younger recruits. Abbott's account (made anonymous) of decline in the United States from 1960 to 1990 was put to respondents and they were asked whether it fitted the British experience over the same period. He had postulated four reasons. The British professors, especially the young ones, disagreed that the subject had lost excitement over these years. Only among those who graduated before 1951 was there a majority who agreed with him. On the other hand, Abbott's second and third suggestions, that policy advice had moved outside the discipline and that the subject had become fragmented, were overwhelmingly supported. As to student quality, a slight majority thought that it had declined but there is no discernable trend of opinion (Table 8.8).

Finally, when asked whether, given the opportunity to start afresh, they would choose another discipline or another profession, the answers were strongly negative (Table 8.9). Again, with respect to discipline, it was the younger professors, born after the Second World War, who in over 85 per cent of the cases rejected the idea of a different subject. The people born before the War were less certain about changing their discipline (over a quarter said yes) and said that they would have chosen a non-academic profession if they could begin their career again. Most respondents thought that public respect for academics had declined during the 1990s and since they themselves had been undergraduates. A larger proportion of those born after rather than before the Second World War held this view, but a yet larger proportion of those born during the War years. And it was the younger men and women who were more disillusioned by poorer working conditions and salaries and less sure than their elders that they wished to stay in the academic profession of sociology, a third opting for a change of profession if they could start again.

TABLE 8.8 *Decline of sociology 1960–90*

Agree with Statement	Birth cohort			
	<1930 (%)	1931–44 (%)	1945–9 (%)	1950+ (%)
Quality of students declined	42	58	53	45
Policy advice from others	72	77	79	80
Fragmentation increased	80	85	79	75
Excitement declined	61	44	40	26

Source: As for Table 8.4.

TABLE 8.9 *Attitudes to career in British sociology*

Agree that	Birth cohort			
	<1930 (%)	1931–44 (%)	1945–9 (%)	1950+ (%)
Quality of teaching in the 1990s declined	24	31	17	15
Quality of teaching since respondent was undergraduate declined	14	32	19	25
Public respect for academics declined	47	72	59	65
Public respect declined since respondent was undergraduate	68	83	71	72
Research quality declined during 1990s	19	29	21	24
Research quality declined since respondent was undergraduate	22	26	10	18
Chair should be normal part of career	25	22	18	23
Choose another discipline if could start again	29	28	13	13
Choose another profession if could start again	29	26	30	33

Source: As for Table 8.4.

Administrative Posts

The reader may have gained the impression from this chapter that the professorship is the highest possible destination and that to rest in a chair of sociology is a terminal position before retirement. If so there has been a mistake. Analysis of the questionnaire demonstrates that a minority have taken administrative posts beyond the headship of a department. They have accepted appointments as deans, pro-vice-chancellors, heads of colleges, or vice-chancellors of universities, usually after but sometimes instead of holding a chair.

Motives for seeking or accepting a vice-chancellorship are beyond the reach of a simple survey of the kind reported here. Some like Newman in Ireland or Humboldt in Berlin or possibly Hutchins at Chicago may be servants of a mission to realize their particular idea of the university. Others may seek petty power. Yet others may desire the personal satisfaction that goes with marble halls, a fat salary, secretary between outsiders and the inner sanctum, and all the paraphernalia of superior status. Others again may have come to dislike teaching their subject or to decide that they have nothing further to add to it by way of research or innovation. Questionnaires will not easily reveal conscious, leave alone unconscious, motives.

TABLE 8.10   *Comparison of vice-chancellors and professors*[a]

	VCs Valid *N*	VCs %	Profs Valid *N*	Profs %
Do you think of yourself primarily as a sociologist?	15	83	189	83
Political party preferred				
Conservative	0	0	5	2
Labour	10	56	144	62
Liberal Democrat	2	11	25	11
Others	1	6	12	5
None	5	28	41	19
Political spectrum				
Far left	0	0	26	11
Mod. left	14	78	160	72
Centre	4	22	30	14
Mod. right	0	0	5	2
Quality of students declined at entry				
Undergraduate	3	43	74	45
Graduate	1	13	36	21
Quality of students declined at exit				
Undergraduate	3	38	48	30
Policy advice from others	12	80	155	77
Fragmentation increased	11	69	165	44
Excitement declined	5	33	83	42
Agree that				
Quality of teaching in the 1990s declined	4	27	45	23
Public respect for academics declined	10	67	125	63
Public respect declined since respondent was undergraduate	13	87	149	75
Research quality declined during 1990s	4	27	46	24
Choose another discipline if could start again	3	18	45	21
Choose another profession if could start again	3	6	64	29
Oxbridge undergraduate	6	33	55	24
Oxbridge doctorate	3	23	30	15
Independent-school educated	3	17	41	18
First-class degree	12	75	77	45
More than 20 papers published	16	89	201	88
More than 20 books published	3	17	18	8

Note: [a] As a percentage of valid cases.

Source: As for Table 8.4.

The question may, however, be reasonably put as to whether the rate of transfer or escape from professorship to administration denotes changes in the attractiveness of a professorial career. We know that appointment to higher administrative posts was never absent from the first cohort (Dahrendorf became Director of LSE, Stewart Campbell became vice-chancellor of Keele, and Jean Floud became the principal of Newnham College, Cambridge). We also know from the survey that the rate of transfer into administration has increased in the later cohorts at least in absolute terms. Giddens (LSE), Finch (Keele), Newby (Southampton), Bell (Bradford and Stirling), Bernbaum (South Bank), Whitty (Institute of Education, London) Burgess (Leicester), and Marshall (Reading) are all cases in point. But we do not and cannot know from the evidence whether the academic career for sociologists has become less or more attractive compared with either non-academic careers or other university social sciences or other university staff in all subjects. The survey results are set out in Table 8.10. What is most remarkable is that the background of vice-chancellor sociologists and those who occupy other posts in the high administration of universities is similar to that of their colleagues who devote themselves to teaching and research. They broadly share the social and educational upbringing of the professors. They have a similar political outlook (moderate left) with slightly less tendency to extreme opinion. A fair minority on both sides of campus management believe that the quality of sociology students at entry and at exit fell during the 1990s along with the quality of sociological research and teaching. A heavy majority of both vice chancellors and professors saw public respect for academics as having declined since their own undergraduate days.

There are however two noticeable differences. Very few of the high administrators would choose another profession if they could start again. This hardly needs explanation. It is perhaps surprising that, given our account of a quarter of a century of uncertainty for sociology, as few as 29 per cent of its chairholders would choose to avoid the scholarly life. The other difference is possibly significant. Vice chancellors from sociology have a distinctly higher proportion of first-class degrees. Perhaps therefore ability is linked to administrative elevation in the university.

9

Celebrated Sociologists

In the last chapter we portrayed the changing character of the professors of sociology in the United Kingdom. We can now ask who among them and their colleagues overseas are held *by them* in the highest respect either as teachers or as researchers, as mentors or as models. Both the choosing constituency and the chosen group can be differently defined. Widening of the constituency suggests a poll of all qualified sociologists or an even wider group of students or the widest possible group of compatriots. Narrowing of the chosen ones suggests fellowship of the British Academy or inclusion in the list of civil honours or of the presidents and executive committee members of the British Sociological Association (BSA). To mention such alternatives is to call attention to the advantages and disadvantages of any particular method and particularly to our own which is, in effect, the composited opinion of past or present chair holders in the subject. Other methods assuredly would bring other results. The outcomes of election, selection, co-optation, or any process of achievement will differ not only among themselves but also from any process of ascription such as caste, primogeniture, or gender. In this context our methods are of two kinds. The first is a form of restricted co-optation—the pattern of answers by serving professors to two questions. The second is a form of selection by the three mainstream sociology journals in Britain through their editors, their editorial boards, and their invited referees.

The Professorial Survey

The survey of professors[1] of sociology included two questions aimed at discovering who had taught or inspired and who had impressed these chair holders as contributors to contemporary sociology. The questions were:

1. Who have been your most important mentors during your career?
2. In the world as a whole which sociologists of the twentieth century have contributed most to the subject?

Space was provided for three 'mentors' and three 'models'. Of the 255 respondents there was a significant minority who did not give a full reply. The maximum

---

[1] For details of this survey see Appendix 1.

possible number of 'votes' for each of the two was 765 whereas the actual number of 'votes' recorded was for mentors 554 and for models 578. Thus, one in four of the professors were unwilling or unable to name a mentor and a slightly smaller proportion either did not name three models or rejected the question.

Mentors

Most holders of sociology chairs in the UK universities, in 2001, had been educated in Britain. Accordingly, the mentors named in Table 9.1 are themselves likely to have held British posts. The twelve who received the most 'votes' include three (Hall, Shils, and Neustadt) who, though of foreign birth (West Indies, United States, and Russia), held posts at The Open University, London School of Economics (LSE), and Leicester. Otherwise the hierarchy of names is neither especially interesting nor easy to interpret. Time or period is a dominant factor: Glass could not have been taught by Lockwood nor Lockwood by Giddens nor could any of the three have taught Westermarck. A more revealing array of mentors appears in the first four columns of Table 9.1 where succeeding birth cohorts name their favourites.

TABLE 9.1 *Who have been your most important mentors during your career?*

Name	Birth cohort of respondent				
	Up to 1930	1931–44	1945–9	1950 on	Total
Glass, David	10	2	1	0	13
Titmuss, Richard	6	3	3	0	12
Halsey, A. H.	0	4	4	2	10
Hall, Stuart	0	3	3	3	9
Lockwood, David	0	4	3	2	9
Bernstein, Basil	0	4	3	0	7
Neustadt, Ilya	1	5	0	1	7
Townsend, Peter	4	3	0	0	7
Shils, Edward	0	5	2	0	7
Elias, Norbert	1	5	0	0	6
Giddens, Anthony	0	1	5	0	6
Macrae, Donald	2	2	1	1	6
Worsley, Peter	1	5	0	0	6
Bauman, Zigmunt	1	2	1	1	5
Cohen, Stanley	0	3	1	1	5
Gellner, Ernest	0	4	0	1	5
Ginsberg, Morris	4	1	0	0	5
Gluckman, Max	4	1	0	0	5

Note: Respondents were asked to name three mentors and the table shows all those individuals receiving five or more nominations.

Source: A. H. Halsey survey, 2001.

Inevitably, with time, mentors come and go. Hobhouse, Westermarck, and possibly Geddes were presumably the only available tutors in Britain before the First World War. In our survey, in 2001, Westermarck and Geddes disappeared and Hobhouse got only one 'vote' from the survivors of the first cohort (those born before 1931). The rows of Table 9.1 show the rise and fall of individuals through career, retirement, and death, with Stuart Hall, Lockwood, and Halsey as the most conspicuous long-distance runners.

Those respondents who were born up to 1930 almost invariably attended LSE as undergraduates or graduate students where Glass, Titmuss, Shils, and Ginsberg taught. Max Gluckman, though an anthropologist, was still remembered by as many future professors of sociology as anyone who taught this cohort except for Glass and for Titmuss who, though not appointed to his LSE chair until 1950, taught or influenced several later holders of chairs in social policy.

The second cohort (born 1931–45) mostly entered chairs in the 1970s and remembered tutelage most fondly from Shils (LSE), Worsley (Hull and Manchester), Elias and Neustadt (Leicester), Bernstein (Institute of Education, London), Lockwood (Cambridge and Essex), Gellner (LSE), and Halsey (Birmingham and Oxford). The third cohort (1945–9) began its professorial life in the 1980s and looked back most frequently to supervision from Halsey and Giddens (Cambridge). The fourth cohort (1951 +), the professorial recruits of the 1990s, had a wider tutelage than their predecessors with Hall, Halsey, and Lockwood as their favourite mentors.

All those named as past mentors have now died or retired, except for Giddens who became the director of LSE and served in that capacity for his last year in 2002–3.

What is most striking about the overall picture? Three things. First is the infrequent mention of any given person. Even the leader of the hierarchy, Glass, received only thirteen 'votes' and only ten out of a possible sixty-eight from the survivors of the first cohort. Famous names other than those listed in Table 9.1 certainly appear—Dore, Rex, Pahl, Goldthorpe, Burns, Abrams. Yet none of these attract more than four votes. Perhaps one has to conclude that these early (i.e. twentieth century) recruits to sociology chairs in Britain were largely self-taught. Influences, by direct teaching rather than the printed word, also tended to disappear among the younger professors who were born after 1949 and appointed to their chairs in the period after 1980.

Second, women are seldom named. Margaret Stacey, Jean Floud, Barbara Wootton, and Joan Woodward were all mentioned by the first cohort; Janet Finch, Margot Jeffreys, Mary Douglas, Sarah Arber, Claire Callender, and Leonora Davidoff by second cohort; Marie Jahoda by third cohort; Jennifer Platt, Jane Lewis, and Patricia Carlen by the fourth cohort. But in almost every case there was no more than one vote.

Foreign mentors are also rare, except those like Popper or Gellner who were refugees from the Nazis. From America Shils is prominent, though some British professors have been exposed to American teaching in US universities as graduate students. Hence, the admittedly rare appearance of names like Lipset, Bendix, or Merton.

Models

The story about models is quite different from that about mentors, and underlines the international character of sociology as a discipline. It is presented arithmetically in Table 9.2.

The balance of cited models (those who contributed most to the subject) was overwhelmingly in favour of foreigners, especially the German Max Weber (ninety-two 'votes'), the Frenchman Emile Durkheim (forty-three 'votes') and the American Talcott Parsons (thirty-seven 'votes'). By comparison with the hierarchy of mentors it must be noted that the top three of the latter (Glass, Titmuss, and Halsey) disappeared and were replaced by the distinguished foreign fathers of the subject.

The only Briton to offer a serious challenge in the opinion of the British professoriate of 2001 was Anthony Giddens. Giddens' international fame is remarkable: he appears in Table 9.2 in sixth place below Weber, Durkheim,

TABLE 9.2 *In the world as a whole, which sociologists in the twentieth century have contributed most to the subject?*[a]

Name	Birth cohort of respondent				
	Up to 1930	1931–44	1945–9	1950 on	Total
Weber, Max	16	31	27	18	92
Durkheim, Emile	14	14	12	3	43
Parsons, Talcott	5	12	13	7	37
Merton, Robert	5	15	5	5	30
Goffman, Erving	1	11	7	7	26
Giddens, Anthony	0	4	9	6	19
Mills, C. Wright	4	9	4	2	19
Bourdieu, Pierre	2	3	10	3	18
Simmel, Georg	2	4	5	4	15
Habermas, Jurgen	0	2	7	4	13
Foucault, Michel	2	6	3	1	12
Becker, Howard	0	5	2	3	10
Marx, Karl[b]	5	2	2	1	10
Lockwood, David	0	5	2	0	7
Bauman, Zigmunt	2	1	2	2	7
Elias, Norbert	0	5	0	1	6
Castells, Manuel	0	3	3	0	6

Notes:

[a] Respondents were asked to name three contributors and the table shows all those individuals receiving six or more nominations.

[b] Not, of course, a twentieth-century figure, but nevertheless given ten votes by our learned professors.

Source: A. H. Halsey survey, 2001.

Parsons, Merton, and Goffman. He attracted nineteen 'votes' and ties with the American C. Wright Mills, beating the Frenchman Bourdieu (eighteen) and the Germans Simmel (fifteen) and Habermas (thirteen), as well as the Frenchman Foucault (twelve) and the American Howard Becker (ten). Not until we get down to seven 'votes' does another Englishman appear—Lockwood in a tie with Bauman for the thirteenth place in the hierarchy. It is not that other famous British people were never cited; Hobhouse, Spencer, and Beatrice Webb were remembered, if only by one respondent in each case. It is that no one received even five 'votes', not even Goldthorpe or Runciman. And no other woman got more than one, indeed only Mary Douglas and Margot Jeffreys received even that marginal level of recognition as an outstanding contributor.

Citation Analysis

To gain a snapshot of influences we sampled the core British sociology journals in every decade of the twentieth century: the *Sociological Review*, the *British Journal of Sociology* (*BJS*), and *Sociology*.[2] The three journals we use are 'assumed to reflect in a significant way the pattern of British sociological research' and, while these journals are not the only form of sociological writing,[3] and academics from other fields publish in sociology journals and vice versa, 'research work reported in article form and of central interest to sociologists will tend to find its way to one or other of them' (Collison and Webber, 1971: 522).[4]

We selected all articles that were ten pages or more in length (including notes), and so a few review articles are included. The sample totals 399 papers but, once we subtract twenty-eight articles that do not have a bibliography, endnotes, or footnotes, this number falls to 371. Data were collected from the bibliographies of articles from the first volume of 2000 onwards, when this style of referencing became standard in all journals. In the earlier years, either bibliographies, endnotes, or footnotes were used. All referenced works were added to our database, although editors of books are excluded as we have taken citations to book chapters to belong to the author(s) alone.

Our data differ from those which would be gained from the Institute of Scientific Information (ISI) methods. For example, in the case of co-authorship, ISI provides data for the first author only, while we include a weighting for all authors. We take a cited book or paper as a 'text unit' (Collison and Webber, 1971) and allocate a single author one point for a work, two joint authors half a point each, three authors a third of a point each, and so on. Like ISI, we include

---

[2] A more general discussion of the techniques of citation analysis and their limitations by Claire Donovan appears below at Appendix 3.

[3] Books are excluded as sources of data, and there is no existing database of references from books (Hicks, 1999). While we acknowledge that a mainstream journal-based analysis does not represent the whole of British sociology's output, journal bibliographies do cite books so we are at least able to chart their impact in this context.

[4] We did not sample specialist journals.

TABLE 9.3 *A comparison of ISI methods with the Donovan/Halsey method applied to the 1990 and 2000 sample*

Year	Name	ISI%	Rank	Name	New%	Rank
1990	Goldthorpe, John H.	36	1	Giddens, Anthony	17	1
	Weber, Max	32	2	Weber, Max	16	2
	Giddens, Anthony	27	3	Goldthorpe, John H.	15.5	3
	Turner, Bryan S.	25	4	Goffman, Erving	15	4
	Marshall, Gordon	23	5	Marshall, Gordon	14 (s)	5
2000	Bourdieu, Pierre	66	1	Giddens, Anthony	37	1
	Giddens, Anthony	63	2	Bourdieu, Pierre	27	2
	Castells, Manuel	42	3	Castells, Manuel	25 (s)	3
	Beck, Ulrich	32	=4	Bauman, Zigmunt	21	4
	Foucault, Michel	32	=4	Beck, Ulrich	17.5 (s)	5

Note: (s) = 1 self-citation.

self-citation in our data, although we show where this occurs should anyone wish to exclude them from our findings. While there is a distinct upward trend in levels of self-citation within our sample, this does not significantly affect the outcome of our analysis.

In comparison with ISI methods, the most striking difference is that we take into account the distribution of citations. Like ISI we only allow a paper to make one citation to a specific work, and while we also record every reference a paper makes, unlike ISI our analysis allows for only one citation to a solo author or a particular writing collaboration. This method enables us to assess how citations are distributed throughout the whole sample and we avoid simply recording the total frequency of citations, which are liable to be skewed by one or a few bibliographies. Table 9.3 demonstrates how the ISI method compares with our study for 1990 and 2000.[5]

That the names of the top five closely overlap reflects the tendency of citation analysis to favour a handful of highly cited researchers. Although we are dealing with a relatively small number of papers (seventy-five in 1990 and 100 in 2000), different results emerge and it is clear that ISI methods can mislead in any attempt to measure the breadth of influence of certain sociologists. The inclusion of self-citations is controversial. ISI practice is to include self-referencing but not to indicate where this occurs. Our approach allows for, and identifies, self-citation. This is particularly significant in 1990 when Bryan Turner wrote two articles and cites himself nine times. Using our approach the nine citations become two (one for each paper) and, when other multiple citations are accounted for, Turner falls out of the top five (to joint ninth or, should self-citation be excluded, to tenth position).

[5] For Table 9.3, 1990 and 2000 data were collected manually and analysed using standard ISI techniques and the Donovan/Halsey method.

Accounting for the distribution of citations produces the most marked difference between ISI practice and ours. ISI findings may give the impression that an author is very widely cited when only mentioned by a few people many times (perhaps including himself or herself). Studying only the frequency of citations does not allow us to understand levels of influence across the discipline, but when one author or one particular writing collaboration is counted only once per sample paper, patterns of influence can be distinguished. The result is that the number of citations is greatly reduced as this reflects the percentage of papers which cite an individual. When we add a weighting for joint works, giving equal credit to all contributors, this may boost or reduce people's citation counts. Thus, in 1990, Goldthorpe and Giddens exchange places and Goffman displaces Turner. The impact is more marked in 2000 where Bourdieu is demoted to second place and is replaced by Giddens, while Foucault disappears altogether and Bauman becomes the fourth most cited sociologist.

Combining both author weightings and the distribution of citations provides a different picture of the development of sociology in Britain from that offered by ISI. Once we establish who were the most widely cited sociologists we work backwards to reveal their most influential works. Tables 9.4 and 9.5 show the most widely cited authors in our sample, and for each year the authors are ranked from one to ten.

Pre-1950 Citations

In the period before 1950, the only journal was the *Sociological Review*, and it was not a convention for journal articles to have a bibliography although some papers use footnotes for referencing. In 1910, 1920, and 1930 there is no replication of names between the references of sample papers, although we can find common influences within the text of the papers in 1930 when four cite Patrick Geddes (50 per cent) although one counts as a self-reference, a further four cite Le Play (50 per cent), three mention Comte and Plato (38 per cent), while two refer to Hobbes, Marx, J. S. Mill, and the French historian Lucien Romier (22 per cent). These shared references reflect the common interests of a small group of writers bound together by their belief in Le Playism and Geddes' version of evolution. Classical references are common. There is no apparent shared interest in contemporary empirical research, although it is noteworthy that the foundational works of Comte and Marx are cited. There is no such consensus in 1940, where the only replicated name is Geddes who is mentioned in two papers, and the only journals to receive shared references belong to anthropology.

Post-1950 Citations

Table 9.4 presents the results of a citation analysis for 1950, 1960, and 1970. In these years the numbers are very small, a fact often lost when citation analyses

TABLE 9.4 *The most highly cited authors 1950–70*

Year	Rank	Name	N citation weighting	% distribution
1950	1	Ginsberg, Morris	4.5	21
	=2	Hogben, Lancelot	3	14
	=2	Malinowski, Bronislaw	3	14
	=2	Mill, John Stuart	3	14
	=3	Blackburn, Julian M.	2	10
	=3	Burt, Cyril	2 (s)	10
	=3	Cattell, Raymond B.	2	10
	=3	Centers, Richard	2	10
	=3	Eysenck, Hans	2 (s)	10
	=3	Galton, Francis	2	10
	=3	McDougall, William	2	10
	=3	Thompson, Godfrey	2	10
	=3	Toynbee, Arnold	2	10
1960	1	Parsons, Talcott	4	16
	2	Merton, Robert K.	2.3	9
	3	Young, Michael	2	8
1970	1	Parsons, Talcott	21.5	39
	2	Merton, Robert K.	12	22
	3	Durkheim, Emile	10	18
	4	Weber, Max	9	17
	5	Lockwood, David	8.75	16
	6	Gouldner, Alvin	8	15
	=7	MacIntyre, Alasdair	6	11
	=7	Mills, C. Wright	6	11
	=9	Aron, Raymond	5	9
	=9	Goode, William J.	5	9

Note: (s) = one self-citation.
Source: Analysis of core British sociology journals.

present percentages only. The findings should therefore be treated with appropriate caution.

1950 saw the introduction of a new mainstream sociology journal, the *British Journal of Sociology*. Twenty-one papers are sampled in this year and two factors are immediately apparent: one is the influence of the LSE and the other is the fact that only one of the thirteen authors, Morris Ginsberg, would now be counted as a sociologist. Several papers discuss psychology and education, particularly IQ and heredity, accounting for the high number of psychologists cited. The impact of the LSE is apparent in the top three most cited authors, with Ginsberg mentioned by 21 per cent of papers, followed jointly by Hogben and Malinowski with 14 per cent each. However, the actual distribution of

TABLE 9.5 *The most highly cited authors 1980–2000*

Year	Rank	Name	N citation weighting	% distribution
1980	1	Marx, Karl	15	20
	2	Weber, Max	12	16
	3	Giddens, Anthony	11	14
	4	Parsons, Talcott	10	13
	5	Parkin, Frank	9	12
	=6	Lukes, Steven	8	10.5
	=6	Mills, C. Wright	8	10.5
	8	Goldthorpe, John H.	7.5	10
	=9	Douglas, J.	7	9
	=9	Hindess, Barry	7	9
1990	1	Giddens, Anthony	12.3	17
	2	Weber, Max	12	16
	3	Goldthorpe, John H.	11.5	15.5
	4	Goffman, Erving	11	15
	5	Marshall, Gordon	10.25 (s)	14
	=6	Douglas, Mary	9	12
	=6	Pahl, Ray	9	12
	8	Parsons, Talcott	8	11
	=9	Saunders, Peter	7 (s)	10
	=9	Turner, Bryan S.	7 (ss)	10
2000	1	Giddens, Anthony	37	37
	2	Bourdieu, Pierre	27	27
	3	Castells, Manuel	25 (s)	25
	4	Bauman, Zigmunt	21	21
	5	Beck, Ulrich	17.5 (s)	17.5
	6	Foucault, Michel	15	15
	=7	Goldthorpe, John H.	14	14
	=7	Habermas, Jurgen	14	14
	9	Hall, Stuart	13	13
	10	Latour, Bruno	12.5 (s)	12.5

Notes: (s) = one self-citation, (ss) = two self-citations.

citations is small, with Ginsberg receiving 4.5 'points', and only two for the same text, *Reason and Unreason in Society*. Hogben's *Political Arithmetic* was the key text of 1950 with three citations, while Malinowski was mentioned for *Scientific Theory of Culture* twice. Although we may infer little from such low numbers it is noteworthy that references to Ginsberg are shared almost evenly between the *Sociological Review* and the *BJS*, while the former cites Malinowski and the latter Hogben, hinting perhaps at an early qualitative and quantitative divide.

In 1960, the sample size is twenty-five, only three authors were cited twice or more, and they are recognized readily today as sociologists. We begin to chart the rise of American functionalism, though while Parsons and Merton are the most widely cited sociologists the numbers are again small and none of their works are referred to more than once. Michael Young receives a weighting worth two full citations, although half of his total derives from Young and Willmott's *Family and Kinship in East London* (1957), which is mentioned twice.

In 1970, the sample increases to fifty-five papers, including the fourth volume of *Sociology*. American functionalism was again a dominant influence as Parsons is cited by 39 per cent of papers and Merton by 22 per cent, followed by European functionalism as expressed by Durkheim (18 per cent). Parsons' most widely used works were his *Structure of Social Action* (1937) and *The Social System* (1951), while Merton's core text was *Social Theory and Social Structure* (1949), and Durkheim's influence is found in a fairly broad range of references although *The Elementary Forms of Religious Life* (1915) and *The Rules of Sociological Method* (1938) dominate. Similarly, several of Weber's texts were referred to but *The Theory of Economic and Social Organisation* (1964) was favoured. David Lockwood was mentioned for two main works, a paper in the *Sociological Review* entitled 'Sources of Variation in Working Class Images of Society' (1966) and his *The Black-Coated Worker* (1958). There were some collaborative efforts cited several times such as the *Affluent Worker* (1968/9) series (9 per cent) and Burns and Stalker's *The Management of Innovation* (1961) (9 per cent). It is noticeable that in 1970 anthropology and urban sociology were reasonably fashionable areas of study.

Table 9.5 presents the findings of the citation analysis from 1980 onwards, and the sample size rose to seventy-seven, seventy-five, and then 100 papers. This table brings out the importance of foundational European sociology with Marx at 20 per cent and Weber at 16 per cent.[6] It also signals a break with the dominance of functionalism in favour of radical and interpretive sociology. Marx's most cited work was *Capital* (1933) and Weber's was *Economy and Society* (1968), while Giddens lies in third place with 14 per cent of papers citing his work, most notably *The Class Structure of Advanced Societies* (1973) and *New Rules of Sociological Method* (1976). The year 1980 was the last sample year in which a non-European sociologist appears, when Parsons was the fourth most cited sociologist (13 per cent) although no particular text was favoured. Stratification and the study of the workplace and occupations were favoured research areas, and Frank Parkin attracted a 12 per cent citation rate with his *Class Inequality and Political Order* (1971) while the *Affluent Worker* study was the most cited collaborative work (6.5 per cent).

The year 1990 was the first in which a native sociologist was the most widely cited, and while Weber was second (16 per cent), other classic authors such as Marx and Durkheim did not figure at all. Weber was the only foreign sociologist

---

[6] The number of citations of Weber is significantly boosted by a special edition of the *BJS* 'Aspects of Weberian Scholarship' 31/3, September 1980.

among the top ten. Giddens was cited in 17 per cent of the sample papers for a wide range of his writings, but mostly for *The Constitution of Society* (1984), while Weber was cited mostly for *Economy and Society*. John Goldthorpe was third (15.5 per cent) and is unusual because, in addition to his books, he was cited for various contributions to debates on stratification in *Sociology*. He was followed by Goffman (15 per cent), usually for *The Presentation of Self in Everyday Life* (1971), while Gordon Marshall on stratification (14 per cent) was mentioned in several journal articles and a co-authored book *Social Class in Modern Britain*, the most widely cited joint work in this year (9 per cent). In 1990 also there was a strong field of British sociologists, and alongside an enduring preoccupation with social theory there was a resurgence of research into social stratification, largely manifested by a series of debates in *Sociology*, the journal which cites Giddens, Goldthorpe, and Marshall more often than the other journals combined. The *BJS* cites Weber and Goffman most highly (albeit marginally), again demonstrating that empirical work most often finds its way to *Sociology* while the *BJS* remains the likely although not exclusive home of interpretive sociology, and the *Sociological Review* occupies a middle ground.

In 2000, the most highly cited sociologists were European and mostly representing social theory, particularly modernist and postmodernist debates. In this final year of the twentieth century, there was most consensus within the distribution of citations with over a third of papers citing Giddens (37 per cent), over a quarter citing Bourdieu (27 per cent) and Castells (25 per cent), a fifth mentioning Bauman (21 per cent), and almost one in six papers referring to Beck (17.5 per cent). A very wide range of Giddens' books was referred to, in particular *The Constitution of Society* (1984), *The Consequences of Modernity* (1990), *Modernity and Self Identity* (1991), and *Central Problems in Social Theory* (1979). Several of Bourdieu's texts were noted, particularly *Distinction: A Social Critique of the Judgement of Taste* (1984a), while Castells' *The Rise of the Network Society* (1996) was his most popular work. Bauman's favoured publication was *Globalization: The Human Consequences* (1998) and Beck's was *Risk Society: Towards a New Modernity* (1992). There were several frequently cited collaborative works including Scott Lash and John Urry's *Economies of Signs and Space* (1994) (8 per cent), Held *et al. Global Transformations* (1999) (6 per cent), Beck *et al. Reflexive Modernisation* (1994) (5 per cent), and, surprisingly, Berger and Luckmann's *Social Construction of Reality* (1967) (6 per cent). With the exception of Bourdieu, the *Sociological Review* was the least likely to cite the top five sociologists, and a high proportion of reflexive social theory found its way to *Sociology*, whereas previously this would have been the *BJS's* preserve. The year 1990 finds the only woman, Mary Douglas, in the rankings for various works, particularly those associated with the sociology of religion.

The post-1950 trend was away from the institutional dominance of the LSE, to a theoretical preoccupation with American functionalism, which was in turn replaced by attention to the European 'founding fathers', to British interests in either social theory or empirical sociology (directed to stratification and occupational sociology in particular) and to some symbolic interactionism.

Then from around 1980 there was a flirtation with British and European social theory concerned with modernity and postmodernity. There was less reference to American sociology than might be expected. The rankings were completely male dominated with the exception of Mary Douglas in 1990. The most widely cited texts were books and not journal papers, although there was a tendency for highly cited empirical sociology to appear in journal form. While there was some separation between the kinds of sociology we would expect to find in the journals, with *Sociology* representing more empirical work, the *BJS* publishing more interpretive studies, and the *Sociological Review* maintaining a middle ground, this division appears to have broken down by 2000. While widely mentioned sociologists were valued for their books rather than papers, the trend was away from reference to foundational works and towards contemporary debates. This contradicts the recent view (Hargens, 2000) that sociology is out of touch with contemporary thought.

Future research may reveal precisely how twentieth-century sociologists used citations. Whether or not authors refer to empirical evidence or make totemic genuflections to their 'models' or 'mentors', our analysis presents the sum total of individual choices and is a map of influence that draws together an often divided discipline.

Conclusion

To sum up this chapter, a survey of all UK professors and a citation analysis of British sociology journals reveal who were the most celebrated sociologists in this country during the twentieth century. While British names dominate those who have taught or inspired (Glass, Titmuss, Halsey, Hall, Lockwood), the survey and the citation study combine to demonstrate that, in terms of their contribution to the subject, the most influential sociologists in Britain were increasingly German (Weber, Marx, Beck, Habermas) and French (Durkheim, Bourdieu, Foucault). American impact waned and a new generation of European figures emerged. The notable British figure is Giddens, both for his role as mentor and model and his leading position in citation patterns.

Influential sociologists, 'models' rather than 'mentors', are characterized by their contribution to social theory more than by specialized empirical work. It may be hoped that, in the twenty-first century, the link between theory and research will bring this division to an end; that theory may become more exact and rigorously tested by evidence.

10

The Shape of Sociology

Introduction

W E HAVE already seen how the institutional shape of sociology in Britain changed from 1900 to 2000. There was a bright start at LSE, with Hobhouse and Urwick before the Great War. It stagnated in the inter-war years and then was admitted belatedly to academic respectability: the number of students grew after Robbins in the 1960s, faltered in the 1970s and 1980s, and expanded in the 1990s with the incorporation of the polytechnics and the other institutions of higher education. Research resources and institutes also multiplied, funded by departments of government, the University Grants Committee (UGC), the Social Science Research Council (SSRC), and the private foundations such as Rowntree, Leverhulme, and Nuffield. In this chapter we turn to substance. Did not only people multiply but also their theories?

Compare the content of the first British sociology journal, the *Sociological Review*, launched by the Sociological Society in 1908 with its Volume 48 published in 2000. At first glance the reader is faced by two totally different worlds and certainly in the early years the net was cast wider to include anthropology, economics, political science, social psychology, and history. At second glance, however, the difference seems to be more linguistic than conceptual. The Edwardians were addicted to classical allusion and traditional English:[1] the late Elizabethans used strange new words and phrases such as structuration (taken from Giddens), governmentality (taken from Foucault), class-specific habitus (taken from Bourdieu), and the cultural turn (taken from philosophy). In this chapter, we can pursue this general hypothesis: that people came in increasing numbers but that their ideas and explanations were static or oscillating through fashion as the century wore on. For example, there was an article published by F. G. D'Aeth in the *Sociological Review* of 1910 which had been delivered as a paper before the Sociological Society in the previous year. Compared with any contemporary paper in the field of stratification, it illustrates our general thesis that people and methods change but ideas remain much the same. The modern reader is struck by its amateur quality, its bold, wide coverage of the field, its presentation of empirical evidence describing the 'old' and the

---

[1] Thus, Hobhouse in his editorial reminds the readers that 'nothing that is human is foreign' and space is found for advertising French, German, Italian, and other sociological journals of the day.

'new' class structure of Britain, its use of income statistics and of marriage registers presented confidently without any notion of percentages, representation, or the need for large-scale surveys, the absence of explanatory and methodological concepts now taken for granted, like meritocracy, perfect mobility, inflow and outflow, and so on. And yet at the same time marriage, size of town, education, and ambition as causal variables or determinants of mobility are all included without hesitation in his analysis.

Over the course of the century this topic-cum-sub-discipline was to become specialized and statistically sophisticated in method without discernible advance in theory, but with continuing commitment to empiricism, to increasing precision, and perhaps also to the moral search for a classless society. Thus, by 2000, Geoffrey Evans and Colin Mills were writing in the *BJS* a careful assessment of Goldthorpe's classificatory schema of classes and Adam Swift contributed an article on 'Class Analysis from a Normative Perspective' in which he specifies the concept of equality (Swift, 2000). All authors, 1910 and 2000, are widely if differently read, but those writing at the end of the century are professionalized in that they refer exactly and copiously to the relevant literature and they use or assume knowledge of sophisticated statistical methods. More generally our narrative history has provided evidence on which we shall draw. But now we can exploit a further source of evidence bearing on our general thesis—the content analysis of journals.

The new source, however, is not comprehensively adequate to our purpose. The journals lack books which, as a medium of communication, have been estimated to total one-third of social science publication, more than the natural sciences but less than the humanities. It may be that, in the early decades of the twentieth century when sociology was dominated by Hobhouse's orthogenic evolutionism, the impact of the books mentioned in Chapter 3 was paramount. Certainly the description below of the first half of the century as dominated by empiricism is based on articles in the *Sociological Review* rather than on books. The Hobhousian legacy, though backed always by empiricism, was first and foremost one of anti-Spencerian evolution.

Missing too are specialized journals which multiplied to over 160 during the century, mainly to meet the needs of newly fashionable or newly developed perceptions of society, such as *Marxism Today* or *Feminist Review* or *Work, Employment and Society*. Multiplication of specialist journals accelerated towards the end of the century, aided by advances in printing technology but driven by a constant flow of innovatory methods, or areas of study, or at least new words. For example, the disputed fashion of interest in globalization led to an advertisement by Blackwell in association with the Economic and Social Research Council (ESRC) for a new journal beginning in 2001 under the title '*Global Networks: A Journal of Transnational Affairs*'. Moreover there are further limitations of content analysis discussed by Claire Donovan below in Appendix 3.

We cannot emphasize too much the limitations of content analysis. Mary Douglas (1987: 69) has maintained that 'the construction of past time . . . has very little to do with the past at all and everything to do with the present'. The element of truth in this observation bears on our construction of categories whether of topics, methods, or 'isms' (the underlying ideology that determines the substance of an article). Take, for example, the noticeable decline in the 1980s and 1990s in research on the sociology of industry and the switch of attention to economic organization. Behind this labelling change lies a marked fall in recruitment of students and scholars to sociology in the 1980s and a no less marked rise of management courses. Martin Parker at the University of Keele has turned an analysis of terminology into reflections on his own identity as one who used to be a sociologist but now earns his living in a business school (Parker, 2000). What emerges is an interesting account of shifting disciplinary boundaries, the creation of a new sub-discipline, the process of forgetting as an aid thereto, and the intellectual costs and benefits involved.

Parker is at pains to point out that no sin of neglect in scholarship is alleged, and he is sensitive to the danger of dismissal as a deserter from sociology to management. But the consequence of this institutional shift for students may be an impoverishment of their historical knowledge along with a distancing, even hostile distancing, of the 'old' from the 'new' discipline. Thus, he recounts the rise of 'organisational culture' to replace the sociology of organization. The eighty years of sociological literature from Weber to such modern writers as Fox, Gallie, and Edwards tends to be ignored or represented as structuralist (i.e. concerned with rational models, organization charts, formal systems) and 'progress' is learnt as the recognition of cultural forces which are deemed to be essential to explain behaviour in factories and offices. He finds it easy to correct this misrepresentation, pointing to Weber's industrial studies and the widespread former use in sociology of such notions as 'climate', 'atmosphere', 'personality', 'informal structure', and Gouldner's 'natural system'—a body of work constituting serious discussion of the aspects of organizational life now allegedly 'discovered' as 'organisational culture'.

He asserts that, like himself, many staff of the business schools find it more difficult to publish in the three main British journals of sociology or in *Work, Employment and Society* than in *Organisation, Organisational Studies*, and a wide selection of journals with management in the title.

This is one example of the multiplication of sub-disciplines or even of entirely new disciplines, of which social policy is the obvious example, as the map of knowledge has evolved and is redrawn in response to an ever more complicated division of academic labour. Sociology itself was the product of such a process. It was, before Comte, the nameless outcome of developments in economics, politics, philosophy, and history. There is an analogy with Christianity which spread as Catholicism throughout Europe and beyond, was beset by schism, especially the Reformation of the sixteenth century, and subsequent further schisms within Protestantism into distinct sects and denominations. The break up of an ill-defined sociology has followed a similar pattern in the second half of the twentieth century, following an expansive initial invasion into the territories of economics, politics, genetics, and history. Social psychology has established itself as a discipline, anthropology and demography have maintained a separate existence, and history has differentiated a separate sub-discipline of social history.

From the same ill-defined sociology there has also arisen the question of whether any new movement is destined to be either first a mere fashion, or second a more established sub-discipline, or third even a new separate discipline. In the relatively brief history of sociology in Britain there have been five such movements with serious impact: Marxism, social policy, ethnomethodology, feminism, and cultural studies. The content analysis reported below offers clues as to whether the answers in each case lie clearly in one of the three directions.

The Journals and their History

Before presenting the evidence, however, a brief word on the history and editorship of the three main journals may be helpful. Volume 1 of the *Sociological Review* appeared in 1908 in place of the previously published papers of the Sociological Society and was edited by Hobhouse who resigned in 1910 and was succeeded by S. K. Ratcliffe and Victor Branford. The journal lived, like the subject itself, through hard times in the inter-war period, moved to Le Play House in 1920, and was run from 1934 by an editorial board made up of Carr-Saunders, Alexander Farquharson, and Ginsberg until after the Second World War. In 1953, it was taken over by the new University College of North Staffordshire (Keele) and run by senior members of the academic staff including W. A. C. Stewart, Ronnie Frankenberg, and John Eggleston. In the last four years of the century the managing editors were Sharon Macdonald and Dennis Smith.

The second main periodical, the *British Journal of Sociology* (*BJS*), was launched in 1950 at London School of Economics (LSE) by the then three professors, Ginsberg, Glass, and Marshall. In 1956, Macrae took over as managing editor followed by Terence Morris in 1965 and Angus Stewart in 1975. From 1981 Christopher Badcock, Leslie Sklair, and Percy Cohen served for shorter periods until Paul Rock was appointed in 1988, helped first by Ian Roxborough and then from 1991 by Stephen Hill who succeeded as editor in 1996, until 1999 when John Urry steered the journal to the end of the century.

Sociology was the third of the journals, appearing first in 1967. It was later to become the official journal of the British Sociological Association (BSA) in place of the *BJS*. Its first editor was Michael Banton followed by Goldthorpe in 1970 and Horobin in 1973.[2] The editorship was later scattered over the universities, and beginning with Abrams, followed the presidency of the BSA. Thus the original *Sociological Review* stemmed early in the century from the *Sociological Society*, the *BJS* was started at the LSE after the Second World War

---

[2] Philip Abrams took over in 1976, Martin Albrow 1982–4, Jennifer Platt 1985–8, Janet Finch and Nick Abercrombie 1989–90, David Morgan and Liz Stanley 1991–3, Joan Busfield and Ted Benton 1994–7, David Mason and Joan Chandler 1998–9, and Tony Spyby and Maggie O'Neill in 2000.

with the newly found confidence in sociology of that institution while the *Review* was resuscitated by enthusiasts at Keele. Then *Sociology* began in the late 1960s, independent of either the LSE or Keele but with ties to the BSA which transferred its patronage from the *BJS* and recruited editors from the country at large.

This history is worth recapitulating because a new editor and editorial board and the chosen referees will tend to shift the content of a journal from one area of research to another, and to favour or resist some new or revived interest or theoretical approach. A new movement will tend to differentiate itself from the tradition out of which it sprang. The word 'new' symbolizes or labels such a movement. Thus, the 'new criminology' and the 'new sociology of education' of the 1970s announced themselves more or less plausibly as departures from the established sub-disciplines of sociology against which they, more or less, successfully rebelled. Altogether then the results reported below must be interpreted with all the caution implied by the method employed.

Our analysis falls into three parts. We first consider continuities and shifts in the areas studied while fashions, sub-disciplines, and new disciplines have appeared. Second, we turn to the still hotly disputed question of whether to use quantitative and/or qualitative methods in the study of society. Third, we try to relate both methods and substance to the ideological approaches of journal authors.

Areas of Study

Sociology in the twentieth century has been made up of descriptions and theories about stratification, politics, religion, education, and the division of labour economically and domestically. Following established practice (Collison and Webber, 1971) we expanded the Sociological Abstracts Classification Scheme (SACS) adopted by Bath Information Data Services (BIDS) and divided sociology into thirty-eight fields (listed in Appendix 3), but in the text we refer only to those appearing most frequently in the three main sociology journals in Britain in the twentieth century. Eight of the thirty-eight stand out in this context. They are stratification (including social differentiation, class, status, mobility, and occupational scales), social theory (papers that do not use or discuss the use of sociological data), social policy, political sociology, religion (including paranormal behaviour and beliefs), education, economic organization (including industrial relations), occupations, and gender.

Table 10.1 and Fig. 10.1 show the trends from 1910 to 2000. The century as a whole was dominated by stratification, politics, and social theory. Stratification was the most popular subject in the post-war years followed by occupations and social theory, then political sociology was the strongest field in 1990 followed by social theory, stratification, gender, and economic organization which all featured in around 20 per cent of papers, and by 2000 social theory was the most popular field followed most closely by political sociology and gender.

TABLE 10.1 *Popular areas of sociology 1910–2000*

Area	1910–40		1950–70		1975–85		1990–5		2000		Total	
	%	Rank	%	Rank	%	Rank	%	Rank	%	Rank	%	Rank
Social theory	15	=2	17	3	24	1	25	2	31	1	23	1
Stratification	3	=8	31	1	22	2	24	=3	14	5	22	2
Political sociology	21	1	10	6	16	5	24	=3	25	2	19	3
Economic organization	9	4	12	5	19	4	17	5	16	4	16	4
Gender	3	=8	3	9	9	7	28	1	24	3	15	=5
Occupations	6	=5	19	2	20	3	12	8	7	7	15	=5
Education	6	=5	15	4	8	8	8	7	13	6	10	7
Religion	15	=2	7	8	11	6	6	9	4	=8	8	8
Social policy	6	=5	8	7	4	9	7	8	4	=8	6	9

Note: This table lists only the most numerically significant areas in each period.

Source: Content analysis of *Sociological Review, British Journal of Sociology*, and *Sociology*.

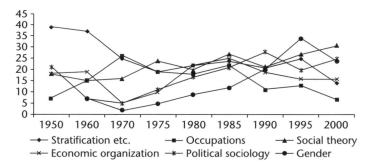

FIG. 10.1 Key trends 1950–2000, in per cent

Political sociology became increasingly popular after 1950, reaching a low of 5 per cent in 1970 and a high of 25 per cent in 2000. Social theory also climbed from 18 per cent in 1950 to 31 per cent in 2000, and was the most popular sociological field in 1975, 1985, and 2000. There was a rise in popularity of gender as a field of study from its beginning in 1970 to a peak of 34 per cent in 1995. However, some may ask at what point do considerations of gender constitute a specialist field or become the norm in sociological enquiry? Perhaps this is evidence of the assimilation rather than acceptance of an interest. In the case of social policy, as we shall see below, it was separation rather than assimilation that prevailed.

Figure 10.1 shows the six most highly featured fields of sociology since 1950 (stratification, occupations, social theory, economic organization, political sociology, and gender) and their distribution throughout the sample years. This chart demonstrates that the major preoccupations of sociology were linked with the division of labour in society, its organization and management, and its impact upon the social structure. Is it possible that Fig. 10.1 demonstrates the earlier ascendancy and later decline of the dominant sociology of the twentieth century, and that this old orthodoxy is being replaced by social and cultural theory?

In favour of this possibility it may be noted that John Urry introduced the first number of the *BJS* in the year 2000 (vol. 51: 1) noting 'a widespread sense that social-material transformations (were) occurring around the millennium that indicate a break in the development of human societies' and asking how 'sociology' was facing up to the challenge. He referred to 'the most recent analysis of such major social-material transformations, namely Castells' three-volume account of the "information age"'. Urry himself, in an article in the same number, advocated a 'post-societal sociology' with approving references to Castells' networks. Gosta Esping-Anderson contributed a notable further paper in which he opposes 'post something' sociology and urges the renewed use of serious comparative method. Recognizing the salute to Castells as 'the new Max Weber', he suggests that, if Castells succeeds, 'it may be because he is a Spaniard working in the USA'. But, in a footnote, Esping-Anderson adds the caution that 'it is not easy to establish whether one has got Castells' work right....Everything appears related to everything, and all of it seems of equal relevance'. Peter Abell and Diane Reyniers in the final number of *BJS* for 2000 went much further. In their 'On the failure of social theory' they acknowledged Castells' international fame, but put forward a blistering attack on his 'profoundly unclear' style of writing, 'the evocation of neologism and epigrammatic phrases... (timeless time).... This volume (vol.1) provides nothing but unendurably extended description without any form of analysis or attempt at formulating a genuine theory' (Abell and Reynier, 2000). Here is the authentic voice of 'classical' sociology. It challenges any 'broad church' view of social theory and cultural studies as permissible variants of sociology.

At root we are again confronted with the original struggle between two definitions of sociology—the scientific search for explanation and the literary effort towards interpretation. This was our second theme in the introduction, elaborated in Chapters 1 and 2. We have now added evidence from a content analysis of the three main journals of sociology in Britain. Table 10.1 and Fig. 10.1 do not demonstrate an unequivocal victory for either side. Both explanatory studies (especially of stratification and the division of labour) *and* interpretative essays in social theory have flourished with fluctuating fortunes throughout the twentieth century. Like the Chinese historian who was asked to decide on the success of the French Revolution of 1789, we can only say that it is too early to judge whether social (interpretative) or sociological (explanatory) theory is the victor. We are, nonetheless, left with the question of future institutional unity or schism. Meanwhile we can turn to the related third theme of our introduction.

Methods of Study

Our approach here derives from Martin Bulmer's exploration of the relation between theory and method in the British sociology of the 1980s. From an examination of the *BJS* in 1986 and 1987 he reported (1989) that twenty-one out of fifty-two articles were classified as purely theoretical, that is, concerned exclusively with abstract and general issues or with issues in the history of social thought. *All* lacked significant empirical data, whether historical or contemporary. Articles with titles such as 'Weber and Mommsen: Non-Marxist materialism', 'Recent Marxist Theories of Nationalism and the Issue of Racism', and 'The Idea of Crisis in Modern Society', Bulmer argues, may make important contributions to internal theoretical debates but they do not *directly* illuminate the state of contemporary society. There were, he notes, a further twenty-four articles which did contain systematically assembled empirical data, on the basis of which more general interpretations were advanced. There were seven historical articles.

He observes that theory (of a particular kind) made a strong showing, but method was almost totally absent as a topic in its own right. In the two years examined, there was only one substantial article on method, concerned with social class classification. No doubt this reflected submissions, but it is also evidence of a wider malaise. He identifies this as an ambivalence of British sociologists towards quantification, which is one aspect of methodological competence. The report of the ESRC study group on *Horizons and Opportunities in the Social Sciences*, examining their medium-term future, had observed in 1987 that: 'There is a real worry that in some subjects (sociology and political science for example) researchers are not as numerate as their colleagues overseas and that the gap is widening... at worst some social scientists appear to show not only indifference but disdain for statistical training' (ESRC, 1987: 7).

Thus, Bulmer comments that, in the *BJS* issues studied, twenty out of the twenty-four articles with systematic empirical data contained some quantitative material, but only eight of these were by British sociologists. There was a greater likelihood of the author of such articles being based either outside Great Britain or if in Britain coming from another discipline such as demography or economic history.

Bechhofer too has interested himself in the question of the use of empirical data and of advancing quantitative technique in sociology. He extended Bulmer's coverage to study the three main British journals in 1977–9 and 1992–4 and arrived at similar conclusions, sharing Bulmer's alarm. He noted that the published articles had become more empirical over the fifteen years between his first and second enquiries (Bechhofer, 1981, 1996), but that the increase was attributable to qualitative rather than quantitative studies. And he agreed with Bulmer that a substantial proportion of the more sophisticated statistical articles were of foreign authorship. He emphasized particularly that undergraduates were not normally and systematically trained in advanced techniques, quantitative or qualitative.

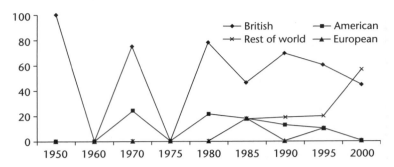

FIG. 10.2 Nationality and high quantification, in per cent

Bulmer and Bechhofer make a strong case but it has to be modified by the wider coverage of our content analysis below and by the ESRC initiative on research training mentioned at the end of Chapter 2 above. Let us look first at the evidence on origins of contributors.

Though the records before 1960 are unreliable, it is clear from our more extended analysis that UK authorship was dominant, although North American contributions remained significant along with European and Australian efforts. The use of high quantification such as log linear modelling and regression analysis, though a minority of contributions since 1950, has been predominantly of British as distinct from of American, European, or other foreign origin (Fig. 10.2).

An Extension of Bulmer

Looking back at the journals before the Second World War is to see a weird world of incoherent method in sociology. We should not be surprised. There was only one academic institution, LSE, in which sociology was formally recognized[3] and only one journal, the *Sociological Review*, which was increasingly centred on the interests of Geddes in Le Play. In 1910, there were twelve papers, half of which would not be called sociological as now (2004) understood but rather representing political theory, anthropology, history, or political advocacy. Nevertheless we treated them all as sociology, allocating them all to our present day (2000) categories. Not one of the 1910 authors would be recognized as a sociologist in recent times. W. H. R. Rivers was a distinguished anthropologist and J. A. Hobson a no less famous political economist but all the others, including S. K. Ratcliffe, have now disappeared from view. Nor did the scene seriously change in the inter-war years, when Geddes contributed an

---

[3] When we consider the impact of particular institutions we see that British universities provided most contributors. The LSE was invariably the institution that provided the most authors. During the period 1940–2000 the stated department or discipline of authors was never solely 'sociology'. Explicit identification with 'sociology' was at its lowest in 1940 (11 per cent) and its highest in 1990 (59 per cent). In 2000, half of the authors of the papers in our sample labelled themselves 'sociologists'.

article in 1920 and Branford in 1930. Only in 1940 was there the hint of the future in store when Ginsberg and Mess each published an article.

Using our extended sample we can comment on developments of method in what we may term 'mainstream journal British sociology'. Bulmer classified three main types of paper:

- Theory only—where the article has no empirical content.
- Empirical—where the paper provides some systematic observation. This includes qualitative as well as quantitative research.
- Quantitative—where the paper uses a sophisticated analysis or manipulation of data, that is, it goes beyond description. Again, this category may include qualitative research.

We chose to expand the range of Bulmer's categories to include:

- Theory only—where the article offers no empirical content (the remaining papers are necessarily 'empirical').
- Quantitative—any paper that uses quantitative methods alone (later divided into descriptive, low, and high quantification).
- Qualitative—any paper that employs solely qualitative methods.
- Both—work that combines quantitative and qualitative methods.

The categories used in the 649 papers in our sample are summarized in Table 10.2.

During the twentieth century 'theory only' papers tended to dominate the journals, except for the years 1940, 1960, and 1995. These articles discuss social

TABLE 10.2 *Methods used in British journal articles 1910–2000*

Methods	1910–40		1950–70		1975–85		1990–5		2000		Total	
	N	%	N	%	N	%	N	%	N	%	N	%
Theory only	25	74	56	50	138	59	80	47	54	54	353	54
Quantitative	6	18	28	25	37	16	34	20	17	17	122	19
Descriptive	8	100	31	58	44	63	33	59	15	60	131	62
Low	0	0	13	25	6	9	5	9	1	4	25	12
High	0	0	7	13	19	27	16	29	9	36	51	24
Theory & high quant.	0	0	2	4	1	1	2	4	0	0	5	2
Qualitative	1	34	8	7	32	14	38	22	22	22	101	16
(a) Anthropological	3	100	12	41	34	59	45	80	26	93	120	69
(b) Other	0	0	17	59	24	41	11	20	2	7	54	31
Both qual. and quant.	2	6	20	18	25	11	18	11	8	8	73	11

Notes: 'Quantitative' and 'qualitative' include papers that are both quantitative and qualitative, as do quantitative (descriptive, low, and high) and qualitative (anthropological and other).

Source: See Table 10.1.

theory or sociological theory, assess the state of a particular field of sociology, or review the literature in an area of sociology. In the period since 1950, 1975 is the year when, as a proportion of each journal's output, the most theory only papers were published. The *BJS* tended to publish more theoretical work, while *Sociological Review* and *Sociology* were the more likely homes for empirical research.

Papers published in the three journals, therefore, moved gradually as the twentieth century wore on away from a focus on theory towards an equal division of purely theoretical work and empirical research. The role of female contributors was important here. Since 1950, women have made a larger contribution to all sociological approaches and have been more likely to engage in work that combines both quantitative and qualitative methods, followed by purely qualitative research. Women's contribution to theory rose from 13 to 22 per cent, while their previously small representation in the proportion of qualitative papers grew to 44 per cent in 2000. They were more active in empirical than theoretical work, and increasing numbers were involved in quantitative projects (either purely quantitative or combined with qualitative methods), and in this respect women departed from the conventions of journal publishing in science and the humanities in that they were more and more likely to write 'scientific' papers.

Quantification

While noting that qualitative papers outnumbered quantitative papers in 1995 and 2000, we now concentrate on quantitative methods, which are divided into four main categories:

Descriptive	The simple presentation of figures in the form of tables, diagrams, or within the text. Includes percentages, median, mean, and simple correlations.
Low quantification	Includes chi square, significance, etc. Standard deviation and coefficients may be included depending on the level of difficulty.
High quantification	Includes sophisticated data manipulations such as log linear modelling and regression analysis. Several papers that do not use this kind of analysis are included if the discussion assumes knowledge of them.
Theory and high quantification	Includes papers that deal with abstract and mathematical issues underpinning quantitative work.

Articles were classified according to the highest level of quantification used. (Table 10.2). Few papers were 'theoretical and highly quantitative' and there was a diminishing proportion of research relying on 'low' levels of quantification. Most quantitative research was descriptive, but the most significant finding is that levels of 'high' quantification increased after 1975, accounting for a third of quantitative papers in 2000. So the last quarter of the twentieth century must somewhat have allayed the fears of Bulmer and Bechhofer. Taking all papers

TABLE 10.3 *Qualitative methods 1910–2000*

Year	Total papers	Ethnography/ anthropology		Observation (overt)		Interviews		Questionnaires		2 + methods	
	N	N	%	N	%	N	%	N	%	N	%
1910	1	1	100	—	—	1	100	—	—	1	100
1920	0	—	—	—	—	—	—	—	—	—	—
1930	0	—	—	—	—	—	—	—	—	—	—
1940	2	1	50	—	—	1	50	1	50	1	50
1950	4	1	25	1	25	2	50	1	25	1	25
1960	9	4	44	1	11	6	67	3	33	4	44
1970	15	3	20	4	27	7	47	8	53	5	33
1975	21	2	10	5	24	12	57	4	19	5	24
1980	17	3	18	5	29	10	59	4	24	5	29
1985	19	1	5	5	26	11	58	4	21	6	32
1990	17	4	24	4	24	13	76	2	12	6	35
1995	39	5	13	10	26	26	67	11	28	16	41
2000	30	10	33	5	17	24	80	3	10	13	43

Source: As for Table 10.1.

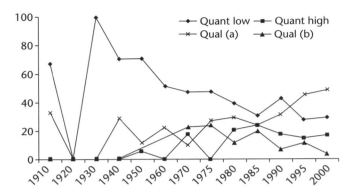

FIG. 10.3 Empirical papers by method 1910–2000, in per cent

using quantitative methods, our analysis demonstrates that, while lower levels of quantification remained most frequent, mainstream sociological articles slowly became increasingly numerate.

Nevertheless, one of the most surprising results of our analysis is the rise in the use of qualitative methods, especially ones using ethnographic and anthropological techniques [Qual (a)] as opposed to open questionnaires and interviews [Qual (b)] which have been used relatively less and less since 1970. Women have contributed strongly to this trend. Table 10.3 presents the figures for papers that have employed qualitative techniques (these are qualitative only papers and papers that combine both qualitative and quantitative methods) divided into ethnography/anthropology, overt observation, interviews, questionnaires, and papers that use more than one of these methods. 'Ethnography/anthropology' includes covert participant observation, and both 'interviews' and 'questionnaires' refer to papers that go beyond merely quantifying findings.

In the discussion of method, the refinement of qualitative methods and their popularity tends to be ignored, while attention is focused on the evolution of sophisticated quantitative techniques. There was a rise in levels of quantitative and qualitative expertise, but the use of 'high' quantification peaked in 1985, and with the exception of 1970 and 1985 has been outstripped in popularity by qualitative [Qual (a)] approaches. After 1995 qualitative work [Qual (a)] dominated mainstream sociology in the leading journals (Fig. 10.3).

Ideology and Sociology

As to the ideologies that underlay the development of sociology and its offshoots, we must first return to the classifications used (or 'isms') in our analysis of the journals. Many definitions of various 'isms' are self-evident, but several need further clarification as their meaning may be contentious and several categories have been merged together (e.g. interpretivism).

Table 10.4 *Ideology in sociology*

Ideology	1910–40		1950–70		1975–85		1990–5		2000		Total	
	%	Rank	%	Rank	%	Rank	%	Rank	%	Rank	%	Rank
Empiricism	26	1	56	1	39	1	34	2	24	2	38	1
Interpretivism	3	2	15	4	32	2	41	1	46	1	32	2
Functionalism	0	—	22	2	8	5	6	7	2	7	9	5
Weberianism	0	—	18	3	16	4	9	5	5	6	10	4
Marxism	0	—	3	5	21	3	10	4	6	5	13	3
Feminism	0	—	0	—	3	6	11	3	8	4	5	=6
Postmodernism	0	—	0	—	1	7	8	6	18	3	5	=6

Notes: This table represents the most numerically significant areas in the sample only.

Source: As for Table 10.1.

Our system of classification, admittedly modern but modifying the Bulmer technique, yielded 'empiricism' as the only perspective in the pre-war articles. Le Playism had disappeared, though it endured in the form of regional surveys designed to influence the direction of social change. Freudianism had become a perspective in 1930 and also 11 per cent of the articles discussed Marxism, feminism, interpretivism, or relativism. But in the journals, as distinct from the most influential books, ideological approaches were rarely consciously adopted in that period. Empiricism was the tacitly agreed definition of approaches to sociology.

The trends in ideology are summarized in Table 10.4 for the period 1910–2000. The empiricist approach continued to dominate the main journals until 1990 when interpretivism became the most used or discussed approach. Seven of the ideologies appear. It should be noted that positivism, relativism, and rational action/choice disappeared because they all fell below 10 per cent of the papers published in our sample years, except that positivism reached 12 per cent in 1975. Apart from empiricism and interpretivism, the most frequent ideological approaches were functionalism, Weberianism, Marxism, feminism, and postmodernism.

The evidence is of a gradual displacement of empiricism by interpretivism. At lower levels there was also a decline of functionalism from around 1970, a rise and subsequent fall of Marxism and Weberianism in the 1980s, and the appearance of feminism in the 1970s followed by postmodernism in the 1990s.

The three sociology journals have not contributed equally to these trends. Though not shown here, the *BJS* tended to be representative of what at least some will regard as the more conservative elements of sociology—functionalism, Weberianism, and empiricism—though at the end of the century, it became the most likely journal for research carrying postmodernist assumptions. *Sociology* stood out as a publication concerned with Weber and with empiricism. The *Sociological Review* was the most hospitable to papers dealing with interpretivism.

Meanwhile the main shifts in the specialist social policy journals were away from the small empirical studies of particular services in Britain towards more theoretical and comparative work about the nature, development, and consequences of the many varieties of welfare societies.

Social Policy as a Separate Discipline

The expansion of the academic study of social policy led to its separation as a recognized new discipline and to the emergence of four associated journals. *Social and Economic Administration* appeared first, in 1967, with Michael Cooper at Exeter as managing editor. It intended to draw on work in the social sciences—especially economics and sociology—in so far as those subjects might be applied to the task of defining and modifying policy, as well as social and public administration. The development of the idea of the welfare state, the editor declared, demanded not only more professional training but also research into the character of modern society and 'current trends in thought about human need and balancing sometimes conflicting values'.

The outcome was a collection of nineteen articles during the first year of publication, mainly focused on Britain and on particular services. The two more theoretical studies discussed ways of analysing health service systems and the sources of change in formal organizations, respectively. Different aspects of health services attracted most attention, with only a couple of articles dealing with social security or income levels, a couple with local government, a couple of historical case studies of women in public service, one piece on education, and one on urban problems. In 1970, the concentration on Britain remained evident, with only one contribution, on housing in Yugoslavia, dealing with another country. Virtually all the articles were empirical studies of particular areas of policy or administration—and most often of the personal social services.

By 1980, the journal had changed its name to *Social Policy and Administration*. It remained heavily concentrated on Britain and on specific services, the personal social services still attracting most attention. By the end of the century, with Catherine Jones-Finer as editor at Birmimgham University, the balance had shifted. Only half the articles in the volume for 2000 were primarily concerned with Britain. The rest examined particular problems in other countries—Australia, Israel, China, Japan, and New Zealand—or theoretical questions to do with welfare states, including the impact of globalization. In the same year, a special issue of the journal was devoted entirely to research— its funding, management, and relation to policy making.

The *Journal of Social Policy*, with D. E. G. Plowman of LSE as editor, was second on the scene in 1972, concerning itself with all aspects of social policy: with ideologies and values; with historical developments; with pressure groups and the formation and implementation of policy; and with the effects of government legislation in Britain and other countries. In the first volume roughly one-third of the sixteen articles were general discussions of values in social policy, and the remaining studies of particular services were mostly concerned with social security, low pay, or poverty. Only about a quarter were specifically tied to Britain. In 1980, there were fewer general or theoretical articles, the great majority being analyses of particular policies or problems and mostly relating to Britain. Ten years later the pattern was similar, most contributors discussing British problems or policies—especially those concerned with children or old people.

The volume marking the beginning of the twenty-first century, edited by Michael Hill and Helen Jones at Goldsmith's College, was also largely devoted to empirical studies of social problems or the administration of social services, but, in 2000, a third of the articles were concerned with countries other than Britain. The subjects discussed ranged from children's services and the long-term care of old people, to drug–crime links, urban deprivation, policies for lone mothers, and housing policy.

In 1981, came *Critical Social Policy*. It was run by an editorial collective of fifteen as 'A Journal of Socialist Theory and Practice in Social Welfare', intending to develop understanding of welfare from socialist, feminist, and radical perspectives. The editorial in the first issue declared opposition to the radical right and an 'awareness of inadequacies' of Fabian and other orthodox approaches.

The journal was aimed at academic social scientists, at workers and practitioners in the welfare state, and at people 'involved in welfare issues'. The first eight articles were mainly about social policy and politics—whether labour, feminist, new right, or socialist. There were only a couple of empirical studies; of migrant workers in the NHS and of the sale of council houses. By 2000, the publication had dropped the appellation 'socialist', describing itself as 'A Journal of Theory and Practice of Social Welfare', though still run by a collective widely drawn from the universities. Interest in the politics of welfare remained evident, in articles on New Labour and the Third Way, on 'sexual citizenship', and on the utility of the government's Social Exclusion Unit, for example. The more empirical studies were mostly concerned with housing, health, and urban policies, and mainly in Britain. One whole issue in 2000 was devoted to disability and the restructuring of welfare, employment benefits, and the law.

Finally, the advent of the *Journal of European Social Policy* in 1991 with Graham Room at Bath as editor marked the growing significance of developments in other parts of Europe for academic and policy discussion in Britain. The first editorial noted the moves to political integration in the European Commuity and the 'turmoil' in Eastern Europe as representing challenges to policy making and to academic analysis, raising questions about the role of social policy in protecting living standards, supporting economic efficiency, and securing political consent during a period of major reconstruction. The central interests of the journal would be the implications of economic and political change for social welfare; the redistribution of social policy decision making between national and supranational authorities and efforts to establish common standards; the reasons for convergence or divergence in welfare strategies; and the methods appropriate for cross-national and supranational studies of social policy and social welfare. The editor proposed that priority be given to analyses of comparative developments in Europe, and said that articles combining theoretical and empirical studies would be especially welcome. Ten years later the volume for 2000 appeared to fulfil these expectations. One whole issue was given to problems of globalization and its effects on the growth of welfare states. And the others contained comparative studies of problems and policies relating to gender and family matters and to various aspects of social security, housing, and employment.

R. M. Titmuss

The influence of R. M. Titmuss is crucial to this prime example of the splitting off of a distinct discipline. Titmuss had immense academic and political influence as writer and teacher of social policy and administration during the 1950s and 1960s after being elected to the first chair at LSE in 1950. His first book, *Poverty and Population* (1938), commended by Lord Horder, Harold Macmillan, Eleanor Rathbone, and the liberal intellectuals of the day established his place in the English tradition of political arithmetic and responsible social criticism based on private enquiry into public issues. After Tawney and the Second World War, Titmuss became the main bearer of this tradition.

His second book, *Problems of Social Policy*, the volume on the Ministry of Health in the series of histories of the Second World War, brought him national and international acclaim. In the Ministry of Health, he grew familiar with the social services, and was recognized as possessing 'really creative insight into human problems' and 'the most unusual gift for asking the right questions'.

These experiences led Titmuss from his earlier allegiance to the Liberal Party to the Fabian wing of the Labour Party. His commitment to social justice and equality were displayed in his academic work rather than in political agitation. He was an 'ethical socialist', no Marxist, regarding capitalism as not only economically wasteful but threatening social integration as markets 'drove out altruism'. This conviction was powerfully expressed in *The Gift Relationship: From Human Blood to Social Policy* (1970), where he argued that the buying and selling of blood undermined altruism, the readiness to give freely to others without any expectation of reward that was the essential mark of a civilized society.

Titmuss wrote persistently about equality and its many meanings; the distinction between equality of condition, of opportunity, and of outcome, and the strategies for attaining whichever might be desired. Treating people equally, he argued, would not necessarily produce more equality. In an unequal society equal provision would leave original inequalities undisturbed. They might even widen, as the middle classes tended to make better use of medical care and education. If people were to benefit equally from the welfare state, some form of positive discrimination, or selectivity, might well be needed, though such arrangements were in danger of stigmatizing the recipients (Titmuss, 1968: part III). These questions remain a vital part of social policy discussion. Underlying the ongoing debates about the relative merits of selective or universal services were not only questions of stigma, but also fears of rising costs and excessive redistribution, memorably expressed by Ian Macleod and Enoch Powell in a pamphlet in 1949. 'Why,' they demanded, 'should any social service be provided *without* test of need'.

It was partly in response to this sort of question that Titmuss set out a more theoretical approach to the nature and ethical basis of the welfare state in his Eleanor Rathbone Memorial Lecture in 1955 (Titmuss, 1958). There were three welfare systems, he asserted. First were the public arrangements for social security; second, the fiscal system distributing 'benefits' through tax allowances; and third, the occupational system where benefits attached to particular jobs. But while the public welfare system tended to redistribute resources to the poor, fiscal and occupational arrangements redistributed money to the better off—to those with high incomes and secure, well-paid work. Interest in the extent and direction of redistribution arose partly from the wish to discover where the true costs of the welfare state actually lay; but it also reflected concern about inequality—its nature, its degree, its causes, and its consequences—and how public services affected it. A powerful strand in the development of state welfare had been the desire for a more equal society. The continuing moral debate was joined by Tawney in the 1930s (Tawney, 1931) and after the Second World War by Michael Young (Young, 1958). It was further stimulated at the end of the twentieth century by Gordon Marshall and Adam Swift (1996, 1997), in response to Peter Saunders (1995).

Preferences for more or less equality are not only moral. They also relate to arguments about the preconditions for a healthy economy. The slowing of economic growth in the 1970s coupled with ageing populations and the rising costs of public services produced the spectre of a 'crisis' of the welfare state—in other rich European countries as well as in Britain. On the one hand were those of an individualist tendency who held that high taxes and generous public services reduced work incentives, stifled initiative, encouraged dependency, and damaged the economy. On the other hand were those taking a more collectivist stance who asserted that, as one of the rich nations of the world, Britain could well afford its welfare state and that, in any case, spending on health and education was essential for economic efficiency and social integration.

In the first twenty years or so after the Second World War, teaching and research in social policy and administration in Britain were largely concerned with the practicalities of social services in this country, and this was reflected in the journals. But, during the 1960s, the emphasis was beginning to change. A more theoretical approach was emerging and producing more sophisticated analyses of welfare arrangements and of the relation of social theory and social values to social policy (Pinker, 1971, 1979). And at the same time, linked to the development of 'theories' of welfare, more attention began to be paid to the welfare systems of other nations.

Titmuss shared with T. H. Marshall a concern with social justice and inequality, the delineation of the social rights of citizenship, and a 'commitment to welfare' (Titmuss, 1968), and this was reflected in teaching and research through the second half of the twentieth century. In 1967, Titmuss defined the 'unifying interest' of social administration as centred on those social institutions that fostered integration and discouraged alienation (Titmuss, 1968: 22), claiming that the subject had begun to develop a body of knowledge and a related set of concepts and principles.

International Studies

In the immediate aftermath of the Second World War the study of social policy had been parochial in Britain. It became 'globalized'. Titmuss and Marshall both recognized the importance of understanding developments in other countries, and after the 1960s the number and variety of studies using comparative material grew rapidly. Prominent among them was historical and theoretical work exploring the origins of welfare states and variously linking their development to industrialization, to labour movements, to social structure, to pressure groups, or to political ideology (Wilensky and Lebaux, 1958; Wilensky, 1975; Rimlinger, 1971; Room, 1979; Flora and Heidenheimer, 1981). In some cases historical enquiry merged into model making, as with Esping Anderson's (1998) study distinguishing 'laissez-faire', 'liberal', and 'social democratic' welfare states—essentially an elaboration of Titmuss's earlier analysis. And, not surprisingly, examination of the growth of welfare states also raised questions about their possible decline. Social, economic, and political changes stimulated considerable debate about the viability or 'crisis' of welfare states in the 1980s and later years (OECD, 1981; Hills, 1993).

Teaching and Research in Social Policy

The Social Administration department at LSE remained the leading department in Britain through the second half of the century. In the nineteen-fifties Professor Titmuss was delivering ten introductory lectures on Social Policy, dealing with 'concepts of social need', the causes of need, and its changing nature. In addition there were twenty-five lectures on the development and principles of social administration and a further twenty-four entitled 'Aspects of Social Policy', which included comparative social security, education, and old age.

By 1970, the number of social policy lectures had doubled, with ten of them devoted to the history of changes in theory and practice before 1939, and Titmuss was now adding discussion of the use of welfare models. After Titmuss died, Brian Abel-Smith took over the introductory lectures, now specifically including the contribution of social and political theorists and economists to social policy, and also indicating that, while the main focus would be Great Britain, comparative material would also be used. There were in addition five distinct series of lectures with complementary classes on different aspects of social policy and administration. By now the potential audience included candidates for a master's degree as well as a diploma in Social Policy and Administration, and in 1990 an undergraduate B.Sc. in Social Policy and Administration had appeared in the LSE Calendar.

At the end of the twentieth-century there were over eighty courses listed in the social policy section of the LSE Graduate handbook. Introductory lectures dealt with the 'mixed economy of welfare'; the relative importance of the state, family, market, and the voluntary sector; and explanations of the development of social policy in Britain and other European countries. Students were also asked to consider the concept of social rights, and the possible conflicts between social classes, races, generations, and the sexes.

All this amounts to a very substantial enterprise, but LSE had also developed more than twenty research centres by 2000, variously funded and producing regular publications. Of special interest for social policy were the Suntory and Toyota International Centres for Economics and Related Disciplines (STICERD), the more recent Centre for Analysis of Social Exclusion established in 1997, LSE Housing, the Greater London Group, and the Personal Social Services Unit. Among the eighteen academic departments listed in the LSE handbook, Social Policy came second only to Economics, with forty-three teachers and researchers—compared with forty-seven economists. Developments in Glasgow, Kent, Sheffield, and Bath were similar, if less impressive in scale than those at LSE.

Conclusion

Our conclusions from the foregoing content analysis of the three main British journals of sociology must be tentative because the material is limited. Within those limits it is reasonable to infer that ideas have not multiplied at the same rate as the numbers of authors. Which is in no way to deny that sociological writing has expanded or that sociologists have become more professional or more sophisticated in their statistics.

The most outstanding feature of article production in 2000 compared with a century or even 50 years previously is its fragmentation. The evidence for this trend is strong. Scores and scores of new journals have appeared catering for new tastes, new areas of the subject, and new methods of dealing with an increasing diversity of topics. Fragmentation is a fact. Whether it implies cumulating theory, as it clearly does in the natural or laboratory sciences, must remain dubious. In part it may be a response to demand for social policy advice in various areas ranging from management to medicine. Where this is true the conditions for development of separate disciplines are likely to be met. Where, however, it is untrue the possibility of a temporary fashion such as postmodernism may be suspected or of new or renewed enthusiasm for a theory like Marxism or a movement like Feminism.

As to the original struggle over science or literature, explanation or interpretation, our content analysis records continuing warfare for space with some advance for quantitative analysis by British sociologists but also, somewhat surprisingly, a trend towards the use of qualitative methods. The outcome may well be to transform the traditional struggle between scientific and cultural study.

Part IV

Conclusion

11

Epilogue in Eight Essays

A. H. Halsey

O NLY AFTER I had invited the seven essayists who together make up this final chapter or epilogue to offer their views did it occur to me that I too ought to answer my own question: what, in the light of the foregoing, and with a second chance, would I have done to put together a history of sociology in Britain? Books evolve. On rereading this one I now see more clearly than I did at the planning stage that it is not a true history in the sense of systematic perusal of documents. I could, and perhaps should, have worked through the records of the relevant institutions, whether universities like Warwick, Essex, or Glasgow, or research organizations like Rowntree, the Fabian Society, or the Institute of Economic Affairs: I knew that Jennifer Platt was writing a history of the British Sociological Association (BSA) but I could have searched more diligently than I did through the official sources like the Higher Education Statistical Agency (HESA), the Economics and Social Research Council (ESRC), or the Office for National Statistics (ONS) and their predecessors. Instead I have relied on my own memory and on personal correspondence and interviews with other sociologists, with all the dangers of bias and unrepresentativeness to which such unreliable and unsystematic sources are notoriously heir.

On the other hand, I have produced new data, partly from a survey of all twentieth-century professors of sociology in the United Kingdom, to which Jennifer Platt has since added material on members of the BSA (Platt, 2003) and, with Claire Donovan's help, a content and citation analysis of the three main British sociology journals. These extra sources add to the historical literature and to them I also bring a lifetime of reading. Is that, I wonder, adequate? I am increasingly doubtful. The history of a subject is composed, presumably, of people, institutions, and ideas. I have taken pains to cover people, especially the earlier sociologists from Hobhouse to Glass and Shils. And then the professors of the second half of the twentieth century, growing in numbers beyond 250, were covered by survey and correspondence. People and perhaps institutions are thereby dealt with. Nevertheless, I cannot pretend to have written a definitive account of all the theories or all of the numerous specialisms into which sociology fragmented in the course of the century—education, religion, economy, polity, stratification, family, media, etc. In any case such an enterprise would necessarily have gone beyond the limits of a single volume.

Have I passed the three tests set by Kelsall for the history of a subject (Preface)? I doubt it. Rereading only reinforces the doubt and confirms my inclination to see sociology as 'a moment in history'. My generation, as Chapters 4 and 5 make clear, began its career in an intense period of high excitement. My knowledge of the thoughts and feelings of the London School of Economics (LSE) 1950s group is inevitably strong. I knew that world and, for better or worse, it has been a touchstone of interpretation of all events, people, writing, and institution-building from the 1960s through the rest of the twentieth century. It overwhelms the evidence subsequently collected from the survey, the content analysis, and the official and other records. None of these 'data', however painstakingly used, have the vibrancy, the persuasiveness, the evidential compulsion of early personal experience. One is always something of a prisoner of autobiography, not least when the period covered and the trade followed happen also to be one's own lifetime.

All these limitations granted, I have left the reader with at least one major unanswered question. Does the twentieth bequeath to the twenty-first century a clear agenda for sociology? My implicit answer is that it does not. Put it another way: is there a definable subject properly called sociology or was it a 'moment in history' which convinced would-be sociologists that they were the inheritors and possessors of a new and integrated discipline? The leading lights of the subject such as Goldthorpe, Giddens, or Runciman offer conflicting answers.

The first generation of professional sociologists in Britain after the Second World War saw their world as a *tabula rasa* of bomb-cleared societies in Europe and Asia and themselves as among the intellectual agents of a new order of planned, free, democratic countries. The aftermath of that War was certainly such a moment, just as the 1870 war gave rise to Durkheim and his followers in France. Was it these circumstances which enabled sociologists to raise important questions about society—questions of social order, of urban and industrial welfare, of planning, of the liberties to be attached to citizenship, of the opportunities to be yielded by education, of inequalities to be overcome by political and macroeconomic management? Surely such challenges were at the heart of the motives driving many if not most young sociologists at that time. Or was it, as some still argue, that the Victorian dream of a science of society was to be crowned by a Comtean, regal sociology at the head of the social sciences if only the diabolical forces of unreason, of relativism in all its forms, could be banished and replaced by the rule of reason? Or was it, thirdly, that the subject was doomed to be marginalized as the depository of resentment, the study of oppressed groups—ethnic, class, gender—or sects? Could the post-war impulse itself be interpreted as the release of powerful class resentments from an inter-war traditional Britain to be dissipated and eventually marginalized by new 'minorities' like women, immigrants, the uneducated, the disabled, or the old?

For Goldthorpe (2000) the outlook is dire and the solution essentially Popperian. Sociology is split between theory and research. Theory is by definition explanatory and, on Popperian principle, to be tested by empirical research following a unity of method, the method of conjecture and refutation. With Popper he argues that too much is made of the differences between natural and social sciences. There are, he writes, 'clear warning signs that the present state of the discipline may not be sustainable and that the future of sociology, both intellectually *and* institutionally, is indeed problematic' (Goldthorpe, 2000: 11).

Goldthorpe along with Gellner (1992) directs his fury against postmodernism, which holds that the Western tradition of rational thought is wrong. Postmodernists hold that there is no world 'out there' which exists independently of our representations of it. We construct it socially through our language. Truth is not discovered but made. So all truth is local and contextual. No knowledge can claim priority or universality. There are only 'knowledges' which are local or cultural or partial views of the world. No science of society can decide between them.

Postmodernism is now in retreat. Only one respondent to the professorial survey confessed adherence to it. The rout was dramatically effected by Alan Sokal, a physicist from New York University, who sent in and had published by a prestigious journal of cultural studies a grandiloquently titled article 'Transgressions into Boundaries: Towards a Transformative Hermeneutics of Quantum Gravity' (*Social Text*, Spring/Summer 1996). Sokal's successful spoof called into question the intellectual standards of the whole field of cultural studies. Yet, I have also argued the historical strength of the sociological novel and of literature as social criticism. The conflict is surely about the place of pernicious forms of relativism in future scholarship.

In the subsequent years the warfare continued until Max Steuer, the LSE economist, published his *The Scientific Study of Society* (2003) attacking 'pretend social science' by tracing the record in five disciplines, including sociology, of articles published in the leading journals on six topics about which something significant might be expected (crime, migration, housing, money, the family, and religion). His argument, covering a vast territory, is nowhere *ad personam* and everywhere simple and civilized in his hatred of fraudulence and his love of knowledge. He concludes that, though also explanatory sciences, the achievements of the social science disciplines are both modest and variable and seriously threatened by 'pretend social science'.

A comparable pessimism is also to be found among some of the supporters of cultural studies, especially in America. Peter Berger, for example, the author of *Invitation to Sociology* (1963), a still popular text in 2000, has bewailed the fate of sociology to which he was so enthusiastically drawn in the 1950s. He believes that the discipline has fallen victim to two serious deformations. The first he calls 'methodological fetishism', the more and more sophisticated quantification of more and more trivial topics. The second was the cultural revolution that started in the late 1960s, seeking to transform sociology from a science into an instrument of ideological advocacy. Typically, the ideology is of the left. Marxism was the first to revolt against Parsonian structural-fuctionalism, but was subsequently transformed into criticism of a Marxisante type aided by ethnomethodology and abetted by feminism in the 1970s. We have traced the course of these movements in Britain in earlier chapters. Berger stresses the American consequences of declining status for the discipline, the poorer quality of students and recruits to the profession, and restricted funding for sociological research. Steuer puts forward some of the same set of arguments for the English-speaking world and for the social sciences as a whole. Our British findings confirm the 'ideological advocacy' and the restriction of governmental funding in the 1980s but are much less clear on the quality of students and teachers.

There is no doubt that sociology is in peril in the twenty-first century, at least in Britain and America. But it is clear that a scientific basis for the development of the discipline does exist and could be strengthened. Britain, on the foregoing account, never rose so fast or so high nor fell so low as France, Germany, and the United States. Our historical explorations have not revealed so strong a denial of scientific objectivity or so frenzied a fanaticism. As to the consequences for institutions and ideas I must remain sceptical. It will be interesting to know what the seven voices have to say. They follow in alphabetical order.

Zygmunt Bauman

That Professor Halsey is an insider of British sociology (more correctly, *the* insider—the standard by which the very meaning of 'being an insider' needs to be measured), and that therefore there is no one to match his knowledge and insight—is a banal observation as much as a sordid understatement. My place is at the opposite pole: an outsider who doesn't even fit any of Halsey's age/service cohorts (a member of the oldest cohort by the date of birth, but barely making it into the middle one if judged by the birth date of my Britishness). No wonder that I failed to take note of what to Halsey was dazzlingly evident, whereas my foreigner's eye focused on such features of British sociology as stood out from the familiar realities of its continental counterpart. I perhaps followed the pattern set by Talcott Parsons who, when asked by the Allied Commission to report on the state of German society, composed a list of America's attributes that Germany in his view missed. . . .

Coming to Britain in the early 1970s, I was struck by the demographic composition of British sociology: a few old men (much fewer old women) who in most cases wandered into the newly mushrooming sociology departments from outfits with different remits and names—separated by the huge age gap from lecturers, recruited in most cases from the ranks of the recent alumni of the brand new, post-Robbins sociology courses, and all apparently born at almost the same time (I remember worrying that by the end of the century the whole sociological establishment would retire simultaneously and without progeny . . .). Hand in hand with the uncannily wide age gap went the enormous difference of *Weltanschauungen*; discontinuity made generations matter more than among the continental practitioners of sociology. I had sometimes an impression that when the word 'sociology' was spoken on two sides of the age divide it meant different things...

It was probably the relative novelty of the discipline (heretofore scattered and hiding from view in other compartments of the *academe* and only beginning to appear on the public stage under its own name) that made the British public uneasy and suspicious—another oddity when gleaned from my continentally trained viewpoint. The coincidence between sociology exploding into public view and the countless traumas caused by the confidence-sapping disintegration of the received certainties and daily routines did not help either (Raymond Aron famously explained the modern spread of anti-semitic sentiments by the Jews emerging from the ghettos and mixing with the street crowds at a time of the most destructive and painful transformation of life conditions). To say that sociology had a 'bad press' would be to play down that mixture of hostility and ridicule in which it seemed to be held. 'He is studying sociology' was the soap-operatic formula for a family black sheep, while it seemed natural for a perceptive mind like Bradbury's to assume that the cynical, trouble-making 'history man' must have been a sociologist. Once more, I was shocked: how remarkably prestigious the public position of sociology was by comparison in France, Germany, or indeed my native Poland, where it settled in the public worldview on the tide of the late-nineteenth century rising optimism and self-confidence.

Nothing much seemed to be expected by the British public from the new-fangled discipline (and no useful services would, given its unprepossessing provenance and the widespread suspicion of its unsavoury intentions). Again, a sharp contrast with the esteem in which sociological know-how was held in continental Europe. There, sociology was by common consent a repository of important wisdom: a sort of non-governmental brain-trust whose practitioners were the obvious people from whom to seek clarification of the itinerary and advice about next steps to be taken at each successive junction. In Britain, I did not notice much interest in the sociologist's opinion. Hardly ever was it sought by the norm-setting media (except perhaps by a few off mainstream periodicals, most notably *New Society*—but even there sociology was living out its original public administration and social policy incarnation) and in times of crises or 'moral panics' they were the 'experts' least likely to be asked to voice it. From the public arena sociology was by and large absent. Or rather it served as the outer limit of the relevant and the attention-worthy.

Perhaps in the end that 'internal exile' turned to be British sociology's good luck. Neither spoiled by excessive public demands nor rushed by overblown and impossible-to-gratify public expectations, insured against the dangers awaiting the academics seduced into the corridors of power, sociology was free to select its own topics and could be guided by social and cultural criteria of relevance. This chance has been taken, and to great effect. I was profoundly impressed by the intellectual ferment notable in numerous sociological gatherings (though in the small scattered chapels rather than in the opulent High Churches in places like Leicester, Durham, Warwick, or Goldsmiths' College), by students challenging and pressing their teachers to focus on the task to illuminate the fast changing social conditions and to make sense of unfamiliar life experience, by ethical sensitivity of most even narrowly professional debates and sometimes an almost missionary zeal of their participants, by the (often excessive) openness and (on occasion unwarranted and gullible) curiosity for new ideas, and by the immense volume of self-reflection and self-scrutiny in developing a social knowledge fit for the changed social realities. There was a widespread—exciting—feeling of 'catching up' with the lost time and of a new beginning—unpolluted by the long record of the alleys proved to be blind, of frustrations and betrayed promises that cooled the fervour and held back the ambitions of continental sociologists.

This handful of observations is not meant to question the truth of Halsey's analyses, let alone to 'correct' his depiction of sociology's realities. At best it may remind us (if such reminder is called for, that is) that the world we try to penetrate and portray is one of multiple realities, that each reality's risk is another beholder's eye, and that the objective intelligibility of the world we share would be somewhat diminished if not for its many beholders sharing their, incurably subjective, experiences.

Colin Crouch

An important educative experience for the expatriate is the discovery that features of one's native environment which one had thought to be distinctive and had attributed to rather specific, local causes are in fact far more general. In that case the causes must be less specific too. My main complaint against British sociology had always been that it had allowed itself to become a marginal discipline studying marginal groups. It has been rich in the study of crime and deviance, ethnic and cultural minorities, minority sexual orientations, single mothers, and victims of various kinds. Studies of occupational structure (apart from class), the organization of firms, the architecture of the welfare state were not lacking, and when one found them they were often of very high quality, but they were hard to find. They certainly did not dominate the contents lists of UK sociology journals, or the sociology pages of publishers' catalogues, or the conference proceedings of the BSA. Work on the 'non-marginal' has been marginal to recent British sociological enterprise, and one would often find such work outside the walls of sociology departments themselves: in departments of geography or industrial relations, increasingly in business schools.

One could give a plausible local account of why British sociology had these characteristics. As Halsey's history shows, sociology always was, still is, marginalized by the British academic and political establishment; and, as victimology teaches us, excluded groups tend to behave in the manner that they are treated. An additional local cause was that, from the 1970s on, beleaguered by teeming hordes of ethnomethodologists and methodologically flaky researchers, hard-edged empiricists with an eye fixed on the core phenomena of social structure took a Calvinist approach. They constructed a few exclusivist redoubts and defined all other than true disciples as enemies. That was how the main hope that British sociology might emerge from the margins actually marginalized itself. Then, during the 1980s, establishment exclusion became downright political persecution. Sociologists either ran for cover within other departmental labels or buried themselves further in the world of other excluded minorities, reinforcing both tendencies that have weakened the discipline's autonomous profile.

Neither the local stereotype nor its local explanations are false: a turning away from the study of core institutions does seem to characterize British sociology more than those of other parts of western Europe or the United States. But it is important to see these characteristics as a virulent form of a far more general phenomenon, rather than an exception, a *Sonderweg*. Further, not only are there other national variants of the British story of establishment exclusion and internecine strife, but the preoccupation with the marginal and the marginalized is also found elsewhere, and has deeper and more general intellectual causes. In his account of the historical development of *economic* sociology— itself a major attempt at reorienting sociology towards central themes—Carlo Trigilia (1999) confronts the puzzle of how a sub-discipline which had been so important within the subject virtually disappeared after the Second World War. He finds part of the explanation in the widespread belief that, in the dynamic industrialism of the post-war decades, economic activity no longer presented any sociological puzzles. This account finds support in the fact that economic sociology continued to thrive in the specific field of development studies—focused on parts of the world where many such puzzles remained— and has now reappeared as Western economic success can no longer be taken for granted.

Trigilia finds a further explanation of sociology's neglect of the economic in Talcott Parsons's (1951) assignment of roles to the different branches of the social sciences. Although Parsons regarded sociology as the over-arching discipline, he conceded economics and political science full autonomy in the study of the phenomena within their defined domains. Of course, economics would have gone its own way whatever Parsons had said. But he profoundly influenced the way sociologists viewed the limits of their own discipline, not only within the United States but in many parts of western Europe, especially in Germany and in other places within the former sphere of German intellectual dominance. Following the Nazi period there was profound mistrust of anything in that country's cultural past, and Parsons's essentially German but Americanized approach represented something familiar but safely reprocessed. At the same time Parsonian sociology represented an over-arching edifice that could challenge Marxism, the only other such edifice readily available to the discipline.

The Parsonian sociological empire came to resemble the Holy Roman Empire: retaining purely nominal superiority over territories/disciplines which in fact had total autonomy, both concentrated their attention on smaller, marginal lands/topics. Although Parsons cannot be held responsible for contemporary sociologists' preference to study marginal groups, he curiously prepared the ground for such a turn. For a period Marxist sociology remained a major exception to all this, but that only exacerbated the problem. Marxist study itself remained dogmatic and largely incapable of intellectual innovation, leading non-Marxists to flee from the research areas where it was dominant. Then, as their privileged historical subject, the industrial working class, declined in size, Marxists themselves began to seek out the marginal.

This account has a very broad application, both within western Europe and in the United States as well. Of course, many local specificities exist and often counter the main trends. Scandinavian and Dutch sociology remain impressively quantitative and concern themselves with broad ranges of themes. France exhibits its familiar mix of sophisticated empirical demography and heavily philosophical social analysis. With some exceptions, like the impressive research-oriented schools of Trento and the Instituto Juan March at Madrid, Italian and Spanish sociology remain close to political theory. The vast enterprise of German sociology seems to find space for every form of the subject. But our task here is to make more precise our location of British sociology within the general framework. And here we encounter an interesting paradox. Although it suffered particularly strongly from local causes of marginalization, British sociology was more immune from these general trends. Its blunt empiricism produced an aversion to Parsonian structural functionalism, which never became dominant there as it did in the United States or some other European countries. Marxism having been weaker, non-Marxists among British sociologists felt less need to avoid topics dominated by Marxists. Therefore, the British tradition of studying social class remained strong, clearly differentiated from US social stratification research, and continuing today to produce results superior to much of what is found elsewhere. Class analysis is also a very big exception to the tendency to study the margins—provided its practitioners are willing fully to acknowledge the implications for their models of the decline of industrial employment.

More Recent Trends

The general situation is changing now; it is increasingly difficult, both intellectually and in the real world, to compartmentalize the social, the economic, and the political. Something similar to the creativity engendered when molecular research broke down barriers between chemists and biologists of various kinds is emerging in the social sciences. But, where macro- (though not micro-) phenomena are concerned, the leading role is being taken by political science, not sociology. Economists, outside France, prefer to move ever closer to mathematics and therefore away from engagement with other social sciences; and sociologists seem reluctant to leave the margins. Therefore, when what was in reality a new economic sociology emerged in the late 1970s, it often called itself political economy and much of the best work was done by political scientists. Similarly, leadership in research in the rapidly developing field of governance—a concept that rests by definition in the space where political science and sociology meet—is firmly in the hands of the former discipline.

However, the fact that economic sociology has now emerged from its disguise as political economy, and that at least some sociologists are engaged in governance research, shows that matters are at last improving. There are now courses in economic sociology in France, Germany, and Italy. Special sections for it have been formed within at least the German and US national sociological associations.

But here there is a final paradox revealed by a view from abroad of British sociology today. The response to these new developments from within British sociology seems considerably weaker than that in a number of other places—unless one looks to sociologists working in business schools and within other disguises. The University Grants Committee (UGC) review of the subject in the late 1980s noted how, following the political attack on it, sociologists had taken refuge in inter-disciplinary work (UGC, 1989; Westergaard and Pahl, 1989). Oddly, while sociology departments themselves were being decimated, sociology courses were growing fast within schools of medicine, engineering, geography, accountancy, and several other unlikely places. Westergaard and Pahl, commenting favourably on this spread of sociological understanding across the educational spectrum, nevertheless wondered anxiously how the discipline would reproduce itself if it lost its own autonomous core and became primarily a service subject.

We are now seeing the fulfilment of this anxiety. The exciting new work in the social sciences is happening at disciplinary interfaces, so British sociologists within business schools and elsewhere are very well placed to share in it. But this innovation will not feed back into the renewal of the structure of the discipline itself if those central to it, those in the sociology departments as such, are detached from the sites of innovation. Since the decimation of the 1980s was largely, though not entirely, a British experience, it is British sociology which is now feeling this new source of marginalization particularly keenly.

Giddens

I became a sociologist, like so many others of my generation, largely by default. I had barely heard of sociology when I went up to the University of Hull as an undergraduate at the end of the 1950s. I originally wanted to study philosophy, but Hull being a small university, with a tiny Philosophy Department, my luck wasn't in—or maybe it was. There was only one main lecturer in philosophy, and the year I got to Hull he happened to be on sabbatical. So I had to look around for something else. I wanted to study a subject or subjects that one couldn't do at school—and the only ones I could find were sociology and psychology. So that is where I ended up. I liked sociology the better of the two, and so concentrated on that. However, sociology at Hull wasn't taught by a sociologist, but by an anthropologist, Peter Worsley.

I mention this story because it shows something about the state of sociology in the country at the time. The subject was virtually unknown in schools, and outside of the LSE was only available in a handful of other departments. And almost all of those teaching it were refugees from other subjects. If my experience were any guide, many of those studying sociology came into it much by chance.

I started teaching sociology at Leicester University early in 1961. Sociology at that time in the United Kingdom was quite heavily Americanized. I knew a fair bit about the British traditions of sociology and their connections with Fabian socialism. I have still got a tattered copy Hobhouse's *Morals in Evolution* on my shelves. The Continental sociological classics—Marx, Durkheim, and Weber—already brooked large.

But it was to the United States that most of us looked, albeit with a critical eye. Parsons and Merton had in fact filtered the reception of the classical authors into contemporary sociology; but of course they had also developed striking positions of their own. Most of the best empirical sociology, and the most advanced techniques of data analysis, emanated from the United States.

The late 1960s, of course, was a breakthrough period for sociology in the United Kingdom. At Leicester, in terms of applications received, it became the most popular subject in the whole of the university. There was an integrated first-year social science course, after which students were required to choose one area in which to specialize. Hardly anyone wanted to do economics or politics—80 per cent chose sociology.

Sociology became massively popular at the same time as it was in turmoil. Some of the 1968 radicals made sociology a special focus of attack—not just American sociology, but the whole of the discipline. For them it was a bourgeois speciality, a sanctification of the status quo—an ironic fate for a discipline that had never achieved much respectability within academia. So sociology suffered from both sides. In the academic world it was seen as an upstart, while to its leftist critics it was the opposite, a set of establishment doctrines. It is this conjunction of circumstances that explains the chequered history of sociology in this country after that point. Sociology had no steady build up of popularity. Its rise was steep and sudden, and its appeal diminished when the wider climate of social ferment that had fostered it declined.

Yet, this was also the time at which British sociology staked a claim to greater international pre-eminence than it had ever achieved before. Sociology had never previously had a cluster of thinkers to rival those in anthropology—E. E. Evans-Pritchard, Audrey Richards, Meyer Fortes, Edmund Leach, Raymond Firth, and many others—but now it began to develop one. On the level of theory, there were those such as Steven Lukes, Garry Runciman, Perry Anderson, and, in a slightly later generation, Michael Mann; and on the more empirical level, scholars like David Lockwood, John Goldthorpe, or John Westergaard. Feminist authors, such as Sheila Rowbotham, Ann Oakley, and Juliet Mitchell, working in or close to sociology, although of course critical of some of its emphases, rose to great prominence.

So far as social theory goes, there was a particular reason for the growth of a distinctively British set of contributions. For British sociologists were well versed in American sociology, but became increasingly interested in Continental thought too—not just the classical authors, but more contemporary thinking. It is hard to remember now, but even in the late 1970s writers such as Jurgen Habermas, Michel Foucault, and Pierre Bourdieu were not really very well known in the English-speaking world. British authors helped promote an understanding of them, and at the same time produced something of a synthesis of their ideas both with indigenous traditions and with American thought.

I was one of the founders of Polity Press, a social science publisher set up in 1984. We established Polity partly in order to help connect Anglo-Saxon thought to Continental perspectives. So we did (and still do) a lot of translations, especially from French, German, and Italian. We initiated translations of many works by Habermas, Bourdieu, and their contemporaries; and we also sought to introduce newer authors who at that time were not known in the Anglo-Saxon world at all, such as Ulrich Beck. I followed a similar trajectory in my own writings, drawing extensively upon these and other authors to try to produce a new approach to sociological thinking. I called this structuration theory for want of a better term. The word structuration I took from French, and I have to admit that it sounds much more elegant in that language. It was originally used, I believe, by Jean Piaget; at any rate, that was where I originally discovered it.

Sociology remains very popular in the United States, especially at an undergraduate level. In the United Kingdom, in spite of the fact that it is firmly established as a school subject, it has never approached the level of popularity it reached three decades ago. I have indicated the reasons why. But what has also happened is a process of differentiation. Some areas that were once part of sociology and which today are highly popular—such as business, media, cultural, or feminist studies—have become separated out. Students at the moment are not so interested in the core traditions of sociology, the study of industry, organizations, class, and so forth.

What of the future? Will there be a new growth of interest in sociology as an academic discipline? As the wag has it, one shouldn't try to predict anything, least of all the future. But I'll chance my arm anyway. I think it is quite likely that there will be a resurgence of sociology over the next few years. The past two decades or so have seen the dominance of two types of intellectual perspective—market fundamentalism and genetic or biological approaches to the explanation of human behaviour. Each in a different way tends to downplay the impact of social institutions and social learning upon human life. The first is plainly on the wane.

Maybe, as some say, genetics and evolutionary thinking will actively contribute to a new wave of interest in sociology, as some of their ideas and findings become absorbed within it. But sociology has always been driven on mainly by the need to interpret social change. And there is plenty of that to feed on, with the rise of new social conflicts, disputes about globalization, the influence of fundamentalism, changes in family structure worldwide, and the persistence of structural inequalities. It is fresh ideas about these issues, and also a practical engagement with them, that could achieve again a more central intellectual role for sociology.

That engagement should also be focused upon Britain itself. Fabianism will never again have the closeness of connection with sociology it once enjoyed. Yet, along with the other industrial countries, Britain is changing as rapidly today as it ever has done in the past. Sociologists should not only provide an account of how and why, they should try to have an impact upon how society responds. Here I see at least some connection with sociology's Fabian traditions. The Fabians were public intellectuals. I am a believer in the importance of the public intellectual—someone who makes academic thinking accessible to a wide public audience, and thereby influences the social world. Quite apart from anything else, it is one main way in which a discipline registers in people's consciousness. I don't think that in recent years sociologists have been as prominent as they could and should be—and hopefully will become again.

Ann Oakley

Many people wrestle with a sense of being caught between two worlds. This is particularly true of women and other migrants and asylum-seekers: it is also the hallmark of the history inherited by sociologists brought up in the twin British traditions of well-meaning empiricism and privileged academic obscurantism. Is sociology a socially useful activity? Should it be? What is the role of the academic professor, confined in the narrow spaces of 'his' university and deeply committed to the value of ideas?

Having decided I wanted primarily to be a creative writer, I went to Oxford in 1962 to study Philosophy, Politics, and Economics in the mistaken belief that these subjects constitute a form of social science which, as we all know, is close to fiction. At Oxford, I had the good fortune to be taught by Chelly Halsey in the first year in which sociology was considered sufficiently respectable to be taught to Oxford undergraduates. Perhaps this was its downfall—at least in Oxbridge.

Over the ensuing forty years I have been successively impressed by four aspects of British sociology. The first is its masculinity. The second is its addiction to theory for theory's sake; the third is the impressive neglect by British sociologists of well-designed experiments as an aid to sociological understanding; and the fourth, linked, issue is that of methodological warfare, which has been (and remains) a major distraction.

Masculism

The key founding fathers, mentors, and practitioners introduced to me as a student were all men; and masculine names, theories, and positions have continued to dominate. Halsey's own survey for this book supports this view. Tables 9.1 and 9.2 which list the important mentors and key twentieth-century sociologists named by 216 living British sociology professors (themselves 81.1 per cent male) are also all male. But, of course, who does sociology and is remembered for having done it is only one index of its character. What matters much more is the systematic and sustained way in which sociological theory, research, and teaching is informed by the perspectives of the socially powerful, who therefore lack any incentive to understand or amend the distortions that may be consequent on this process. To put it differently, the problem noted by feminists and other enthnomethodologists, that knowledge is reached through *everyone's* experience of everyday life, is not a perspective which has been incorporated into modern mainstream sociology.

An account of women's studies in British sociology I offered in 1989 ended with Sylvia Walby's (1988*b*) four stages of the response of sociology to feminism: neglect of women's position; recognition of fallacies and gaps; adding women in; and full integration of gender analysis into the discipline. Thirty years on we remain fixed at stage two.

Theory

One important reason for this stasis is an over-attachment to theory. Too often theory is just speculation; definitions are arbitrary; subjectivity is extolled tokenistically; and we never know what difference a good theory might make. Postmodernism and other post-isms have brought a newly suicidal relativism to the sociological preoccupation with theory, and this has effectively closed off the attention of the sociological community from pursuing a scientific understanding of society. The 'flight from universals'—the view that human beings and their ways of being are fictions, and all that sociology can do is tell stories (Assiter, 1996)—decisively removes sociology from the field of practical public policy.

When positivism becomes a form of abuse, and anti-realism fosters the position that statements about being are always contingent, conditional, and partial, the danger is that sociology will disappear down the plug hole of theory and philosophy instead of contributing to the intellectual housekeeping of the policy-making process. In the face of global poverty, inequality, murderous aggression, and environmental collapse (Oakley, 2002), this retreat from reality is more worrying than merely protracted self-abuse.

Evidence and experimentation

The malaise of anti-realism is aligned with a third feature of British sociology which increasingly preoccupies me and other social scientists interested in the rise of the 'evidence' movement as a new moment in the complex relationship between social research and policy making. 'Evidence-based' or 'evidence-informed' policy and practice is a child of mixed parentage, its father the evidence-based health care movement which, since the 1980s, has inspired doctors to consider a sounder basis than expert judgement for professional action (Maynard and Chalmers, 1997), and its mother the Blair Labour government's invention of the mantra 'what matters is what works' as a cover for discarding the old politics of identity and class (Solesbury, 2002). Reliable evaluations of public policies have not been the forte of British sociology, despite the clarion calls of some early social scientists, such as the Webbs and Barbara Wootton, for sociologists to engage in controlled experiments capable of yielding sound and cumulative knowledge. The need for such practices across sectors as diverse as criminal justice, housing, social care, transport policy, and education is being very clearly articulated by many social scientists today (see, for example, Davies *et al.*, 2000). Controlled experimentation is distinct from the uncontrolled experimentation that constitutes the normal social policy process. It remains a puzzle, as Martin Bulmer (1991) has noted, as to why British social scientists have so ignored the possibilities for large-scale social experimentation, especially when the history of sociology elsewhere is littered with successful examples (see Oakley, 2000).

Of course, the rejection of experimental methods is part of (British) sociology's old identity crisis: science or literature? An inventive response to this would outline a new conceptual framework for the activity of science itself. Such a framework would privilege the highly contextualized knowledge which has traditionally been sociology's forte, and which is probably increasingly going to be a requirement of good non-social science (Nowotny *et al.*, 2001).

Methodological wars

The fourth notable aspect of British sociology—that of general methodological warfare—is one with which my own work has been particularly aligned. Disputes about the relative values of 'qualitative' and 'quantitative' methods have enhanced many CVs over the last half century, but what they have not done is contributed much of lasting value to the sociologist's tool kit. What matters most is the fit between the research method and question, and the steps researchers take to minimize the chances of their research findings simply reflecting their own selective perception. Systematic reviews—another giant leap for sociology (Boaz *et al.*, 2002)—are currently revealing how poorly designed and/or reported much British social research is (see, for example, Oakley, 2003). An enormous, as yet unmet, challenge concerns 'qualitative' research, whose parallels with fiction can be truly frightening. All of this is (in my view) a serious indictment of professional sociology, and it cannot just be rebuffed by epistemological excuses.

In his *The Scientific Merit of the Social Sciences*, Cho-Yee To, a Professor of Education at the Chinese University of Hong Kong, identifies three obstacles in the path of improvement: uncritical attachment to theory, the entrapment of methodology, and unsystematic poorly executed social research. To this I would add reluctance to entertain in anything other than a rhetorical fashion the prospect of an emancipatory sociology which is for, rather than about, its subjects. Halsey notes (Chapter 2, p. 30) the importance of asking the question, 'what's right with sociology?' What sociology has got right in the past is, I suggest, what it needs most to nurture for the future: an extension of the Enlightenment project from the natural to the social world; an engine of moral progress; and an intellectual aid to the young capable of promoting them to understand the changes, continuities, and challenges of living on planet earth.

Jennifer Platt

History written from different angles gives a different perspective on the same events, and brings into focus aspects which might otherwise not be noticed. I take my function here as being to draw attention to the history of British sociology from the angle of organizational structures and policies and their consequences.[1] Those I shall mention are disciplinary bodies and universities, the employing organizations for most sociologists.

The BSA has been of central relevance. It articulates with a range of other organizations—the International Sociological Association (ISA) and the European Sociological Association, the ESRC, the learned societies of related disciplines—the set of which can be seen as constituting a loose system, whose members cannot be fully understood without taking into account their relations to other members of the set. Other bodies—the Teachers' Section of the 1960s for 'professional sociologists', Sociologists in Polytechnics when the BSA was seen as not meeting their needs, the Heads of Departments of sociology— have represented particular groups of British sociologists, but all these have eventually become associated with or absorbed into the BSA.

The BSA is not a certifying body, and so membership has been truly voluntary; whatever the definition of sociologist, not all have belonged, and the proportion of members has fluctuated. It cannot, thus, be taken as representing the profession in that sense,[2] though it has played a formal representative role and, in that and other ways, has affected non-members too. I am probably a member of the last generation to have been able to know 'everybody' in British sociology—because one met them at BSA meetings. In 1964, 73 per cent of university sociologists belonged while, in the much larger profession of 1997, the proportion was only 50 per cent. (One reason for that is presumably that larger numbers can support more specialized groups of those working in particular areas.) The BSA has been vital in creating a sociological community, and its membership does not sufficiently indicate the role of its conferences, study

[1] Space does not permit the presentation of data, although data on some of the points made is available elsewhere: Platt (1998, 2000, 2003).
[2] It has been seen as weakened by the absence from it of the most senior members of the discipline; they certainly have not all consistently belonged, but through the period 1972–81, when the folk myth suggests that many resigned in protest at developments, the proportion of professors belonging was consistently c.30 per cent higher than that of non-professors.

groups, and summer schools in establishing intellectual networks. Another way in which it has supported community has been by the promulgation of codes of practice, which specify norms of sociological behaviour; probably the most influential of these have been successive editions of its ethical code and guide to good professional conduct, its guidelines on non-sexist language, and its statements of good practice in the treatment of graduate students and part-time staff. Very important in other ways have been its journals *Sociology*, the only general British sociological journal not tied to a particular department, and *Work, Employment and Society*. It has helped individuals in their careers by providing a range of training activities and helpful publications for junior people; less intentionally, it gave several future vice-chancellors valuable early administrative and leadership experience.

The most active members cannot be taken as typical of the whole membership, but the changing pattern of BSA executive membership tells one something about wider changes in British sociology. Initially the executive was almost entirely male, but gradually it became more feminized, until by the later 1980s men were in the minority. The women's movement since the 1970s has made gender issues salient, and alternation of men and women in office has become conventional. The proportion of members from polytechnics, later the 1992 cohort of new universities, has also risen markedly over time. These patterns reflect demographic change in the profession, but also a politically egalitarian ethos which has made the BSA work quite differently from the elitist model of a learned society, in ways ranging from the structure of its subscription rates to the organization of its conference programmes.

One of the most striking features of the post-war history of sociology has been the fluctuation in the labour market for university sociologists, in response to changes in government policy and student fashion. The enormous expansion of the 1960s and 1970s brought in many young people with little sociological training, and compelled them to concentrate on building departments and on teaching; the social integration into the discipline of this surge was inevitably problematic. The youthful intakes of the 1960s and 1970s then grew grey together through the 1980s, when recruitment virtually ceased, and when it started again in the 1990s a distinct new cohort was created. The generational composition of the discipline and of departments has affected the relative chances of institutionalization of different intellectual currents. In addition some departments, if not all, have had a pronounced individual character, affecting both the wider system and individual careers, occupational and intellectual. Halsey has discussed the LSE department. Its early formation positioned it to play a prominent role in the founding days of the ISA, and to initiate the creation of the BSA; its institutional location in the system of external degrees, and then the participation of its members in the Council for National Academic Awards (CNAA) and on appointing committees for other institutions, was very influential. Expansion elsewhere undermined this leading role, and it turned more inwards. Leicester under Elias is another famous case— though perhaps the practical significance in recruitment to the profession of its system of tutorial assistantships should be emphasized here as much as its intellectual style? The role of departments remains to be systematically researched.

Also relevant to intellectual life has been the internal organizational structure of universities: where have sociologists been institutionally located? Important differences are created between those with relatively autonomous sociology departments and those, mainly in the newer universities, within inter-disciplinary frameworks; more recently, the growth of sociology teaching for nurses and medical students has located some sociologists in their schools, and the development of new fields such as women's studies and media studies has taken others out of the sociology departments. This can be seen as weakening the sociological centre—but it can also be seen as extending sociology's influence. Perhaps 'uncertainty' should be read as diversification?

W. G. Runciman

Mine is an outsider's contribution in a double sense: first, because I learned my sociology not in Britain but in the United States; and second, because I have never held a normal university post in a British department of sociology. That said, my personal picture of British sociology in the second half of the twentieth century is, institutionally speaking, one of disappointment at opportunities missed, which I believed could, and therefore should, have been taken. But I must emphasize the 'institutionally speaking'. Nobody can seriously dispute that valuable contributions were made by British sociologists during that period across the standard agenda of the discipline—social stratification, social mobility, political behaviour, deviance and social control, education, religion, trade unionism, feminism, ethnicity, and so on. But as a collective national enterprise, British sociology did not achieve the recognition and influence that I would (if asked) have predicted when I returned to my Cambridge college in 1960 at the conclusion of a Harkness Fellowship held at Harvard, Columbia, and the University of California at Berkeley.

Given the distribution of resources, influence, and prestige between the British universities of the time, much was inevitably bound to depend on what happened at three places in particular: Oxford, Cambridge, and the LSE. But each, in their different ways and for their different reasons, failed to do for British sociology what might have been expected of them.

At the LSE, Morris Ginsberg had for many years held the Martin White chair in succession to his mentor Leonard Hobhouse. But to contrast his influence with that of Malinowski or Oakeshott or Popper is to bring out how relatively little he achieved for British sociology as such. (Did he really say of *Wirtschaft and Gesellschaft*, as Edward Shils once told me, 'I've read all that stuff and there's nothing in it'?) Ginsberg's sociology was what he himself was willing to call 'social philosophy', which meant a theory of progressive evolution which had nothing in common with authentic neo-Darwinian theory and a theory of social justice which, although his book *On Justice in Society* came out in 1965, took no account of the then available articles of John Rawls. David Glass was a figure of international reputation, but as a demographer rather than a sociologist, and his relations with other sociologists were known to be often uneasy. (I remember happening to talk to him at the time the Oxford mobility study was getting under way, when his remarks about it were not merely unconstructive but, as it seemed to me, gratuitously hostile.) Donald Macrae, like Shils, was a sociologist whose creative output fell short of his impressive erudition and unquestioned commitment to the subject. And T. H. Marshall, after two years in the Martin White chair in succession to Ginsberg, left the LSE in 1956 for UNESCO, where he remained until he retired.

Meanwhile, at Cambridge, it was widely believed that Talcott Parsons had been invited for a year as a deliberate tactic to forestall the recognition of sociology for which Noel Annan, in particular, had been campaigning. Whether or not that is true, Parsons did the cause of sociology in Cambridge no good, and the well-entrenched dominance of economics and anthropology virtually guaranteed that if it was admitted at all, it would be as an adjunct to one or other of them. A move to create a professorship which Marshall would be invited to occupy was—lamentably—defeated. Sociology was finally admitted under the wing of the economists and David Lockwood and Michael Young appointed as lecturers. But the university still declined to create a chair, and by the time, in due course, that it would have been handed to Lockwood on a plate he had—understandably—no inclination to leave the University of Essex. It was symptomatic, too, that Cambridge's first Professor of Sociology was an anthropologist. Not that John Barnes's achievements or qualifications were in doubt—far from it. But his appointment sent an ambiguous message about the university's attitude to sociology to the wider world. And to this day, sociology in Cambridge remains yoked in an uncomfortable multi-disciplinary troika in a way that no other university I can think of would contemplate.

At Oxford, by contrast, it was the dominance of philosophy and politics with which sociology's advocates had to contend, including not least the majestic opposition of Isaiah Berlin, for whom sociology was a subject, as he used to say, still awaiting its Copernicus, let alone its Newton. (When, years later, I learned to my surprise that he approved of a Spencer Lecture which I had given at Oxford, it was only because I had explicitly disavowed any pretence that Marxist or any other sociology is or could be a predictive science.) Coupled with this was a widespread opinion that sociology was an adjunct to, if not actually a form of, social administration in the tradition of Booth, Rowntree, and Titmuss which ought therefore to be taught as such. As at Cambridge, the establishment of a chair took an unconscionably long time, and when it came was deliberately not accompanied by the creation of an autonomous sociology department. There was always Nuffield College. But the Official Fellows of Nuffield were, and are, under no formal obligation whatever to the university: any undergraduate teaching they do or graduate students whose research they supervise is a matter of pure goodwill. Viewed from outside, it looked as if only

Chelly Halsey's personal standing and powers of persuasion were keeping Oxford (as distinct from Nuffield) sociology on the road at all.

There had, to be sure, been established the Social Science Research Council (SSRC) with Michael Young, who enjoyed the friendship and backing of Anthony Crosland as Secretary of State for Education, as its first head. But its funds were, in the spirit of the times, too widely and therefore thinly dispersed for maximum effect, and Michael Young, for all his many achievements and the acknowledged contributions of his Institute of Community Studies, was not someone who could be expected to overcome the hostility of those members of the British academic establishment for whom sociology had still to prove itself as a discipline in its own right. The SSRC, although it survived the politically motivated attacks subsequently directed against it, spent too much of its money providing too many graduate students with inadequate training for careers which turned out not to be there at all after the first heady, over-expansionist days of the new universities. However strong the argument of principle for giving smaller sums to more institutions rather than larger sums to less, a concentration on a few chosen centres of excellence would have done more to give British sociology not merely the sustainable funding but the reputation for intellectual professionalism which it still seemed to lack. It is not as if there were no established departments in universities outside of Oxford, Cambridge, and London which could have put extra resources to effective use in a more closely controlled and carefully thought out expansion. Nor were matters helped if Harold Wilson as Prime Minister really believed, as I once heard him say to a private gathering, that the student unrest of 1968 and thereafter was all the fault of sociologists.

There remained, too, the perennial problem of defining the relation of sociology to the other disciplines institutionally demarcated within the humanities and social sciences. Inaccurate as the image might be, the practitioners of the better-established disciplines could sometimes be forgiven for thinking that British sociology was a mixture of reformist practical policy making on the one hand and political–philosophical speculation about the Good Society on the other. The irritating question 'What *is* sociology?' became less frequently and less aggressively asked as the years went by. But there remained a problem of both academic and public perception of its distinctiveness which American sociologists had long been spared. It was not that similar disagreements over the scope, methods, and aims of sociology were (or are) absent from the American scene. But the much greater resources, both in money and people, which supported the sociology departments of the major American universities, the volume of their output of high-quality research, and the quality of the training given to their successive generations of Ph.D. students all combined to dispel any similar scepticism which might have arisen there about the solidity of the intellectual and organizational foundations on which they had been built.

However much more might have been done for British sociology by those in a position to do so between 1950 and 2000, that is no reason for being pessimistic about its prospects in the twenty-first century. But it will need to be

provided with the resources both to train and then to support in their subsequent careers the researchers of the future on which its reputation as a distinctive
discipline of unchallenged scientific and scholarly standing will depend—
a discipline, that is, which leaves 'social philosophy' to the philosophers and
does as well as, or better than, anthropology, economics, psychology, and history
in discovering new, true, and interesting things about human social behaviour.

John Westergaard

Is the story of sociology, as Chelly Halsey incitingly tells it for twentieth-
century Britain, one of cumulative growth? In part yes, he says: in respect of
methods of enquiry, despite curious delays en route. Otherwise, only debatably
so. Focused more on critique than steady brick-building, sociological theory in
particular leans to the arts rather than the sciences; and it still keeps somewhat
aloof from empirical research.

Fair judgement, I'd say. True, one may detect trends of wider accumulation
within this period or that. The 1950s-into-1960s thus arguably showed
a sequence from first-step broad mapping of socio-structural contours to second-
step in-filling of detail about hows and whys; and theoretical grounding came
to loom larger in the process. The claim would need elaboration to stand. But it
is in any case overshadowed by the rest of the story—a story surely more about
shifts of themes and paradigms than plain accumulation, those shifts set going
by larger movements of societal climate.

After all the putative knowledge-building period of the 1950–60s, too, bore
a clear imprint of time and place. Its first-step sociography was geared to post-war
(and post-depression) 'social reconstruction': this in Britain by contrast with
the complacency that coloured leading structural-functionalism (and 'mindless empiricism'?) in the United States, less warworn while more afflicted by
cold war paranoia. Steady boom then helped to waft straws of complacency
across the Atlantic, in the form of conjectures about 'embourgeoisement' and
transpolitical societal 'convergence'; yet here only against vehement and
empirically argued rebuttal. But it was the signal paradigm-shift of the 1960s
into the 1970s that shattered any image of cumulative continuity in sociology.

Hot war in Vietnam, civil rights campaigning in America, militancy resur-
gent far and wide, and feminism's new wave pressed prognoses for an 'end of
ideology' out of sociological agendas. Divisions of power and social condition
took the lead there again. Largely to good effect, I still think. Economic and
political sociology gained fresh edge; development studies shook off the earlier
bland evasions of 'modernization' scenarios; criminology was radicalized and
're-sociologized'. . .and gender set to pervade social enquiry. Yet, there were
debit-side effects that came to haunt sociology over the two decades ahead.

In particular, the new iconoclasm tripped over itself in declaring war on 'positivism'. The sources of that were paradoxically diverse: primarily in the hyper-
structural abstractions of neo-marxist theory; subsidiarily in opposing denials

of structure fostered by ethnomethodology and symbolic interactionism. From bird's-eye view or worm's-eye view, the outcome was to turn reasoned caution about conventional means of research into wide scorn for empirical, especially quantitative, enquiry. Bordering on relativism—a line continued into later 'postmodernism'—this implied a confession of bankruptcy, and did its bit to give sociology a poor press.

A 'poor press'—and for subversion more generally—certainly figured in the next shift. But this was a shift less of paradigm than of political and institutional context: authoritarian neo-liberalism's ascendance, in but also beyond Britain; governmental promotion of a philistine programme for higher education, in though also beyond social science. To Chelly's Chapter 7 account of these Thatcher-era traumas one might add some smaller episodes: Sir Keith Joseph's forays, for example, against the CNAA over a polytechnic study programme in sociology suspected of 'political contamination' and against The Open University, similarly accused over the economics strand in a sociologically oriented foundation course. Both ministerial exercises were thwarted. But they were telling signs of the 1980s' pressures.

Sociology was more a token scapegoat than main, let alone sole, target of such pressures. But it suffered cuts, feared more, and responded variously. One response, positive if slow and externally prompted, was a reacknowledgement of empirical research. Others were more contestable: a diversification into sub-specialisms, some dropping the name-tag of sociology; new caution over research agendas; a set of 'cultural turns' inclined to see 'culture' as free of 'structure'; similarly market-attuned, a focus on 'underclass' formation with scant attention to class and class power more widely... Yet, to the subject's credit, never without solidly argued dispute; and sociology survived in fair shape. Perhaps it did so in good part, again, for reasons of institutional context: policy changed to allow new growth, though underfunded, and the subject proved too well ensconced in British higher education for drastic measures of 'cut and concentrate'. I note the contrast with Denmark at much the same time, where sociology, thinly spread yet, was suspended from significant university presence over several years by a Thatcher-like government.

Rather than continuous build up, then, we see shorter cumulative runs between major shifts of orientation, theme, and interpretation. What else in social science, when the very ground studied itself periodically shifts? But the point of course highlights a perennial dilemma: how to stay alert to the scenery changes on the social stage where we are bit-actors ourselves, yet also observers who must bring convincing impartiality to that job. Ideological disengagement is no part of my own answer, an implausible and self-defeating prescription. I look instead to two safeguards: the nurture of professionally collective heterodoxy, to challenge individual and factional partiality; and the nurture, above all, of common respect for factual evidence.

The cumulative advance of research methods has more than technical significance on that last score. Turn the initial question to ask, not so much how far we have built brick steadily on brick, but, more modestly rather, how far we have learned by empirical testing to discard demonstrable untruths, delusions, and blind alleys? If so, then progress at least by cumulative refutation; and I think the answer, on balance, is positive. Specific examples would grow to a long list. But to generalize, sociology has surely come to some common acknowledgement of the messy realities of multicausality as against the alluring simplicities of monocausality, for one thing. And for another, while dispute rightly remains our life-blood, its range has surely become better disciplined by respect for trial by evidence. If theory can be brought closer into that frame, so much the better.

Appendix 1

The Professorial Survey 2001

This survey was carried out in 2001. Names were taken from the Commonwealth Universities Year Book to which were added (from the reading and memory of A. H. Halsey) those who had died during the twentieth century. They are listed below alphabetically with their last (British) institution where they held full professorial status or its equivalent, and whether serving (S), retired (R), dead (D), or not known (NK). Table A1.1 below also records the respondents who completed and returned their questionnaire (C), questionnaires that were completed on behalf of dead Professors using public or private records (C*), one Professor who refused to participate in the survey, and those who did not respond at all or were not traced (NR/NT).[1] Every effort was made to trace respondents including three reminders. Professors who were VCs or heads of colleges are listed against that particular institution. Visiting Professors are not included.

Name	Institution	S/R/D/NK	C/C*/Ref/NR/NT
Abell, Peter	LSE	S	C
Abel-Smith, Brian	LSE	D	C*
Abercrombie, Nick	Lancaster	S	C
Abraham, John	Sussex	S	C
Abrams, Philip	Durham	D	C*
Acton, Thomas	Greenwich	S	C
Albrow, Martin	Roehampton	S	C
Allcock, John	Bradford	S	C
Allen, Sheila	Bradford	R	C
Anderson, P.	LSE	S	C
Andreski, Stanislav L.	Reading	R	NR/NT
Anthias, Floya	Greenwich	S	C
Arber, Sarah	Surrey	S	C
Archer, Margaret	Warwick	S	C
Ashton, David	Leicester	S	C
Bailey, Joe	Kingston	S	C
Baldamus, Wilhelm	Birmingham	D	C*
Banks, Joe	Leicester	R	C

[1] Some of the respondents may have changed institution after the Year Book was published.

Name	Institution	S/R/D/NK	C/C*/Ref/NR/NT
Banks, Olive	Leicester	R	C
Banton, Michael	Bristol	R	C
Baric, Lorraine	Manchester	S	C
Barker, Eileen	LSE	S	C
Barnes, J. A.	Cambridge	R	C
Barnes, Barry	Exeter	S	NR/NT
Barrett, Michele	City	S	Ref
Bauman, Zygmunt	Leeds	R	C
Bean, Philip	Loughborough	S	C
Bechhofer, Frank	Edinburgh	S	C
Beckford, Jim	Warwick	S	C
Bell, Colin	Stirling	S	C (Died 2003)
Bennett, Tony	Open	S	C
Benton, Ted	Essex	S	NR/NT
Bernbaum, Gerry	South Bank	S	C
Bernstein, Basil	Institute of Education, London	D	C*
Beynon, Hew	Cardiff	S	NR/NT
Birrell, Derek	Ulster	S	C
Blaikie, Andrew	Aberdeen	S	C
Bonney, Norman	Robert Gordon	S	C
Booth, Tim	Sheffield	S	C
Bottomore, Tom	Sussex	D	C*
Boyne, Roy	Durham	S	C
Bradshaw, Jonathan	York	S	C
Breen, Richard	Oxford	S	C
Brewer, John	Queen's, Belfast	S	C
Brown, George W.	Bedford College	R	C
Brown, Phil	Cardiff	S	C
Brown, Richard	Durham	R	NR (too ill)
Bruce, Steve	Aberdeen	S	C
Bryant, Christopher	Salford	S	C
Bryman, Alan	Loughborough	S	C
Bulmer, Martin	Surrey	S	C
Burgess, Robert	Leicester	S	NR
Burns, Tom	Edinburgh	D	C*
Bury, Michael	Royal Holloway	S	C
Busfield, Joan	Essex	S	NR/NT
Byron, Reginald	Swansea	S	C
Callender, Claire	South Bank	S	C
Carlen, Pat	Bath	S	C
Chaney, David	Durham	S	C
Cherns, Albert	Loughborough	D	C*
Child, John	Aston	S	NR/NT
Clarke, Simon	Warwick	S	C

Name	Institution	S/R/D/NK	C/C*/Ref/NR/NT
Cohen, Percy	LSE	D	C*
Cohen, Robin	Warwick	S	C
Cohen, Stan	LSE	S	NR
Collison, Peter	Newcastle	R	C
Cormack, Robert	Queen's Belfast	S	C
Cotgrove, Stephen	Bath	NK	NR/NT
Coxon, Tony	Essex	S	C
Craft, Maurice	Goldsmiths	S	C
Craib, Ian	Essex	S	C
Crompton, Rosemary	City	S	C
Crouch, Colin	Oxford	S	C
Dahrendorf, Ralf	LSE	R	C
Dale, Angela	Manchester	S	C
Davidoff, Leonora	Essex	R	C
Davies, Christie	Reading	S	C
Davis, Howard	Bangor	S	C
Deacon, Alan	Leeds	S	C
Dingwall, Robert	Nottingham	S	C
Donnison, David	Glasgow	R	C
Dore, Ronald	LSE	R	C
Downes, David	LSE	S	C
Drewry, Gavin	Royal Holloway	S	NR/NT
Dunning, Eric	Leicester	R	C
Edgell, Stephen	Salford	S	NR/NT
Edwards, John	Royal Holloway	S	NR/NT
Edwards, Rosalind	South Bank	S	C
Edwards, Paul	Warwick	S	C
Eggleston, John	Warwick	R	C
Eldridge, John	Glasgow	S	C
Elias, Norbert[2]	Leicester	D	C*
Ermisch, John	Essex	S	C
Evans, Mary	Kent	S	C
Evans, Roger	Liverpool John Moores	S	NR/NT
Evetts, Julia	Nottingham	S	C
Fielding, Nigel	Surrey	S	C
Finch, Janet	Keele	S	C
Fitzpatrick, Ray	Oxford	S	C
Fletcher, Ronald	York	D	C*
Floud, Jean	Cambridge	R	C
Flynn, Rob	Salford	S	C
Frankenberg, Ronald	Keele	R	C
Franzosi, Roberto	Reading	S	C
Frisby, David	Glasgow	S	NR/NT

[2] Not formally a professor: included in error.

Name	Institution	S/R/D/NK	C/C*/Ref/NR/NT
Fuller, Steve	Warwick	S	C
Gallie, Duncan	Oxford	S	C
Geddes, Patrick	Dundee	D	C*
Gellner, Ernest	Cambridge	D	C*
Gershuny, Jonathan	Essex	S	C
Giddens, Anthony	LSE	S	C
Gilberts, Nigel	Surrey	S	C
Gilroy, Paul	Goldsmiths	S	C
Ginsberg, Morris	LSE	D	C*
Glasner, Peter	UWE	S	C
Glass, David	LSE	D	C*
Glass, Ruth[3]	UCL	D	C*
Glucksman, Miriam	Essex	S	C
Golding, Peter	Loughborough	S	C
Goldthorpe, John	Oxford	S	C
Goulbourne, Harry	South Bank	S	C
Gould, Julius	Nottingham	R	C
Grebenik, Eugene	Leeds	D	C*
Halfpenny, Peter	Manchester	S	NR/NT
Hall, Stuart	Open	R	NR/NT
Halmos, Paul	Open	D	C*
Halsey, A. H.	Oxford	R	C
Harrison, Barbara	East London	S	C
Hawthorn, Geoffrey	Cambridge	S	C
Heath, Anthony	Oxford	S	C
Hill, Stephen	LSE	S	C
Hills, John	City	S	NR/NT
Hobbs, Richard	Durham	S	C
Hobhouse, Leonard	LSE	D	C*
Holdaway, Simon	Sheffield	S	C
Holland, Janet	South Bank	S	C
Holmwood, John	Sussex	S	C
Hopkins, Mark	Cambridge	S	NR/NT
Hornsby-Smith, Mike	Surrey	R	C
Hough, Mike	South Bank	S	C
Hughes, John	Lancaster	S	NR/NT
Illsley, Raymond	Bath	R	C
Irwin, Alan	Brunel	S	C
Jackson, John	Trinity, Dublin	R	C
Jaques, Elliott	Brunel	R	NR/NT
Jenkins, Richard	Sheffield	S	C
Jenks, Chris	Goldsmiths	S	C
Jessop, Bob	Lancaster	S	C
Jones, Gill	Keele	S	C

[3] Not formally a professor: included in error.

Name	Institution	S/R/D/NK	C/C*/Ref/NR/NT
Kelly, Mike	Greenwich	S	C
Kelsall, Keith	Sheffield	D	C*
Kendall, Ian	Portsmouth	S	C
King, Roy	Bangor	S	C
Klein, Rudolf	Bath	R	C
Lacey, Colin	Sussex	S	C
Lane, David	Cambridge	R	C
Larrain, Jorge	Birmingham	S	C
Lash, Scott	Goldsmiths	S	NR/NT
Lauder, Hugh	Bath	S	C
Law, John	Lancaster	S	C
Layder, Derek	Leicester	S	C
Lewis, Jane	Oxford	S	NR
Lockwood, David	Essex	R	C
MacRae, Donald	LSE	D	C*
McRae, Susan	Oxford Brookes	S	C
McCrone, David	Edinburgh	S	C
McGregor, Oliver (Lord)	Bedford College	D	C*
McIver, R. M.	Aberdeen	D	C*
McKenzie, Robert	LSE	D	C*
McKie, Linda	Glasgow	S	C
McLennan, Gregor	Bristol	S	C
McPherson, A. F.	Edinburgh	R	C
Madge, Charles	Birmingham	D	C*
Mannheim, Karl	Institute of Education, London	D	C*
Manning, Nick	Nottingham	S	C
Marsden, Dennis	Essex	R	C
Marshall, Gordon	Oxford	S	C
Marshall, T. H.	LSE	D	C*
Martin, David	LSE	R	C
Martin, John	Southampton	D	C*
Martin, Rod	Oxford	NK	NR/NT
Mason, David	Plymouth	S	C
May, Tim	Salford	S	C
Miles, R. F.	Glasgow	NK	NR/NT
Millar, Jane	Bath	S	C
Mitchell, G. Duncan	Exeter	D	C*
Mitchell, J. Clyde	Oxford	D	C*
Modood, Tariq	Bristol	S	C
Moore, Robert	Liverpool	R	C
Morgan, David	Manchester	R	C
Morris, Lydia	Essex	S	C
Morris, Terence	LSE	R	C

Name	Institution	S/R/D/NK	C/C*/Ref/NR/NT
Morton-Williams, Peter	Ulster	NK	NR/NT
Mouzelis, Nicos	LSE	S	C
Mulkay, Michael	York	S	C
Neustadt, Ilya	Leicester	D	C*
Newby, Howard	Southampton	S	C
Nichols, Theo	Cardiff	S	C
Oakley, Ann	Institute of Education, London	S	C
O'Dowd, Liam	Queen's, Belfast	S	C
Oliver, Michael	Greenwich	S	C
Orr, John	Edinburgh	S	C
Outhwaite, William	Sussex	S	C
Pahl, Ray	Essex	S	C
Payne, Geoff	Plymouth	S	C
Peel, John	SOAS	S	C
Phillipson, Chris	Keele	S	C
Phizacklea, Annie	Leicester	S	NR/NT
Pinker, Bob	LSE	R	C
Platt, Jennifer	Sussex	S	C
Plummer, Ken	Essex	S	C
Pringle, Rosemary	Southampton	S	C
Raffe, David	Edinburgh	S	C
Ray, Larry	Kent	S	C
Rex, John	Warwick	R	C
Richardson, Linda	Newcastle	NK	NR/NT
Roberts, Ken	Liverpool	S	C
Rock, Paul	LSE	S	C
Room, Graham	Bath	S	C
Rose, David	Essex	S	C
Rose, Michael	Bath	NK	NR/NT
Rothman, Harry	UWE	S	C
Rucht, Dieter	Kent	S	C
Runciman, W. G.[4]	Cambridge	S	C
Saunders, Peter	Sussex	S	C
Savage, Mike	Manchester	S	C
Sayer, Andrew	Lancaster	S	C
Scott, John	Essex	S	C
Seidler, Vic	Goldsmiths	S	NR/NT
Shanin, Teodor	Manchester	R	C
Shapiro, Dan	Lancaster	S	C
Sharrock, Wes	Manchester	S	C
Shilling, Chris	Portsmouth	S	C
Shils, Edward	Cambridge	D	C*
Silverman, David	Goldsmiths	R	C

[4] Not formally a professor: included in error.

Name	Institution	S/R/D/NK	C/C*/Ref/NR/NT
Silverstone, Roger	LSE	S	C
Simey, Tom (Lord)	Liverpool	D	C*
Skeggs, Beverley	Manchester	S	C
Smart, Barry	Portsmouth	S	C
Smart, Carol	Leeds	S	C
Smith, John	Southampton	R	NR/NT (Died 2002)
Snowden, Robert	Exeter	S	NR/NT
Solomos, John	South Bank	S	C
South, Nigel	Essex	S	C
Sprott, W. J. H.	Nottingham	D	C*
Stacey, Margaret	Warwick	R	C
Stanley, Liz	Manchester	S	C
Stewart, W. A. Campbell	Keele	D	C*
Stimson, Gerry	Imperial	S	C
Tarling, Roger	Surrey	S	NR/NT
Taylor, Ian	Durham	D	C*
Taylor, Laurie	York	R	C
Tester, Keith	Portsmouth	S	C
Thompson, Kenneth	Open	S	C
Thompson, Paul	Essex	S	C
Timms, Duncan	Stirling	S	C
Titmuss, Richard	LSE	D	C*
Townsend, Peter	Bristol	R	C
Tropp, Asher	Surrey	R	C
Tumber, Howard	City	S	C
Turner, Bryan	Cambridge	S	C
Turner, C.	Stirling	NK	NR/NT
Ungerson, Clare	Southampton	S	NR/NT
Urry, John	Lancaster	S	C
Vannelli, Ron	Central England	S	C
Waddington, P. A. J.	Reading	S	C
Wakeford, John	Lancaster	S	C
Walby, Sylvia	Leeds	S	C
Walker, Alan	Sheffield	S	C
Walklate, Sandra	Manchester Metropolitan	S	C
Wallis, Roy	Queen's, Belfast	D	C*
Walsh, David	Glasgow Caledonian	S	C
Warde, Alan	Manchester	S	C
Webb, Adrian	Glamorgan	S	C
Webster, Frank	Birmingham	S	C
Wedderburn, Dorothy	Royal Holloway	R	C
Weeks, Jeffrey	South Bank	S	C

Name	Institution	S/R/D/NK	C/C*/Ref/NR/NT
Wenger, G. Clare	Bangor	S	C
Westergaard, John	Sheffield	R	C
Westermarck, E. A.	LSE	D	C*
Westwood, Sallie	Manchester	S	C
Whitty, Geoff	Institute of Education, London	S	C
Williams, Fiona	Leeds	S	C
Willis, Paul	Wolverhampton	S	C
Witkin, R.	Essex	S	NR/NT
Woodiwiss, A.	City	S	NR/NT
Woodward, Joan	Imperial	D	C*
Woolgar, Steve	Brunel	S	NR/NT
Wootton, Barbara	Bedford College	D	C*
Worsley, Peter	Manchester	R	C
Yeandle, Sue	Sheffield Hallam	S	C
Yearly, Steve	York	S	C
Young, Jock	Middlesex	S	C
Young, Michael[5]	Institute of Community Studies	S	C
Yuval-Davis, Nira	Greenwich	S	C

TABLE A1.1 *Survey of British professors of sociology 2001*

Professors	N	%	Questionnaires	N	%
Serving	202	69	Completed by respondent	216	73
Retired	46	16	Completed using records	40	14
Dead	40	14	Refused to participate	1	0.3
Not known	8	2	Not traced or not returned	32	13
Total	296		Total	296	

[5] Not formally a professor: included in error.

Appendix 2

Students Numbers and Quality
1950–2000

In this appendix, we assemble the twentieth-century numbers and explore the quality of students in sociology, in social science faculties, and in universities in the United Kingdom. The task is not easy as the numbers are not readily available from official sources. A fully developed 'science of society' would require not only an Office of National Statistics (ONS) but records agreed with and freely available to academic social researchers. So many hours must be spent searching through the statistics with their ever-changing administrative responsibility and apparently arbitrary shifts in relevant definitions. And to all this has to be added the labours of civil servants who have been unfailingly helpful in my experience over many years.

Figures A2.1–4 present the total number of students from 1950 to the end of the twentieth century and Figures A2.5–A2.9 detail those studying sociology. They should be read with due attention to the appended notes. Even so, however, the story of growth is remarkable. It represents an expansion of education beyond school in response to the opportunities and demands of modern industrialism. In that process, the relevant vocabulary has been transformed. From the economically marginal university with its dons and undergraduates and its theology and associated arts in the service of church and state there has rapidly emerged a mass system of tertiary education with its students, graduate students, teachers, and researchers and its applied sciences serving the competitive needs of a modern, secular, perennially innovating society. The medieval university has come to occupy a small space in a vast international apparatus of 'continuing education' and research. In 1900, the British universities had about 20,000 students and yet in 2000 there were more than 70,000 university teachers. At that point there were about 5 million students in higher and further (i.e. tertiary) education and the Prime Minister, Tony Blair, promised the 1997 Labour Party Conference that 'we will lift the cap on student numbers and set a target for an extra 500,000 people in tertiary education by 2002'. Thus, in 1900, the universities took in 0.8 per cent of the relevant age group. By 1954, when sociology was beginning to be recognized, it was 3.2 per cent; in 1972 it was 6.0 per cent. Now, according to Dearing (1997), it is to be 50 per cent. So whereas only one person in eighteen went through tertiary education at the beginning of the twentieth century, it is to be one in two in the twenty-first.

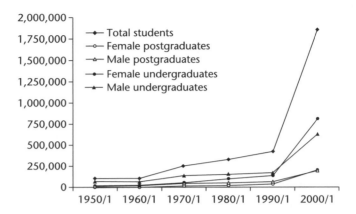

FIG.A2.1 UK universities all students 1950–2000/1

Notes

'Undergraduate' = first degrees, first diplomas, and other courses.

For sociology students: 1950/1—data for postgraduate students only (defined as 'sociology and criminology').

There are no decennial data for sociology students in 1960/1 or 1970/1. We have the total number of sociology students for 1972/3, and the number of sociology undergraduates and postgraduates for 1980/1.

1972/3 sociology numbers are given for universities and not all HE institutions. The figures are for full-time students only.

1980/1 and 1990/1 cover sociology undergraduates by UK domicile only, so foreign students are excluded. However, foreign students are included in the part-time figures for 1990/1.

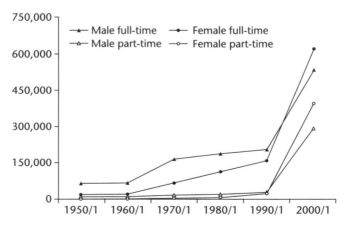

FIG.A2.2 UK universities all full-time and part-time students
1950/1–2000/1

Note: See Fig. A2.1.

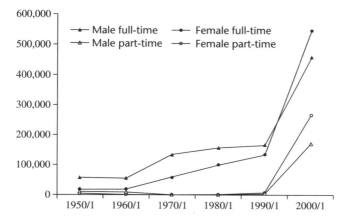

FIG.A2.3 UK universities all undergraduates 1950/1–2000/1
Note: See Fig. A2.1.

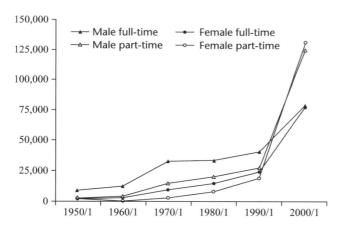

FIG.A2.4 UK universities all postgraduates 1950/1–2000/1
Note: See Fig. A2.1.

This is the background against which the expansion of sociology has to be assessed. We have attempted this numerically in Figs. A2.5–A2.9. Before 1950 the numbers were trivial, by 1970 they were 6,228, by 2000 they were 24,080. By the end of the century, sociology was being taught in 114 (out of 165) higher educational institutions in the United Kingdom. Of these, sixty-five were made universities after the 1992 decision to 'elevate' to university status ninety-six polytechnics or other tertiary colleges. There were more sociology students in these recently promoted institutions (14,824) than in the previously established universities (9,256) and they were made up disproportionately of women and part-timers. Before 1992, through the 1980s, the number

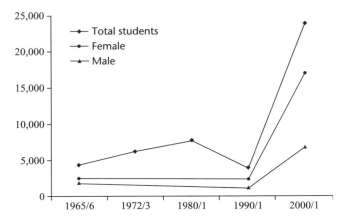

FIG.A2.5 UK universities all sociology students
1965/6–2000/1

Note: See Fig. A2.1.

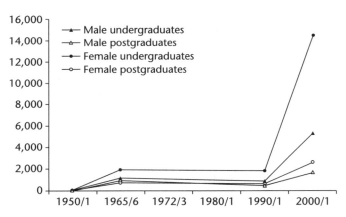

FIG.A2.6 UK universities sociology students 1950/1–2000/1
Note: See Fig. A2.1.

of male graduate and undergraduate students had been falling; after 1992 the number of men rose but the number of women rose even faster. Female sociology students, undergraduate, postgraduate, part-time, or full-time, had slightly outnumbered male students from early in the 1960s. After 1992, they outdistanced the men heavily among undergraduates, less so among graduates.

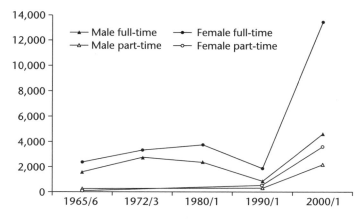

FIG.A2.7 UK universities part-time sociology students
1965/6–2000/1

Note: See Fig. A2.1.

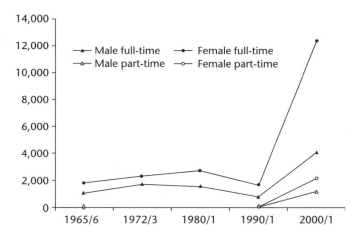

FIG.A2.8 UK universities sociology undergraduates
1965/6–2000/1

Note: See Fig. A2.1.

With respect to the figures it should be noted that the effect of decennial readings is to smooth out the trends. Thus, neither the Robbins Report of 1963 nor the 1992 decision show as points of acceleration. In both cases, however, and especially the latter, there was a definite increase in the rate of growth on these two dates. Among graduates, part-time students increased most rapidly after 1992, followed by full-time women and full-time men.

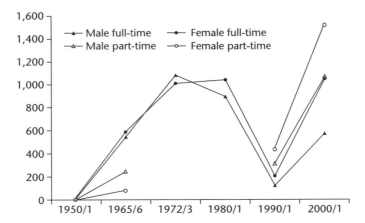

FIG.A2.9 UK universities sociology postgraduates 1950/1–2000/1
Note: See Fig. A2.1.

The Quality of Sociology Students

We discussed the quality of sociology staff in Chapter 8 and came to an indeterminate conclusion, partly through lack of survey evidence. There is,
however, an indirect approach by considering the quality of students at entry
and exit. Ideally, what is required is a comprehensive record of the school,
university, and occupational careers of all students in order to place the sociologists in the wider picture. In practice this is not possible. We cannot, to start
at the beginning, measure the extent to which talent (however defined) has
switched from one path to another. Have talented people moved from the staff
of universities and the civil service to other economic sectors during the
twentieth century? Some believe so but no one can be sure.

At the point of entry to British universities we do have records of A-Level performance among home (i.e. UK) applicants who were accepted. They are shown
in Table A2.1 as mean scores at GCE A-Level for sociology compared with students of other subjects. Sociology students, as defined by A-Level performance,
are poorer than the general run of entering undergraduates, distinctly so compared with those studying medicine or mathematics, slightly so compared with
economists, historians, or psychologists, and superior to those reading social
policy, social work, or education. The gap (i.e. the relative scores of average
entrants to these various disciplines) shows a tendency to shrink during the
1980s and 1990s, but the ordering of disciplinary quality remains the same.

In the spring of 2003, Derek Leslie (2003) published a study of the 2.3 million
home-based (UK-domiciled) applicants to higher educational institutions who
went through the UCAS system in the six years 1996–2001. He divided them
into 170 subject groups and ranked the subjects by quality. Medicine and
Dentistry came first. Mathematics was 8th, economics 20th, politics 40th,

TABLE A2.1   *A-level scores at entry 1970–2000*

	1970	1975	1978	1980	1985	1990	1995	2000
Medicine	27.6	57.4	60.2	12.7	13.3	26.7	17.4	19.4
Engineering and technology	15.5	19.3	22.3					
Agriculture and vets	9.5	19.3	20.5					
Maths	34.1	53.4	29.3	10.8	12.2	23.2		
Sociology	12.8	5.6	4.1	7.3	9.0	19.8	14.8	16.8
Economics	12.4	16.7	22.0	9.1	10.9	23.5		
Psychology (social)	14.3	8.9	7.1	8.8	10.7	21.9	23.1	
History	33.8	24.9	21.8	10.3	11.1	39.0		
Education	—	—			8.3	2.4		
All social sciences							10.3	10.0
All subjects	21.5	22.2	23.3	9.7	11.0	21.1	17.4	19.2
% Sociology of all					75	85	94	85	88

Source: University Statistics vol. 1, Students and Staff (published by Universities Statistical Record).

law 43rd, sociology 115th, social policy and administration 153rd, and social work 170th.

But, *pace* Rothschild's witness, the evidence is flimsy. Quality is bound to be subjective in academic matters generally, and perhaps especially in the social studies. Suppose the implausible, that we were able to define and measure talent and its conversion into performance. In practice, this usually means reputation in the first case and number of books and articles in the second. Both are endlessly controversial. We already know that there is a correlation between class of degree and research productivity; but we also know that it is a low one. Rothschild's witness could or should have known the results of the analysis made by the University Central Council of Admissions (UCCA) statisticians and published in their supplement to the Sixth Report (UCCA *Statistical Supplement*, 1967). The connection is there shown to be tenuous. For candidates entering UK universities in 1963 who graduated in 1966 with first-class honours, the array was as shown in Table A2.2.

Thus, performance at entry is associated with performance at exit and the sciences are, on average, more 'talented' than undergraduates in arts or in social studies. So 'talent' at entry can be used as a predictor of talent at graduation which is better than tossing a coin. But how much better?

The UCCA statisticians worked out the correlations as in Table A2.3.
The answer is 'not much'. The higher correlation (r) for the sciences presumably reflects less subjective assessments at both ends and the relative lack of continuity between school and university courses in the arts and social studies.

We are reminded that A-level is not the sole criterion of undergraduate performance. Age, gender, zeal, and other personal and environmental characteristics are together more closely associated with degree results.

TABLE A2.2   *Entry and graduation quality in the United Kingdom 1963–6*

	% with firsts	% with firsts	
		With 3 A-levels	With 2 A-levels
Pure science	9.5	12.5	7.1
Engineering and technology	11.2	16.5	12.5
Arts	3.9	4.9	4.1
Social studies	3.3	4.9	2.2

Source: UCCA Statistical Supplement, 1967.

TABLE A2.3   *Correlation of entry score with class of degree*

	Mean A-level score	Class of degree	Correlation (r)
Pure science	13.684	3.917	0.27
Engineering and technology	13.830	3.583	0.33
Arts	13.850	3.894	0.18
Social studies	13.768	3.689	0.17

Source: As for Table A2.2.

TABLE A2.4   *First-class graduates from UK universities (% with firsts)*

Students	1994/5	2000/1
Sociology	3.5	4.0
All social sciences	4.5	6.5
All	7.0	8.9

Note: Post-1992 universities awarded markedly less firsts in both years.

Source: HESA.

All this must be taken into account in any interpretation of the limited figures set out in Table A2.1. More recently the Higher Education Statistical Agency (HESA) has reported that a considerably greater proportion of first-class degrees was awarded in mathematical sciences (e.g. 23.7 in 2000/1), engineering and technology (14.5), and physical sciences (14.4). The lowest proportions were in the social sciences.

Table A2.4 shows that sociology students at the end of the twentieth century were being awarded half (1995) or less than half (2001) the percentage of firsts received by students in the tertiary system as a whole.

Appendix 3

Citation and Content Analyses

Claire Donovan

Citation Analysis

The professors' survey (Chapter 8 and Appendix 1) shows who, for them, were the most influential and celebrated sociologists in the twentieth century. Of course, the preferences of the professors do not necessarily reflect the views of the profession at large today or throughout various stages of the twentieth century. A citation analysis of British sociology journals may appear to provide an alternative 'objective' measure of influence but (and this may at first seem counter-intuitive) citation analysis is not as straightforward a measure of influence as the professors' survey. While citation analysis quantifies citation patterns, the methods and interpretations of such analyses have been hotly contested. It is therefore necessary to explain our particular choices of method, and how this affects the outcomes of our study and what realistically can be measured.

Citation analysis is familiar through the efforts of the Philadelphia-based Institute of Scientific Information (ISI)[1] established by Eugene Garfield in 1958, and through such resources as the *Web of Science*.[2] The ISI compiles the Science Citation Index (SCI), the Social Science Citation Index (SSCI), and the Arts and Humanities Citation Index (AHCI) from references to journal articles and some edited collections of papers published as books. The analysis operates by recording the references made in the footnotes, endnotes, or bibliographies of these papers and presents the total frequencies (and source details) of citations of authors, books, papers, and journals. For the social sciences, ISI (in the form of SSCI) covers 1,725 journals which span fifty disciplines and add to over 30.15 million entries. ISI data were originally employed in the late 1960s and early 1970s by historians of science and sociologists of science. But what precisely does citation analysis measure?

Citation analysis is used to indicate relative levels of impact by particular researchers or particular works in certain subjects. How often an author or a work is cited is treated as a gauge of influence and of research quality. Citation

---

[1] http://www.isinet.com/isi/   [2] http://wos.mimas.ac.uk/

patterns are taken as an objective measure of research quality free from any subjective biases, providing a simple empirical record of who influences the work of others in their field (Bavelas, 1978). So far so good. However, the production and interpretation of citation analyses have not only been the object of sociological use but also the subject of sociological investigation, so we should expect to find that these processes are not as straightforward as they may at first appear. The traditional view takes for granted the question of what citation analysis really is, something that has become by default 'embodied in the procedures of ISI' (Hicks and Potter, 1991: 481). Critics have seized upon two areas of weakness, with citation analysis generally (Phelan, 1999) and ISI procedures in particular (Chapman, 1989).

In the late 1970s, citation analysis was criticized by 'new' sociologists of science who linked attitudes towards citation to competing philosophies of science. The traditional and social constructivist views are 'two entirely different accounts of the validity and function of citation where on the one hand citations are unproblematic and citation analysis provides valid data for analysis, and on the other hand citations are seen as a deeply problematic basis for data evaluation' (MacRoberts and MacRoberts, 1996: 438). While some critics believe that despite some obvious flaws, if handled correctly, citation analysis remains a fairly reliable measure of research impact, constructivists largely dismiss citation analysis as an indicator of anything concrete. The social constructivist approach thus entails a sceptical view of the worth of citation analysis as its basic assumptions 'are clearly false' (1996: 422) and we must question citation data as a true measure of the value of a work or as a means of bestowing credit on colleagues.

The constructivist approach mentioned above differs from the traditional perspective because it is concerned with social aspects of citation; 'a scientific contribution does not become legitimised until it has been endorsed by other scientists' (Baldi, 1998: 829–30). Thus, scientific progress is part of a socially constructed pattern of agreement and endorsement. Attention is given to the context of citation or '*how* authors use their colleagues' work' (Hargens, 2000: 857), and social science is thought to differ from natural science (the model of disciplinary organization upon which the traditional approach depends) because social scientists tend to cite foundational rather than recent publications. In this light, citations are taken to have a rhetorical use and social scientists in particular use citations to justify and contextualize their work by aligning their efforts with influential texts and authors. This has become part of the expected 'packaging' for journal articles because social science is written for a 'heterogeneous' audience of allegiances and fields. If there is little assumed shared knowledge the author is obliged to go back to first principles to explain why his or hers is a significant contribution (Hargens, 1991, 2000).

Several authors note that when social scientists refer to foundational or 'classic' works, in contrast to natural scientists they rarely cite empirical evidence to elaborate research methods and they instead tend to cite general themes, sometimes mistakenly (Platt, 1984; Chapman, 1989; Delamont, 1989). Citations are often used as 'totemic representations' of general approaches initiated by foundational works and become 'shorthand markers of general perspectives' (Hargens, 2000: 859–60), while past empirical results are, it seems, 'delivered to an empty house' (Cozzens, 1985: 147). It is felt that there is often citation without knowledge: 'No doubt some authors sometimes cite in a perfunctory fashion, without themselves having more than a superficial knowledge of particular papers in their reference lists' and this may add to the citation counts of 'established, cited works and eminent persons' (Chapman, 1989: 341).

Critical concerns with citation analysis may be divided into two areas: 'conceptual concerns'—what citation analysis truly measures—and 'methods'—the technicalities of how citation analyses should be conducted.

Limitations of citation analysis: conceptual concerns

An issue of fundamental importance is what citation analysis really measures. The traditional ideal is that citation levels point to the inherent quality of the research cited but quantity does not simply mean quality. For example, there is the idea of negative citation, that referring to a work 'does not necessarily denote approval' as some highly cited research may be 'poorly regarded, perhaps defective' if 'there has been a failure to replicate or verify' or 'even because the research is known to be fraudulent'. Yet negative citations do indicate the impact of research as academics tend to ignore unimportant work and negative citations may indicate that 'a piece of work has substance' as a valuable step in the development of knowledge (Chapman, 1989: 341). An alternative approach is to accept that citations measure 'impact' so that uncertainties surrounding any unrecognized or inherent qualities of a piece of work may be avoided (Martin, 1996). Judgements of research 'quality' are beyond the scope of what citation analyses can measure, while assessments of 'impact' are not.

Yet this approach too has its shortcomings. Although we may accept that citation analysis is a reasonable indicator of research impact, there are many influences that it cannot measure. There is the phenomenon of 'obliteration' where original sources are no longer cited because sociological concepts and methods have become assumed knowledge (Hicks and Potter, 1991; Hargens, 2000). This is an important consideration because the traditional view assumes that scientists cite work that has influenced them, yet MacRobers and MacRoberts (1996) found that bibliographies typically cover only 30 per cent of the influence evident in the body of a paper, a figure they maintain applies equally to natural science and to sociology. Indeed, their analysis finds one-third of references credited to someone other than the original researcher. In this sense, citation is a far more complex process than assumed by the traditional approach, particularly when we add that informal influences, such as the views of colleagues, go uncited (Cronin et al., 1993) and influence credited in the acknowledgements section of a paper may be more significant than a particular reference made or the efforts of a co-author. Citation patterns may also be distorted by the activities of invisible colleges or networks, although it is fair to say that where these exist they are 'little more than a manifestation of the power relations existing within that field. That citation counts reflect this reality is not a methodological shortcoming' (Phelan, 1999: 124).

When considering 'impact' a further factor is the assumption that 'all papers have the same probability of being cited, the same potential citing audience'. However, while sociologists working in a small specialist area may gain few citations, this does not mean that their work has relatively low impact, but reflects the fact that in a narrow field of research there are few people to cite and to be cited by. It follows that, if we are to 'determine if a paper...has received the proper number of citations, [we] would first have to know its potential audience. This is never known' (MacRoberts and MacRoberts, 1996).

Limitations of citation analysis: methods

Alternative methods will yield different results. For example, the range of sources from which bibliographies are drawn will affect the outcome of any study. Moreover the question arises as to whether all the works cited in chosen bibliographies should be included for analysis. As potential sources, should all journal entries be treated equally, irrespective of length and content? Should research papers, review articles, and short book reviews be equally weighted? Are reviews original research? The ISI includes all types of journal entries, and while incongruities will occur because it is 'unavoidable that very large-scale, computerised enumeration lacks sophistication', we may remain uncomfortable with the idea that all journal contributions are treated equally (Chapman, 1989: 341). As a crude measure of the significance of a contribution, smaller-scale citation analyses often exclude bibliographies that, for example, belong to papers less than ten pages long, although it is unusual to exclude any work cited by an accepted bibliography. The ISI does not include all the fringe journals of various disciplines or fields, and the efforts of editors of journals and books may go without credit, factors that all smaller-scale analyses must grapple with.

One of the most pressing issues, particularly when dealing with the social sciences, is that bibliographies of monographs are not included as sources for ISI information. Citation analysis based upon journal publications evolved from the study of publishing patterns in the natural sciences where the dynamic of research compels scientists to report their findings quickly before they are 'scooped': so they publish in journals. Social scientists, according to some, are not so concerned about this speed of publication and often prefer 'lengthy exposition and extensive reference to past work' in book form (Hargens, 1991). In this light the SSCI is 'asymmetric' as the impact of books is greatly underestimated (Clemens *et al.*, 1995). It may, however, be noted that while the SSCI does not include the bibliographies of books, it does represent the impact of books that are cited by papers.

Various approaches to recording authors' details will affect the outcome of citation analyses. ISI lists only the first author of a work rather than all named contributors. So, for example, in the *Affluent Worker* series, Goldthorpe gains the full ISI citation and Lockwood, Bechhofer, and Platt go uncredited, while for a later joint publication with Erikson, Goldthorpe is unrecognized. This is clearly a problem when attempting to assess the influence of particular persons. Too great or too small a weighting may be given to an individual's contribution. A moot point is whether reference to one's own work should be allowed. At an aggregate level this may not be a problem, although 'removing self-citations is an important prerequisite when comparing the performance of specific reearchers' (Phelan, 1999).

A crucial consideration is that ISI does in some respects, and not in others, take account of the *distribution* of references. For example, ISI will allow only one citation per work no matter how many times it is cited by one source, but will allow the same source to provide numerous citations to an author or journal if different works are mentioned. Chapter 9 demonstrates that this has dramatic consequences in frequency counts.

While there is suspicion of the value of international data sets, an emerging counter-trend within the recent literature is to develop alternative bibliometric approaches designed for specific purposes, and small-scale nationally oriented studies are proving to be more revealing than ISI data alone (Hicks, 1999; Phelan, 1999). In spite of various criticisms of citation analysis, this self-aware, smaller-scale approach is a simple empirical measure of the most cited individuals and works in particular contexts, and whatever motivations may or may not lie behind citation behaviour, the outcome is representative of sociologists' citation choices at given times.

Citation analysis: our approach

So how did we grapple with the various conceptual and methodological concerns about citation analysis? And how did we shape our research design? We followed the lead of Hicks and Phelan and set out to construct a small-scale, nationally oriented study designed to overcome the perceived shortcomings of the ISI approach.

Our sources were the three mainstream British sociology journals: *Sociological Review*, the *British Journal of Sociology*, and *Sociology*, taken decennially from 1910 to 2000. We included all types of journal entries that were at least ten pages in length (including notes and bibliography). The result was a sample of 371 papers.

The credit for jointly authored papers was divided equally between all authors rather than purely on a first author only basis. Self-citation was allowed and noted so that the number of self-citations could be subtracted if required. The distribution of references in each paper was limited to one per journal, author, and specific collaboration, although the unweighted totals were recorded for comparison. Our main concern was with the number of citations to authors and journals, and once the most highly cited authors were listed their most cited texts were identified. This revealed that the impact of books is not lost in a journal-based analysis.

Our citation study provides a snapshot of the *influence* of particular sociologists and specific texts on the citation habits of sociologists in Britain in different decades of the twentieth century. Our methods modify and improve traditional approaches and, because we measure the direction of sociology through the sum total of citing authors' actions, constructivist arguments about their underlying motivations become redundant.

Content Analysis

In contrast to citation analysis, content analysis of journal papers is a less common activity and perhaps as a consequence has historically been less controversial. Content analysis does not derive its data from bibliographies—the object of study is the construction and content of articles. Past examples of the content analyses of sociology papers tend to be allied to the history of sociology and trace the popularity of various areas or fields of sociology (Carter, 1968; Simon, 1969; Collison and Webber, 1971) and study the research methods employed by sociologists (Bechhofer, 1981, 1996; Bulmer, 1989; Gartrell and Gartrell, 2002). Our content analysis expands and modifies these approaches, largely by extending coverage from 1910 to 2000. We also include an original study of the ideologies which underpin the sample papers, mapping the rise and fall of various sociological perspectives (or 'isms') throughout the twentieth century. Thus our content analysis provides a comprehensive empirical study of the development of research methods, the changing fashions in popular areas of sociological enquiry and shifts in ideology, and how these interact, as represented by the mainstream journals for the century that sociology has existed in Britain.

Our starting point was to analyse the papers originally used in our citation analysis. In order to further analyse trends we extended the years covered to include quinquennial years from 1975 onwards, yielding a sample of 649 papers. The detail of our analysis meant that each paper had to be individually scanned and while this process was intense and lengthy it produced a rich and valuable resource.

Our analysis was constructed on a 'text unit' basis (Collison and Webber, 1971) so that each paper is a potentially divisible unit. So, for example, when we calculate the number of women who employ highly quantitative methods in a particular year, if a paper is a female/male joint collaboration this will equal 0.5 of a text unit. All variables were treated in this manner, where appropriate. In addition to the variables listed below, data recorded for each sample paper included: year of publication, journal, journal number and volume, name(s) of author(s), gender, institutional affiliation, discipline, and nationality.

Methods used by sociologists

The previous studies mentioned above are confined to particular periods of time and tend to focus on 'positivism' or empirical methods, and quantification in particular. Our aim was to extend the coverage for the period 1910–2000 and to study the development of both quantitative and qualitative research methods and levels of technical sophistication or otherwise. Sample papers were categorized under the following headings: theory only, empirical, quantitative, qualitative, and both quantitative and qualitative. Quantitative papers were further divided into: descriptive, low, high, and high and theory only. Qualitative papers were classified as belonging to either the survey or anthropological tradition. (See Chapter 10 for further elaboration.)

Areas studied by sociologists

Past studies of the areas that sociologists choose to study are based upon categories developed by the Sociological Abstracts Classification Scheme (SACS),[3] which divides sociology into a number of areas. We modified this starting point so that, for example, we could distinguish between social theory and sociological theory, and we both expanded and compressed several SACS classes to better handle and interpret our data. Our aim was to provide a map of the ebb and flow of interest in the various sociological fields for the whole of the last century as represented by the core journals. The areas covered include:

Ageing—includes generations, gerontology, the elderly
Biology and behaviour
Sociology of the body
Comparative sociology
Consumption
Culture—includes museums, music
Demography—includes migration
Economic organization—includes industrial relations, political economy, development theory
Education—includes universities
Ethnicity and race
Family—includes marriage, divorce
Gender—also includes masculinity
Health and medicine—includes deviance and labelling 'in terms of mental health', addiction, accidents, death
History of sociology—includes the contemporary state of sociology, the future of sociology
Sociology of knowledge
Law and crime—includes deviance and labelling connected with law breaking behaviour or perceptions of potential criminality or recidivism, prisons, the police, punishment, crime prevention, surveillance
Leisure—includes tourism
Methods—includes practical issues concerning research methods, research ethics, problems of method, discussion of perceived methodological flaws in sociological research
Media and communication—includes television, censorship

[3] http://www.csal.co.uk/csa/factsheets/saclass/shtml

Occupations—specific to particular occupations and professions (not occupa-
  tional scales, which are classified under stratification/social differentiation)
Organizational theory—includes state level (bureaucracy, corporatism) and
  macro level (individual company structures and management schemes)
Political sociology—includes political theory, nationalism
Religion—includes paranormal behaviour/beliefs
Rural sociology
Science and technology
Social anthropology
Social geography—includes ecological sociology and environmentalism,
  regional sociology and planning (rural planning is classified as 'social
  geography' and 'rural'), community studies
Social history
Social movements
Social policy
Social psychology
Social theory—theoretical papers that do not use or discuss the use of socio-
  logical data
Sociological theory—theoretical papers that use or discuss the use of socio-
  logical data
Social welfare—includes social work
Sociology of sport
Stratification/social differentiation—includes class, occupational scales,
  mobility
Urban sociology—includes town planning
Youth

The sample papers could belong to more than one of these areas. The list was
reduced to cover any area that was represented by 5 per cent or more papers in
any given sample year.

Sociologists and ideology

As far as we are aware, this aspect of our citation analysis is a unique attempt to
chart the rise and fall of ideological interests (sociological perspectives or 'isms')
for the duration of the twentieth century. We took our starting point as the commitment to ideologies expressed in the professors' survey and we added new
categories as we encountered them in our sample. The resulting list is as follows:

Action/agency/structuration theory—includes Parsonian/positivist action
  theory, agency and structure (again in the positivist sense), holism v. individualism debate, structuration
Critical theory—includes critical realism
Empiricism—this does not include all articles that use quantitative empirical
  evidence, but refers to work that is explicitly empiricist or that may be
  placed in this paradigm

Exchange theory—includes the Mauss/Levi-Strauss collectivist approach, whereas the individualist approach is classified under 'rational action/choice'

Feminism

Foucauldianism

Freudianism

Functionalism

Interpretivism—includes interactionism, ethnomethodology, hermeneutics

Le Playism

Marxism—includes neo-Marxism

Positivism—includes papers that discuss positivism or that make statements that support or are commensurate with the view that social science should aspire to equivalence with the natural and physical sciences

Postmodernism—includes post-industrialization and post-Fordism

Poststructuralism—includes intertextuality, anti-humanism

Rational action/choice—includes rational action theory, rational choice theory, methodological individualism, individualist exchange theory

Rationalism/realism—excludes critical realism which is classed as 'critical theory'

Relativism

Social constructionism

Structuralism (a)—the view that society is prior to individuals

Structuralism (b)—unobservable social structures that generate observable social phenomena (e.g. Levi-Strauss)

Weberianism—includes neo-Weberianism

Papers could subscribe to one, several, or none of these perspectives. Again, this list was reduced to ideologies covered by at least 5 per cent of the sample papers in any year.

REFERENCES

Abbott, A. (1999), *Department and Discipline: Chicago Sociology at One Hundred* (Chicago: University of Chicago Press).

Abell, Peter, and Reyniers, Diane (2000), 'On the Failure of Social Theory', *British Journal of Sociology*, 51/4: 739–50.

Abel-Smith, B., and Townsend, P. (1965), *The Poor and the Poorest* (London: Bell).

Abrams, Mark (1951), *Social Surveys and Social Action* (London: Heinemann).

Abrams, P. (1968), *The Origins of British Sociology 1834–1914* (Chicago: Chicago University Press).

—— *et al.* (1981), *Practice and Progress: British Sociology, 1950–1980* (London: Allen and Unwin).

Agresti, A., and Finlay, B. (1997), *Statistical Methods for the Social Sciences*, 3rd edn. (Upper Saddle River, NJ: Prentice Hall).

Anderson, O. W. (1972), *Health Care: Can there be Equity?* (New York: Wiley).

Anderson, Perry (1992), *English Questions* (London: Verso).

—— (1968), 'Components of the National Culture', *New Left Review*, No. 50, July/August.

Annan, N. G. (1955), 'The Intellectual Aristocracy' in J. H. Plumb (ed.) *Studies in Social History: a tribute to G. M. Trevelyan* (London: Longman, Green, Co.).

—— (1990), *Our Age* (London: Weidenfeld & Nicholson).

Archbishop of Canterbury's Commission on Urban Priority Areas (1985), *Faith in the City: A Call for Action by Church and Nation* (London: Church House Publishing).

Assiter, A. (1996), *Enlightened Women: Modernist Feminism in a Post-modern Age* (London: Routledge).

Atkinson, A. B. (1969), *Poverty in Britain and the Reform of Social Security* (Cambridge: Cambridge University Press).

Avineri, Shlomo (1967), 'Feuer on Marx and the Intellectuals', *Survey*, 62: 152–5.

Baldi, S. (1998), 'Normative Versus Social Constructivist Processes in the Allocation of Citations: A Network–Analytic Model', *American Sociological Review*, 63: 829–46.

Balzac, H. (1928), *Comédie Humaine* (Paris: L. Conard).

—— (1899), *Eugénie Grandet* (Paris: Calmann-Lévy).

Banks, Olive (1955) *Parity and Prestige in English Secondary Education* (London: Routledge and Kegan Paul).

—— (1981), *Faces of Feminism* (Oxford: Martin Robertson).

Banks, J. (1954), *Prosperity and Parenthood* (London: Routledge and Kegan Paul).

Barker, P. (1991) 'Painting the Portrait of "The Other Britain", New Society 1962–88', *Contemporary Record*, Col. 5, No. 1: 45–61.

Barnett, C. (1986), *The Audit of War* (London: Macmillan).

Barry, B. (1988) 'The Continuing Relevance of Socialism' in Skidelsky, R. (ed.) *Thatcherism* (London: Blackwell), pp. 143–58.

Bauman, Z. (1992), *Risk Society: Towards a New Modernity* (London: Sage).

—— (1997), *Postmodernity and its Discontents* (Oxford: Polity Press).

Bauman, Z. (1998), *Globalization: The Human Consequences* (New York: Columbia University Press).

Bavelas, J. B. (1978), 'The Social Pyschology of Citations', *Canadian Psychological Review*, 19: 158–63.

Bean, P., and Whynes, D. (1986), *Barbara Wootton: Social Science and Public Policy Essays in her Honour* (London: Tavistock).

Beauvoir, De, Simone (1949), *The Second Sex* (London: 1966 Four Square Books edition).

Bechhofer, F. (1981), 'Substantive Dogs and Methodologial Tails: A Question of Fit', *Sociology*, 15/4: 495–505.

—— (1996), 'Quantitative Research in British Sociology: Has it Changed since 1981?', *Sociology*, 30/3: 583–91.

——, Giddens, A., and Lash, S. (1994), *Reflexive Modernisation: Politics, Tradition and Aesthetics in the Modern Social Order* (Cambridge: Polity Press).

Beerbohm, M. (1919), *Seven Men and Two Others* (London: Penguin Books edition (1954)), p. 33.

Bendix, R. (1960), *Max Weber: An Intellectual Portrait* (London: Heinemann).

Berger, Peter (1963), *Invitation to Sociology* (Garden City, NY: Doubleday).

—— and Luckmann, T. (1967), *The Social Construction of Reality* (New York: Doubleday).

Bernal, J. D. (1939), *The Social Function of Science* (London: G. Routledge & Sons Ltd).

Bernard Shaw, G. (1965), *The Complete Prefaces of Bernard Shaw* (London: Hamlyn).

Beveridge, W. (1942), *Social Insurance and Allied Services* (London: HMSO Cmd 6409).

Birrell, W. D. *et al.* (1973), *Social Administration: Readings in Applied Social Science* (Harmondsworth: Penguin).

Birnbaum, N. (2001), *After Progress: American Social Reform and European Socialism in the Twentieth Century* (Oxford: Oxford University Press).

Blackstone, Tessa *et al.* (1970), *Students in Conflict LSE in 1967* (London: Weidenfeld and Nicolson).

Blume, S. (1982) in G. Oldham (ed.) *The Future of Research* (London: SRHE).

Boaz, A., Ashby, A., and Young, K., (2002), 'Systematic Reviews: What have they got to Offer Evidence-based Policy and Practice?', ESRC UK Centre for Evidence Based Policy and Practice: Working Paper 2.

Bock, Kenneth (1978), Theories of Development and Evolution in Bottomore and Nisbet, *History of Sociological Analysis* (1978: 39–79).

Booth, C. (1902–3), *Life and Labour of the People of London*, 17 Vols. (London: Macmillan).

Bottomore, T. B., and Nisbet, R. A. (1978), *History of Sociological Analysis* (London: Heinemann).

Bottomore, T. B., and Rubel, M. (1956), *Karl Marx: Selected Writings in Sociology and Social Philosophy* (London: Watts).

Bourdieu, P. (1984*a*), *Distinction: A Social Critique of the Judgement of Taste* (London: Routledge and Kegan Paul).

—— (1984*b*), *Homo Academicus* (Paris: Ed. De Minuit).

Bowley, A. L., and Burnett-Hurst, A. R. (1915), *Livelihood and Poverty. A Study in the Economic Conditions of Working Class Households in Nottingham, Warrington, Stanley and Reading* (London: Bell and Sons).

Bradbury, Malcolm (1975), *The History Man* (London: Secker and Warburg).

Briggs, Asa (1961), *Social Thought and Social Action. A Study of the Work of Seebohm Rowntree* (London: Longman).

Briggs, Asa (2002), *Michael Young: Social Entrepreneur, the Prolific Public Life of Michael Young* (Basingstoke: Palgrave).

—— and Mcartney, Anne (1984), *Toynbee Hall: The First Hundred Years* (London: Routledge and Kegan Paul).

Brock, W. R. (2002), 'James Bryce and the Future' (London: Proceedings of the British Academy 115/3: 30).

Brown, G., and Harris, T.O. (1978), *The Social Origins of Depression* (London: Tavistock).

Buffon, G. L. L. (1749), *Histoire Naturelle, Générale et Particulaire* (Paris: F. Dufart, an 1808).

Bulmer, M. (1985), *Essays on the History of British Sociological Research* (Cambridge: Cambridge University Press).

—— (1986), *Social Science Research and Social Policy* (London: George Allen & Unwin).

—— (1987a), *Social Policy Research* (London: Macmillan).

—— (1987b), *Social Science Research and Government: Comparative Essays on Britain and the United States* (Cambridge: Cambridge University Press).

—— (1989), 'Theory and Method in Recent British Sociology: Whither the Empirical Impulse?', *British Journal of Sociology*, 40: 394–418.

—— (1991), 'National Contexts for the Development of Social-Policy Research: British and American Research on Poverty and Social Welfare Compared', in P. Wagner, C. H. Weiss, B. Wittrock, and H. Woolman (eds.) *Social Sciences and Modern States: National Experiences and Theoretical Crossroads* (Cambridge: Cambridge University Press).

Bulmer, M., and Rees, A. M. (eds.) (1996), *Citizenship Today: The Contemporary Relevance of T. H. Marshall* (London: UCL Press).

——, Jane Lewis, and David Piachaud (eds.) (1989), *The Goals of Social Policy* (London: Unwin & Hyman).

——, Bales, K., and Sklar, K. K. (eds.) (1993), *The Social Survey in Historical Perspective, 1880–1940* (Cambridge: Cambridge University Press).

Bunyan, J. (1678), *The Pilgrim's Progress from this World to that which is to Come,* ed. by J. Blanton Wharey (1960) (Oxford: Clarendon Press).

Burawoy, M. (1989), 'Two Methods in Search of Science: Skocpol versus Trotsky', *Theory and Society*, 128: 759–805.

—— (1998), 'Critical Sociology: A Dialogue between two Sciences', *Contemporary Sociology*, 27: 12–20.

Burns, T., and Stalker, G. M. (1961), *The Management of Innovation* (London: Tavistock).

Butler, C. V. (1912), *Social Conditions in Oxford* (London: Sidgwick & Jackson).

Butterfield, H. (1963), *The Whig Interpretation of History* (London: G. Bell and Sons).

Calder, A., and Sheridan, D. (eds.) (1984), *Speak for Yourself: A Mass-Observation Anthology 1937–49* (London: J. Cape).

Carnegie UK Trust (1993), *Life, Work and Livelihood in the Third Age: Final Report* (Dunfermline: Carnegie UK Trust).

Carr- Saunders, Alexander, M. (1922), *The Population Problem* (Oxford: Clarendon Press).

—— (1933), *The Professions* (Oxford: Clarendon Press).

—— and Caradog Jones, D. (1927), *The Social Structure of England and Wales* (London: Oxford University Press).

Carter, M. P. (1968), 'Report on a Survey of Sociological Research Data in Britain', *Sociological Review*, 16: 5–40.

Castells, M. (1996), *The Rise of the Network Society* (Cambridge, MA: Blackwell).

—— (1999), *The Information Age: Economy, Society and Culture* (Oxford: Blackwell 3 Vols.).

Chadwick, E. (1842), *Report on the Sanitary Conditions of the Labouring Population of Great Britain* (ed. by M. W. Flinn) (1965) (Edinburgh: Constable).

Chapman, A. J. (1989), 'Assessing Research: Citation-count Shortcomings', *The Psychologist*, 8: 336–44.

Chatterjee, S. K. (2002), *Statistical Thought: A Perspective and History* (Oxford: Oxford University Press).

Clapham Report, The (1946), Cmnd. 6868.

Clemens, E. S., Walter, W. P., McIlwaine, K., and Okamoto, D. (1995), 'Careers in Print: Books, Journals and Scholarly Reputations', *American Journal of Sociology*, 101/2: 433–94.

Cohen, Stan (2001), *States of Denial* (Cambridge: Polity Press).

Cole, S. (2001), *What's Wrong with Sociology?* (New Brunswick, NJ: Transaction).

Cole, D., and Utting, J. E. G. (1962), *The Economic Circumstances of Old People* (Wellwyn: Codicote P).

Coleman, D. (1991), 'Policy Research—Who needs it?', *Governance: An International Journal of Policy and Administration*, 4/4: 420–56.

Coleman, James (1979), 'Sociological Analysis and Social Policy' in T. B. Bottomore and R. A. Nisbet (eds.) *A History of Sociological Analysis* (London: Heinemann), pp. 677–703.

Coleman, Peter (1989), *The Liberal Conspiracy: The Congress for Cultural Freedom and the Struggle for the Mind of Postwar Europe* (New York: Free Press).

Collini, S. (1979), *Liberalism and Sociology: L.T. Hobhouse and Political Argument, 1880–1914* (Cambridge: Cambridge University Press).

Collison, P., and Webber, S. (1971), 'British Sociology, 1950–1970: A Journal Analysis', *Sociological Review*, 19/4: 521–42.

Cozzens, S. E. (1985), 'Comparing the Sciences: Citation Context Analysis of Papers from Neuropharmacology and the Sociology of Science', *Social Studies of Science*, 15: 127–53.

Cronin, B., McKenzie, G., Rubio, L., and Weaver-Wozinak, S. (1993), 'Accounting for Influence: Acknowledgements in Contemporary Sociology', *Journal of the American Society for Information Science*, 44/7: 406–12.

Crouch, Colin (1970), *The Student Revolt* (London: Bodley Head).

—— (1999), *Social Change in Western Europe* (Oxford: Oxford University Press).

—— (2000), *Coping with Post-democracy* (London: Fabian Society).

Cullen, M. (1975), *The Statistical Movement in early Victorian Britain* (Hassocks: Harvester).

Cullingworth, J. B. (1965), *English Housing Trends* (London: G. Bell).

D'Aeth, F. G. (1910), 'Present Tendencies of Class Differentiation', *Sociological Review*, III/4: 267–76.

Dacre, Lord (1996), 'Edward Still 1910–1995', *Minerva*, XXXIV, No. 1 Spring. 89–93.

Dahrendorf, R. (1988), *The Modern Social Conflict* (London: Weidenfeld & Nicholson).

—— (1959), *Class and Class Conflict in an Industrial Society* (Stanford: Stanford University Press).

—— (1995), *The London School of Economics, 1895–1995* (Oxford: Oxford University Press).

Danchev, A. (1993), *Oliver Franks: Founding Father* (Oxford: Clarendon Press).

Darwin, C. (1859), *The Origin of the Species* (London: John Murray).

Darwin, F. (ed.) (1887), *The Life and Letters of Charles Darwin* (London: John Murray).

Davidoff, Leonore, and C. Hall (1987), *Family Fortunes: Men and Women of the English Middle Class 1780–1850* (London: Hutchinson).

Davies, B. (1968), *Social Needs and Resources in Local Services* (London: Michael Joseph).

Davies, H. T. O., Nutley, S. M., and Smith, P. C. (eds.) (2000), *What Works? Evidence Based on Policy and Practice in Public Services* (Bristol: Policy Press).

Dearing, R. (1997), *Higher Education in the Learning Society* (London: NCIHE/97/849–852, 856–861).

Defoe, D. (1927), *The Fortunes and Misfortunes of the Famous Moll Flanders* (Oxford: Basil Blackwell).

Delamont, S. (1980), *The Sociology of Women* (London: Allen & Unwin).

—— (1989), 'Citation and Social Mobility Research: Self-defeating Behaviour?', *Sociological Review*, 37/2: 322–37.

Dench, Geoff, Flower, Tony, and Gavron, Kate (1995), *Young at Eighty* (Manchester: Carcanet).

Dennis, N. (1970), *People and Planning* (London: Faber).

—— (1980), 'Sociology, Education and Equality', *Oxford Review of Education*, 5/2: 114.

Dennis, N., and Halsey, A. H. (1988), *English Ethical Socialism* (Oxford: Clarendon Press).

Dennis, N., Henriques, F., and Slaughter, C. (1956), *Coal is Our Life* (London: Eyre and Spottiswode).

Dickens, C. (1854), *Hard Times* (London: J.M. Dent, 1907).

—— (1839), *Oliver Twist* (London: Richard Bentley).

—— (1857), *Little Dorrit* (London: Bradbury and Evans).

—— (1865), *Our Mutual Friend* (London: Chapman and Hall).

Disraeli, B. (1871), *Sybil: or The Two Nations* (London: Longmans, Green).

Donnison, D.V. (1954), *The Neglected Child and the Social Services* (Manchester: Manchester University Press).

—— (1989), 'Social Policy: The Community based Approach', in Bulmer *et al.* (eds.) 1989.

Donovan, Claire (2002), *Government Policy and the Direction of Social Science Research*, D.Phil. Thesis, University of Sussex.

Douglas, J. (1967), *The Social Meaning of Suicide* (Princeton: Princeton University Press).

Douglas, Mary (1987), *How Institutions Think* (London: Routledge and Kegan Paul).

Durkheim, E. (1915), *The Elementary Forms of the Religious Life: A Study in Religious Sociology* (London: G. Allen & Unwin).

—— (1938), *The Rules of Sociological Method* (Glencoe, IL: Free Press).

—— (1947), *The Division of Labour in Society* (Glencoe, IL: Free Press) (First published 1893).

Easthope, G. (1974) *A History of Social Research Methods* (London: Longman).

Eldridge, J. E. T. (1980), *Recent British Sociology* (London: Macmillan).

Eliot, G. (1861, 1967), *Silas Marner: The Weaver of Raveloe*, ed. by Q. D. Leavis (Harmondsworth: Penguin).

Eliot, T. S. (1948), *Notes Towards the Definition of Culture* (London: Faber).

Engels, Friedrich (1892), *Conditions of the Working Class in England in 1844* (London: Allen & Unwin).

Esping-Anderson, Gosta (1990), *The Three Worlds of Welfare Capitalism* (Cambridge: Polity Press).

—— (2000), 'Two Societies, One Sociology, and No Theory', *British Journal of Sociology*, 51/1: 59–77.

ESRC Study Group (1987), *Horizons and Opportunities in the Social Sciences*, Economic and Social Research Council.

Evans, G., and Mills, C. (2000), 'In the Search of the Wage–Labour /service contract: New Evidence on the Validity of the Goldthorpe Class Schema', *British Journal of Sociology*, 51/4: 641–61.

Fitzpatrick, E. (1990), *Endless Crusade: Women Social Scientists and Progressive Reform* (Oxford: Oxford University Press).

Fletcher, R. (ed.) (1974) , *The Science of Society and the Unity of Mankind* (London: Heinemann).

Flora, P., and Heidenheimer, A. J. (1981), *The Development of Welfare States in Europe and America* (New Brunswick: Transaction).

Floud, J., Halsey, A. H., and Martin, F. M. (1956), *Social Class and Educational Opportunity* (London: Heinemann).

Fox, A. (1985), *History and Heritage: The Social Origins of Britain's Industrial Relations System*, (London: Allen & Unwin).

Freud, S. (1933), *New Introductory Lectures on Psycho-analysis*, tr. by W. J. H. Sprott (London: Hogarth Press).

Garfinkel, H. (1967), *Studies in Ethnomethodology* (Englewood Cliffs, NJ: Prentice Hall).

Gartrell, C. D., and Gartrell, A. W. (2002), 'Positivism in Sociological Research: USA and UK (1966–1990)', *British Journal of Sociology*, 53/4: 639–57.

Gellner, Ernest (1959), *Words and Things* (London: Gollancz).

—— (1992), *Post Modernism, Reason and Religion* (New York and London: Routledge).

—— (1995), 'Review of Ralf Dahrendorf's *LSE*' in *Times Literacy Supplement*, 26 May.

Gerth, H., and Mills, C. W. (1948), *From Max Weber: Essays in Sociology* (London: Routledge and Kegan Paul).

Giddens, A. (1973), *The Class Structure of the Advanced Societies* (London: Hutchinson).

—— (1976), *New Rules of Sociological Method: A Positive Critique of Interpretative Sociologies* (London: Hutchinson).

—— (1979), *Central Problems in Social Theory: Action, Structure and Contradiction in Social Analysis* (London: Macmillan).

—— (1984), *The Constitution of Society: Outline of the Theory of Structuration* (Cambridge: Polity Press).

—— (1990), *The Consequences of Modernity* (Cambridge: Polity Press).

—— (1991), *Modernity and Self-Identity* (Cambridge: Polity Press).

Ginsberg, M. (1940), 'The Life and Work of Edward Westermarck', *Sociological Review*, XXVII/182: 1–28.

—— (1944), *Moral Progress: The Frazer Lecture 1944* (Glasgow: Jackson).

—— (1947), *Reason and Unreason in Society, Vol. 2* (London: London School of Economics).

—— (1953a), *The Idea of Progress: A Revaluation* (London: Methuen).

—— (1953b), *On the Diversity of Morals: Huxley Memorial Lecture 1953* (London: Royal Anthropological Institute).

—— (1965), *On Justice in Society* (London: Heinemann).

Glass, David, V. (ed.) (1940), *Population, Policies and Movements in Europe* (Oxford: Clarendon Press).

—— (ed.) (1954), *Social Mobility in Britain* (London: Routledge and Kegan Paul).

Glass, David (1978), Obituary, *The Times,* 27 September.

Glass, Ruth (1955),'Urban sociology in Great Britain: A Trend Report', *Current Sociology*, 4.

Goffman, E. (1971), *The Presentation of Self in Everyday Life* (Harmondsworth: Penguin).

Goldman, Lawrence (1983), 'The Origins of British "Social Science", Political Economy, Natural Science and Statistics, 1830–1835', *The Historical Journal*, 26/3: 587–616.

—— (1986), 'The Social Science Association, 1857–1886: A context for mid-Victorian Liberalism', *English Historical Review*, Vol. CI, No. 433: 95–134.

—— (1987), 'A Peculiarity of the English?, The Social Science Association and the Absence of Sociology in nineteenth-century Britain', *Past and Present*, 114: 133–70.

—— (1991), 'Statistics and the Science of Society in Early Victorian Britain: An Intellectual Context for the General Register Office', *Social History of Medicine*, 4/3: 415–34.

—— (2002), *Science, Reform and Politics in Victorian Britain* (Cambridge: Cambridge University Press).

Goldthorpe, J. H. (1980), *Social Mobility and Class Structure in Modern Britain* (Oxford: Clarendon Press).

—— (2000), *On Sociology: Numbers, Narratives, and the Integration of Research and Theory* (Oxford: Oxford University Press).

—— (1973), 'A Revolution in Sociology', *Sociology*, Vol. 7: 449–62.

Goldthorpe, J. H., Lockwood, D., Platt, J., and Bechhofer, F. (1968*a*), *The Affluent Worker: Industrial Attitudes and Behaviour* (London: Cambridge University Press).

—— (1968*b*), *The Affuent Worker: Political Attitudes and Behaviour* (London: Cambridge University Press).

—— (1969), *The Affluent Worker in the Class Structure* (London: Cambridge University Press).

Gorer, Geoffrey (1955), *Exploring English Character* (London: Cresset).

Gould, J. (1977), *The Attack on Higher Education: Marxist and Radical Penetration* (London: Institute for the Study of Conflict).

Graunt, John (1662), *Natural and Political Observations made upon the London Bills of Mortality* (London: E. Cotes).

Hall, John A. (1981), *Diagnosis of Our Time* (London: Heinemann).

Hall, Penelope (1952), *The Social Services of Modern England* (London: Routledge and Kegan Paul).

Halliday, R. J. (1968), 'The Sociological Movement, The Sociological Society and the Growth of Academic Sociology in Britain', *Sociological Review*, 16/3: 377–98.

Halsey, A. H. (1972), *Educational Priority* (London: HMSO).

—— (1976), *Traditions of Social Policy* (Oxford: Basil Blackwell).

—— (1995*a*), *The Decline of Donnish Dominion*, 2nd edn. (Oxford: Oxford University Press).

—— (1995*b*), 'Education and Ethical Socialism', 129–34 in Dench *et al.* (eds.), *Young at Eighty*.

—— (1996), *No Discouragement: An Autobiography* (Basingstoke: Macmillan).

—— and Floud, J. E. (1961), *Education, Economy and Society: A Reader in the Sociology of Education* (London: Macmillan).

—— and Webb, J. (ed.) (2000), *Twentieth-Century British Social Trends* (Basingstoke: Macmillan).

—— , Trow, M., and Fulton, O. (1971), *The British Academics* (London: Faber).

—— , Heath, A. F., and Ridge, J. M. (1980), *Origins and Destinations* (Oxford: Oxford University Press).

Hankins, F. H. (1908), *Adolphe Quetelet as Statistician* (New York: Columbia University Studies in History, Economics, and Public Law).

Hardy, G. H. (1977, 1942), *Bertrand Russell and Trinity: A College Controversy of the Last War*, (Cambridge: CUP, 1942, New York, Arno).

Hargens, L. L. (1991), 'Impressions and Misimpressions about Sociology Journals', *Contemporary Sociology*, 20/3: 343–9.

—— (2000), 'Using the Literature: Reference Networks, Reference Contexts, and the Social Structure of Scholarship', *American Sociological Review*, 65/6: 846–65.

Harris, J. (1977), *Willam Beveridge: A Biography* (Oxford: Clarendon Press).

—— (1989), 'The Webbs, The Charity Organisation Society and the Ratan Tata Foundation' in Bulmer *et al.* (1989), 27–63.

Harrison, Royden (2000), *The Life and Times of Sidney and Beatrice Webb 1858–1905: The Formative Years* (London: Macmillan).

Hawthorn, G. (1976), *Enlightenment and Despair: A History of Sociology* (Cambridge: Cambridge University Press).

Hayek, F. A. von (1945), *The Road to Serfdom* (London: Routledge and Kegan Paul).

Hayward, Jack *et al.* (eds.) (1999), *The British Study of Politics in the Twentieth Century* (Oxford: Oxford University Press).

Held, D., McGrew, A., Goldblatt, D., and Perraton, J. (1999), *Global Transformations: Politics, Economics and Culture* (Cambridge: Polity Press).

Hellevik, D. (1997), 'Class Inequality and Egalitarian Reform', *Acta Sociologica*, 40/4: 377–97.

Heyde, C., and Seneta, E. (eds.) (2001), *Statisticians of the Centuries* (New York: Springer).

Hicks, D. (1999), 'The Difficulty of Achieving Full Coverage of International and Social Science Literature and the Bibliometric Consequences', *Scientometrics*, 44/2: 193–215.

—— and Potter, J. (1991), 'Sociology of Scientific Knowledge: A Reflexive Citation Analysis *or* Science Disciplines and Disciplining Science', *Social Studies of Science*, 21/3: 459–501.

Hills, J. (1993, 1997), *The Future of Welfare: A Guide to the Debate* (York: Joseph Rowntree Foundation).

Hilts, Victor (1970), 'William Farr (1807–1883) and the "Human Unit"', *Victorian Studies*, 14/2: 145–6.

Hindess, B. (1973), *The Use of Official Statistics in Sociology—A Critique of Posivitism and Ethno Methodology* (London: Macmillan).

Hobhouse, L. T. (1901), *Mind in Evolution* (London: Macmillan).

—— (1906), *Morals in Evolution* (London: Chapman and Hall).

—— (1907), Inaugural Lecture.

—— (1909), *Sociological Review*, 2/402—review of Westermarck's *The Origin and Development of Moral Ideas* (London: Macmillan).

—— (1911), *Liberalism* (London: Oxford University Press).

—— (1913), *Development and Purpose: An Essay Towards a Philosophy of Evolution* (London: Macmillan).

—— (1918), *The Metaphysical Theory of the State: A Criticism* (London: Allen & Unwin).

——, Ginsberg, M., and Wheeler, G. C. W. C. (1915), *The Material Culture and Social Institutions of the Simpler Peoples* (London: Chapman & Hall).

Hogben, L. (1937), *Mathematics for the Million: A Popular Self Educator* (London: George Allen & Unwin).

—— (1938a), *Science for the Citizen: A Self-educator based on the Social Background of Scientific Discovery* (London: George. Allen & Unwin).

Hogben, L. (1938*b*), *Political Arithmetic: A Symposium of Population Studies* (New York: Macmillan Co.).

Hoggart, R. (1957), *The Uses of Literacy* (London: Chatto & Windus).

—— (1991), *Life and Times, Vol. 4, An Imagined Life 1959-1991* (London: Chatto & Windus).

Homans, George C. (1962), *Sentiments and Activities* (London: Routledge and Kegan Paul).

Horowitz, D. L. (2001), *The Deadly Ethnic Riot* (Berkeley: University of California Press).

Husbands, C. (1981), 'Sociologies and Marxisms: The Odd Couples', in Abrams *et al.* (eds.) *Practice and Progress: British Sociology 1950-80*, 163-7.

International Journal of Public Opinion Research (2001), 13/3.

Janowitz, M. (1970), *Political Conflict: Essays in Political Sociology* (Chicago: Quadrangle).

Jeffrey, T. (1978), *Mass Observation: A Short History* (Birmingham: Centre for Contemporary Cultural Studies, University of Birmingham).

Jones, D. C. (1934), *The Social Survey of Merseyside, Liverpool* (Liverpool: Liverpool University Press).

—— (1948), *Social Surveys* (London: Hutchinson).

Jones, K., and Sidebotham, R. (1962), *Mental Hospitals at Work* (London: Routledge and Kegan Paul).

Kelsall, R. K. (1970), 'Review of G. Duncan Mitchell, A Hundred Years of Sociology', *Sociology*, 4: 137-8.

Kent, R. A. (1981), *A History of Empirical Sociology* (Aldershot: Gower).

Kerr, C. (1963), *The Uses of the University* (Cambridge, Mass: Harvard University Press).

Ketchum, John Davidson (1965), *Ruhleban, a Prison Camp Society* (Toronto: University of Toronto Press).

Kevles, D. J. (1985), *In the Name of Eugenics* (New York: Knofp).

Kretschmer, E. (1925), *Physique and Character: An Investigation of the Nature of Constitution and of the Theory of Temperament*, tr. by W. J. H. Sprott (London: Kegan Paul, Trench, Trübner).

Kuhn, T. S. (1962), *The Structure of Scientific Revolutions* (Chicago, London: University of Chicago Press).

Kumar, Krishan (2001), 'Sociology and the Englishness of English Social Thought', *Sociological Theory*, 19/1: 41-64.

Lash, S., and Urry, J. (1994), *Economies of Signs and Space* (London: Sage).

Laslett, Peter (1989), *A Fresh Map of Life: The Emergence of the Third Age* (London: Weidenfeld & Nicholson).

Lazarsfeld, Paul (2001) 'Articles, Appreciations and a select Biography of his Work', *International Journal of Public Opinion Research*, 13: 3.

Leavis, F. R. (1963), *The Great Tradition: George Eliot, Henry James, Joseph Conrad* (Harmondsworth: Penguin in association with Chatto & Windus).

—— (1962), *Two Cultures? The Significance of C.P. Snow* (London: Chatto & Windus).

Lepenies, W. (1988), *Between Literature and Science: The Rise of Sociology* (Cambridge: Cambridge University Press).

Leslie, D. (2003), 'Using success to measure quality in British Higher Education: which subjects attracts the best qualified students?', *Journal of the Royal Statistical Society Series A (Statistics in Society)*, 166: 3.

Lewis, Jane E. (1989), 'Introduction' in Bulmer M. *et al.* (eds.) *The Goals of Social Policy* (London: Unwin Hyman), 121-40.

Lipset, S. M., and Reisman, D. (1975), *Commission on Higher Education: Education and Politics at Harvard* (New York: McGraw Hill).

Lister, R. (ed.) (1996), *Charles Murray and the Underclass: The Developing Debate* (London: IEA Health and Welfare Unit).

Lockwood, D. (1956), 'Some Remarks on "The Social System"', *British Journal of Sociology*, 7: 22, 134–46.

—— (1992), *Solidarity and Schism* (Oxford: Clarendon Press).

—— (1958), *The Black-Coated Worker* (London: George Allen and Unwin).

—— (1966), 'Sources of Variation in Working Class Images of Society', *Sociological Review*, 14: 249–67.

Lukes, S. (1973), *Emile Denkheim: His Life and Work: A Historical and Critical Study* (London: Allen Lane).

Macfarlane, A. (1978), *The Origins of English Individualism: The Family, Property and Social Transition* (Oxford: Basil Blackwell).

MacIver, R. M. (1937 and 1949), *Society* (London: Macmillan), rewritten with Charles Page in 1949.

—— (1968), *As a Tale that is Told* (Chicago: Chicago University Press).

Mackenzie, Norman, and Jeannette (eds.) (1978), *The Letters of Sidney and Beatrice Webb*, Vols I, II, III (Cambridge: Cambridge University Press).

—— (1982–4), *The Diary of Beatrice Webb*, Vols I–III (London: Virago).

Macrae, Donald (1970), *New Society*, 387.

MacRoberts, M. H., and MacRoberts, B. R. (1996), 'Problems of Citation Analysis', *Scientometrics*, 36/3: 435–44.

Madge, C. (1937), *The Disappearing Castle* (London: Faber and Faber).

Madge, C., and Harrison, T. (1939), *Britain by Mass-Observation* (Harmondsworth: Penguin).

Mairet, P. (1957), *Pioneer of Sociology: The Life and Letters of Patrick Geddes* (London: Lund Humphries).

Malinowski, B. (1944), *A Scientific Theory of Culture and Other Essays* (Chapel Hill: University of North Carolina Press).

Malthus, T. R. (1798), *An Essay on the Principle of Population* (London: J. Johnson).

Mannheim, Karl (1936), *Ideology and Utopia: An Introduction to the Sociology of Knowledge* (London: Routledge and Kegan Paul).

Marsh, Catherine (1982), *The Survey Method: The Contribution of Surveys to Sociological Explanation* (London: George Allen & Unwin).

Marshall, G. (ed.) (1994), *The Concise Oxford Dictionary of Sociology* (Oxford: Oxford University Press).

Marshall, T. H. (1925), *James Watt (1736–1819)* (London: Parsons).

—— (ed.) (1938*a*), *Class Conflict and Social Stratification* (London: Le Play House Press).

—— (ed.) (1938*b*), *The Population Problem: The Experts and the Public* (London: Allen & Unwin).

—— (1947), *Sociology at the Crossroads*, (London: Longmans, Green).

—— (1950), *Citizenship and Social Class* (Cambridge: Cambridge University Press).

—— (1967), *Social Policy in the Twentieth Century* (London: Hutchinson).

—— (1973), 'A British Sociological Career', *British Journal of Sociology*, 24: 399–408.

—— (1981), *The Right to Welfare: And Other Essays* (London: Heinemann).

Marshall, G., and Swift, A. (1996), 'Merit and Mobility: A Reply to Peter Saunders', *Sociology*, 30/2: 375–86.

Marshall, G., Rose, D., Newby, H., and Vogler, C. (1988), *Social Class in Modern Britain* (London: Unwin Hyman).

Martin, B. R. (1996), 'The Use of Multiple Indicators in the Assessment of Basic Research', *Scientometrics*, 36: 343–62.

Martins, H. (ed.) (1993), *Knowledge and Passion: Essays in Honour of John Rex* (London: I. B. Taurus & Co.).

—— and Rex, J. (eds.) (1974), *Approaches to Sociology: An Introduction to Major Trends in British Sociology* (London: Routledge and Kegan Paul).

Marx, K. (1933), *Capital* (London: J M Dent).

Masterman, C. F. G. (1909), *The Condition of England* (London: Methuen).

Mayhew, Henry (1851–62), *London Labour and the London Poor* (London: Griffin, Bohn & Co.).

Maynard, A., and Chalmers, I. (eds.) (1997), *Non-Random Reflections on Health Services Research* (London: BMJ).

McConica, James (1986), *The History of the University of Oxford Vol. III: The Collegiate University* (Oxford: Oxford University Press).

McDonagh, E. C., and Simpson, J. E. (eds.) (1965), *Social Problems: Persistent Challenges* (New York: Holt, Rinehart, and Winston).

McGlone, F., and Cronin, N. (1994), *A Crisis in Care?: The Future of Family and State Care for Older People in The European Union* (London: Family Policy Studies Centre).

Mearns, Andrew (1883), *The Bitter Cry of Outcast London* (London: Jason Clarke).

Merton, R. K. (1949), *Social Theory and Social Structure* (Glencoe, IL: Free Press).

Mess, H. (1928), *Industrial Tyneside* (London: Benn).

Mills, S., and Wright, C. (1959), *The Sociological Imagination* (New York: Oxford University Press).

Mitchell, G. D. (1968), *A Hundred Years of Sociology* (London: Duckworth).

Mitchell, Juliet, and Oakley, Ann (eds.) (1981), *What is Feminism?* (Oxford: Basil Blackwell).

Modgil, C., Modgil, S., and Clark, J. (1990), *John H Goldthorpe: Consensus and Controversy* (London: Fulmer).

Morris, L. (1994), *Dangerous Classes: The Underclass and Social Citizenship* (London: Routledge, Kegan Paul).

Morris, Terence (1989), 'In Memoriam: Barbara Wootton 1897–1988', *British Journal of Sociology*, 40/2: 310–18.

Moser, Claus (1958), *Survey Methods in Social Investigation* (London: Heinemann, 2nd edition 1971 with Kalton, G.).

Muggeridge, M. (1975), *The Infernal Grove: Chronicles of Wasted Time Vol. 2* (London: Fontana).

Mullen, H. (1987), *Sociologists on Sociology* (London: Croom Helm).

Murray, Charles, A. (ed.) (1990), *The Emerging British Underclass* (London: IEA Health and Welfare Unit).

Network (2001), 80.

New Society, 8 April 1982.

Nevitt, A. A. (1966), *Housing, Taxation and Subsidies* (London: Nelson).

Nowotny, H., Scott, P., and Gibbons, M. (2001), *Re-Thinking Science: Knowledge and the Public in an Age of Uncertainty* (Cambridge: Polity Press).

Oakley, Ann (1989), 'Women's Studies in British Sociology: To End at Our Beginning?', *British Journal of Sociology*, 40/3: 442–70.

—— (2000), *Experiments in Knowing: Gender and Method in the Social Sciences* (Cambridge: Polity Press).

—— (2002), *Gender on Planet Earth* (Cambridge: Polity Press).

Oberschall, A. (1972), *The Establishment of Empirical Sociology* (New York: Harper and Row).

OECD (1981), *The Welfare State in Crisis* (Paris: OECD).

Oromaner, M. J. (1970), 'Comparisons of Influentials in Contemporary American and British Sociology: A Study in the Internationalisation of Sociology', *British Journal of Sociology*, 21: 324–32.

Orwell, G. (1933), *Down and Out in Paris and London* (London: Gollancz).

—— (1937), *The Road to Wigan Pier* (London: Gollancz).

—— (1970), *The Collected Essays, Journalism and letters of George Orwell* (Harmondsworth: Penguin).

Pahl, R. (1984), *Divisions of Labour* (Oxford: Basil Blackwell).

Parker, J. (1998), *Citizenship, Work and Welfare: Searching for the Good Society* (Basingstoke: Macmillan).

Parker, Martin (2000), 'The Sociology of Organisations and the Organisation of Sociology: Some Reflections on the Making of a Division Labour', *Sociological Review*, 48/1: 124–46.

Parkin, F. (1971), *Class Inequality and Political Order: Social Stratification in Capitalist and Communist Societies* (London: MacGibbon and Kee).

Packman, J. (1968), *Child Care: Needs and Numbers* (London: Allen & Unwin).

Parsons, T. (1937), *The Structure of Social Action: A Study in Social Theory with Special Reference to a Group of Recent European Writers* (New York: McGraw Hill).

—— (1951), *The Social System* (London: Routledge and Kegan Paul).

Peel, J. D. Y. (1971), *Herbert Spencer: The Evolution of a Sociologist* (London: Heinemann).

Perkin, H. (1969), *Key Profession: The History of the Association of University Teachers* (London: Routledge and Kegan Paul).

—— (1989), *The Rise of Professional Society: England since 1880* (London: Routledge).

Phelan, T. J. (1999), 'A Compendium of Issues for Citation Analysis', *Scientometrics*, 45/1: 117–36.

Phillipson, C., and Walker, A. (1986), *Ageing and Social Policy: A Critical Assessment* (Aldershot: Gower).

Pilcher, Jane (1994), 'Mannheim's Sociology of Generations: An Undervalued Legacy', *British Journal of Sociology*, 45/3, 481–95.

Pinker, R. (1971), *Social Theory and Social Policy* (London: Heinemann).

—— (1979), *The Idea of Welfare* (London: Heinemann).

Platt, J. (1971), *Social Research in Bethnal Green: An Evaluation of the Work of the Institute of Community Studies* (London: Macmillan).

—— (1976), *Realities of Social Research* (London: Chatto & Windus).

—— (1984), 'The Affluent Worker Re-visited', in C. Bell and H. Roberts (eds.) *Social Researching: Politics, Problems, Practice* (London, Boston: Routledge and Kegan Paul).

—— (1998), *A Brief History of the ISA: 1948–1997* (Madrid: International Sociological Association).

—— (2000), 'Women in the British sociological labour market 1960–1995', *Sociological Research Online*, 4/4: 16.

—— (2003), *The British Sociological Association: A Sociological History* (Durham: Sociology Press).

Popper, K. R. (1945), *The Open Society and its Enemies* (London: Routledge and Kegan Paul).
—— (1959), *The Logic of Scientific Discovery* (London: Hutchinson).
—— (1957), *The Poverty of Historicism* (London: Routledge and Kegan Paul).
Pratt, J. (1997), *The Polytechnic Experiment, 1965–1992* (Buckingham: Society for Research in Higher Education).
Prendergast, C. (1990), *Introduction to the World's Classics Series* (OUP) of Balzac Eugénie Grandet 1833, Mme Béchet, Paris.
Quetelet, L. A. J. (1842), 'Sur l'Homme et le Développement de ses Facultés: Physique Sociale' (Brussels 1835 English edn, translated by J. Knox as *A Treatise on Man and the Development of his Faculties*, Edinburgh, 1842).
Ratcliffe, S. K. (1910), 'Sociology in the English language', *Sociological Review*, 3: 126–36.
Rex, J., and Moore, R. S. (1967), *Race, Community and Conflict: A Study of Sparkbrook* (London: Publication for the Institute of Race Relations by Oxford University Press).
Rimlinger, G. V. (1971), *Welfare Policy and Industrialization in Europe, America and Russia* (London: Wiley & Sons).
Roberts, D. (1960), *Victorian Origins of the British Welfare State* (New Haven: Yale University Press).
Rodgers, B. N., and Dixon, J. (1960), *Portrait of Social Work* (London: Oxford University Press).
Rojek, C., and Turner, B. (2000), 'Decorative Sociology: Towards a Critique of the Cultural Turn', *Sociological Review*, 48/4: 629–48.
Room, G. (1979), *The Sociology of Welfare* (Oxford: Basil Blackwell).
Roseneil, Sarah (1995), 'The Coming of Age of Feminist Sociology: Some Issues of Practice and Theory for the Next Twenty Years', *British Journal of Sociology*, 46/2: 191–205.
Rothschild, Lord (1971), 'The Organisation and Management of Government Research and Development' *A Framework for Government Research and Development*, Cmnd 4814, (London: HMSO).
—— (1982), *An Enquiry into the Social Science Research Council*, Cmnd 8554 (London: HMSO).
Rowntree, B. S. (1901), *Poverty. A Study of Town Life* (London: Macmillan).
—— and Lasker, B. (1911), *Unemployment. A Social Study* (London: Macmillan).
Royal Statistical Society (RSS News) 29/8, April 2002.
Runciman, W. G. (1972), *Relative Deprivation and Social Justice* (Harmondsworth: Penguin).
—— (1983/97), *Treatise on Social Theory* (Cambridge: Cambridge University Press).
—— (1989), *Confessions of a Reluctant Theorist: Selected essays of W. G. Runciman* (London and New York: Simon & Schuster).
—— (1998), *The Social Animal* (London: HarperCollins).
Rutter, M., and Madge, N. (1976), *Cycles of Deprivation* (London: Heinemann).
Saunders, Peter (1990), *Social Class and Stratification* (London: Routledge).
—— (1995), 'Might Britain Be a Meritocracy?', *Sociology*, 29/1: 23–41
—— (1997), 'Social Mobility in Britain: An Empirical Evaluation of Two Competing Theories', *Sociology*, 31: 261–88.
Selvin, H. (1985), 'Durkheim, Booth and Yale: The Non Diffusion of An Intellectual Innovation', in M. Bulmer (ed.), 1985.
Sen, A. K. (1983), 'Poor, Relatively Speaking', *Oxford Economic Papers*, 35: 53–169.
—— (1985), 'A Sociological Approach to the Measurement of Poverty: A Reply to Professor Townsend', *Oxford Economic Papers*, 37/4: 669–76.

Shanas, E. *et al.* (1968), *Old People in Three Industrial Societies* (London: Routledge and Kegan Paul).

Shaw, G. B. (1965), *Prefaces*.

Shaw, Martin (1976), *Sociology*, 10/3: 519.

Shils, E. (1948), *Present State of American Sociology* (Chicago: Chicago University Press).

—— (1956), *The Torment of Secrecy: The Background and Consequences of American Security Policies* (Glencoe, IL: Free Press).

—— (1961), 'The Intellectual between Tradition and Modernity: The Indian Situation', *Comparative Studies in Society and History*, supplement no. 1 and The Hague: Mouton.

—— (1975), *Centre and Periphery: Essays in Macrosociology* (Chicago: University of Chicago Press).

—— (1992), 'The Sociology of Robert E. Park', *Sociologica*, IX: 32.

—— (1997), *Portraits: A Gallery of Intellectuals* edited by Joseph Epstein (Chicago: Chicago University Press).

Shils, E., and Janowitz, M., (1948), 'Cohesion and Disintegration in the Wehrmacht in World War II', *Public Opinion Quarterly*, XII: 280–315.

—— and Blacker, Carmen (eds.), (1996), *Cambridge Women: Twelve Portraits* (Cambridge: Cambridge University Press).

Simey, T. S., and Simey, M. B. (1960), *Charles Booth: Social Scientist* (Oxford: Oxford University Press).

Simon, B. (1991), *Education and the Social Order, 1940–1990* (London: Lawrence & Wishart).

Simon, R. J. (1969), 'A Comment on Sociological Research and Interest in Britain and The United States', *Sociological Review*, Vol. 17 No. 1, 5–10.

Skidelsky, R. (1992), *John Maynard Keynes, Vol. 2.* Two *The Economist as Saviour* (London: Macmillan).

Small, Albion (1924–5), *AJS* Review of Hobhouse's *Social Development*.

Smith, A. (1950), *An Inquiry into the Nature and Causes of the Wealth of Nations* ed. by E. Cannan (London: Methuen).

Smith, D. J. (1992), *Understanding the Underclass* (London: Policy Studies Institute).

Smith, H. L. (1930–5), *The New Survey of London Life and Labour* (London: P.S. King).

Snow, C. P. (1959), *The Two Cultures and the Scientific Revolution* (Cambridge: Cambridge University Press).

Soares, J. (1999), *The Decline of Privilege: The Modernisation of Oxford University* (Cambridge: Cambridge University Press).

Soffer, R. N. (1978), *Ethics and Society in England: The Revolution in the Social Sciences, 1870–1914* (Berkeley, London: University of California Press).

—— (1982), 'Why do Disciplines Fail? The Strange Case of British Sociology', *English Historical Review*, 97: 767–802.

Sokal, Alan (1996), 'Transgressions into Boundaries: Towards Transformative Hermeneutics of Quantum Gravity', *Social Text*, Spring/Summer.

Solesbury, W. (2002), 'The Ascendancy of Evidence', *Planning Theory and Practice*, 3/1: 90–6.

Solzhenitsyn (1974–8), *Gulag Archipelago, Vol. III* (London: Ellins/Fontana).

Spencer, H. (1860–2), *First Principles* (London: G. Mainwaring).

—— (1884), *The Man Versus the State* (London: Williams & Norgate).

Spencer, J. (2000), 'British Social Anthropology: a Retrospect', *Annual Review of Anthropology*, 29: 1–24.

Sprott, W. J. H. (1949), *Sociology* (London: Hutchinson's University Library).

—— (1954), *Science and Social Action* (London: Watts).

—— (1962), *Sociology at the Seven Dials* (London: University of London, Athlone Press).

Stedman-Jones, G. (1971), *Outcast London: A Study in the Relationship between Classes in Victorian Society* (Oxford: Clarendon Press).

Stedman-Jones, G., Barnett, A., and Wengraf, T. (1967), 'Student Power: What is to be Done?', *New Left Review*, 43, May–June.

Steuer, M (2003), *The Scientific Study of Society* (London: Kluwer).

Stone, P. A. (1970), *Urban Development in Britain* (Cambridge: Cambridge University Press).

Swift, Adam (2000), 'Class Analysis from a Normative Perspective', *British Journal of Sociology*, 51/4: 663–79.

Swift, A., and Marshall, G., (1997), 'Meritocratic Equality of Opportunity', *Policy Studies*, 18/1: 35–48.

Swingewood, A. (1970), 'Origins of Sociology: The Case of the Scottish Enlightenment', *British Journal of Sociology*, 21: 164–80.

Tawney, R. H. (1931), *Equality* (London: Allen & Unwin).

The Times 22 July 2002, Obituary of Royden J. Harrison.

Titmuss, Richard (1938), *Poverty and Population: A Factual Study of Contemporary Social Waste* (London: Macmillan).

—— (1950), *Problems of Social Policy* (London: Longmans and Green & Co).

—— (1958), 'Eleanor Rathbone Memorial Lecture', *'The Social Division of Welfare: Some Reflections on the Search for Equity'* (Liverpool: Liverpool University Press).

—— (1968), *Commitment to Welfare* (London: Allen & Unwin).

—— (1970), *The Gift Relationship: From Human Blood to Social Policy* (London: Allen & Unwin).

To, C.-Y. (2000), *The Scientific Merit of the Social Sciences: Implications for Research and Application* (Stoke-on-Trent: Trentham).

Townsend, Peter (1957), *The Family Life of Old People* (London: Routledge and Kegan Paul).

—— (1962), *The Last Refuge* (London: Routledge and Kegan Paul).

—— (1979), *Poverty in the United Kingdom* (London: Allen Lane).

—— and Davidson, N. (eds.) (1982), *Inequalities in Health: the Black Report* (Harmondsworth: Penguin Books).

Townsend, P., and Wedderburn, D. *et al.* (1965), *The Aged in the Welfare State* (London: Bell).

Trevino, A. Javier (eds.) (2001), *Talcott Parsons Today: His Theory and Legacy in Contemporary Sociology* (London and New York: Rowman & Littlefield).

Trigilia, C. (1999), *Sociologia Economica* (Bologna: II Mulino). Translated into English as *Economic Sociology* (Oxford: Blackwell, 2002).

Tropp, A. (1956), *The School Teachers* (London: Heinemann).

Truscot, B. (1945), *Redbrick University* (London: Pelican).

Turner, S. P., and Turner, J. H. (1990), *The Impossible Science: An Institutional Analysis of American Sociology* (Newbury Park, CA: Sage).

University Central Council on Admissions (UCCA) (1967), *Statistical Supplement*, 1967.

University Grants Committee (UGC) (1989), *Report of the Review Committee on Sociology* (London: HMSO).

Urry, John (2000), 'Introduction', *British Journal of Sociology*, 51/1: 1–3.

—— (2000), 'Mobile Sociology', *British Journal of Sociology*, 51/1: 185–201.

Van Creveld, Martin, L. (1982), *Fighting Power: German and US Army Performance 1939–1945* (Greenwood Press: Westport).

Walby, S. (1988*a*), 'Gender Politics and Social Theory', *Sociology*, 22/2: 215–32.

—— (1988*b*), *Gender Segregation at Work* (Milton Keynes: Open University).

Wallace, R. A. (1989), *Feminism and Sociological Theory* (Newbury Park: Sage).

Ward, Mrs Humphrey (1888), *Robert Elsmere* (London: Smith Elder).

Warner, G. T. (1924), *Landmarks in English Industrial History* (London: Blackie).

Webb, B. P. (1926), *My Apprenticeship* (London, New York: Longmans, Green and Co.).

—— (1948), *Our Partnership*, ed. by B. Drake and M. I. Cole (London: Longmans, Green and Co.).

Webb, Jo (2003), D.Phil Thesis *Always with Us? The Evolution of Poverty in Britain, 1880–2002* (Oxford University).

Webb, B., and Webb, S. (1929), *English Poor Law History Part II: The Last Hundred Years* Vol. 11 (London: Frank Cass, 1963).

—— —— (1932), *Methods of Social Study* (London: Longman).

Weber, M. (1964), *The Theory of Social and Economic Organisation* (New York: Free Press).

—— (1968), *Economy and Society: An Outline of Interpretative Sociology* (New York: Bedminster).

Weiner, M. J. (1985), *English Culture and the Decline of the Industrial Spirit 1850–1980* (London: Pelican).

Wells, A. F. (1935), *The Local Social Survey in Great Britain* (London: Allen & Unwin).

Wells, H. G. (1907), 'The So-called Science of Sociology', *Sociological Papers* III, 357–78.

—— (1911), *The New Machiavelli* (London: John Lane).

Westergaard, John, (1979), 'In Memory of David Glass', *Sociology*, 13: 173–8.

—— and Resler, H. (1975), *Class in a Capitalist Society* (London: Heinemann).

Westergaard, J., and Pahl, R. (1989), 'Looking Backwards and Forwards: The UGC's Review of Sociology', *British Journal of Sociology*, 40/3: 374–92.

Whitty, Geoff (1997), *Social Theory and Education Policy: The Legacy of Karl Mannheim* (London: Institute of Education).

Wilensky, H. L. (1975), *The Welfare State and Equality* (Berkeley: University of California Press).

—— and Lebaux, C. N. (1958), *Industrial Society and Social Welfare* (New York: Free Press).

Williams, K. (1981), *From Pauperism to Poverty* (London: Routledge).

Williams, R. (1961), *The Long Revolution* (London: Chatto & Windus).

Wilson, W. J. (1987), *The Truly Disadvantaged: The Inner City's the Underclass and Public Policy* (Chicago: Chicago University Press).

Wootton, Barbara (1959), *Social Science and Social Pathology* (London: Allen & Unwin).

—— (1967), *In a World I Never Made* (London: Allen & Unwin).

Yeats, W. B. (ed.) (1936), *The Oxford Book of Modern Verse, 1892–1935* (Oxford: Clarendon Press).

Young, M. (1958), *The Rise of the Meritocracy, 1870–2023: An Essay On Education and Equality* (London: Thames and Hudson).

—— and Halsey, A. H. (1995), *Family and Community Socialism* (London: Institute for Public Policy Research).

—— and Willmott, P. (1957), *Family and Kinship in East London* (London: Routledge and Kegan Paul).

Yule, G. U. (1911), *An Introduction to the Theory of Statistics* (London: Griffin).

NAME AND SUBJECT INDEX